D0813828

BAD

THE **SUNY** SERIES

CULTURAL STUDIES IN CINEMA/VIDEO

WHEELER WINSTON DIXON | EDITOR

BAD

Infamy, Darkness, Evil, and Slime on Screen

edited by

MURRAY POMERANCE

STATE UNIVERSITY OF NEW YORK PRESS

UNIVERSITY H.S. LIBRARY

Cover photograph by Chris Buck. Copyright © 2004 by Chris Buck. Used by kind permission of the photographer.

Published by
State University of New York Press, Albany

© 2004 State University of New York

All rights reserved

Printed in the United States of America

No part of this book may be used or reproduced
in any manner whatsoever without written permission.
No part of this book may be stored in a retrieval system
or transmitted in any form or by any means including electronic,
electrostatic, magnetic tape, mechanical, photocopying, recording,
or otherwise without the prior permission in writing of the publisher.

For information, address State University of New York Press,
90 State Street, Suite 700, Albany, NY 12207

Production by Marilyn P. Semerad
Marketing by Fran Keneston

Library of Congress Cataloging-in-Publication Data

Bad : infamy, darkness, evil, and slime on screen / edited by Murray Pomerance.
    p. cm. — (The SUNY series, cultural studies in cinema/video)
    Includes bibliographical references and index.
    ISBN 0-7914-5939-X (alk. paper) — ISBN 0-7914-5940-3 (pbk. : alk. paper)
    1. Evil in motion pictures. 2. Sensationalism in motion pictures. 3. Social problems in motion pictures. I. Pomerance, Murray, 1946– II. Series.

PN1995.9E93B33 2003
791.43'653—dc21
                                                                    2003042556

10 9 8 7 6 5 4 3 2 1

791.43653
B14 p

Uni High

for Mike and Syd Pomerance
who gave me the movie world,
in loving memory

. . . this thing of darkness I
Acknowledge mine.

—Shakespeare,
The Tempest V.i.275–76

CONTENTS

List of Illustrations   xiii

Acknowledgments   xvii

INTRODUCTION   1
From Bad to Worse
MURRAY POMERANCE

I. IT'S A SLIMY WORLD, AFTER ALL

CHAPTER ONE   21
Flickers: On Cinema's Power for Evil
TOM GUNNING

CHAPTER TWO   39
Monstrosity and the Bad-White-Body Film
GWENDOLYN AUDREY FOSTER

CHAPTER THREE   55
Beyond the Thin Line of Black and Blue:
Movies and Police Misconduct in Los Angeles
AARON BAKER

CHAPTER FOUR   65
Genocidal Spectacles and the Ideology of Death
CHRISTOPHER SHARRETT

CHAPTER FIVE   79
Bad, Worse, Worst:
8MM and Hollywood's Bad Boys of Porn
PETER LEHMAN

CHAPTER SIX   93
Toxic Corps: Rage against the Corporate State
KIRBY FARRELL

CHAPTER SEVEN   109
The *Ghost World* of Neoliberalism:
Abandoning the Abandoned Generation
HENRY A. GIROUX

II. AUTEURS OF NEGATIVITY, ICONS OF DARKNESS

CHAPTER EIGHT   127
"How Will I Get My Opium?":
Jean Cocteau and the Treachery of Friendship
WHEELER WINSTON DIXON

CHAPTER NINE   143
The Sweeter the Kitten the Sharper the Claws:
Russ Meyer's Bad Girls
KRISTEN HATCH

CHAPTER TEN   157
Wanted for Murder: The Strange Case of Eric Portman
TONY WILLIAMS

CHAPTER ELEVEN   173
The Arch Archenemies of James Bond
STEVEN WOODWARD

CHAPTER TWELVE   187
From Fu Manchu to *M. Butterfly* and *Irma Vep*:
Cinematic Incarnations of Chinese Villainy
GINA MARCHETTI

CHAPTER THIRTEEN   201
On the Bad Goodness of *Born to Be Bad*:
Auteurism, Evaluation, and Nicholas Ray's Outsider Cinema
DANA POLAN

CHAPTER FOURTEEN   213
The Villain in Hitchcock: "Does He Look Like a 'Wrong One' to You?"
WILLIAM ROTHMAN

III. THE CHARISMA OF VILLAINY

CHAPTER FIFTEEN   225
The "Evil Medieval": Gender, Sexuality,
Miscegenation, and Assimilation in *Cat People*
ALEXANDER DOTY AND PATRICIA CLARE INGHAM

CHAPTER SIXTEEN   239
Wicked Old Ladies from Europe:
Jeanne Moreau and Marlene Dietrich on the Screen and Live
E. ANN KAPLAN

CHAPTER SEVENTEEN   255
Darkness Visible: Images of Nazis in American Film
LESTER D. FRIEDMAN

CHAPTER EIGHTEEN   273
"The Whole Fucking World Warped around Me":
Bad Kids and Worse Contexts
CYNTHIA FUCHS

CHAPTER NINETEEN   287
Searching for Blobby Fissures: Slime, Sexuality, and the Grotesque
REBECCA BELL-METEREAU

CHAPTER TWENTY   301
Crazy Like a Prof: Mad Science and the Transgressions of the Rational
INA RAE HARK

CHAPTER TWENTY-ONE   315
Tom Ripley's Talent
MURRAY POMERANCE

List of Contributors   331

Index   337

ILLUSTRATIONS

𝔖

FIGURE 1. "Magic tricks operated like commodity capitalism through   20
an occluding of labor, concealing the actual effective gesture and
seeming to produce things 'by magic.'" Nosferatu (Max Schreck) rises
from his coffin in *Nosferatu, eine Symphonie des Grauens* (F. W. Murnau, Jofa-Ateler/Berlin-Johannisthal, 1922). (Frame enlargement)

FIGURE 2. "Wholly amoral and sexually obsessed" white scientists   38
(Leslie Daniels, l.; Jason Evers, r.) with the triumph of their careers,
"the white thing," Jan in the Pan (Virginia Leith) in Joseph Green's
The Brain That Wouldn't Die (AIP/Warner Bros., 1962). Somewhere
a suitable body will be found. (Collection Gwendolyn Audrey Foster)

FIGURE 3. *L.A. Confidential* (Curtis Hanson, Warner Bros., 1997)   54
shows the L.A.P.D. as "dysfunctional due to higher-ups who tolerate officers involved in illegal activity for personal gain because of the
need for the 'effective' policing that such bad cops provide." James
Cromwell as Captain Dudley Smith, a particularly "effective" and
particularly "bad" cop, obsessed with personal gain. This film, among
many others, endorses violence as a solution to police corruption.
(Frame enlargement)

FIGURE 4. "The forms of violent expression not sanctioned by the   64
official culture are almost invariably those forms that run against the
grain of dominant ideology, although not always with anything like
a conscious political program." *Bonnie and Clyde* (Arthur Penn,
Warner Bros./Seven Arts, 1967) apotheosizes the unsanctioned
nature of Bonnie Parker's (Faye Dunaway) violence through its
depiction of her gory demise. (Frame enlargement)

FIGURE 5.   Pic-within-pic. What could be more depraved, Joel   78
Schumacher would have us wonder in his *8MM* (Columbia, 1999),
than "arranging the death of a teenage girl so that one can watch it
being filmed?" Machine (Christopher Bauer, r.) "actually killing"
Mary Anne Mathews (Jenny Powell, l.) for the viewer's pleasure—as
depicted by Schumacher in what may be "the most pornophobic film
ever made." (Frame enlargement)

FIGURE 6.   Creative control: *The Truman Show* (Peter Weir,   92
Paramount, 1998) "plays on anxieties that consumer utopia has co-
opted autonomy, hyperrationalizing and numbing life . . . the corporation and the client are symbiotic but also parasitic and alienated,
not to mention vacuous." Stage-managing the co-optation of autonomy is Christof (Ed Harris), who is directing the protagonist's everyday reality in a gargantuan television program of which he does not
know that he is the star. (Frame enlargement)

FIGURE 7.   Utopian possibilities need to be reclaimed against an   108
"utterly privatized notion of resistance." Enid (Thora Birch, r.) and
her friend Rebecca (Scarlett Johansson), come across an older man
sitting at a bus stop that has been closed for years in Terry Zwigoff's
Ghost World (Jersey Shore/United Artists, 2001). Enid tells him the
bus route has been cancelled, but he tells her to leave him alone.
(Frame enlargement)

FIGURE 8. Jean Cocteau (1889–1963), a model in many ways for the   126
artiste of the twentieth century. His allegiances and friendships "were
often only matters of convenience or self-advancement, to be broken
off on a whim," yet "everywhere Cocteau appeared he charmed his
audiences into imagining that his affections and attentions were
directed to them alone." (Collection Wheeler Winston Dixon)

FIGURE 9. Russ Meyer "brought sexploitation into the mainstream,"   142
moving it "out of the male-only grindhouse circuit and into first-
class theaters." Indeed, until the release of his *Beyond the Valley of the
Dolls* (20th Century Fox, 1970), in which Edy Williams plays porn
star Ashley St. Ives, Meyer's films were "understood in relation to the
framework of the stag film." (Frame enlargement)

FIGURE 10. Eric Portman (1903–1969) as Lieutenant Hirth in *Forty-*   156
Ninth Parallel (Michael Powell, Ortus/Columbia, 1941). "Portman so
impressed his more eminent costars with the intensity of his perfor-

mance that they began a campaign to give him costar billing." The director notes that the performance exuded religious fanatacism. (Frame enlargement)

FIGURE 11. Producers of James Bond films, "ever aware of the need   172
to address a global market with their British-produced product . . .
have been careful to craft for Bond antagonists who present a threat to
all governments whether democratic or communist. Max Zorin
(Christopher Walken) intimately unsheathing his malevolence in *A
View to a Kill* (John Glen, United Artists, 1985). (Frame enlargement)

FIGURE 12. Yellow Peril: a Chinese master criminal with a heritage   186
of European violence and a good Western education. Boris Karloff in
the title role in *The Mask of Fu Manchu* (Charles Brabin, MGM,
1932), a character with "enduring global appeal." (Frame enlargement)

FIGURE 13. Gobby (Mel Ferrer) with his painting of a "resourcefully   200
resilient figure whose sins are unstoppable" in the coda to Nicholas
Ray's *Born to Be Bad* (RKO, 1950). On the canvas at least, Christabel (Joan Fontaine), "a perfect embodiment of the notion of the
scheming adventuress," has increasing value "since the scandals of
her trajectory will obviously continue and give her a marketable reputation." (Frame enlargement)

FIGURE 14. In *The Birds* (1963), a mother (Doreen Lang) accuses   212
Melanie Daniels ('Tippi' Hedren) of causing the bird attacks. "In a
shot framed from Hedren's perspective, the hysterical woman screams
right into the camera (symbolically, right at us, right at Hitchcock), 'I
think you're *evil!*'"—perhaps "the only occasion . . . when a Hitchcock character utters the word *evil.*" (Frame enlargement)

FIGURE 15. Irena Dubrovna (Simone Simon) in *Cat People* (Jacques   224
Tourneur, RKO, 1942): her efforts to become a modern American
wife are haunted by the memory of a suppressed female cultural history. In the end, she shares "the common fate of pathetic or dangerous homosexuals in literature, theatre, and films," invoking a
"medieval evil," the queer possibilities of which fascinated American
viewers. (Frame enlargement)

FIGURE 16. The fetishizing of the youthful body presents us with the   238
evil specter of aging. Late in her career, as Tanya in Orson Welles's
Touch of Evil (Universal, 1958), Marlene Dietrich still adored being the
"adored object" of the male gaze and the camera. (Frame enlargement)

FIGURE 17. The Fuehrer has been the butt of satire and humor in   254
film. Adenoid Hynkel (Charles Chaplin) plans to take over the world
in Chaplin's *The Great Dictator* (United Artists, 1940). This film "discusses anti-Semitic activities more openly than might have been possible in more realistic melodramas." (Collection Lester D. Friedman)

FIGURE 18. "Please, whatever I did, I'm sorry!" whines Bobby Kent   272
(Nick Stahl) but in a murder scene that is "alarmingly, and appropri-
ately, graceless and stupid" Marty (Brad Renfro) slits his throat.
Bully (Larry Clark, Lions Gate, 2001). (Frame enlargement)

FIGURE 19. A paragon of the "bug-eyed monsters, hideous and gen-   286
erally not to be trusted" who have infiltrated the culture in Barry
Sonnenfeld's *Men in Black* (Columbia/Amblin, 1997) is Mikey, who
has just snuck across from Mexico and been recognized by the border patrol as a different kind of "alien," indeed. (Frame enlargement)

FIGURE 20. Despite his knowledge that the Krell must have called   300
up something monstrous, Morbius (Walter Pidgeon) blindly believes
that he is immune to whatever evil haunts the *Forbidden Planet* (Fred
M. Wilcox, MGM, 1956). (Frame enlargement)

FIGURE 21. Tom Ripley (Matt Damon) suffers an "explosion of   314
shame and humiliation as he is rejected by the object of his amorous
suit," Dickie Greenleaf, in Anthony Minghella's *The Talented Mr.
Ripley* (Paramount, 1999). In a social climate where homosexuality is
openly shunned, there is also intense fear. (Frame enlargement)

ACKNOWLEDGMENTS

Working on this book has been a *baaaaaad* experience, by which I mean, lest there be any ambiguity at all in a vital and confusing matter of contemporary lingo, it has been wonderful. To edit a gathering of zestful, charming, and learned individuals such as one finds in these pages is the sort of delight for which an editor yearns but cannot expect to experience, and so I am moved to a very special gratitude. The contributors here have worked not only with grace and acumen but also with considerable wit and good humor, a major contribution because this book was produced during a time of profound and widespread social and personal stress that in one way or another has affected us all.

My efforts have been cheered and assisted by several sweet friends and generous colleagues, among whom I particularly wish to thank Keith Alnwick, Toronto; David Del Valle, Beverly Hills; Wheeler Winston Dixon, Lincoln; Lucy Fischer, Pittsburgh; Lester Friedman, Chicago; Frances Gateward, Ann Arbor; Barry Keith Grant, St. Catharines; Kirsty Henderson, Toronto; Nathan Holmes, Toronto; David Kerr, Montreal and Toronto; Marcia Landy, Pittsburgh; Robin MacDonald, Toronto; Charles Oberdorf, Toronto; Davina Pardo, Toronto; Ellen Seiter, San Diego; Vappu Tyyskä, Toronto; Tony Williams, Carbondale; Carolyn Zeifman, Toronto; and Kate Zieman, Toronto. I am especially thankful to Chris Buck, Brooklyn, Toronto, and Los Angeles, not only for his kindness but also for his keen eye. Andrew Hunter, Toronto, has been a warm-hearted chum and also a high-level sounding board—the latter very often without having been so informed, since I almost never like to talk openly about current writing projects while at the same time I love to have consultation.

The Office of Research Services at Ryerson University, especially Robert Dirstein, Mary Jane Curtis, and Rose Jackson, have generously supported this project.

Curtis Maloley is a research assistant of depth, erudition, precision, affability, and trust. He also has a strength I find continually inspiring, and one without which I think no volume such as this could really succeed, and that is genuine curiosity.

Steven Alan Carr, Fort Wayne and Washington, has given substantially of his time and expertise, his cheer, and his encouragement, for all of which I cannot fully enough say thank you. And my friend Peter Lehman, Tempe, has given his wise wit—which is something very genuine and quite immense; without him, my Energizer bunny would have hit the dirt, I fear. My amicable colleagues at State University of New York Press, James Peltz and Marilyn Semerad, have been stalwart, meticulous, devoted, and utterly responsive to my too multitudinous editorial concerns. Thanks also to freelance copyeditor Therese Myers, and freelance cover designer Amy Stirnkorb. These happy collaborators are in this book as much as those of us whose names are on the pages.

It is, of course, entirely conventional on an Acknowledgments page to acknowledge one's family. Both Nellie Perret and Ariel Pomerance have been with me in my writing for a long time, and simply to mention the fact that I could not have done a stitch of the work this book required without their continuing sacrifice, assistance, good spirit, wit, and love just doesn't come near saying what has to be said. Because it was a family endeavor, this book is of them as much as it is to them.

Yet it was indeed Nellie who shared the birth of this project with James Peltz and myself, improbably enough over very good lemon cake and tea. I hope the delicious piquancy of that snack is still here to be found, and will always be remembered.

INTRODUCTION

From Bad to Worse

MURRAY POMERANCE

That this book was originally conceived and contracted prior to September 11, 2001 has become virtually impossible, even for me, to believe. Since then the invocation of malevolence in political and social life and in our popular cultural fictions has seemed to mushroom, to have spread everywhere, and it is understandable how any discussion of the proliferation of negativity onscreen might be thought inspired by those horrendous events or aimed in response to them. Former Deputy Attorney General Eric Holder's comment September 13, 2001 to ABC, "They are evil in a way that we rarely see in the history of this world," sounds a currently prevailing sentiment, and also echoes and prefigures what has become a standard presidential litany about "Them"—the Taliban, the Palestinians, the Israelis, the Iraqis, the mailers of anthrax, the corrupt CEOs of billion-dollar conglomerates—being "Evil."

But even in the Golden Age before that Turning Point in History—as popular rhetoric is leading us to think of it—the screen had already shifted from a place where conventional dramatic unfoldings were staged with regular use of conflict and a lurking villain, to an unheralded new *topos* where—as the subtitle of this volume suggests—infamy, darkness, evil, and slime resided casually and everywhere as the stuff of the everyday. This book does not pretend to be the history of cinema we would need for showing in detail the long line of thieves, rapists, varmints, codgers, dodgers, manipulators, exploiters, conmen, killers, vamps, liars, demons, cold-blooded maniacs, and warm-hearted flakes that populated cinematic narrative from its earliest days around

1907 onward or for arranging in some sensible order the questioned (and sometimes questionable) screen morality of the precode era; the broad range of dramatic negativity before, during, and soon after World War II (ranging from Rhett Butler's potty mouth through the offscreen torture and murder of the unctuous Bugati in *Casablanca* [1942] through the arrogant murder in *Rope* [1948]); the disintegrating social mores of the 1950s; the chilling and vicious political tactics of the 1960s; the institutional horrors that began to appear in a systematic way in the 1970s (Watergate and beyond); and the new visions of all these, as well as depictions of disconnected personality and fragmented community, that became a screen staple after 1980. This book does, however, intend to present a sketch, as it were, of the range of badness that filmgoers around the world have become accustomed to seeing on the screen and to give some hints as to where screen evil came from and how it functions as a staple of our film diet today. By the turn of the twenty-first century it had become virtually unthinkable to see a film entirely without a moment of egregious— typically fantastic—violence, destruction, immorality, threat, or torture.

A man swallowed whole, on camera, by a mammoth shark (*Jaws* [1975]); a beheading, on camera, followed immediately by a shot of one of the observers biting off, and swallowing, his own tongue (*Merry Christmas, Mr. Lawrence* [1983]); a psychotic slasher murder (*Psycho* [1960]); a crucifixion (*The Last Temptation of Christ* [1988]); a man being presented with his wife's head in a hatbox (*Se7en* [1995]); a metallic insect alien with three drooling mouths popping bloodily out of the chest cavity of a gentle man (*Alien* [1979]); an astronaut exploding inside a space suit when his helmet cracks (*Outland* [1981]); humans tortured by having hideous hungry vermiformities given leave to slither into their orifices (*Star Trek: The Wrath of Khan* [1982], *The Matrix* [1999]); a man being devoured by a giant reptile while he sits on the toilet (*Jurassic Park* [1993]); crowds of innocents butchered by military swordplay or gunfire (*Doctor Zhivago* [1965]); a group of apparent innocents butchered by gunfire (*Three Days of the Condor* [1975]); a crowd of mercenaries butchered by gunfire (*Commando* [1985]); people shot in the head (*Stardust Memories* [1980], *Traffic* [2000], *The Prince of the City* [1981], *Dog Day Afternoon* [1975], *GoodFellas* [1990]); date rape (*Saturday Night Fever* [1977], *Bully* [2001]); dental rape (*Marathon Man* [1976]); ravaging by dogs (*The Boys from Brazil* [1978]); death by ice pick at the back of the neck (*GoodFellas* [1990]); accidental electrocution (*The Ice Storm* [1997]); intentional electrocution (*Goldfinger* [1964]); dis-arming (*Satyricon* [1969], *The Empire Strikes Back* [1980], *Total Recall* [1990]); malevolent bisection (*The Phantom Menace* [1999], *Black Hawk Down* [2001]); diabolical explosions (*Darkman* [1990], *Swordfish* [2001], *Blown Away* [1994], *The Sum of All Fears* [2002]); casual planetary vaporization (*Men in Black II* [2002]); being dropped into a pool of piranhas (*You Only Live Twice* [1967]); being tossed from a building (*The*

Man Who Fell to Earth [1976]); slow death by poison (*The Bride Wore Black* [1967]); quick death by poison (*Gosford Park* [2001]); being secretly impregnated (*The Astronaut's Wife* [1999]); being brainwashed (*The Manchurian Candidate* [1962]) . . . all this hardly constitutes even the tip of the iceberg. Speaking of icebergs, how about being shackled to a steam pipe in a ship that is sinking because it has struck the tip of an iceberg, or slowly freezing to death in the icy waters of the Atlantic soon afterward (*Titanic* [1997])? Consider the library of films showing, even centrally turning on, deliberate, brutal, full-frontal scenes of public execution—*The Green Mile* (1999), for example, or *I Want To Live!* (1958), *In Cold Blood* (1967), *Daniel* (1983), *Tom Horn* (1980), and *Dead Man Walking* (1995). Recall putrescent bodies, exploding bodies, bullets to the eye, castrations, rapes brutal (*The Accused* [1988]) and under sedation (*Kids* [1995]), embezzlement, fraud, class warfare, diabolical possession, gay bashing, wife bashing, child bashing, racial and ethnic violence, wanton destruction, cannibalism . . . not to mention mental torture, sadism, humiliation, the myriad ways of producing social death. This is now the *materiel* out of which shots—very often close-ups—are constructed, so that we have increasingly, for the last thirty years, been coming face to face with a vision of conflict and decay that had heretofore been scarcely imaginable in such detail, suggested and implied rather than directly shown. Nor does badness, in life and onscreen, invariably and inevitably bleed, suppurate, and grimace. Out of the shiniest skyscraper, to be sure, the shiniest villainy can routinely emerge, if not to butcher or devour then to exploit, enslave, and politically terrorize. That evil is very often linked to dirt should caution us to search for it, too, in cleanliness.

For an example of the contrast between "old" and "new" screen malevolence, examine the difference between the circumferential way rape is treated by John Ford in *The Searchers* (1956)—John Wayne riding into a gully looking for Pippa Scott and forbidding Harry Carey Jr. to come with him, then showing up a little later without his coat and saying quietly, with a certain cold look in his eye ("When I looked up at Duke during [the first] rehearsal," remembered Harry Carey Jr., "it was into the meanest and coldest eyes I have ever seen" [Eyman 1999, 444]) that he found her and covered her with his coat and buried her—and the on-camera shot near the end of Larry Clark's *Kids* (1995) where Leo Fitzpatrick finds Chloë Sevigny stoned unconscious on a sofa at a party, deftly removes her panties, gently spreads her legs and penetrates her (giving her AIDS) while she sleeps and we hermetically observe. More is at play in this contrast than just the demise of the Production Code in 1964. When *The Searchers* was being filmed, the frankness of *Kids* and its civilian abuse was inconceivable onscreen. Consider, too, the difference between the military killing on Omaha Beach in Sam Fuller's *The Big Red One* (1980)—dangerous, tactical, strategic, adventuresome, individualistic, frightening—or in Spielberg's *Saving Private Ryan* (1998) or Verhoeven's even more graphic *Starship Troopers* (1997), in both of which thousands of young men are chewed up in a moment, the precise equivalent of cannon fodder, yet in shots graphic enough to reveal gore, dismemberment, and agony up close, one body part at a time. Or note the relatively antiseptic mob shootings in *Some Like It Hot* (1959), the camera modestly turning away from the slaughter in the garage; and the graphic drive-by and casual brutality in *Falling Down* (1993); the off-screen murders in *Key Largo* (1948) or the onscreen ones in Scorsese's *Good-Fellas* (1990). In the 1960s, screen torture lasted a couple of minutes—the laser creeping into James Bond's crotch in *Goldfinger* (1964)—but by *Mission Impossible II* (2000) it is extended to last through the last two thirds of the film, as Thandie Newton is injected with an explosive that will rip her apart unless Tom Cruise solves the riddle and finds her in time. The reader will no doubt recollect hundreds of examples to better these.

Even if such an achievement were possible it would not be the intention of this book to make a neat catalog of the many kinds of film and the many kinds of filmic treatment that make for what might now, fashionably, be called "bad" film—that is, popular and pleasurable screen presentation of evil, nefariousness, monstrosity, darkness, negativity, slime, and the uncouth. The territory is vast. As avid viewers, we have surfed happily from Tinker Bell's bottom wagging mockingly in our face in *Peter Pan* (1953) to the chilling killing in *Murder by Numbers* (2002), flashing by countless mafia films, cop films, action films, sci-fi and western films, not to mention the slavish depravity in social commentaries such as *The Magnificent Ambersons* (1942) or melodramas such as *Leave Her to Heaven* (1946), kidpix such as *Home Alone* (1990) or docufictions such as *The Contender* (2000). And in taking our pleasures with such films, we have hardly needed a schema for understanding the structure of presented evil, nor has it made much difference to us as an audience in terms of box-office figures and wider, deeper impacts on the culture, whether we gagged and goggled at heroic struggles against evil—*The Mask of Zorro* (1998), for example, or *The Guns of Navarone* (1961)—or at the kind of quasi-animated, purely speculative characterization of badness typified by *The Silence of the Lambs* (1991). If only to see the cleanup that follows it, we have sat quietly for the spilling of an ocean of blood (screened as such, quite literally, in *Deep Impact* [1998], where the entire east coast of North America is seen from a stratospheric vantage to disappear), massive limb-pruning (in *Star Wars: The Phantom Menace* [1999] the limbs belong to battle droids, and so we need not feel a thing—a great comfort), the sly insinuation of doubt into the minds of characters who seemed untouched by life (Juliet Lewis's seduction by Robert De Niro in *Cape Fear* [1991], as well as the wholesale destruction of public and private property (*Independence Day* [1996] and *Zabriskie Point* [1970], among many others).

The concerted movement in Hollywood from social reality and myth toward action films that choreograph negativity onscreen, beginning roughly with *Rambo: First Blood* in 1982, is due in large part to the economic need of producers—after the breakup of the big studios as production giants—to presell distribution rights to their films internationally. The presale of foreign rights has been lucrative, to understate, and has led not only to steadily increasing star salaries and production costs more generally but also to a need for scripts and mise-en-scène that can satisfy global audiences regardless of variations in cultural knowledge, education, and religion. Sex and violence sell virtually everywhere, and to amplify the film product so that it can be appreciated (that is, bought) by the largest possible audience it helps to detach the appealing sexual and violent treatment from a bed in the plot; plots require thought. Hence the egregious use of sex and violence onscreen—placing it in diegetic contexts where it may seem to have little reason to be. When, more and more, the chance to recoup costs on big budget pictures is restricted to the opening weekend, the size of the audience must be vast, and the people in that audience must be different from one another in taste, background, and sensitivity. Little education or cultural awareness is needed to appreciate the dramatic pungency of a bomb going off, as Orson Welles demonstrated, with elegance, in *Touch of Evil* (1958).

Some further impetus toward the production of films that make extensive use of hideousness and slime has been provided by the development and wide availability of new, more easily manipulable and decorable forms of latex; new explosive and pyrotechnologies; advances in makeup. Anything we see must be capable of being shown. And the more advanced the technology for faking decrepitude—Dick Smith was one of the great pioneers in makeup—the more audiences have been moved to deep-seated delight, but also moral panic, because the corruption that is a pleasure to gawk at is also, in the end—at least as signification—corruption, and therefore something to fear.

Surely, however, it is only an extremely conventional, indeed conservative, notion of organized social life that underpins the kind of moral panic we have seen in criticism of the violence, moral turpitude, and conflict onscreen. In such a perspective, the world is in its ideal state a blissful and rather pretty arrangement of cooperating, harmoniously interrelated, and successfully wishful beings (who are also often complacent, satisfied, and aggressively happy)—the sort of pastoral idyll depicted in the Beethoven sequence of Disney's *Fantasia* (1940). Beside the fact that such an ideal, if it is any ideal at all, is preindustrial and hardly relevant—as moral critics imply it is—to all social systems in all circumstances, the picture of world harmony and bucolic social tranquility that is contradicted by the dark ugliness we are seeing onscreen everywhere now is also impossible to conceive as an objective rendering of things as they "are" or ever "were." Indeed, the idea that the world is essentially orderly, aesthetic, civilized, and beautiful in the precise way it is necessary to understand "beauty" if one is to see criminal underlife as "ugly," is itself only a hegemonic construct, one that "secures its ascendancy by representing itself as a 'natural' order. . . . Through hegemony, ideology is naturalized as history, beauty, order, 'common sense,' and, on the level of psychology, sanity and maturity" (McKelly 1996, 107). Embedded as we are in the logic that the pictures we see of evil and nefariousness onscreen are only so many obvious and direct representations in fiction of what is "obviously," "already," "directly," "clearly," "plainly," and "unmistakably" evil and nefarious in real life, we think it only "mature" and "sane" to enunciate critical disapproval of, say, the extramarital sex in *Fatal Attraction* (1987) or the rampant gunplay in *The Quick and the Dead* (1995) or the disrespectful and visceral anticlericism in *The Exorcist* (1973).

The view of natural social life as a harmony and the contention that evil and violence are inevitably willful, malevolent disruptions of that life is a kind of advertisement. It consciously and intentionally denies the inequalities of power and privilege, and the consequent social conflicts, produced in a social structure manipulated by big corporations and a tiny number of the superrich who persist in milking social benefits—thus, directly and adversely affecting the lives of the poor, the disabled, the uneducated, the sick, the alienated in general—to maximize profit. The state, operating as an extension of this power base, must help in the accumulation of profit, produce an ongoing rhetorical discourse to legitimate capitalism and capital accumulation, and coercively repress threats to these activities (Naiman 2000, 194–211). Coercive repression, indeed, is a power vital to state interests exactly because it is necessary to the smooth, uninterrupted functioning of multinationals and corporate giants. Yet the open assertion of violence in the name of bourgeois interests is ultimately unproductive—it decimates the workforce, for one thing, and demoralizes generally. Far more successful is the coercive function of subtle propaganda, the utile picture of the world in which certain undesirable but safe activity can be promoted as thrillingly marginal whereas other undesirable and dangerous activity can be cast in shadow as frightening, horrifying, disgusting, insane, idiotic, demonic, and uncivilized. Also central to a picture of the world that will be useful in terms of the overall repressive scheme of the state is the depiction of grassroots rebellion and weapons use as uncool, naughty, illegal, and un-American at the same time—often in the same shot—while "official" possession and use of weapons and aggressive activity is taken for granted as logical, noble, and heroic. When aggression is displayed by well-organized bureaucratically organized Others—enemy armies, the militias of Colombian drug cartels, the limitless factotums of megalomaniac "bad guys"—it is easily delegitimized by being labeled as "enemy" action.

All of which suggests that nothing is obvious or natural about the darkness of screen darkness, the evil of screen evil, the sliminess of screen slime. In order for the social order to be maintained and supported, the population must be brought to understand and accept certain configurations as holy and beautiful and others as repugnant, no structure functioning more deftly to accomplish this proscriptive education than a dramatic one and no drama being so cost efficient as a world-scale drama, highly amplified, with mass audiences and—joy!—opportunity for immense profit. Marvin Harris describes the need for proscription in an interesting ancient Middle Eastern case this way:

> The greater the temptation, the greater the need for divine interdiction. This relationship is generally accepted as suitable for explaining why the gods are always so interested in combating sexual temptations such as incest and adultery. Here I merely apply it to a tempting food. The Middle East is the wrong place to raise pigs, but pork remains a succulent treat. People always find it difficult to resist such temptations on their own. Hence Jahweh was heard to say that swine were unclean, not only as food, but to the touch as well. Allah was heard to repeat the same message for the same reason: It was ecologically maladaptive to try to raise pigs in substantial numbers. Small-scale production would only increase the temptation. Better then, to interdict the consumption of pork entirely, and to concentrate on raising goats, sheep, and cattle. (1989, 44)

To paraphrase Harris, people also find it difficult to resist the temptation to make a mess, to take apart, to reduce, shatter, disunite, strive for power, and otherwise uncontrollably play with the world in a manner that might jeopardize corporate arrangements. Or to put this a little differently, corporate arrangements are more precarious than they at first appear. Calling Hannibal Lecter an epitome of evil is a way to help people organize themselves morally in a way that doesn't jeopardize the plans of MacDonald's and Burger King. To insist on asking whether or not he *really is* evil in the face of the enormous contribution that calling him so can make to the state of social order is, in a way, naïve. What is most chilling about his cannibalism, in the end, is its distance from our regular way of handling cuisine, its revolutionary character, its reflection of the social organization of our own food gathering and thus of our social organization altogether. In most circumstances where food is available (such as those described in *Silence of the Lambs*) one can make arrangements to forego cannibalism, teach it as morally problematic and socially dangerous, and urge people to deny themselves its pleasures, whatever those may be, without at the same time requiring to turn one's exemplification of a cannibal into a hideous, depraved, ravenous, immoral, and diabolical reprobate. The chill in the spine that Anthony Hopkins was able to help provide for us, the chill that we called our pleasure and that was held out to us as a lure—"What stirs him is art and music. But what compels him is evil. *Hannibal"* (television ad for *Hannibal* [2001])—was the agency of our sentimental education.

More generally, the squeamishness that delights audiences when they watch the impenetrable darkness in *The Blair Witch Project* (1999) or the blood slurping in *Dracula* (1992) or a little fuzzy demon Osterized in *Gremlins* (1984) or two grown men surgically exchanging faces in *Face/Off* (1997) or a fellow asking to have his eyes plucked out in *Minority Report* (2002) is an emotional support for the indoctrination being dosed. Following Harris, one may conclude that the more tempting the pleasure against which society deems it necessary to provide indoctrination, the more intense—and therefore the more emotional—the indoctrination needs to be. It is emotion, not logic, that galvanizes, enchants, and engages. A philosophy of film must approach feeling and experience, not just plot.

Philosophy can be a method of denial, however, and much is denied by seeing film evil and ugliness *only* as ideological. To put this differently: film is brainwashing, to be sure, and yet brainwashing is also experience. The pervasiveness in critical (even pop critical) circles of the idea that screen "evil" is never to be seen as anything but an agency of brutalizing hegemonic manipulation, never other than an arbitrary politico-cultural fix on activity that in itself has no inherent moral value does raise the heuristic problem of establishing a true ground for cultural and artistic value outside of film once we have discarded it all as ideological drivel—everything in culture, after all, is equally ideological; yet it also raises the problem of elitism because one of film's great potentials is to harbor not only ideology but also the deep, perhaps transgressive, thought that cannot express itself in the sanctora of approved official culture. When "dark" film distances certain persons and activities, political stances, aesthetic configurations, and human choices as nauseating, sickening, disgusting, and abysmal, it is true that social forces achieve control to a degree; but we are also engaged with a vision of the world that, as André Bazin once put it, "accords with our desire." The debunking approach, useful as it may be, blinds us to that desire, thus turning us away from something that is elemental, fascinating, and worth study.

For an interesting example of how debunking can be blinding, and of how one's moral commitment or detachment can affect the way one sees a film, take the case of Freya Johnson's 1997 Internet comments on Spielberg's *Schindler's List* (1993). The Third Reich was an enterprise quite real in history (regardless of how silly it has often been made to seem onscreen) and most certainly one that was not merely "seen as" bad by a liberal U.S. government favorable to Jewish interests and hungry itself to dominate Germany. The systematic murder of millions of people is no neutral activity vulnerable to the application of pejorative labels—is not "bad" only because Jewish apologists say it is. When Johnson writes that Spielberg's Nazis "are not only evil, sadistic, sexually perverted, and well-dressed—all the things we have come to expect from them—they are also wildly *counter-productive;* they would rather kill off their workforce for the sake of ideology than merely exploit it as Capitalism dictates they ought," she seems a trifle too tongue-in-cheek, as though only in the crass manipulative perspective of an inauthentic type such as Spielberg could such august agents be seen as so craven. The "we" who have come to expect sadism, sexual perversion, and good clothing, after all, are precisely the readership in need of Johnson's informed point of view; in short, misperceivers. Without her "help," we might fall into the "trap" of thinking the Nazis "really were evil." By implication, the Nazis must not have been evil at all. Only the questionable, wildly Capitalistic, and notably productive Spielberg, the text seems to cry, could animate these rational beings as "wildly counter-productive," knocking them for not being what he is—all too unfortunately—himself. Although Johnson's point of view is stimulating, it is also a denial of history, and thus, of the present, and an expression of a desire to make these denials. It is also innocent, of course, attributing denial to Spielberg instead. In this case, I would argue, the filmmaker has gone beyond covering up real social forces with obfuscating stereotypes and filmic technique; and the presumptive objectivity of Johnson's critical point of view here is the coverup. Spielberg has at least acted from a more committed position than has Johnson in taking him to task.

So, understanding screen malevolence requires feeling, sensitivity, political savvy, and a commitment to careful sight and thought: taking a position. Sharon Stone's remorseless Catherine Tramell in *Basic Instinct* (1992) was widely regarded as depraved and antisocial. Yet one could argue that her willingness to murder men while copulating with them is "obviously" problematic and "obviously" unthinkable as direct representation only for smug (male) viewers who have never contemplated what women routinely suffer through the enforcement of male-dominated heterosexuality in presumably cleaner films where only females are the (systematic) victims: *Cinderella* (1950), *The Stepford Wives* (1975), *Heavenly Creatures* (1994). She seems a transgressive figuration. But why the long copulation scenes as settings for the murders? Can it be to hook our pornographic imaginations into alignment with exactly the misogyny she may be fantasized to revenge? Although this book is not an express statement of position about screen violence, it is intended to be a provocative collection of inquiries that suggests approaches and questions such as this.

It is worth suggesting that not every inquiry into infamy, darkness, evil, and slime onscreen need occupy itself with the presumption of a basic duality—that there is negativity or positivity (and nothing else); evil or goodness; darkness or light; ugliness or beauty. Binary thinking and depiction by chiaroscuro lend themselves handsomely to a certain style of dramatization of conflict, a style that is ultimately not dialectical and in which one side of the equation invariably dominates. From a screenwriter's perspective, binary logic makes possible the swift, if shallow, mobilization of audience engagement with character, and it is not accidental that contemporary binary representations of screen malevolence are character- (which is to say, actor-) centered in construction. If beauty and ugliness are only to be seen as polar opposites, and so too goodness and evil, the same can be said for heroism and villainy with the result that a plot can revolve on a convenient battle between singular forces, a scene can be composed in alternating close shots, and in the end the cult of personality so dear to consumerist logic can be nourished and maintained. Although situations in real life are far more complex than this, nevertheless the easy division made possible by binary logic makes for enjoyable—if also idiotic—films to watch. I think that, in the end, considering how these films, unrepresentative though they are of real experience, manage to excite us when we view or remember them is far more interesting than elaborating on how they are simplistic, trivial wastes of time. Very often, I would say, the more ridiculous the representation, the less being engaged in it actually feels to viewers actually viewing like a waste of time.

An exploration of screen evil must therefore navigate between two dangers, what might be called the structural and the phenomenological problems: first, an inability to see social structural formations because of a too-ready armature of received ideas about what is and is not bad, a too-pious commitment to the hegemony; secondly, an inability to be true to the deepest sensations and experiences of a viewer's vision of cinema, because of an overinvestment in ideological analysis. To be sure, in this book we have steered *toward* that ideological analysis with some favor, because in an individualizing society where the broad-based issues and formations that shape culture and modern life are systematically hidden much cultural experience is officially masked as personal and idiosyncratic. Yet while there is plenty of ideology around us, there is not only ideology. That "evil" or "ugliness" may seem evil or ugly only because we have been induced to think of them that way does not in the end make us shudder less. Many of the writers here attend to the quality and extent, the ramification, the historical shape, the felt nuance of our experience when we see what we would call bloody deformation, destruction, malevolence, hideousness, shadow, corruption, manipulation, violation, and villainy onscreen. These things of darkness we must acknowledge ours.

The chapters you will find here, that try to come to terms with our experience of watching films, are all original to these pages, and each is written to explore either a single film or a few related films, or a genre, or some facet of the production of what I am calling "bad" movies. Certainly, no single overriding theme interconnects them all except that in them malevolence of some kind is prominent in an interesting way. The writing, lively and pointed, should engage anyone who loves film and anyone who is fascinated by the way Hollywood has moved to extend moral boundaries, multiply and ambiguate screen treatment of evil, extend the forms of representation, and mass market blood and gore around the world. We are living, certainly, in a world where moral problematization is the running theme: the war against terrorism, the reinflamed war in Iraq, the war against immorality in a Catholic Church beset by what the Pope, on March 21, 2002, called "the most grievous forms of the mystery of evil at work in the world" (CNN.com). We are enduring a war of capital against the environment, a war of conglomeration against local interest and small business, a war against disease and at the same time a war against drugs, a war against crime and at the same time a war against decency, and a war against illiteracy and also a war against text. We are, in short, in a state of global and multivariate war with little perspective on resolution—and, I might add, with little sense of stability. Already by April 2002 *Vanity Fair* reported that "9/11" was "out," along with snowboarding, dissing Oprah, and Greta Van Susteren.

Part I, "It's a Slimy World, After All," collects a group of broadly conceived chapters, sociologically or historically based, that examine screen evil and violence as a reflection of broader cultural concerns and technical developments in a world where moral absolutes are crumbling and where ethical conduct is under threat. To begin, Tom Gunning's masterful "Flickers: On Cinema's Power for Evil" is an engaging exploration of the idea that cinema is inherently evil, an idea implicit in the 1915 U.S. Supreme Court decision separating cinema from First Amendment rights. Tracing the history of the regard for cinema as evil from Manicheanism through Cartesian epistemology, parlor magic, and early cinema to Theodore Roszak's book *Flicker*, the author shows that any film "could be ideologically complicit if it was projected in a darkened room with the illusion of motion and the viewer positioned in front of the screen." If the trick of cinema offered neither demystification nor redeeming allegory, if it supported neither science nor religion, visual illusion "might maintain a dangerous anarchic force, an undermining of authority itself in favor of the pure play of sensation." Vulnerable audiences thus "risked being subjected to the 'evil demon of images'" produced by a hungry industry "deviating from the tradition of print culture."

Gwendolyn Audrey Foster's "Monstrosity and the Bad-White-Body Film" examines *Attack of the 50 Foot Woman, The Incredible Shrinking Man,* and several other films that concentrate on the bad-white body, associating whiteness with badness and with war against the self, murder, destruction, and hypersexuality and showing how in these films "the terrain of conquest is the white body, over which whiteness attempts to display mastery." A particular focus of these films, shown in *The Amazing Colossal Man* and *War of the Colossal Beast*, is "problematic liminal whiteness," in the sense that whiteness as performed "underscores the unstable configuration of whiteness at odds with itself." Foster shows how cheap sci-fi exploitation cinema "allowed for a space in which the social conduct of white society could be critiqued" in the 1950s, when women's liberation and civil rights were in their early stages and attitudes toward minorities and women were in retrenchment.

Aaron Baker's "Beyond the Thin Line of Black and Blue: Movies and Police Misconduct in Los Angeles" is a study of systematic police racism in *Colors, Internal Affairs, L.A. Confidential, Training Day,* and other films. By maintaining essentialist notions about race, such films typically advocate the need for "rough justice," sometimes going as far as to suggest that the moral corruption of the police is a straightforward outcome of the increase in non-white police personnel. "Bad cop" films are therefore a screen for the hidden promulgation of racial essentialism. Baker writes, "Because Hollywood is not good at representing systemic problems and is even worse at showing structural solutions, the response these films offer is mostly the individual heroism of a good cop."

Hollywood cinema has a long tradition of representing mass murder. Christopher Sharrett's "Genocidal Spectacles and the Ideology of Death" discusses films from *The Birth of a Nation* to *Black Hawk Down* in terms of the utility of mass violence onscreen in the American imperialist project and the neoliberal ideology on which it depends. Commenting on the disjunction between official, state-sanctioned violence and the representation of unsanctioned violence in cultural media, Sharrett notes governmental concern to stage-manage cultural displays of violence: "the annihilation of the racial Other is a staple of the commercial entertainment industry." That mass destruction onscreen might be so graphic is seen by Sharrett to collude with "the postmodern conceit that all human experience (or at least all experience worth writing criticism about) is mediated."

Peter Lehman's "Bad, Worse, Worst: *8MM* and Hollywood's Bad Boys of Porn" is a discussion of the presumptive moral superiority of mainstream Hollywood filmmakers depicting the "bad" porn industry in mainstream, "good" narratives. With specific focus on *8MM* as seen in comparison to *The People vs. Larry Flynt* and *Boogie Nights,* Lehman gives a precise reading that reveals the angling and exaggeration necessary for construction of a portrait of the porn world as a thoroughly morally suspect universe. Perverse and widely varying depictions of the "bad boys of porn" from filmmakers such as Joel Schumacher, Milos Forman, and Paul Thomas Anderson can be understood best through an examination of the relationship between the porn industry and mainstream Hollywood, which includes attention to the move from film to video, the filmmaker's position on First Amendment rights, and what Lehman calls "dominant cultural fears about pornography."

In "Toxic Corps," Kirby Farrell muses upon the "bewilderingly equivocal" relation to historical reality of the Hollywood trope he calls "rage at the corporate state." Corporations are "enabling fictions" making possible risk, responsibility, and resource sharing, but they also diminish responsibility. Seen in films from *Intolerance* and *Metropolis* through *King Kong* to *The Atomic Cafe, Kalifornia,* and *Titanic,* the state and its institutions are increasingly and pervasively corporate. Although rage against this development "underlies consumer rights advocacy and anti-globalization protests," Farrell shows that it serves, at the same time, "specific groups as different as Al Qaeda terrorists and right-wing militias in the United States."

And Henry A. Giroux, in "The *Ghost World* of Neoliberalism: Abandoning the Abandoned Generation," assesses *Ghost World*'s attempt to address the question of how popular representations of youth use a discourse of privatization to signal social crisis. For Giroux, our public, "emptied of any social content," has been "reduced to a phantom sphere largely dominated by the vocabulary of the private." Politics has become disengaged from power and has turned inward, and youth "have become a target of disciplinary control, surveillance, and punishment, especially on the streets and in the public schools." This chapter illuminates the simplistic notion of the "bad kid" and its function for hiding broadly developed and pernicious social formulations that imperil democracy. *Ghost World* "points to crucial problems without fully engaging them."

Part II, "Auteurs of Negativity, Icons of Darkness," focuses on screen darkness and immorality as particularized in particular motion pictures or in the work of particular filmmakers. Wheeler Winston Dixon's "'How Will I Get My Opium?': Jean Cocteau and the Treachery of Friendship" is a biographically focused reading of the important film work of Jean Cocteau (1889–1963). A paragon of the twentieth century *artiste,* Cocteau is shown through analysis of his life and work to have been willing to go to extraordinary lengths to find "new material." Here, the artist is analyzed as morally culpable, rather than the neutral medium through which social morality is filtered and depicted. Dixon's analysis of Cocteau's apparent perfidy in his working method brings new insight to the appreciation of works such as *La Belle et la Bête, Orphée, Les Enfants terribles,* and *Le Sang d'un poète* among others.

Russ Meyer was a significant contributor to the history of the exploitation film and to the 1970s eruption of hard-core porn. In "The Sweeter the Kitten the Sharper the Claws," Kristen Hatch analyses his midcareer work, notably *Vixen!, Motor Psycho, Lorna,* and *Faster, Pussycat! Kill! Kill!,* among other films, to show that what seems to be transgressive in Meyer may be counterhegemonic: systematically in his work, "the patriarchal family structure is shown to be perverted." Although conventional critique of exploitation cinema rests on a claim for its endorsement of patriarchy, Hatch convincingly shows that in the case of Meyer, that dominant structure is no more supported than it is symbolically overthrown.

In "Wanted for Murder," Tony Williams examines the revealing and peculiar case of Eric Portman, who figured prominently, very often playing nefarious and twisted villains, in 1940s and 1950s British cinema. Although Portman never achieved major star status, his performances are consistently noteworthy—in such films as *The Colditz Story, Wanted for Murder, A Canterbury Tale,* and *Forty-Ninth Parallel.* Williams explores the possibility that the "obsessional" acting style Portman used may have been related to his secret homosexual orientation, problematized by repressive British cultural codes of the era. The actor qualifies as an auteur of negativity, Williams asserts, "especially if we place Portman within the specific cultural context of repressive British social life."

James Bond films have typified Hollywood's vision of immorality and evil in a coherent way since 1962. Steven Woodward's "The Arch Archenemies of James Bond" explores the treatment of villainy in the twenty-two James Bond films so far, arguing that ultimately the Bond villain, "surrounded by beautiful women who do not love him, comfortable with wealth although obsessed with its acquisition, connoisseur of food and wine although ascetic to a fault," constitutes the real enigma in Bond narratives. As our moral landscape has grown "hazier, the distinction between dignity and depravity less easy to make in everyday life," Bond films have sustained the portraiture of villainy in terms of sexual coding and Oedipal drama, "primarily through the self-conscious irony embodied in Bond himself."

Gina Marchetti's "Cinematic Incarnations of Chinese Villainy" examines the Oriental evil on Hollywood screens with specific focus on the treatment of Orientalism in two contemporary films, David Cronenberg's *M. Butterfly* and Olivier Assayas's *Irma Vep,* with performances by John Lone and Maggie Cheung. In both films, masking is associated with the construction of villainy—in *Butterfly* invoking a notable performance of gender. As with Fu Manchu, these characters openly suggest a fear of colonial hybridity and European violence, and give us to see how "the Yellow Peril/Red Menace combination of the Cold War continues to endure in contemporary figurations of Red China. Marchetti provocatively suggests that if the Orient has lost its power to be our "underground self," it follows that "the projected fantasy of imperial ambition, colonial conquest, and patriarchal privilege loses its screen in the Other and must ricochet back onto the white male."

Dana Polan's "On the Bad Goodness of *Born to Be Bad:* Auteurism, Evaluation, and Nicholas Ray's Outsider Cinema" is a metacritique of our procedures for distinguishing "bad" from "good" films, and at the same time a close reading of an underexamined film, Nicholas Ray's *Born to Be Bad*. Contrasting moral and aesthetic badness in terms of this film, Polan shows how the narrative reflects changing moral attitudes in the 1950s. If *Born to Be Bad* has been "declared aesthetically bad by auteurists," because of the conventional morality underpinning its aesthetic, Polan finds it fascinating because it evidences the "pressures toward conformity to the dominant system in action." That *Born to Be Bad* was not sanctioned by auteurists sheds light on auteurism as much as on the film.

No study of screen evil could miss an exploration of the director Andrew Sarris has called "the supreme technician of American cinema" (1968, 57). William Rothman's "The Villain in Hitchcock: Does He Look Like a 'Wrong One' to You?" explores a wide range of Hitchcockian films with some focus on *The 39 Steps* and *The Lodger* and their implication of the viewer in a moral position. Rothman shows how Hitchcock affiliates the eye of the camera with the eye and "I" of the protagonist, in situations where the characters and the audience are similarly trapped in the filmmaker's device. Unable to "self-nominate" as villain, the screen character is very different from the protagonist of stage melodrama—a human being, ongoingly mysterious. Hitchcock's mastery included his special sensitivity to *the camera*'s nomination of villainy.

The final part, "The Charisma of Villainy," has contributions that focus on particular characterizations or characterizational types. Alexander Doty and Patricia Clare Ingham give an extended queer reading of *Cat People* in "The 'Evil Medieval,'" suggesting that the film can be read as a tale of the conflict between a heterocentric power structure and a transgressive cultural tradition that emphasizes women's pleasure and liberation. The "badness" of the cat women is portrayed narratively as a cultural strategy for containing those who threaten the dominant order. However, in a "shift to biological essentialism" that highlights the protagonist's natural essence, the film suggests that our racial and ethnic past is ineluctable. In its panther imagery, the film alludes to the "troubled and troubling" past of U.S. race relations as well.

E. Ann Kaplan concentrates on the later careers of Marlene Dietrich and Jeanne Moreau in "Wicked Old Ladies from Europe." Postmenopausal screen characters are almost invariably seen in negative light. Dietrich can be seen in Chris Hunt's *Marlene Dietrich: Shadow and Light* and Maximilian Schell's *Marlene* attempting to repress her aging, maintaining her youthful screen allure well into old age. Moreau, on the other hand, often contradicts powerful cultural assumptions about old women, most specifically when she plays the principal role in *La Vieille qui marchait dans la mer*. Here, "outrageous" in her desires for a young man, she "has her own morality, her own limits, and above all her own perspective on herself."

Lester D. Friedman provides a penetrating overview of Nazis in Hollywood film in "Darkness Visible." The author begins by reflecting in depth upon the attractions of Nazi imagery, suggesting the importance of Nazi image power; our "sympathy for the devil" attitude with respect to villains; the erotic appeal of Nazi imagery; the Holocaust culture that grounds our perception of screen Nazis; and our fear that we might be *them*. He then proceeds to a systematic overview of the vast array of American screen treatments of Nazism, categorizing them as period pieces—those made immediately before or during World War II; as retrospectives—films set in World War II but made after that time; as humoresques and satires; as fantasies; and as victimization narratives—particularly Holocaust stories. In this sweeping and galvanizing view, we are brought from *Confessions of a Nazi Spy* to *Apt Pupil* and *Schindler's List* with a stunning awareness of the pervasiveness and power of the Nazi as an icon of evil on the Hollywood screen.

Cynthia Fuchs's "'The Whole Fucking World Warped around Me': Bad Kids and Worse Contexts" examines two ostensibly different yet deeply related films about kids: Larry Clark's *Bully*, set in a dreamlike world of "speed and immobility, boredom and overstimulation, expectation and hopelessness, affluence and pretense"; and David Gordon Green's *George Washington*, recounting the story of young people who live among wrecked cars, with constant noise from trains, "crossing bells ringing, wheels grating and squealing, truck beds heaving." Both films deal with sudden death—in one by murder, in the other by accident—and the moral world the kids inhabit as in their very different ways they come to terms with it. *Bully* raises questions about "social responsibility and ethical definitions," whereas *George Washington* suggests that moral comprehension is a personal experience that "can be affected by contexts, but is not determined by them."

Rebecca Bell-Metereau examines the hideous monstrosities that people sci-fi and horror film in "Searching for Blobby Fissures: Slime, Sexuality, and the Grotesque," an exploration through the territory defined by such films as *The Fly, Men in Black, The Blob, Carrie,* and *The Elephant Man* to discover what accounts for the allure of "disgusting" sights onscreen. Bell-Metereau connects the grotesque body to the abjectness of femininity, but her analysis shows that screen uses of bodily fluids, orifices, and membranes differ. Although the ultimate taboos of menstruation and castration certainly help underpin the chilled response of many viewers to grotesque imagery, we must also note that female viewers may "take vicarious pleasure" in the release of aggression that permits them to find themselves empowered in "identifying with the monster or killer and in the shock and horror of the victim."

The mad scientist as a screen convention is discussed in Ina Rae Hark's "Crazy Like a Prof: Mad Science and the Transgressions of the Rational." With specific attention to a close reading of *Forbidden Planet* and the role in that narrative of exceptional intelligence as a harbinger of pure "evil," Hark suggests that mad scientists are more often "bad" than "mad" and that the mad badness they display is typically configured as contention with the powers of divinity. In *Planet,* the blasphemy of the mad scientist is punished as his creation turns on him.

And finally, in my own "Tom Ripley's Talent" I consider an unconventional reading of *The Talented Mr. Ripley* that takes the protagonist's social class and sexual identity as structural forces. More important than what Tom Ripley does in this story is the way he is seen and framed, the consequences that beset him because of the economic advantages he does not have. That the "criminal" aspect of the film is so tightly wedded to a portrait of class distinction suggests that "evil" is a label we can conveniently and systematically apply to those we wish to keep down.

Screen malevolence provides a sense of power exactly to the measure that we can alienate ourselves from it by watching, then climb above it by finding it disgusting. A sense of power, but not power. "Badness" onscreen therefore helps produce a society in which individuality and personal sanctimony are heightened at the expense of group relations, where individualistic sensuality and sensitivity are played up at the expense of humanity, recognition, and deep understanding. The villain we abhor is precisely the figuration we cannot accept as a version of ourselves, the screen on which we cannot see ourselves—our discrete and self-absorbed selves—projected. And the gorier the image—by the end of the twentieth century screen imagery had reached new heights of gore—the more easily we can deny it, withdraw into a narcissistic paradise where the world is perfect as long as we do not have to reach out and touch it.

Badness on film may be a repository of our most important secrets.

WORKS CITED

Anonymous. 2002. "Vanities: Hollywood Rule Book," *Vanity Fair* No. 500 (April), 322.

CNN.com. 2002. "Pope Responds to Sex Abuse Cases." *www.cnn.com* (March 21).

Eyman, Scott. 1999. *Print the Legend: The Life and Times of John Ford.* New York: Simon & Schuster.

Harris, Marvin. 1989. *Cows, Pigs, Wars, and Witches: The Riddles of Culture.* New York: Vintage.

Johnson, Freya. 1997. "Newt's Nazis: Pop Culture's 'High Other.'" http://eserver.org/bs/33/johnson.html.

McKelly, James C. 1996. "Youth Cinema and the Culture of Rebellion: *Heathers* and the *Rebel* Archetype." In Murray Pomerance and John Sakeris, eds., *Pictures of a Generation on Hold: Selected Papers,* Toronto: Media Studies Working Group, 1996, 107–14.

Naiman, Joanne. 2000. *How Societies Work: Class, Power, and Change in a Canadian Context.* Toronto: Irwin.

Sarris, Andrew. 1968. *The American Cinema: Directors and Directions 1929–1968.* New York: Dutton.

PART I

It's a Slimy World, After All

FIGURE 1. "Magic tricks operated like commodity capitalism through an occluding of labor, concealing the actual effective gesture and seeming to produce things 'by magic.'" Nosferatu (Max Schreck) rises from his coffin in *Nosferatu, eine Symphonie des Grauens* (F. W. Murnau, Jofa-Ateler/Berlin-Johannisthal, 1922). (Frame enlargement)

CHAPTER ONE

Flickers:
On Cinema's Power for Evil

TOM GUNNING

They are letters and symbols in a language I don't know; but I
know they stand for evil words.
—G. K. Chesterton, "The Wrong Shape"

There is Power in Evil.
—Herlof's Marta in Carl Theodore Dreyer's *Day of Wrath*

Could cinema in its essence be evil? When Georges Bataille (1981) claims
literature for Evil, he is speaking primarily of the tales that literature tells, of
the importance of transgression to literary narrative (vi). Evil is something literature expresses; it does not inhere in the very signifiers of the text, the materiality and perceptual qualities of literature. But with cinema . . . doubts arise
about its innocence from its origins. This chapter traces what I call an essential suspicion of cinema—a suspicion of cinema's nature—which I find in a
variety of seemingly heterogeneous discourses: U.S. Supreme Court decisions,

A somewhat different version of this chapter was presented as a paper for the Unprin-
cipled Passions Conference, Southampton, England, Feb. 2002. I dedicate this to my
Hollywood friends: Adam Simon, auteur of *The American Nightmare* and E. Elias
Merhige, auteur of *The Sign of the Vampire*.

1970s film theory, and a fairly recent pulp thriller written by an important American thinker. Although I recuse myself from pronouncing final judgment, I think that the suspicion of cinema as somehow essentially evil plays a subterranean—unacknowledged, but often powerful—role in much of contemporary thinking about cinema as an art form and a social force.

Anyone who has ventured into the social and legal history of cinema in the United States knows that until 1952 motion pictures were denied the protection of the First Amendment of the Constitution. For more than half a century, movies shown in the United States were not allowed the privilege of free speech guaranteed to print media. The basis for this judgment, which legalized film censorship in the United States for nearly four decades, came very near to proclaiming motion pictures evil. According to the long-standing Supreme Court decision in the case of *Mutual Film Corporation v. Ohio Industrial Commission*, the new medium of film was "capable of evil, having power for it, the greater because of the attractiveness and manner of exhibition" (McKenna 1915, 3). Supreme Court Justice McKenna inscribed the evil capacity of cinema in his opinion reflecting the February 23, 1915, unanimous Supreme Court decision. The court ruled against the Mutual Film Corporation, a film distribution company, which had asked the court to overturn the film censorship law and board of censors in Ohio. As Garth Jowett (1989) has pointed out, this decision remained in place for the next thirty-seven years, providing the basis for not only various state and local film censorship boards but also the legal definition of cinema's status (or lack thereof) as a medium of public discourse, defining the terms under which the Hollywood system operated during its period of ascendancy and triumph (260).

While this decision primarily addressed issues of censorship and freedom of expression, I want to stress its attempt to grapple with a new medium, with the nature of movies as opposed to the printed word. This case addressed the law instituting censorship in Ohio, but not the banning of a specific film. The court's ruling dealt with the regulation of the film medium rather than a specific film, therefore attempting, at least in passing, to define the nature of film. Not simply the *content* of a film was literally placed on trial here, but the *nature* of film itself, and more specifically its relation to audiences, its unique power of attraction. McKenna freely admitted many films were innocuous and underscored that the censorship statute in Ohio stated that "films of a moral, or amusing and harmless nature shall be passed and approved" (3). Therefore, it was not claimed that cinema by its essence *had* to be evil. However, under the Ohio statute, film would be subjected to prior censorship, the most objectionable and authoritarian form of regulation, not simply entailing prosecution for abusive or obscene films once they were shown but requiring prescreening and judgment by an appointed board of censors on the suitability of films before they were screened for the public. Such treatment differed radically from that accorded constitutionally protected printed material. The lack of prepublication censorship formed a cornerstone of freedom of the press—a point the lawyers for Mutual Film argued strongly, and felt should be applicable to film as a means of expression (McKenna, 3).

The Mutual Film Corporation asserted a shared purpose of expression between movies and print culture and claimed thereby the protection of freedom of speech guaranteed by the First Amendment of the U.S. Constitution (although, for technical reasons, it was the guarantee of the freedom of speech in the Ohio Constitution that was argued). Films, the corporation claimed, "depict dramatizations of standard novels, exhibiting many subjects of scientific interest, the properties of matter, the growth of various forms of animal and plant life, and explorations and travel; also events of historical and current interest—the same events which are described in words and by photographs in newspapers, weekly periodicals, magazines and other publications" (McKenna, 1). Films must be recognized, the Mutual lawyers argued, "as graphic expressions of opinion and sentiment, exponents of policies, as teachers of science and history, as useful, interesting, amusing, educational and moral" (3).

The Supreme Court, however, did not accept this analogy with "the press of the country," instead finding motion pictures more analogous to the theater or circus, to visual spectacles and shows. "We immediately feel that the argument is wrong or strained which extends the guarantees of free opinion and speech to the multitudinous shows which are advertised on the billboards of our cities and towns. . . . They [motion pictures], indeed, may be mediums of thought, but so are many things. So is the theater, the circus, and all other shows and spectacles" (McKenna, 3). Rather than "organs of public opinion," motion pictures, the court claimed, were "mere representations of events, of ideas and sentiments published and known, vivid, useful and entertaining no doubt, but as we have said, capable of evil" (McKenna, 3).

Much of the court's decision undoubtedly depended, Jowett argued (60–63, 71–75), on the nature of the film-going public in 1915, drawing primarily on the segments of the public guardians of traditional culture considered most impressionable: women, children, and the lower classes. Justice McKenna stressed that such audiences were assembled promiscuously, mixing genders, ages, and classes: "The audiences they assemble, not of women alone nor of men alone, but together, not of adults only, but of children, make them the more insidious" (3). Thus the court ruling not only reflected a narrow interpretation of the media by which public opinion was expressed, restricting it to the spoken and written word, but also implied a restrictive understanding of the proper constitution of the public sphere itself. What Miriam Hansen (1991) has called the "alternative public sphere" of motion pictures in the Progressive Era, comprising the working-class patrons and women and children of all classes, the Court and other reformers saw rather as a public in need of special protection due to their low level of education and biological maturity or perhaps even their perceptual, intellectual, and emotional makeup (90–125). Justice McKenna undoubtedly felt this new public was especially susceptible to the evil introduced by the power and attraction of the movies.

Most discussions of this ruling have focused on the issue of this new audience, seeing the call for film censorship as a sign of panic on the part of Protestant white males over their eroding social control by such innovations as commercial mass entertainment (Jowett 1989, 61–63). Although this remains an important issue to investigate, I want to shift focus to the concern over the medium itself, its evil capabilities that are inherently different from the spoken or written word. Whereas McKenna's decision can certainly be understood within a puritanical tradition, generally suspicious of the visual image and especially of theater (what Jonas Barish calls "the anti-theatrical prejudice" [1981]), the force with which this decision brings this tradition to bear on the new medium needs to be stressed. McKenna's concern about the nature of this new medium casts an anxious eye not only on its new form of audience, but also on a new power of attraction.

For a film historian attempting to recover the horizons of reception of early American cinema, McKenna's comments are frustratingly laconic, lacking a detailed phenomenological description of an experience we would love to recover. But while succinct (and at points seemingly ungrammatical!), his language remains revealing. Although McKenna grants laudable uses of motion pictures, he immediately cautions: "But they [motion pictures] may be used for evil, and against that possibility the [Ohio] statute was enacted" (3). The following quotation, a fragment of which I cited earlier, captures something of the power McKenna sensed in motion pictures that gave them a dangerous aspect:

> Their power of amusement, and, it may be education, the audiences they assemble, not of women alone nor of men alone, but together, not of adults only, but of children, make them the more insidious in corruption by a pretense of worthy purpose or if they should degenerate from worthy purpose. Indeed we may go beyond that possibility. They take their attraction from the general interest, eager and wholesome it may be, in their subjects, but a prurient interest may be excited and appealed to. Besides, there are some things which should not have pictorial representation in public places and to all audiences. (3)

Besides invoking motion pictures' strong appeal to what we could call—following a long tradition that has treated this impulse with grave suspicion—curiosity (see Gunning 1995, 124), McKenna recognizes (albeit without detailing) what he calls elsewhere the "attractiveness" of motion pictures. He concludes that the Ohio statute was properly motivated by this power of attraction and its potentially evil applications: "It was this capacity and power, and it may be in experience of them, that induced the state of Ohio, in addition to prescribing penalties for immoral exhibitions, as it does in its Criminal Code, to require censorship before exhibition, as it does in the act under review" (3). The statute merited upholding because it addressed a very real, and basically new, threat: "We would have to shut our eyes to the facts of the world to regard the precaution unreasonable," McKenna concludes (3).

What is cinema's power and what does it have to do with Evil? I would like to broaden the context of this discussion of film's capacity for evil, not by turning to institutional censorship and its discourses, but rather by exploring a deep-rooted suspicion of the nature of cinema and spectacle itself. Rather than simply exemplifying a reactionary scheme by a threatened elite (although certainly that plays a role here), arguments about the nature of the cinema of the sort Justice McKenna introduced derive from long-standing discussions about the nature of vision and visual entertainments and their emotional effects. Claims about the unique nature of the cinema must be situated within a tradition of visual illusion that has long been associated with Evil. These suspicions stretch (in their modern form) from the Enlightenment to, I would claim, the foundational theories of academic film studies. Although in tracing this genealogy I believe I am partly tracing a paranoia about the nature of visual illusion, I should add that I do not entirely dismiss the relation between the cinema and what Jean Baudrillard has termed "the evil demon of images" (1988).

The *Mutual v. Ohio* decision articulates a series of common assumptions about the cinema during the period of its emergence and transformation asserted by journalists and social reformers as well. First, motion pictures were recognized as *different* experientially from other media. Comparisons to the magic lantern, and to various devices that caused the illusion of motion abound, but early accounts recurringly indicate some important novelty in motion pictures, especially in combining photographic images with the illusion of motion. Secondly, this difference had to do with a perceptual *vividness,* an increased power over the viewers' senses, one that was pictorial and visual rather than linguistic and discursive (even if language might be a component), but that also exceeded the impact of ordinary pictures. This power is often described in terms of an intense realism, but even when realist writers such as Maxim Gorky questioned the realism of the silent black-and-white images, they also testified to cinema's power of fascination (1960, 407–9).

The intense effects of motion pictures frequently triggered involuntary physical reactions (jolts, screams, and—less reliably—fainting) in viewers unfamiliar with the new medium, but the effects could also be described more psychologically and more sinisterly. This visually vivid novelty, some reformers and journalists claimed, exerted *undue influence* on its audience, an attraction compared to bewitchment, hypnosis, casting a spell, or putting the viewer/audience into a trance (Curtis 1994, 455–57). This is where cinema's power of attraction, its capacity for evil, takes on a more tangible form than

McKenna described explicitly. A complete survey of these claims of what I am calling "undue influence" would run the gamut of complaints that the cinema adversely affected the viewers' eyesight or other aspects of physical well-being, their nervous states, their dreams or sleep patterns, and their capacity for aesthetic, moral, or political judgments. Less frequently, but garnering a great deal of attention, more extreme claims were made that films had actually compelled viewers to behavior or mental states through a manipulation of their senses or their mental capacities.

Placed in this light, the 1915 Supreme Court ruling clearly did not claim that films should not receive First Amendment protection because they could not adequately convey opinions or emotions the way language can. Rather than a deficiency, their capacity for evil might derive from their ability to convey emotions or opinions *too* effectively, their having a power that might supersede rational argument especially when presented to those presumably less rationally trained or logically skilled. The reformist campaign against the cinema in many countries (from Progressivists in the United States to the Kino reformers in Germany [see Curtis]) during cinema's first decades aimed at restricting or curtailing these baleful physical and psychological effects (hence, their common emphasis on protecting children).

But, in essence, do we not also recognize here the descriptions of cinema as an ideological machine as articulated by Jean-Louis Baudry in the 1970s and embraced to varying degrees by European and American academic film theorists under the rubric of "apparatus theory?" I cannot claim that noting this similarity supplies a full critique of the value of this much-debated theory, but placing its argument within a history of the suspicion of cinema may help us rethink its role in articulating the ideological effects of the cinema. A suspicion of cinema, understood as a visually powerful medium rooted in an illusion of reality and exerting unconscious influences on the viewer, underlies both a conservative antimodern resistance to the new medium at the dawn of the twentieth century and a neo-Marxist ideological critique decades later.

Any sophisticated reader of 1970s film theory recognizes that the critique of cinematic vision offered by apparatus theory was rooted in a broader late-twentieth-century critique of the ocularcentrism and the hegemony of vision, articulated in a variety of ways from Heidegger and Sartre to Foucault and Debord (if such recognition was not immediate, Martin Jay's masterful explication of this modern suspicion of the visual in *Downcast Eyes* [1993] could supply it). But, as Jay reminds us, a particular reified sort of vision, the rationalized, aggressive, knowledge- and mastery-seeking vision associated with Western metaphysics, formed the target of this critique (435–91). Recent work by theorists such as Jonathan Crary (1990) has focused new attention on the history rather than the theory of vision, or the transformations that took place within both theories and practices of vision. Crary has described the nineteenth-century appearance of the conception of an embodied sight, displacing the disembodied panoptic eye of earlier metaphysics. In investigating this new embodied vision, the cinema, as representative of a long tradition of popular visual devices, has much to teach us, rather than simply being identified with dominant visual reification and the age of the world picture. Certainly we must avoid merely inverting the terms of the denigration of vision with a valorization of the visual. Such an inversion would risk losing important critical insights. Nonetheless, a dialectical model seems to be called for that does not reduce vision to one monolithic metaphysical conception. To envision this alternative visual tradition and its relation to cinema's power of attraction, let us probe further Justice McKenna's and the early film reformers' suspicion as well as its peculiar, belated echo in 1970s film theory.

Clearly for the reformers the new popularity of the cinema threatened a dethronement of the rational and the verbal, especially as the tutor of youth (and women and the working class). The terms of this concern, although not directly articulated in the 1915 decision, do not simply lie in a fear that cinema might overwhelm rationality by arousing irrational emotion, but rather target an even more dangerous (and modern) short circuit, which we could call "sensationalism." I do not mean by this a form of eighteenth-century philosophy, but rather a late-nineteenth-century transformation of aesthetics into a sensual rather than an intellectual process, bypassing even the carefully trained "sensibility" of the earlier part of the century and perhaps even replacing the passions of the romantics with a nearly physiological concern with the bodily senses. Crucially, this phenomenon takes place on both the popular and the avant-garde levels, while middle class (and middle brow) art theorists proclaim it an assault on civilization itself. The "sensation novel" and the "sensation drama"— such as the melodramas of Boucicault ("The Poor of New York") or the novels of Wilkie Collins *(The Woman in White)*—exemplified a popular taste for a direct, almost physical, experience from forms of entertainment (see Gunning 1994, 52). Aestheticians and critics roundly condemned such strong stimulus as beyond the pale of art. However, the unheard-of popularity of the sensational created both a new mass audience and a commercial conception of artistic production. Lagging slightly behind the mass audiences and the entrepreneurs of entertainment, the avant-garde also offered artistic and theoretical practices based in sensation. For example, Rimbaud's call for a systematic derangement of the senses, Seurat's exploration of the effects of color, Wagner's *gesamkunstwerk,* the experiments in synesthesia of the Symbolists all began to replace traditions of representation with a new address to the senses, albeit senses of an altered sort, including vision.

The commercial art of sensationalism in the nineteenth century was identified with the apparent chaos of modern life, with a new shallow and inauthentic existence. In many ways the suspicion of cinema as a new, vividly visual, and sensual technology with mass appeal (articulated by the 1915 decision) repeats the derision heaped upon the new techniques for reproducing color painting supplied earlier in the nineteenth century by the chromolithograph. Garish and supposedly exaggerated in its use of color, making visual art available to almost everyone, and—worst of all—offering images produced by machines rather than an artist's hand, the chromolithograph aggressively threatened the aura of traditional painting. Attacked as the antithesis of true art, the chromolithograph became an emblem for everything inauthentic in modern life. Thus a New York newspaper editorial condemning the involvement of Rev. Henry Ward Beecher, the revered spokesman of New York Protestantism and a popular orator, in an adulterous affair, referred to a new "chromolithographic culture" in which all values had been cheapened and overturned (see Marzio 1979, 1, 205–11).

Although equating the radical Marxian ideological critiques of the 1970s with these conservative jeremiads may seem too simple, I have always suspected that beneath the proclaimed radicalism of apparatus theory lay an inherent puritanism, suspicious not only of ideological representation but also of sensual or visual pleasure. Whereas apparatus theory proclaimed an attack on the "realism" of the cinematic image and called for a radical undermining of the metaphysics of identity and coherence, it frequently described the cinematic image as an "illusion" or "hallucination," as if these theorists possessed a hidden card of apodictic truth hidden up the sleeve in readiness to trump the Hollywood moguls. Although claiming materialist inspiration, Baudry more or less directly announced his ambitions to deliver us from our absorption in the shadows passing on the screen of Plato's subterranean screening room, leading us into the effulgence of the truth. Indeed, the evil of cinema in apparatus theory as well as in the discourse of earlier reformers seems to lie precisely in its power to deceive via its direct relation to the senses and the unconscious.

Let me deepen the historical context of this argument. Cinema, understood as part of the centuries-old "great art of light and shadow," displays a truly dialectical and perhaps even contradictory relation to the project of Enlightenment. As an optical device, cinema and its visual ancestors derive from the new science of optics that fascinated Descartes and other Enlightenment figures, including Christian Huygens, the most likely inventor of the magic lantern (see Mannoni 2000, 36–45). However, as Barbara Stafford has shown in her study of eighteenth-century visual devices, *Artful Science* (1994), such devices were designed for two rather contrary, yet dialectically related, purposes. The first was scientific and enlightening. By demonstrating the visual logic behind an optical illusion the *savant* or *philosophe* could make scientific demonstration triumphant, dissolving a wondrous illusion into its generative and explicable logic. However, in the hands of a mountebank, these illusions might create nothing but wonder, or, worse yet, superstitious beliefs, especially when presented before a gullible audience.

To a late-nineteenth-century audience, cinema appeared within a tradition of visual magic that had become part of popular entertainment at least since the Enlightenment, reaching a technological climax at the end of the nineteenth century (see Barnouw 1981). Rarely claiming supernatural powers (except, of course, in the fascinating and ambiguous case of the Spiritualist performers, such as the Davenport brothers) nineteenth-century magicians most frequently operated within a realm of demystification. Frequently parodying and mocking their Spiritualist counterparts, such magicians claimed no extrahuman aid, yet fervently concealed the secrets behind their illusions (see Solomon 2001, 11–38). Thus provoking curiosity and astonishment, they produced illusions that entertained not only by denying supernatural revelation or miracles but also by avoiding a fully explicated demonstration of their mysterious processes. The pleasure such illusions offered lay in making the audience attend to their own sensuous experience and asking them to doubt their very eyes.

Magic tricks operated like commodity capitalism through an occluding of labor, concealing the actual effective gesture and seeming to produce things "by magic." A trick acknowledged as a trick might cause no deception and appear as harmless and entertaining as the Chinese conjurer in Vertov's *The Man with a Movie Camera* (1929). Tricks that undo themselves are thus essential to an Enlightenment system that seeks to separate visual illusion from scientific certainty. Likewise, Justice McKenna did not claim that cinema was by nature evil, simply that it had the capacity, the power for it. Films that used their power of attraction harmlessly would not be subject to censorship, the decision stressed, only those that crossed the line.

The enlightenment interest in "philosophical toys"—those visual devices that demonstrated illusions and the manner in which they were caused (including the various motion devices such as the thaumatrope or phenakistoscope to which the origins of the cinema are frequently traced) were designed, as Stafford has shown, primarily for the education of the elite young. Science, while rendered entertaining, nonetheless carried the essential lesson that these illusions were explainable. Thus such demonstrations inoculated the young against the spectacles of superstition that the *philosophes* associated especially with the Catholic Church (Stafford, 58–70). But, in fact, the Jesuits had also used optical devices during the Counter Reformation as visual aids, not simply to convince the ignorant of the powers of God and his Church, but also to reveal to the learned as well the conditional nature of knowledge and perception in the fallen world of creation. Thus an anamorphic landscape painting, which could appear either as a craggy mountain or as the face of an old man, bore the caption, "Your attempts to view me are vain./ If you perceive me, you will not see me anymore" (Stafford and Terpak 2001, 250–51). Demonstrating the oscillation in visual apprehension such visual illusions called perception and knowledge into question. Thus, both rational demystifying demonstration and religiously mystical enigmas used optical illusions as means less to deceive the viewer than to cause her to reflect on the limited and fragile nature of human perception.

Therefore the primary purpose for creating optical illusions may not lie in simple deception, their ability to fool someone into taking them for "reality." Rather, such illusions operate to confound habitual attitudes toward perception, indeed sowing doubts about the nature of reality. These doubts could play a pedagogic role in either rational systems (teaching that perceptual systems are not to be trusted, but must be buttressed by knowledge of scientific causes and the demonstration that the scientific method calls for) or transcendent systems of belief (teaching that mere perception is fallible; only faith in transcendence can make sense of creation). But outside their appropriation by larger pedagogical systems of demonstration or indoctrination, such illusions primarily spawn wonder, astonishment, and curiosity. Rather than buttressing the power of vision, they might call it into question, the essential claim of the conjurer being that "the hand is quicker than the eye." Herein lies the significance of the magician's denial, at least since the age of Enlightenment, of supernatural power, balanced with his refusal to reveal the basis of the trick. The magician's vow never to reveal the trick (admittedly often violated, but what vows are not?) does more than simply preserve a guild practice or professional secret. Fashioning an essential mode of address toward the viewer, this lack of explanatory mechanism maintains an attitude of uncertainty and wonder on the spectator's part, who must always wrestle with what she saw and what she thinks she saw, with both the uncertainty and the power of perception.

Thus, in spite of claims to the contrary by both contemporary theorists and turn-of-the-century reformers, the suspicion of tricks may not only derive primarily from their illegitimate claims to spurious "magical" systems of cause and effect; it may be that there is no "innocent" form of trickery. Thus the inherent suspicion of a visual medium emerges as a concern about the means by which knowledge or opinions are conveyed. Recall again that Justice McKenna did not condemn a specific evil film for its prurient or subversive content. Although he admitted unobjectionable films existed, his decision brackets the medium itself under the sign of capacity for evil. Although he is vague in defining it, visual deception of some sort, independent of specific content, renders film in need of special surveillance. Likewise Baudry revolutionized film theory by focusing on neither the practices of filmmaking (the uses of editing or composition or deep focus that had preoccupied previous film theorists, such as Eisenstein, Arnheim, Bazin, and Mitry), nor the reactionary content and imagery of specific films, but on the film apparatus itself. Any film could be ideologically complicit if it were projected in a darkened room with the illusion of motion and the viewer positioned in front of the screen. Although we have seen that trickery can be rendered inoffensive, this taming of illusion depends either on rational explanation through a scientific analysis or on allegorizing such illusions through a metaphysical interpretation. But if the trick served neither as educational, demystifying demonstration nor as redeeming allegory, as buttress neither to the explanations of science nor to the mysteries of the faith, then trick and visual illusion might maintain a dangerous anarchic force, an undermining of authority itself in favor of the pure play of sensation. The fascination of visual uncertainty remains a potentially dangerous force.

As so often happens with early cinema, a consideration of its genealogy leads us not so much toward the perspectival schemes of Enlightenment optics as to the ambiguous setting of the fairground: cinema as the product not only of scientists and inventors, but also of conjurers and mountebanks. Historically, the conjurer and the juggler compose a single victimized figure in the condemnation and persecution of magic performers by religious and secular authorities (Stafford, 79–85). Before the nineteenth century, legal, religious, and even philosophic institutions condemned the juggler as passionately as the conjurer; sleight of hand generated as much anxiety as (false?) claims of supernatural power. As Stafford points out, manual facility even in the arts was often viewed with suspicion, often seen as a tool of deception. I think that within the suspicion of the cinematic apparatus we find a similar anxiety about the nature of an art of vision that is also, because it is mechanical, quicker than the eye, able to make us see things we know are not there.

Linking the cinema with the juggler, we might consider one magic trick combining manual dexterity and visual illusion, which master conjurer and historian of illusions Ricky Jay terms the "blow book" (Stafford and Terpak, 252), but which I prefer to call by another of its traditional names, the "flick book." As a somewhat more optically primitive ancestor of the later and better known protocinema device (whose history remains to be written) the "flip book," the "flick book" employed notched pages and carefully arranged visual illustrations that a mountebank could manipulate to make images seem to appear, disappear, or transform rapidly and magically. Reginald Scott's sixteenth-century *The Discoverie of Witchcraft* described flick books this way:

> Ye hab they saie a booke, wherof he would make you think first that every leafe was clean white paper: then by virtue of words he would shew your everie leaf to be painted with birds, then with beasts, then with serpents, then with angels etc. (qtd. in Stafford and Terpak, 252–53)

Scott found describing this book, its manipulation and effects, in words nearly impossible, saying, "Best because you will hardlie conceive hereof by this description, you shall (if you be disposed) see or buie for a small value the like booke," giving an address of a book shop where it could be purchased "for your further instruction" (252–53). Existing examples indicate that flick books do not rely on a literal persistence of vision (as do their later offspring, the flip books, in which successive photographs or drawings are rapidly flipped by the thumb so that an optical illusion of motion is produced). However, flick books anticipate this later illusion by rapidly replacing one image with another, creating an illusion of metamorphosis rather than motion (and thus resembling a substitution in a Méliès trick film caused by a splice, or the transformation produced by a trick lantern "slipping" slide).

The term "flick book" also proleptically evokes early cinema, the "flickers," or in contemporary vernacular, "flicks." The derivation of this term bifurcates in an interesting manner. Our conjurer's flick book refers to the deft and rapid movement of the hand, as in the "flick of a wrist." The cinema gained its name through an analogously rapid motion of light, originally describing the behavior of flames or reflection of light: "flickering." The term thus unites the two aspects of optical trickery: the manual skill of juggling and the rapidity of light itself, accenting light's ability not only to reveal, illuminate, and enlighten, but also to conceal, cast shadows, and create illusions. The history of early cinema's imbrication with stage magic is well known; stage magicians such as Felicien Trewey, John Stuart Blackton, or Georges Méliès adopted the cinema as the latest conjuring device, another nineteenth-century example of precision machinery replacing the skilled hand (Barnouw).

But is this historical relation between cinema and magic shows of importance in understanding film's capacity for evil as defined by legal or theoretical discourse, for example, its reliance on visual illusion? I believe metaphysical and philosophical issues subtend this historical genealogy. Much of Western metaphysics derives from reflection upon the fallibility of the senses or human perception. If the meditations of Descartes institute a process of systematic doubt that leads to the apparently apodictic truth of the fact of consciousness, the process begins in the "First Meditation on First Philosophy" by imagining a conjurer of cosmic proportions, the evil demon *(malin geni)* who can create a world of endless deception (Descartes 1985, 15). The ultimate lesson of Descartes's imagined trip to a cosmic magic show is not only to doubt the evidence of the senses but also to found the assurance of knowledge more deeply, simultaneously in the fact of consciousness and in the existence of a God whose goodness guarantees the impossibility of a cosmos of deception. By invoking a God who "would never" deceive, Descartes—like the Enlightenment pedagogues or the Jesuit theologians—provides the reassurance of explaining away the "trick" that the magician obstinately refuses to supply. But in contrast to the assurance of self-evidence of consciousness for Descartes, the fascination supplied by the magician's trick, its contradictory, rather than self-founding, nature, opens a realm of delight in, perhaps even an unprincipled passion for, illusion whose very nature would seem to undermine the metaphysics of reassuring certainty.

Cinema's power for evil may lie precisely in its lack of certainty, its maintenance of a realm of illusion rather than clearcut revelation. However, if this digression on magical illusion may provide a new perspective on the critique of cinema offered by apparatus theory and the suspicion of cinema that provides the countercurrent to cinephilia throughout the history of the medium, does it really apply to Justice McKenna's decision? Returning to our starting point: the evil the Supreme Court felt the need to protect film viewers against lay less in cinema's undermining the reality of the senses or the foundations of certainty than in its direct address to the passions, its ability to excite whether sexually ("a prurient interest may be excited and appealed to") or politically. The Supreme Court knew the cinema did not rest in the hands of a God whose inherent goodness would make it impossible for Him to deceive. Instead, Justice McKenna stressed, "the exhibition of moving pictures is a business pure and simple originated and conducted for profit" (3). It was the lack of an authority beyond the circulation of capital that rendered film's capacity for evil so dangerous in 1915.

Thus the most vulnerable sections of the public risked being subjected to the "evil demon of images," the destabilizing deception and overloaded sensationalism of an industry deviating from the tradition of print culture and deriving instead from a visual tradition whose purchase on actual knowledge was dubious and whose powers of sleight of hand had become rarefied not only by modern commerce, but also by modern industrial technology. Once again the discourse of early film reformers seems to anticipate that of contemporary French theory when in his 1984 lecture, "The Evil Demon of Images," Jean Baudrillard speaks of the "diabolic seduction of images," adding:

> It is precisely when it appears most truthful, most faithful and most in conformity to reality that the image is most diabolic—and our technical images, whether they be from photography, cinema or television, are in the overwhelming majority much more "figurative," "realist," than all the images from past cultures. It is in its resemblance, not only analogical but technological, that the image is most immoral and most perverse. (1988, 13–14)

On the surface Baudrillard reiterates the same discourse we have followed, the suspicion of the visual and magic "sleight of hand" illusion for its appropriation of reality, its deception. But, commenting on his lecture, Baudrillard indicated the demon he invokes here is older than Descartes's *"malin geni."* Baudrillard declares his thought to be Manichean and magical, maintaining that the principle of evil does not derive from disobeying the Good Lord but exists as a coeval power and actual creator of the phenomenal universe that itself is understood as a magical illusion and seduction. As a truly postmodernist thinker, in contrast to Baudry whose critique of cinema's illusory power was ultimately more conservative and idealist, Baudrillard seems to usher in an age of gods and monsters, a return to heretical sources pronounced anathema at the origins of Western thought. The Evil Demon of Cinema is not simply a duplicitous and complicit ideological swindle, but a banished deity of a nearly forgotten, but once worldwide, religion, a deity torn within by a cosmic struggle between Good and Evil, faced with a creation that is itself illusory, the product of demons rather than a beneficent creator.

I will resist indulging my area of undergraduate studies fully and only briefly summarize the Manichean religion. The system of the Prophet Mani (which at one time circled the known world, stretching from Southern and Eastern Europe through its area of origin in the Middle East, then moving along the silk route into China and the Far East) flourished between the third and the thirteenth centuries C.E. Drawing from Persian Zoroastrianism a cosmic dualism of utterly opposed Good and Evil (or Light and Dark) deities, and from the Gnostic systems that were coeval with the origin of Christianity the doctrine that this world was created and dominated by the Evil cosmic forces, Mani created a syncretistic religion. Salvation consisted, first, in recognizing the seduction and enslavement of mankind's souls that the Evil forces had effected through material creation and physical embodiment. Then, by abstaining from procreation and other worldly practices, the enlightened soul could flee this evil cosmos and return to the realm of light outside the physical universe (Lieu). This system strove with Christianity for centuries (St. Augustine began as a Manichean, then, after conversion, undertook a radical polemic against it). Its final drama in the West took the form of the Albigensian Crusade in the early fourteenth century as the Catholic Church waged war against the last vestiges of the Manichean heresy in the Albigensian sect (also known as the Cathars) in the south of France (Oldenbourg). The heresy was wiped out by the combined efforts of military slaughter and the persuasive techniques of the Inquisition. But once again, what does this heretical tradition have to do with cinema and its capacity for evil?

Although magicians have often been suspected of heresy and various conspiracy theories have seen survivals of the Manicheans in modern eras (and a few have attempted outright revivals), no one (that I know of, anyway) had connected the cinema, the art of light and shadow, with this metaphysic of Light and Darkness. That is, until 1991, when Theodore Roszak, one of the first pundits of American counterculture, published a mass-market thriller novel, *Flicker,* which begins with the epigram attributed to Alfred Hitchcock, "The stronger the evil, the stronger the film." A work of profound mythopoetic imagination, *Flicker* takes as its premise that the cinema, or at least "moving pictures" in the form of the "flip book," were invented centuries before Edison or the Lumières by the Albigensians. Although this is a claim of (wild) imagination, it takes inspiration from the fact that the Manicheans were known for the elaborate illustrations of their books (which the Church incinerated in huge pyres) and their belief in the power of visual images to instruct and reveal. I do not know if Roszak knew of the earlier flick book, which would indicate ancestors of the flip book existed centuries earlier than the first examples of philosophical toys, but his thesis has an uncanny plausibility.

Flicker traces this bizarre thesis through a bildungsroman of a film academic in the 1970s (complete with thinly veiled caricatures of Pauline Kael, Raymond Bellour, and even Eileen Bowser), in search of the lost work of a Weimar film director, Max Castle (a sort of amalgam of the émigré master of eerie mise-en-scène Edgar G. Ulmer and slightly later technological trickster William Castle) who has been exiled to making B-films in Hollywood. Unlike most academic research projects, the protagonist's auteur study generates a plot of the most recherché paranoia imaginable. He learns that Castle, an initiate of a secret sect of modern Albigensians, loaded his Hollywood B-films with subliminal images, using the very flicker of the cinema, its primal visual alternation of light and dark, to express the primal dualism of the Manicheans, the struggle between the Gods of Light and Darkness, Good and Evil. Thus Castle used cinema's hypnotic power to convey unconsciously to viewers of his films the illusory and demoniac nature of what appears as reality. Early in the novel a movie projectionist hints at the Albigensian conspiracy underlying the invention of cinema, and he warns the protagonist:

> Sure, the Zoetrope is just a harmless toy, right? But it's based on an illusion. Same illusion this projector's built around. That's what makes this a magic lantern. But what kind of magic? Maybe *black* magic. (Roszak, 58)

Roszak's film scholar protagonist pursues the legacy of Max Castle not only through his uncredited collaboration with Orson Welles and uncredited contribution to *The Maltese Falcon* (1941), but even into a later generation of punk splatter movies, ending with an apocalyptic vision of Castle's final opus (titled appropriately *The End*) in which Betty Boop and Fred Astaire perform a final Shiva-like dance of death over the final dissolution of the cosmos.

Evil, as circumscribed by legal discourse, would seem to proclaim an issue of morality, involving questions of choice and free will. However, when legal discourse justifies censorship, belief in the power of rational choice seems to have been abandoned, or at least redefined. In 1915 the U.S. Supreme Court felt the medium of motion pictures, with its newfound power of attraction, could overwhelm rational thought, especially when projected before mixed audiences. Although I find this extremely disturbing politics, I think it reveals something about a modern conception of evil: a power exceeding and possibly overwhelming reason, a power that institutions of power respond to by invoking authoritarian control. Tzvetan Todorov claims in his classic treatment of the fantastic genre in literature that in the twentieth century the unconscious takes over the role played in earlier works by the devil (1975,

160–61). Whatever terminology is used, however vaguely or systematically it is described, the power of the cinema seems dependent on its connection with unconscious or subconscious reactions on the part of viewers. Rather than evil understood as the result of moral (or immoral) choice, Evil in relation to cinema refers to a power, a capacity. But, as a nonmoral power, it may be best understood in the manner Georges Bataille defines Evil in relation to literature, as a pure intensity, a return, as Bataille would put it, to the pure instincts of childhood. If it is true that society could not survive if left to the untamed excessive instincts of children, it is also true that a return to this instinctual ground, both before and beyond good and evil, constitutes the sort of regression in which both healing and what Bataille calls "hypermorality" are founded.

Cinema may not rest in this Evil, but it returns to it, moving from moments of regression to moments of clarity as the revolving shutter divides projection into instants of obscurity and illumination. In the very pulse of its flicker, cinema breathes, taking its viewers alternately into and out of a realm of Evil and Darkness. Sufficient to each film is the Evil thereof.

WORKS CITED

Barish, Jonas. 1981. *The Anti-Theatrical Prejudice.* Berkeley: University of California Press.

Barnouw, Erik. 1981. *The Magician and the Cinema.* New York: Oxford University Press.

Bataille, Georges. 1981. *Literature and Evil.* Trans. Alastair Hamilton. New York: Urizen Books.

Baudrillard, Jean 1988. *The Evil Demon of Images.* Sydney: Powers Institute Publications.

Baudry, Jean-Louis. 1986a. "Ideological Effects of the Basic Cinematographic Apparatus." In Philip Rosen, ed. *Narrative, Apparatus, Ideology.* New York : Columbia University Press, 286–98.

———. 1986b. "The Apparatus: Metapsychological Approaches to the Impression of Reality in the Cinema." In Philip Rosen, ed. *Narrative, Apparatus, Ideology.* New York: Columbia University Press, 299–318.

Crary, Jonathan. 1990. *Techniques of the Observer: On Vision and Modernity in the Nineteenth Century.* Cambridge MA: MIT Press.

Curtis, Scott. 1994. "The Taste of a Nation: Training the Senses and Sensibility of Cinema Audiences in Imperial Germany," *Film History* 6: 4 (Winter), 445–69.

Descartes, René. 1985. "Meditations on First Philosophy." In *The Philosophical Writings of Descartes* Vol. II. Trans. John Cottingham, Robert Stoothoff, and Dugald Murdoch. Cambridge: Cambridge University Press, 1–62.

Gorky, Maxim. 1960. Appendix 2 in Jay Leyda, *Kino, A History of the Russian and Soviet Film*. London: George Allen & Unwin.

Gunning, Tom. 1994. "The Horror of Opacity: The Melodrama of Sensation in the Plays of André de Lorde." In J. S. Bratton, Jim Cook, and Christine Gledhill, eds. *Melodrama—Stage, Picture, Screen*. London: BFI, 50–61.

———. 1995. "An Aesthetic of Astonishment: Early Film and the [In]Credulous Spectator." In Linda Williams, ed. *Viewing Positions*. New Brunswick NJ: Rutgers University Press, 316–31.

Hansen, Miriam. 1991. *Babel and Babylon: Spectatorship in American Silent Film*. Cambridge MA: Harvard University Press.

Jay, Martin. 1993. *Downcast Eyes: The Denigration of Vision in Twentieth Century French Thought*. Berkeley: University of California Press.

Jowett, Garth. 1989. "A Capacity for Evil: The 1915 Supreme Court Mutual Decision," *Historical Journal of Film, Radio and Television* 9: 1.

———. 1996. "'A Significant Medium for the Communication of Ideas': The Miracle Decision and the Decline of Motion Picture Censorship 1952–1968." In Francis G. Couvares, ed. *Movie Censorship and American Culture*. Washington, D.C: Smithsonian Institution Press, 258–76.

Lieu, Samuel N. C. 1985. *Manichaeism in the Later Roman Empire and Medieval China, A Historical Survey*. Manchester: Manchester University Press.

McKenna, Justice Joseph. 1915. Decision, U.S. Supreme Court, *Mutual Film Corp. v Industrial Commission of Ohio*, 236 U.S. 230 (reproduced at http://caselaw.lp. findlaw.com/getcase.pl?navby=search&court=US&case=/us/236/230.html)

Mannoni, Laurent. 2000. *The Great Art of Light and Shadow*. Exeter: University of Exeter Press.

Marzio, Peter. 1979. *The Democratic Art: Chromolithography 1840–1900*. Boston: David R. Godine.

Oldenbourg, Zoe. 1968. *Massacre at Monsegur: A History of the Albigensian Crusade*. Trans. Peter Green. New York: Minerva Press.

Roszak, Theodore. 1991. *Flicker: A Novel*. New York: Summit Books.

Solomon, Matthew Paul. 2001. Stage Magic and the Silent Cinema: Méliès, Houdini, Browning. Ph.D. diss. University of California at Los Angeles.

Stafford, Barbara Maria. 1994. *Artful Science: Enlightenment, Entertainment and the Eclipse of Visual Education*. Cambridge MA: MIT Press.

Stafford, Barbara Maria and Francis Terpak. 2001. *Devices of Wonder: From the World in a Box to Images on a Screen*. Los Angeles: Getty Research Institute Publications.

Todorov, Tzvetan. 1975. *The Fantastic: A Structural Approach to a Literary Genre*. Ithaca: Cornell University Press.

FIGURE 2. "Wholly amoral and sexually obsessed" white scientists (Leslie Daniels, l.; Jason Evers, r.) with the triumph of their careers, "the white thing," Jan in the Pan (Virginia Leith) in Joseph Green's *The Brain That Wouldn't Die* (AIP/Warner Bros., 1962). Somewhere a suitable body will be found. (Collection Gwendolyn Audrey Foster)

CHAPTER TWO

Monstrosity and the
Bad-White-Body Film

GWENDOLYN AUDREY FOSTER

One of the implications of the whiteness in white culture is its presumed link to purity, innocence, goodness, and truth. We need only think of Shirley Temple's golden curls, Claudette Colbert's alabaster skin, Cary Grant's well-starched style, Clark Gable's radiant poise, or Doris Day's twinkly verve as renditions of white stability and "cleanliness." But, we may well ask, what lies beneath the presumably pristine white surface of white culture?

Science fiction and horror films frequently feature unstable white bodies: white bodies out of control, invisible bodies, bodies missing hands, brains without skulls, monstrous eyeballs, bodies contaminated by nuclear fallout, bodies at war with themselves. Films such as *The Hand* (1960), *The Head* (1959), *The Man Without a Body* (1957), *The Brain That Wouldn't Die* (1962), *Attack of the 50 Foot Woman* (1958), *The Amazing Colossal Man* (1957), *The Incredible 2-Headed Transplant* (1971), and *The Incredible Shrinking Man* (1957) not only problematize whiteness but display the instability of white embodiedness and subjectivity and suggest a postmodern reworking of self with regard to whiteness. Considered to be trivial trash cinema, these films have much to teach us about our attitudes toward the body and the ways in which it is colonized, gendered, raced, classed, and socialized.

In these films of the bad-white body, whiteness is usually associated with badness, war against the self, destruction, murder, death, and hypersexuality.

Exploitation films are seen as tasteless, perhaps because they often show straight white culture in a harsh light. Indeed, suggesting white bodies out of control, these films are white others to whiteness itself. As Thomas Cripps (1993) and others have noted, blackness in cinema is often associated with bad conduct, hypersexuality, monstrous behavior, and the threat of otherness. But what if the monster-other is not only white but also in a struggle with his own body, a self-reflective Janus face interminably attempting to destroy itself? I find it curious that such fascinating exemplars of white-on-white fear have been relegated to the dustbin of culture, enjoyed only at the level of camp, when they should be seriously considered for their problematizing of race, gender, sexuality, and ethnicity, but especially whiteness. Exploitation films are cultural relics, filled with examples of "bad" whites often at war with their own (sometimes) "good" selves.

As Joan Hawkins writes, "film representations can be both subversive and hegemonically contained" (2000, 215). One thing that I find fascinating about bad-white-body films is that they often suggest a postmodern definition of self, as defined here by Linda Hutcheon: "The postmodern way of defining the self (an internalized challenge to the humanist notion of integrity and seamless wholeness) has much to do with [a] mutual influencing of textuality and subjectivity" (1988, 83). Bad-white-body films challenge the integrity of the body and the wholeness of identity as much as they challenge the integrity and wholeness of whiteness. They are also generated from a space that problematizes and fragments the binaries *good* and *bad,* and *moral* and *immoral,* as well as the notion of *a unified performing white self.*

Take, for example, the spectacle of tragedy afforded the viewer in *The Amazing Colossal Man* and its sequel, *War of the Colossal Beast* (1958). The disease of the central character, Lieutenant Colonel Manning (played by Glen Langan in the first film and look-alike Duncan "Dean" Parkin in the sequel), is brought on by exposure to a plutonium bomb explosion. Manning grows taller than fifty feet, the height attained by the main character of *Attack of the 50 Foot Woman;* perhaps his disease is, after all, the burden of whiteness itself and, in particular, of "responsible" white maleness. In *Colossal Man,* Manning's body is burned by radiation (white man's science), and begins to grow completely "out of control," yet for all his size he spends much of the film (until his mind fails him and he is forced to resort to inarticulate grunts in a futile attempt to communicate with the outside world) bemoaning the fact that he is now "less than a man," especially when he's with his sympathetic if bewildered wife, Carol Forrest (Cathy Downs), with whom he can no longer associate as a human, much less as a sex partner. (In the sequel, the Carol Forrest character is replaced by Joyce Manning [Sally Fraser], Lieutenant Colonel Manning's sister, his wife having apparently deserted him.) The source of Manning's pain is white maleness, especially as it is associated with the military, which sanctioned the atomic tests that led to Manning's exposure to radiation. But perhaps the *Colossal* films also deploy Richard Dyer's ideas about the association of whiteness with death:

> The idea of whites as both themselves dead and as bringers of death is commonly hinted at in horror literature and film. . . . It is a cultural space that makes bearable for whites the exploration of the association of whiteness with death. . . . This is the apotheosis of whiteness: to be destroyed by your own kind. (1997, 210–11)

The space of the colossal beast is a zone for the consideration of the power of white America of the 1950s, and it is here, in unusual fantasies, that whites were able to begin to look at the paradoxes of white power and its association with the death and destruction of its own people.

These paradoxes show up clearly in *War of the Colossal Beast*. Whereas in *Colossal Man* Manning went over Boulder Dam and was declared dead (this brief sequence was shot in color, the rest of the film in black-and-white), in *War*, Manning is alive and hiding in the Mexican countryside. Lonely, horribly disfigured, his mind gone, Manning survives by overturning rural grocery trucks and scavenging through the wreckage for food. The viewer sympathizes with him as a grotesque other. White society, even the military, his ostensible home, rejects him just as white society was ill prepared to manage and aid returning veterans from World War II and the Korean War. White "authorities" tranquilize the gigantic Manning and shackle him in chains in a hangar at Los Angeles International Airport, but he later escapes and destroys a good portion of Los Angeles. The sequel contains numerous flashbacks to the first film (no doubt for budgetary reasons because these are some of the more spectacular scenes of destruction): these serve to remind the viewer that Manning's ordeal is unending, cutting him off from society completely. At the end of the film, Manning suicidally walks into a set of high-tension power lines. He is excluded from the white male world.

Paradoxes are part of the postmodern condition. "While unresolved paradoxes may be unsatisfying to those in need of absolute and final answers, to postmodernist thinkers and artists they have been the source of intellectual energy that has provoked new articulations of the postmodern condition" (Hutcheon 1988, 21). *War of the Colossal Beast* refers to the war that one bad-white other wages against society as much as it refers to society's discomfort with returning war veterans. Interestingly, the authorities give up on Manning only when they think his mind has "gone." When he loses his faculties and powers of speech, he seemingly loses whiteness and becomes a liminal other. He loses his white identity as much as his human identity. Now he is seen only as a monster that must be destroyed. Even his own sister encourages him to kill himself, ostensibly to save a busload of children he holds aloft near the Griffith Park Observatory. Although the film seemingly allows for closure, it also problematizes whiteness and white male conduct, specifically blind allegiance to the armed forces. Like postmodern performance studies alluded to by Jon McKenzie, the *Colossal* films work in the space of the liminal and "theorize performative genres as liminal, that is, as 'in-between' times/spaces in which social norms are broken apart, turned upside down, and played with" (1998, 220).

Problematic liminal whiteness is a hallmark of the bad-white-body film. This particular trash film investigates cultural amnesia: forgetting the price of war. Manning is clearly a veteran out of control, yet the authorities neither fault themselves for the nuclear accident that caused his condition, nor credit Manning for his war efforts. When the *Colossal* films are viewed from a postmodern perspective, it is clear that they are in many ways radically subversive for films of the 1950s, reminding us that, as Hutcheon suggests, "The act of problematizing is, in a way, an act of restoring relevance to something ignored or taken for granted. . . . What postmodernism does is not only to remind us of this, but also to investigate our amnesia" (229). The space of enunciation, the performance of whiteness in the *Colossal* films, underscores the unstable configuration of whiteness at odds with itself.

That these films appeared in the 1950s, when social codes were both regressing in terms of attitudes toward women and minorities and advancing with the beginnings of the women's liberation and civil rights efforts is telling. The cheap sci-fi exploitation vehicle allowed for a space in which the social conduct of white society could be critiqued. Culture—especially white male culture—is ultimately constructed as untenable, which demonstrates that the cultural performance of whiteness is subject to instability. In this sense, the films of the bad-white body constitute an expression of the dichotomy inherent in the artificially constructed performance of whiteness.

Grotesque proportions are an important feature in bad-white-body films, just as shrunken bodies and out-of-control body parts are crucial. Repetitive performances of bad-white bodies, grotesque and liminal, disruptive of whiteness, are certainly not rare in American pop culture. These performances represent a norm of othered whiteness. As McKenzie states in a study of performativity, it is "through repeated performances [that] these norms become sedimented as (and not in) gendered bodies" (221). I want to bring up the specter of gender as I move to another film, this one featuring a huge, monstrous, white female body, the infamous *Attack of the 50 Foot Woman*. In the film, Nancy Fowler Archer (Allison Hayes), an alcoholic millionaire unhappily married to worthless fortune hunter Harry Archer (William Hudson), grows to gargantuan proportions after she is raped by a thirty-foot-tall, semitransparent, balding alien (Michael Ross, who also plays Tony, the owner of a sleazy bar and hotel, where much of the film's action takes place) during a nighttime drive in the desert. Just as in the *Colossal* films, the white authorities are stumped by the appearance of an unruly white body, in this case female: a rape victim, an angry woman who finds that her husband is cheating on her with a "lower-class" white woman, Honey Parker (Yvette Vickers). The film has painfully funny scenes of Nancy Archer chained up in her mansion by two befuddled white doctors, who give her massive injections of morphine with an elephant syringe in a futile attempt to keep her under control. In the meantime, her husband, "Handsome Harry," spends all of his time and Nancy's money in Tony's bar, where he is either bedding down Honey Parker in the rooms upstairs or plotting ways to push his wife over the brink of sanity, so that he can inherit the Star of India diamond, along with the rest of her millions. In the film's brutal conclusion, Nancy Archer, like Lieutenant Colonel Manning, finally breaks free of the mansion that has become her prison and stalks into town, where Harry is drinking himself into oblivion at Tony's bar. Without hesitation, the fifty-foot Nancy rips off the roof of the building, grabs Harry with one enormous hand, kills Honey by dropping huge chunks of debris on her, and then commits suicide and murder by walking into a set of high-tension power lines (as in *War of the Colossal Beast*) with the squashed Harry still in her hand.

To analyze the numerous bad-white bodies in *Attack of the 50 Foot Woman*, we must consider white performance of both class and gender. The *Colossal* films deployed a safer response to the angry, unfairly treated, white male veterans of World War II and the Korean War. *Attack of the 50 Foot Woman* is a critique of 1950s gender roles. The film clinically examines 1950s marriage and gender roles, using the schlocky atmosphere of the exploitation vehicle to raise such issues as rape, class difference, and the breakdown of white heterosexual coupling. As is often the case, the exploitation film offers the opportunity to talk about and perform subjects and social issues considered taboo in mainstream culture. Indeed, a white woman is subjected here to rape, a cheating husband, and medical mistreatment at the hands of white culture, a culture ultimately responsible for her alcoholism and death. Few films of the 1950s dealt with rape, with the exception of director Ida Lupino's *Outrage* (1950), which begins with a harrowing white-on-white workplace rape of a young woman by a fellow employee (never named in the film, but played by Albert Mellen). The victim of the assault, Ann Walton (Mala Powers), is more psychically damaged by the disinterest of white society in her plight than she is physically damaged by the attack itself. In cases of rape, particularly in the United States in the 1950s, society blames the female victim. Indeed, *Outrage* is much more critical of white society's inability to deal with the rape of women than of the act of rape itself. Lupino deftly handles the issues that surrounded rape in the postwar era and that still, to a large degree, persist today; women are assumed to have somehow been guilty of "leading on" their own rapists.

Nathan Hertz, who (as Nathan Juran) directed *Attack of the 50 Foot Woman*, and his scenarist, Mark Hanna, also blame the victim. Both the police and her attending physicians suggest that Nancy's gigantism is somehow her own fault (no one but she believes she has been raped), and she must be silenced for suggesting that white men rape and abuse their own white women. The film is rife with mixed messages undermining the supposed stability of white heterocentrism and the institution of marriage. If the film and its characters blame Nancy Archer for her condition, the audience, at least, wants to see her exact vengeance. Nancy, like the colossal beast, becomes a sort of white version of the noble savage. By the film's conclusion, the audience is completely sympathetic as Nancy destroys both herself and the cheating pair, Harry and Honey, themselves embodiments of the sexually out-of-control bad-white body.

Much is made of class in the film. Nancy Archer is coded as upper class by her jewelry, her mansion, her butler, and her cultured behavior. Her educated status is in sharp contrast to that of her husband and the slatternly Honey Parker, who are definitively classed by their behavior, clothing, and performances. The rule of thumb for the working classes in white culture is that they are "not supposed to be seen," according to Peter Hitchcock (2000, 21), but Harry and Honey are constantly on display, flaunting their relationship throughout the town, despite the gravity of Nancy's condition. In an article about the problems inherent in portrayals of working-class whites, Hitchcock writes: "'You're not supposed to be seen,' but the paradox of working-class subjectivity is that you must be seen in order to confirm that class is there and negotiable in stable and unthreatening ways. . . . The 'must be seen' of working-class subjectivity is intimately connected to modes of representation and power" (21).

Harry Archer is a consummate drunk and womanizer; he cares little for his wife and carries on his affair with Honey openly. Their scenes in Tony's honky-tonk are representative of the unseen side of the 1950s American Dream gone bad. Moreover, not only do Harry and Honey choose to live in squalor, but they also treat even each other badly. Parker suggestively hangs on Harry's shoulders or hips in every scene of the film the two share; when they dance, it is always a slow, drunken bump and grind. Their conversation is limited to ordering more drinks, sex, and plotting how to swindle Nancy out of her money, kill her, or both, all the better to get out of town and "live a little." Discouraged from working outside the home, Nancy becomes a 1950s housewife. Bored by her role, she becomes an alcoholic instead of fulfilling the role of the proper heteronormative mate.

Critics might be inclined to overlook class issues in the case of *Attack of the 50 Foot Woman*, but I think class intersecting with gender makes this such an important example of the bad-white-body film. Bad-white-body films allow a culturally agreed on space for those sublimated narratives to be heard. Bad-white-body films expose myths and lies perpetuated by dominant white culture. *Attack of the 50 Foot Woman* is a critique of gendered whiteness, the nuclear family, and all the falsely utopian visions with which these constructs are associated. Seen in this light, the film is a surreal riff on *Outrage*, presenting the white raped woman as an out-of-control gargantuan figure. The white authorities' inability to believe a white raped female is an idea dealt with in serious dramatic fashion in *Outrage;* even so, when the film was released, many critics thought that the subject itself was in such poor taste that the film should never have been produced. In a heterocentric ending imposed on the film because of the censorship constraints of the Eisenhower era, a compassionate psychiatrist helps Ann Walton rejoin society. But in the grade two camp fest favorite *Attack of the 50 Foot Woman* the white woman has revenge on society. She squeezes and electrocutes her husband to death for his cheating and complete lack of regard for her as an alcoholic rape victim. The problem, of course, is that she must die. The narrative demands it; the audience demands it; the Production Code demands it. The formulaic genre of the film demands it. White blood lust demands it. Nancy Archer is a sexual white female who has gone out of control—the ads for the film describe her as "a female colossus . . . her mountainous torso, skyscraper limbs, giant desires" (qtd. in Weldon 1999, 26)—and like Lieutenant Colonel Manning, she must be destroyed. It's obvious: Nancy Archer must die because she cannot perform her white femininity correctly. "For a woman, performing whiteness meant acting out purity and moral virtue" (Williams 1999, 10). Her husband must also die because he has performed male whiteness inappropriately, and he has failed to adhere to a classed gentleman's code of conduct. Bad whiteness, for both, is ultimately out-of-control sexuality, something itself frequently associated with unruly blackness and the lower classes.

Rape is at the center of another important bad-white-body film, *The Beast Within* (1982). In this film, Michael MacCleary (Paul Clemens) is a teenage boy who was conceived when his mother was raped by a swamp monster. At age seventeen, he begins to become an insect and sheds his human skin. *The Beast Within* conflates lower-class behavior (in this case within the bounds of Southern society) with rampant sexuality and animal depravity. The rape in *The Beast Within* is associated with incest, the black male rapist myth, or both; as the young man mutates, he literally sheds his whiteness and becomes the other: an animal who decapitates, kills, and eats anyone who gets in his way. This raises the specter of white women being raped by aliens, swamp monsters, giants—everything but actual white men. Of course, numerous films feature white-on-white rape, which is, in fact, becoming a staple of the postmillennial cinematic consciousness. But that the white woman continues to be at the mercy of the other suggests that American white culture cannot end its fascination with the trope of the quintessential other, the black male rapist who was so definitively ground into the white imagination in such films as *The Birth of a Nation* (1915). Statistics show white women are most frequently raped by white men, often members of white families.

Perhaps deflecting white-on-white rape onto monsters is one way to deflect self-scrutiny. Bad-white-body films that feature nonhuman rapists suggest shame and guilt but in the safe space of the campy exploitation film. Rita Felski has done considerable analysis of shame and guilt in Western societies:

> Guilt is a sense of inner badness caused by a transgression of moral values; shame by contrast is a sense of failure or lack in the eyes of others. It has less to do with infractions of morality than with interactions of social codes and a consequent fear of exposure, embarrassment, and humiliation. (2000, 39)

Many bad-white-body films are steeped in both white guilt and shame. One example is the British film *Dr. Terror's House of Horrors* (1965), which tells the story of five doomed men who share a railway compartment with a tarot reader, Dr. Sandor Schreck (Peter Cushing). One is killed by a female werewolf; another is trapped with his family in his house by an out-of-control vine with paranormal intelligence. A jazz musician is attacked when he appropriates and performs in public secret Haitian music that he has been specifically told not to play. At the subtextual level, these are bad-white-body figures who get their due because they continue to act as colonialists in a world that was increasingly de-colonizing itself as many African countries started to declare their independence in the 1950s and 1960s. Art critic Franklyn Marsh (Christopher Lee) ruins the career of artist Eric Landor (Michael Gough) with a string of negative reviews in the press and then, for good measure, runs down Landor with his car, severing Landor's hand. Landor's severed hand then seeks out Marsh and causes his car to swerve off the road, severely injuring the critic. As the ambulance drivers take Marsh from the scene of the wreck, one of them comments, "He'll never see again . . . still, there are plenty of things a blind man can do," as Marsh screams in agony.

The severed white hand, unswervingly focused on revenge, is prominently featured in a number of bad-white-body films. In *The Hands of Orlac* (1960), concert pianist Stephen Orlac (Mel Ferrer) is given a replacement pair of hands after he loses both of his in an accident. But the hands that are grafted onto his body once belonged to a murderer, and as a result Stephen finds himself compelled to commit a series of crimes. Later, Orlac is blackmailed by the unsavory magician Nero (Christopher Lee), who uncovers Orlac's secret. The discrepancy between the white body of an upper-class pianist and the hands of a lower-class killer places whiteness in conflict with itself within a body that cannot contain both kinds of whiteness. In another version of the same story, *Hands of a Stranger* (1962), pianist Vernon Paris (James Stapleton) has his mutilated hands replaced by a surgeon. Paris finds himself unable to play the piano as a result and seeks revenge on the doctor who performed the surgery. Both films suggest a conflation of guilt and shame, but shame—caused by class conflict that takes place in the bodies of white men—seems to be the dominant emotion.

The Hand is about two British soldiers who are captured in Burma in World War II. After they refuse to give information to the enemy, their hands are brutally amputated. Their captain is a traitor who cooperates with the enemy. Years later, London is plagued by a series of grisly murders in which all of the victims have their hands amputated. A variation on castration anxiety is certainly at work here, but psychoanalytic methodology is not the only effective approach to these films.

I am interested in the manner in which these "amputee films" allow for a sort of splitting of white identity, a space where shame and guilt can be disrupted or identified, a space where white audiences can identify across subjectivities in an intersubjective state with good/bad, classed/not classed, male/female whites. As I noted in *Captive Bodies: Postcolonial Subjectivity in Cinema*, jungle films, such as *She* (which has been filmed numerous times from 1908 to 2001), *Tarzan the Ape Man* (1932), and *Trader Horn* (1931), "exist primarily to construct whiteness" *against* external otherness (1999, 63). Similarly, bad-white-body films exist to construct whiteness through raising the specter of otherness *within* the body of whites.

As Dyer writes in *Stars*, film stars "embody social values that are to some degree in crisis" (1998, 25). Peter Cushing embodies a significant example of such a star. Cushing made a career of horror movies for Hammer Films and their chief competitor, Amicus—British companies that specialized in fantasy and sci-fi films. A frequent player in bad-white-body films, Cushing sometimes performed the bad-white figure and sometimes the good-white figure. He plays both in *The Skull* (1965), as Dr. Christopher Maitland, a professor of metaphysics who buys the stolen skull of the Marquis de Sade from Marco (Patrick Wymark), an unscrupulous antiques dealer, and soon becomes its servant. The skull wills Maitland to commit numerous murders, and the audience is invited to participate vicariously in his crimes through a series of point-of-view shots through the eye holes of the skull. *The Skull* allows the audience both to participate in bad-white performativity and to witness its consequences. This device smacks deeply of white colonial arrogance and traditional Western discourse's reliance on a "darkness within whiteness" (that which is capable of murder, rape, decapitation, dismemberment, and other atrocities). The history of white hegemony is a tale of the conquest and control of space and peoples. In bad-white-body films, the terrain of conquest is the white body, over which whiteness attempts to display mastery. The all-white world inhabited by these films is infected with unspoken desires, sexual jealousies, murderous frenzies, inchoate insanity, and malign evil. Western ideology, dependent on dualism, reinforces the need to produce such performances of whiteness. In such films, the bad-white body is usually conquered. Nevertheless, these films remind whites that dualism exists in the white body and its performances and cannot be summoned without consequences.

This dualism often takes the form of vicious and blatant misogyny, as in the film *The Brain That Wouldn't Die*. Dr. Bill Cortner (Jason Evers) is a white surgeon who accidentally decapitates fiancée Jan Compton (Virginia Leith) in a driving accident. Instead of letting Compton die, Cortner immediately takes her head back to his basement laboratory and keeps it alive in a developing tray, constantly replenished with blood. The desperate Jan wants only to die and eventually complains so incessantly that the surgeon puts tape over her mouth. Cortner has plans of his own; intent on finding a suitable body for his fiancée's head, Cortner begins frequenting a series of sleazy strip clubs, looking for a candidate for his grafting experiment. *The Brain That Wouldn't Die* portrays the white scientist as wholly amoral and sexually obsessed, like the scientists in the *Colossal* films, *The Skull*, and *The Hands of Orlac:* morally bankrupt. Jan Compton, a new bodiless head, a single body part, is a white woman deprived of both agency and ability to alter her circumstances. However, as the film nears its appalling conclusion, Jan develops telepathic power, which enables her to control a half-human, half-beast monster, a "white thing" that Cortner keeps locked in a laboratory closet. The sum total of all his surgical failures to date, the white thing, which possesses superhuman strength, inevitably breaks out of its prison, revealing itself to be a pastiche of arms, legs, eyes, and hands culled from previous surgical experiments. The creature sets the lab on fire, exacting Jan's vengeance, even as the flames consume her bandage-wrapped head.

Another film that features a disembodied head is aptly titled *The Head* (originally titled *Die Nackte und der Satan*), a West German film in which one Dr. Ood (Horst Frank) intentionally removes the head of his aging colleague, Professor Abel (Michel Simon), to keep his mind alive. "Your brain made you great! The rest doesn't count!" Ood shouts. But Abel is unimpressed and implores Ood to end the experiment. Predictably, however,

Ood has other ideas and becomes obsessed with the idea of transplanting the head of his hunchbacked nurse, Irene (Karin Kernke), onto the body of a striptease dancer. Ood cruises strip clubs, looking for the perfect subject for his experiment. Perhaps the most ghastly aspect of *The Head* is not the misogyny of the plot but the fact that Abel is played by the great Michel Simon, who once starred in Jean Renoir's classic *Boudu Saved from Drowning* (*Boudu sauvé des eaux* [1932]). The blatant misogyny of bad-white-body films is also evident in the 1981 version of *The Hand*, directed by Oliver Stone. When comic-book artist Jon Lansdale (Michael Caine) loses his drawing hand in a car wreck, his shrill, unsympathetic wife, Anne (Andrea Marcovicci), calls him a failure and cuckolds him. Unable to continue drawing the comic strip that had brought him to prominence, he is forced to earn a meager living teaching at a community college. As his female students start to disappear, the audience knows Lansdale's hand, of course, is responsible, but Lansdale has no awareness of his severed hand's activities. As with the other films discussed here, the white man is shown as ultimately not responsible for his own body's actions and his own inner desires. This duality allows a splitting of consciousness and conscience. In all these body-part films, white badness is depicted as not being responsible for its actions. Thus Lansdale's misogyny is a function not of the whole man but of only part of his white body.

Whiteness, especially in horror films of the 1960s and 1970s, is often equated with brutality and recklessly ill-advised science. Perhaps bubbling under these films is a hefty dose of colonialist guilt combined with a concomitant fear of medical science and its future. Furthermore, I would suggest that bad-white-body films exist and multiply because of white shame and white fear of hybridity. Whiteness exists only when hybridity and otherness are erased; in a world of rampant hybridity, however, maintaining hegemonic whiteness is impossible. Nowhere is that more true than at the site of the body and the soul, and no one is more at odds—and in touch—with body and soul than the white scientist figure.

White science (read, bad whiteness) has been responsible for the introduction of lethal nuclear radiation, the bad-white science that is at the center of *The Incredible Shrinking Man*. While on a fishing boat in the first few minutes of the film, Scott Carey (Grant Williams) is exposed to a radioactive mist. Instead of growing to an enormous height like the man in the *Colossal* films, Carey begins, ever so gradually, to shrink. At first his clothes are loose, and he thinks he's lost a couple of pounds. Soon he must wear children's clothing. Finally, he must dress in an improvised loincloth cut from a handkerchief. Like the colossal man, the incredible shrinking white man watches helplessly as his marriage to Louise Carey (Randy Stuart) falls apart. He is terrorized by his own cat and is nearly devoured by a spider in the family's basement, where his diminutive size makes it impossible for his wife to locate or even hear him. The film's subtext invokes and displays the fear of a diminishment of whiteness and the power that whiteness conveys. By 1957, black men had attained some degree of equality, in both the military and mainstream society. White maleness was in trouble, or at least white males felt that it was, but women—white women—were beginning to make real strides in the workplace. White men's power was decreasing in proportion to the rise of white women's power, especially as consumers. One could argue that the civil rights movement was beginning to mark a shift in white hegemony, but more important in the reading of this film is the deep-seated fear of whiteness itself as an unattainable phantom construct. Scott Carey's personal narrative in *The Incredible Shrinking Man* begins with a happy white nuclear family. Carey's family and friends are initially supportive, even after he begins to shrink. They abandon Carey, however, when they can no longer see him. *The Incredible Shrinking Man* questions the historical validity of the dominance of white maleness in the 1950s. As Scott says in the film, "Easy enough to talk of soul and spirit and essential worth, but not when you're three feet tall." In a manner that is still striking today, the film encourages the audience to question the "truth" of the primacy of the white nuclear family.

The Incredible Shrinking Man is perhaps one of the more important bad-white-body films because it deals with white culture's lack of compassion for the fallen white hero. Scott Carey's house is no longer a haven; it is a labyrinth of deadly traps. As the film nears its conclusion, Carey, forgotten by his family and friends, continues to shrink with each passing hour, until he is small enough to squeeze through a window screen and leaves the former safety of his split-level home. Only outside this nuclear white family home does Carey experience any sense of hope. Looking up at the stars, Carey decides he's going to continue his struggle as long as he can still see the heavens, and he delivers a compelling voiceover on the value of life, no matter how small it may be.

To this point, I've considered only all-white bad-white-body films. However, many films that include bodies out of control are problematized by being about hybrids of white and black bodies, including *The Cosmic Man* (1959) and *The Thing with Two Heads* (1972). These films remind us that race as an identity is constructed through an agreed-upon relationship:

> An individual is a relationship composed of the different identities which participants in the relationship retain. An individual is, inevitably, an asymmetric relationship. . . . (Monk 1998, 31)

This idea of an agreed-upon relationship is tested in *The Cosmic Man*, another 1950s sci-fi thriller, starring John Carradine as the Cosmic Man, a well-meaning but misunderstood alien who has, at times, black skin and a white shadow. He can pass as white and, if need be, attain invisibility, but he passes, perhaps most interestingly, as *human* by wearing a hat, sunglasses, and trench coat. The film views him as a good alien with a bad body because he has to work at passing as a white human male. He means no harm to humans, and in fact he selflessly cures a quadriplegic child. At the end of the film, he must be destroyed to satisfy the requirements of the genre, but a few sympathetic scientists, Dr. Karl Sorenson (Bruce Bennett) and Kathy Grant (Angela Greene), believe in the alien's mission. *The Cosmic Man* problematizes the usual constructions of race. The film forces the audience to question the validity of race, displaced onto the body of an alien, as a "scientific" category.

John Carradine in *The Cosmic Man* is not unlike the foreigner, the immigrant, the undocumented worker, the nonwhite other who must erase himself and become "white" to thrive. He must learn how to perform whiteness to survive. Whiteness depends on a disavowal of hybridity, an elimination of ethnicity, and an adherence to the othering mechanism of whiteness itself. It depends on correctly performing as white, but in the narrative of *The Cosmic Man* Carradine's alien plays a ludic white who is also black. The film trades on what Peggy Phelan terms "the failure of racial difference to appear within the narrow range of the visible" (1993, 98). We simply do not know his race because we cannot see him, and this leads to the question Phelan poses: "If racial difference is not registered visibly, where is it located? Is it a free floating signifier?" (98). How can the Cosmic Man secure whiteness, much less humanity? And are the two not immutably conflated?

Perhaps the most outrageous and transgressive film of the bad-white body is *The Thing with Two Heads*. In this film, racist white scientist Dr. Maxwell Kirshner (Ray Milland) has a bad body: he has terminal cancer. His brain, however, is unaffected. Kirshner, wanting to avoid the inevitability of death, arranges to have his head transplanted onto the body of a man on death row. Only one candidate steps forward in time for the operation to be successful, and so it is that to save Kirshner's life his head is grafted onto the body of African American prisoner, Jack Moss (Roosevelt Grier). The two heads taunt one another, punch each other in the face, and exchange racist diatribes. One could view *The Thing with Two Heads* as a threat to white and black constructs; after all, if the two heads can live in one body, this forced coexistence potentially threatens the categories of both white and black. *The Thing with Two Heads* disturbs the myth of unsullied and totalized separate white and black cultures, even as it revels in their differences. In doing so, *The Thing with Two Heads* renders cultural diversity as dystopian.

Looking at bad-white-body films, such as *The Thing with Two Heads*, through the lens of postmodernism is important because it makes terms such as *bad* and *body* suspect. In addition, postmodernism does not demand allegiance to matters of so-called taste and aesthetics. A healthy postmodern questioning of the myths that these films explore suggests that we are still in some ways dependent on them, as tools to aid us in examining the routinely accepted—but generally unexamined—world. "The myths and conventions" recycled in popular culture, Hutcheon argues, "exist for a reason and postmodernism investigates that reason. The postmodern impulse is not to seek any total vision. It merely questions. If it finds such a vision, it questions how, in fact, it *made* it" (1988, 48). This chapter suggests some of the ways in which bad-white-body films can be deconstructed to tell us a great deal about the social, racial, and political systems that informed their construction. Although more work remains to be done, this is at least a gesture in the direction future research might take.

WORKS CITED

Cripps, Thomas. 1993. *Making Movies Black: The Hollywood Message Movie from World War II to the Civil Rights Era*. New York: Oxford University Press.

———. 1997. *Slow Fade to Black: The Negro in American Film, 1900–1942*. New York: Oxford University Press.

Dyer, Richard. 1997. *White*. London: Routledge.

———. 1998. *Stars*. London: BFI.

Felski, Rita. 2000. "Nothing to Declare: Identity, Shame, and the Lower Middle Class," *PMLA* 115, 33–45.

Foster, Gwendolyn Audrey. 1999. *Captive Bodies: Postcolonial Subjectivity in Cinema*. Albany: State University of New York Press.

Hawkins, Joan. 2000. *Cutting Edge: Art-Horror and the Horrific Avant-Garde*. Minneapolis: University of Minnesota Press.

Hitchcock, Peter. 2000. "They Must Be Represented? Problems in Theories of Working-Class Representation," *PMLA* 115, 20–32.

Hutcheon, Linda. 1988. *A Poetics of Postmodernism: History, Theory, Fiction*. New York: Routledge.

McKenzie, Jon. 1998. "Genre Trouble: (The) Butler Did It." In Peggy Phelan and Jill Lane, eds., *The Ends of Performance*. New York: New York University Press, 217–35.

Monk, John. 1998. "The Digital Unconscious." In John Wood, ed., *The Virtual Embodied: Presence/Practice/Technology*. London: Routledge, 30–44.

Phelan, Peggy. 1993. *Unmarked: The Politics of Performance.* London: Routledge.

Weldon, Michael. 1999. *The Psychotronic Encyclopedia of Film.* New York: Ballantine.

Williams, Patricia J. 1999. "The Contentiousness of Their Character," *The Nation* (January 4), 10.

FIGURE 3. *L.A. Confidential* (Curtis Hanson, Warner Bros., 1997) shows the L.A.P.D. as "dysfunctional due to higher-ups who tolerate officers involved in illegal activity for personal gain because of the need for the 'effective' policing that such bad cops provide." James Cromwell as Captain Dudley Smith, a particularly "effective" and particularly "bad" cop, obsessed with personal gain. This film, among many others,

Beyond the Thin Line of Black and Blue: Movies and Police Misconduct in Los Angeles

AARON BAKER

[L.A.P.D.] street cops haven't necessarily read the police novels of
Joseph Wambaugh, but they've seen the movies.
—Peter Boyer, "Bad Cops"

The videotape showing Rodney King being forcibly arrested by twenty-seven
Los Angeles police officers in March 1991 was seen around the world. That
videotape, along with the April 1992 acquittal of four officers accused of
excessive force in King's arrest and the widespread violence triggered by the
outcome of their trial, cast a bright spotlight on the deeply rooted tensions
between police in Los Angeles and some of the city's nonwhite residents
(Woods 1993, 283; 291–92).

The recent history of the Los Angeles Police Department (L.A.P.D.)
shows that a primary role of the force has been as "agents of social control"
relative to the city's growing nonwhite population (Escobar 1999, 11). When
the first African American chief of police in Los Angeles, Willie Williams,
took over in 1992 after the fallout from the Rodney King scandal, the
L.A.P.D. had 70 percent white officers in a city with only thirty-seven percent white residents (Woods, 290). This, even though in 1980 the city had
signed a consent decree mandating certain numbers of minority and female

officers be hired. An investigatory commission established after the 1992 civil unrest, and headed by former U.S. Secretary of State Warren Christopher, found widespread instances of misuse of force by Los Angeles police that "ignore written policies and guidelines," and that "racial bias on the part of officers toward minority citizens currently exists and contributes to a negative interaction between police and community" (Woods, 285–86).

Historian Ed Escobar corroborates the commission's findings by presenting evidence that Los Angeles police regard Chicanos and other nonwhites as "criminally inclined" (1999, 3). In his 1990 book *City of Quartz,* Mike Davis reports that William Parker, who was chief of the L.A.P.D. from 1950 to 1966, told the U.S. Commission on Civil Rights that the residents of the barrio in East Los Angeles were "only one step removed from the wild tribes of Mexico" (295). Although Parker testified in 1960, his attitudes toward race have been maintained by men such as his protégé Darryl Gates, who was police chief when Rodney King was arrested, and justified more recently by journalist Peter Boyer, who suggests that the most serious problems the L.A.P.D. has faced in recent years have been the result of criminal behavior by Latino and African American officers. In a spring 2001 *New Yorker* article, "Bad Cops," Boyer shifts the focus of scrutiny away from the racist attitudes that became so public in the Rodney King case or through Detective Mark Furman's role in the O. J. Simpson trial by honing in on three nonwhite officers, Rafael Perez, David Mack, and Kevin Gaines. Perez and Mack were central players in the Rampart district case that began to unfold in 1999 in which L.A.P.D. officers were implicated for stealing drug evidence, and framing and even shooting innocent suspects in what has been called the worst corruption scandal in the history of the L.A.P.D. Boyer ties Gaines to similar criminal behavior, especially when working as off-duty security for Death Row Records founder Marion (Suge) Knight. Aside from these indictments of its nonwhite gangstas, Boyer generally exonerates the L.A.P.D. of racism and concludes that the majority of the force, which he describes admiringly as "the modern L.A.P.D. . . . created in the image of William Parker," has been guilty only of having "countenanced a strain of rough justice in the street" (2, 78).

Four recent films about the L.A.P.D., *Colors* (1988), *Internal Affairs* (1990), *L.A. Confidential* (1997), and *Training Day* (2001), maintain similar essentialist ideas about race, and therefore advocate the need for such "rough justice." *L.A. Confidential* presents the framing of a group of young African American men for robbery and murder as the work of corrupt police, yet it shows these same young men as guilty of gang rape, as if to substantiate the old justification for profiling: even if they did not commit the crime they were stopped for, they have done something else. *Training Day* gives police corruption in contemporary Los Angeles a decidedly nonwhite flavor by drawing on the Rampart scandal. The film therefore echoes Boyer's suggestion that corruption in the force has occurred as the result of the increased presence of nonwhite officers. The characterization in *Training Day* of bad cop Alonzo Harris (Denzel Washington) is a composite of the Rampart villains Perez and Mack: both Latino and African American, part cop and part gang-banger. Like both officers, Harris is a serious player with a Salvadoran mistress who recalls Veronica Quesada, the Honduran *amante* of Rafael Perez. In another specific reference to Perez and Mack, as in real life the corruption of the two officers was revealed by a wild jaunt to Las Vegas, so on film the Harris character is brought down by a gambling trip in which he runs afoul of the Russian mobsters who ultimately kill him. Ethan Hawke as the white hero of *Training Day* who stops Denzel Washington's bad cop underlines its interest in giving a racially tinted picture of current police corruption in Los Angeles.

This kind of essentializing about the criminality of nonwhite cultures can be traced to what Michael Omi and Howard Winant (1994) call *ethnicity theory*. Originating in the Chicago school of sociology in the 1930s and 1940s, such theory understands the experience of European immigrants as defined primarily by their ethnicity, which they overcome by assimilating into mainstream American society. Based on this view of the history of European Americans, ethnicity theory has created the expectation that nonwhites will assimilate in a similar fashion, and if they do not, it explains the failure as being due to "flaws" in their culture. Such thinking has contributed to the link between race and criminality that underlies the police practice of profiling in Los Angeles and elsewhere in the United States (Escobar, 9–10).

Although unjust policing based on these ideas of race has a long history in Los Angeles, relatively few films have represented it as a problem, and most of those that do have been made since the attention generated by the events of the early 1990s. Most films that show police misconduct in Los Angeles assume that it does not result from structural problems such as a lack of nonwhite officers, the prevalence in police culture of prejudicial ideas about the inherent criminality of certain racial groups, or tolerance for excessive force. Instead, the four films from the 1980s and 1990s analyzed here portray the problem as being caused by a dysfunctional law enforcement system that alienates officers—some of whom therefore go bad. This dysfunction is understood in these films as the result of a lack of political will to pursue the solution and punishment of crime. Because Hollywood is not good at representing systemic problems and is even worse at showing structural solutions, the response these films offer is mostly the individual heroism of a good cop. *Colors* establishes a lack of institutional commitment to justice even before the film begins with real-world statistics telling us that 250 L.A.P.D. officers do the impossible work of battling more than 60,000 gang members in an environment in which the previous year saw almost 400 "gang-related killings." *Internal Affairs, L.A. Confidential,* and *Training Day* show the L.A.P.D. as dysfunctional due to higher-ups who tolerate officers involved in illegal activity for personal gain because of the need for the "effective" policing that such bad cops provide. The central paradox in these bad cop films is that individual action offers the only solution to a dysfunctional law enforcement system in Los Angeles. In other words, the best way to repair the system is to go outside it with extralegal violence. One reason for such contradiction is that it fits a central thematic tendency of Hollywood films in which a hero acts outside the law and uses his own (often violent) response to fix what's wrong with the world. Because such individual action appears to help the community, it offers what Robert Ray calls "avoidance of [ideological] choice," allowing us to have both clear and decisive action and community responsibility at the same time (1985, 55–69).

Although it features no corrupt cops, another film set in Los Angeles, *Falling Down* (1993), presents a variation on this paradox of fixing the dysfunctional justice system through the unilateral action of a single officer. Robert Duvall plays a detective named Prendergast who has chosen to retire rather than deal with an insecure and therefore autocratic supervisor and a multicultural mix of incompetent colleagues. Before he goes, however, Prendergast demonstrates that the individual initiative of a good cop is still the best response to crime in Los Angeles, especially when that crime takes the form of an angry white male (Michael Douglas) disgruntled to the point of violence by what he sees as the abandonment of law, order, and justice. The Douglas character in *Falling Down* is a defense industry worker recently laid off, not a cop, yet his criminal actions come from the same alienation from the system (a perception that there is a lack of systemic commitment to those working for a safe, just world) that disillusions both corrupt and good officers in several other films.

Whereas *Falling Down* confidently endorses the reforms enacted by a lone, good cop, *Colors* shows some ambivalence about this mode of policing, yet ultimately affirms it as necessary. *Colors* focuses on two white officers, veteran Bob Hodges (Robert Duvall) and rookie Danny McGavin (Sean Penn), and their conflicts with Latino and African American gang members in Los Angeles. The film initially appears sympathetic to Hodges's patient brand of community policing and not to McGavin's attempts at intimidation. Yet, ultimately the movie discredits the former as a less effective strategy that indicates how Hodges, partly because of his age, lacks the toughness and resolve necessary for the job. The film hints at this inclination in an early scene that shows the two officers at a meeting of residents of a neighborhood overrun with gang violence. While the task-force leader running the meeting asks for information to help police arrest gang-bangers, the residents instead demand larger structural solutions (jobs, social programs, adequate police presence) that the film dismisses as evidence of their angry, irrational unwillingness to work toward improving the neighborhood. Although the film's final scene shows McGavin telling a new partner Hodges's stories about the value of patience, the previous scene in which the Duvall character is shot by a gang-banger and McGavin kills the assailant demonstrates the film's position that the younger cop's quick use of force is necessary for survival. *Internal Affairs*, *L.A. Confidential*, and *Training Day* link unilateral policing directly to the idea of reform by foregrounding officers who state their belief in concepts of process and blind justice, yet ironically support those ideals by going outside the law with vigilante violence. Although *L.A. Confidential* sticks with this idea to an optimistic ending that features one such contradictory cop as an official hero and has another leave for small-town life armed with true love, *Internal Affairs* and *Training Day* qualify somewhat the individualized justice of their protagonists with endings that suggest how it expands rather than ends the noir nightmare. In *Internal Affairs*, bad cop Dennis Peck (Richard Gere) so threatens the Latino masculinity of Detective Raymond Avilia (Andy Garcia) that the latter good cop joins him in his sadistic violence. As a result, Avilia strikes his wife in a crowded restaurant and kills Peck in her presence in their bedroom. In *Training Day*, idealistic rookie cop Jake Hoyt (Hawke) must also adopt the ruthless violence of the story's bad cop to stop him. Whereas the narratives of these two films endorse unilateral violence as the only way to stop the crimes of the bad officer, *Internal Affairs* and *Training Day* also suggest that the solution is so much like the problem that it is clearly not enough of a response.

The critical reflection on police violence in these two films can be found in an earlier film set in Los Angeles, *Chinatown* (1974), yet like the more recent movies it avoids racism as a cause of police misconduct. Instead, *Chinatown* prefers to identify the maintenance of class privilege as the main motive for the repressive violence of law enforcement. It ends with its main character, former cop turned private investigator Jake Gittes (Jack Nicholson), paralyzed in the face of police violence that has been employed to protect the malevolent plans of developer Noah Cross (John Huston). Gittes arrives at a nihilism like that born of the experience of the film's director Roman Polanski, whose mother was killed in the Holocaust and whose wife, Sharon Tate, was murdered by the Manson "family." Like the Nazis who ran the death camps or Manson's followers, the L.A.P.D. in *Chinatown* kill unjustly because they believe in the wrong ideas and serve the wrong master.

Yet, such emphasis on the influence of class privilege in *Chinatown* shifts attention away from the racial dimension of police corruption. Although *Chinatown*, like more recent films such as *Internal Affairs*, *Boyz N the Hood* (1991), and *Training Day*, avoids white racism by representing nonwhite officers who go astray out of selfishness, it also, like these other three, inadvertently indicts an L.A.P.D. in which nonwhites must be predatory to get anywhere. Lieutenant Escobar's respect for the money and influence of Noah Cross in *Chinatown*, the ambitious young black patrolman in *Internal Affairs* who joins the corruption of a senior white officer because it fosters his goal of promotion, the dismissive contempt shown by the African American officer toward South Central blacks in *Boyz N the Hood*, and the arrogance and violence of Detective Alonzo Harris toward working-class African Americans and Latinos in *Training Day*—each of these instances of misconduct comes from a nonwhite officer's sense of class superiority or his ruthless desire for upward mobility.

One film about police corruption in Los Angeles, *The Glass Shield* (1994), adopts neither the melodramatic response of individual officer justice to the cynicism and corruption to be found in *Colors, L.A. Confidential,* and *Falling Down,* nor the nihilism about law enforcement suggested in *Chinatown, Internal Affairs, Boyz N the Hood,* and *Training Day.* Instead, *The Glass Shield* presents police misconduct as motivated by ideas of class, race, and gender that cannot be undone simply by the unilateral actions of a heroic protagonist. Ultimately the film wants to hold onto the hope that justice can be realized, but through the actions of characters who make the legal system function as it promises to, rather than by the imposition of a personal, vigilante sense of justice.

Like *Training Day, The Glass Shield* is inspired by a real-world story, here that of an African American cop named John Eddie Johnson, whose experience sparked a corruption investigation of the California Sheriff's Department in 1980 and who ultimately became its main casualty. Young J. J. (Michael Boatman) is chosen right out of the Police Academy to integrate the previously all-white Los Angeles County Sheriff's station. The film's opening images of African American and white comic-book cops collaborating to get the bad guys represent J. J.'s fantasies of how he will fit in and do good.

We quickly see that J. J. attempts to avoid the determinative power of race and bond with his new colleagues in terms of masculinity and class: J. J. shows his toughness by pounding the dashboard to pump himself up when he and his partner get their first call that may involve violence; he later attempts to establish class camaraderie when asked to fabricate a reason for stopping an African American suspect, Teddy Woods (Ice Cube), accused of murdering a white woman during a robbery: "I got no sympathy for low-life scum," he tells a white deputy.

J. J.'s opportunity to enter the Sheriff's Department represents what Angela Davis describes as the thinking "in the dominant political discourse" that racism "is no longer a pervasive structural phenomenon" (1998, 61). Although this thinking acknowledges that race still informs "a complex of prejudicial attitudes" held by individuals, when J. J. encounters such racist thinking at his new job—for example, on his first day another deputy assumes he is a con, not a cop—he maintains a determined optimism to overcome such thinking by showing what he can do. The lone woman deputy at the station, Deborah (Lori Petty), confronts him with the prejudicial thinking of their coworkers, but J. J. tells her defiantly that they will name the station after him someday.

Yet, as J. J. becomes aware that Teddy Woods has been charged with the shooting for reasons of race rather than evidence, he comes up against the more subtle forms of what Davis calls "camouflaged racism." Davis asserts that the high level of nonwhite, especially African American, young men in the criminal justice system in the United States (32 percent according to a 1995 study) is part of a "war on crime" that assumes that such nonwhite men are "the most likely people to whom criminal acts will be attributed." Davis summarizes that "although black people were 7.8 times more likely to be imprisoned than whites," this imbalance "is not recognized as evidence of structural racism, but rather is invoked as a consequence of the assumed criminality of black people" (63–64).

Once J. J. realizes that he faces not just isolated racist attitudes but this "less visible structural racism," which assumes that black people are the criminal enemy, it becomes clear that he cannot work in the Edgemar station without adopting its dominant mind-set. Not that the adoption of what Davis terms "implicit consent to anti-black racist logic (not to speak of racism toward other groups) . . . among black people," is unprecedented (65). The apathetic African American officer in *Boyz N the Hood* (Jessie Lawrence Ferguson) articulates that view when he tells Furious Styles (Laurence Fishburne) that it is too bad he didn't shoot the young black male who broke into his house because that would have left "one less nigger out here on the streets for us to worry about."

The Glass Shield's rejection of that kind of classist black-on-black racism is further underscored by another reference to *Boyz N the Hood* in the form of the stylized Volkswagen Beetle that Teddy Woods drives. A similar car contributes to the characterization of Tre Styles (Cuba Gooding Jr.), the young African American male who is the moral center of John Singleton's film and whose success does not preclude caring about and helping the less fortunate and even the criminal in his neighborhood. The similar distinctive vehicles in the two films symbolize how the young men both adopt and refashion aspects of the larger culture to fit the needs of African Americans. For Teddy Woods this comes about through how he, his parents, and his attorneys make the system provide justice; for Tre Styles the car alludes to his appropriation, in a manner that is not cold-hearted, of the dominant values of self-discipline and education as the keys to success.

Whereas the strategies used by Teddy Woods and Tre Styles prove effective, the initial middle-class and masculinist attitudes of J. J.—like the gang-banger nihilism of Doughboy (Ice Cube) in *Boyz N the Hood*—prove flawed. Both J. J. and Doughboy react to structural racism with violence; J. J. adds to this strategic mistake bourgeois assumptions of his ability to fight it alone with the aptitude for physical violence that he had hoped would gain him acceptance. Such violence recalls the individualized solutions of other bad cop films, but proves singularly ineffective here, as in one scene in which J. J. angrily attacks the white deputy Bono (Don Harvey)—who asked him to perjure himself to justify stopping Teddy Woods—only to be thrown in a cell by other officers.

J. J.'s confinement in a holding cell foreshadows how he will later face charges for perjury whereas Bono will go free with a plea-bargain arrangement. Therefore, one of the main ways in which *The Glass Shield* marks its difference from other movies about bad cops is its refusal to endorse violence as the solution to police corruption. Although violence in *Colors, Internal Affairs, L.A. Confidential,* and *Training Day* is essential to stopping—or at least reforming—the bad cop, in *The Glass Shield* it is shown only as part of the criminality of corrupt policemen or as part of J. J.'s failed attempt to resist them. The ineffectiveness of violence is emphasized in the film's last scene, in which J. J. boils over in anger and frustration about the perjury charge and breaks the window of his car. The response of his startled girlfriend, as she insists that he calm down and talk to her, sums up what the film has shown about the power of discursive responses to the negative identities the deputies (including J. J.) force on others.

In contrast to J. J.'s individualism and violence, *The Glass Shield* sets up the legal actions of an African American attorney, Locket (Bernie Casey), as more effective. Locket's successful use of legal strategies and his collaboration with both his Latina partner, Carmen Munoz (Wanda De Jesus), and a liberal white female judge to make the system work, counter the racist profiling and sexism of the deputies. *The Glass Shield* underscores the challenge of assigning these analytical and rhetorical skills to an African American male character in a scene soon after Teddy Woods has been denied bail. Teddy angrily tells Locket, "I knew my momma shoulda' got me a white lawyer." Not only does Locket prove the value of his discursive approach to Teddy (and to the film's audience), eventually even J. J. understands the importance of a more strategic, collaborative approach to the racism of the station, teaming up with Deborah to investigate how deputies have blackmailed influential figures in Los Angeles politics to keep them from scrutinizing their corrupt practices. (Indeed, the real L.A.P.D. for years used the Public Disorder Intelligence Division [P.D.I.D.] to keep an eye on what it perceived as its enemies [see Woods 1993, 267–72].)

The Glass Shield's attempt at representing a discursive approach to justice led to the filmic equivalent of profiling and excessive violence. Its production company, Miramax, blocked the film's release for a year after it was completed and forced director Charles Burnett to change the ending and make it less despairing about the chances of police racism and corruption being penalized. Despite these changes, Miramax did very little publicity for *Glass Shield* and gave it a limited release (see Rosenbaum 1997, 161).

Writing just after Rodney King's arrest, Salim Muwakkil predicted that the March 3, 1991, video of the King beating would create at best a "temporary spasm of public concern [that] will do little to alter the racist reality of U.S. law enforcement." To really change the situation, Muwakkil advocates sustained organization and activism within the African American community, and even the outside involvement of the United Nations to investigate and intervene to stop police use of profiling and excessive violence against nonwhites (1991, 7–8).

Muwakkil acknowledges the importance of the Rodney King video, admitting that had it not been made and widely seen, the existence of such excessive police violence would still be doubted by many white Americans. Likewise a film such as *The Glass Shield* by itself—especially considering the lack of support Miramax gave it—can have only limited effect on these problems of race and law enforcement in the United States. Yet, at least the film counters the prevailing assumption in most movies that the best alternative to police misbehavior is the unilateral violence that helped create the problem in the first place.

As part of his supposedly pragmatist justification of the L.A.P.D., journalist Boyer comments that officers "may become cynics, depressives, drunks or bad husbands, but they believe that they form the outer membrane of civilization, and that chaos lies just the other side of the 'thin blue line'—a term coined by . . . William H. Parker" (2001, 5). Out of this "real world" logic comes the assumption that the best way to protect innocent people is to condone ad hoc violence and preemptive actions such as profiling. The reasons for avoiding such thinking are equally pragmatic: as *The Glass Shield* shows, unilateral, vigilante action based on essentialist thinking about race undermines the very foundations of the legal system that forms the basis of the freedoms we promise in American society. Moreover, as J. J.'s experience in the film makes clear, even righteous violence can provide just cause for further repression.

WORKS CITED

Boyer, Peter J. 2001. "Bad Cops," *The New Yorker* (May 21), 2, 78. Also: *www.pbs.org/wgbh/pages/frontline/shows/lapd/bare.html*

Davis, Angela. 1998. "Race and Criminalization: Black Americans and the Punishment Industry." In Joy James, ed., *The Angela Y. Davis Reader*. New York: Blackwell, 61–73.

Davis, Mike. 1990. *City of Quartz*. New York: Verso.

Escobar, Edward. 1999. *Race, Police, and the Making of an Identity: Mexican Americans and the Los Angeles Police Department, 1900–1945*. Berkeley: University of California Press.

Muwakkil, Salim. 1991. "The Racist Reality of Police Culture," *In These Times*, March 27–April 2, 13–15.

Omi, Michael, and Howard Winant. 1994. *Racial Formation in the United States: From the 1960s–1990s*. New York: Routledge.

Ray, Robert. 1985. *A Certain Tendency of the Hollywood Cinema*. Princeton: Princeton University Press.

Rosenbaum, Jonathan. 1997. *Movies as Politics*. Berkeley: University of California Press.

Woods, Gerald. 1993. *The Police in Los Angeles: Reform and Professionalization*. New York: Garland.

FIGURE 4. "The forms of violent expression not sanctioned by the official culture are almost invariably those forms that run against the grain of dominant ideology, although not always with anything like a conscious political program." *Bonnie and Clyde* (Arthur Penn, Warner Bros./Seven Arts, 1967) apotheosizes the unsanctioned nature of Bonnie Parker's (Faye Dunaway) violence through its depiction of her gory demise. (Frame enlargement)

CHAPTER FOUR

Genocidal Spectacles
and the Ideology of Death

CHRISTOPHER SHARRETT

Representations of mass murder and the ideology on which they are based
have held a place of centrality in American media culture since its inception.
From D. W. Griffith's falsified, racist version of the Civil War in *The Birth of
a Nation* (1915) and his Fall of Babylon and persecution of the French
Huguenots in *Intolerance* (1916), the cinema has been intimately associated
with the politics of twentieth-century genocide and with the antecedents of
modern mass murder in earlier epochs. *Intolerance* has a privileged relevance
to my remarks. Griffith's rather pacifist epic, a disingenuous apology for the
racism of *The Birth of a Nation*, was not well received by a U.S. population that
in the first decade of the century had been rather isolationist and pro-labor but
that became steadily more warmongering with the impact of Woodrow Wilson's propaganda machine, designed to stir up hatred against the Central
Powers as the United States prepared to help its friendly rivals in World War
I. This "machine" was the Committee on Public Information, chaired by
George Creel and including pioneering public relations whiz kid Edward
Bernays (Chomsky 1997). The notorious Creel Committee, and the Davis
Committee that in a similar way softened the public for World War II, made
the modern warfare state palatable by tweaking public sensibilities in the
direction of intervention, heroism, and payback.

Griffith's film obliquely references operations of the early public relations industry and its services to state power. In the scenes of strikebreaking

and mass murder by the National Guard at the Jenkins Mill, Griffith embodies the populist furor over the notorious Ludlow Massacre. In 1914, John D. Rockefeller Jr. hired goons and guardsmen to mow down striking workers no longer able to tolerate the barbaric conditions at his mining and chemical interests in Ludlow, Colorado. Rockefeller soon realized that in the age of the emerging electronic media, he had committed a major gaffe, and took the advice of Ivy L. Lee, another founding father of modern public relations, who counseled him to dispense with his robber baron ways and take part in a series of photo ops that would recast him as a friend of the common man.

There are antecedents to that moment of public relations triumph. The death of General George Armstrong Custer and his cavalry brigade at the Little Big Horn River in 1876 ("Custer's Last Stand") became a logo for the Anheuser Busch beer company (Slotkin 1985). Representations of the glorious martyrdom of the outnumbered Custer, butchered by the "devious, bloodthirsty Sioux," became omnipresent in popular culture and an important diversion from the financial panic of the 1870s, not to mention the fraudulent 1876 election, a moment with particular application to our present times. Complementing the death of Custer, and eventually competing for space in popular culture, was the assassination of frontier marshal James Butler "Wild Bill" Hickok in Deadwood, South Dakota (Rosa 1964). Hickok, a psychopath who once shot his own deputy in a manic fit following a gunfight, would become firmly ensconced in the twentieth-century mass media and even have a television western of his own on Saturday mornings to entertain and indoctrinate the children of the Cold War. Hickok had once been a U.S. Army scout who participated in the Indian Removal policies initiated by Andrew Jackson and continued with incremental ferocity throughout the 1800s. One did not find in the accounts of the deaths of Hickok or Custer mention of the sustained genocide of Native Americans that made the white Western expansionism in the United States—and their dramatic involvement—possible: no mention of the Washita River, where in 1869 Custer and his regiment murdered men, women, and children of a wintering Cheyenne village in a near-repeat of the notorious Sand Creek Massacre.

An enormous—and hardly surprising—disjunction continues between official violence, its valorization in the propaganda system of the state and private sector, and the portrayal of violence by artists within and on the margins of the commercial entertainment industry. In the wake of the September 11, 2001 attacks on New York and Washington, members of the George W. Bush brain trust, including chief of staff Karl Rove, met with such Hollywood power brokers as Jack Valenti to decide what television and movie fare would be suitable for the public sensibility during the "war on terrorism." There was some concern that Hollywood should temporarily soft-pedal violence, hence militarist and reactionary dross like the Schwarzenegger vehicle *Collateral*

Damage (2002) should not be released until in February 2002, three months after its proposed date. That this film and dozens like it might be shelved permanently apparently was not a real option. Nor was there undue concern expressed to hold back hyperracist films such as *Black Hawk Down* (2001), which function to fuel patriotic sentiment and the impulse toward genocide in service of state interests. The annihilation of the racial Other is a staple of the commercial entertainment industry, essential, in the neoliberal moment, to a basic ideological dynamic central to the U.S. imperialist project. The black population of Somalia is shown in *Black Hawk Down* from high-angle shots, suggesting a swarm of ants overtaking their white benefactors, who end up fighting a last stand against the swarthy hordes, one wounded soldier positioned in the manner of Jim Bowie at the Alamo (the movie, in fact, borrows a great deal from narratives of that battle and from films such as *Zulu* [1964]). Rigorously excluded from the narrative is any sense of the politics of famine and exploitation during the three centuries of Western colonization of Africa (Davis 2001). This avoidance is quite logical given assumptions about what is acceptable to portrayals of violence and genocide in the entertainment industry throughout the twentieth century and into the twenty-first.

For all the hand wringing within sectors of state and private power about the portrayal of violence in the media, the ideological system clearly permits, indeed encourages, representations of violence, including genocide, if such representations serve the ambitions of the capitalist state. Yet certain specified representations are met with challenges and threats of—or actual—censorship, and clearly cause anxiety to the ideological system.

SANCTIONED VIOLENCE

Cultural representations of violence and genocide exist that explicitly replicate dominant ideology and hence rarely meet with very much moralizing from state power, organized religion, or the private sector. The examples here are so numerous that even a brief rumination on the topic gives the lie to the moralistic pretenses of those political hacks pretending to wish violence excluded from popular art. Most obvious are the spectacles reinforcing competition—the essence of so-called free enterprise—that are axiomatically applauded. These include all sporting contests, including (especially) the most violent and degraded (football, boxing), and even marginal sporting contests that mock sportsmanship (with the notion of fair play under capital now an acknowledged joke), offer base entertainment, and are given a nudge and a wink by the sports industry (TV wrestling, extreme sports, game shows designed to humiliate the contestants, such as "Are You Hot?"). Television shows dealing with "real crime" are permitted ("COPS," "America's Most

Wanted," "The World's Scariest Police Chases," and so forth) because they deal with the underclass getting its just deserts and with assuring the propertied classes that crime is the province of minorities and poor white trash now, as we see on the screen, kept safely at bay by the authorities. The unending action/adventure cycles of the Stallone/Schwarzenegger variety (although these two stars are very much in eclipse, they will no doubt for some time remain as twin emblems of the decay of action cinema) are also within the realm of sanctioned fare because of the acceptable lesson they teach about masculinity in the service of state interests. Their close cousins are the Tom Clancy action films that proliferated in the 1990s, movies that look back nostalgically to the Cold War while assuring the audience that a remilitarization of the nation is important for neoliberal "globalization" (an overworked word that pretends the new hypertechnological form of state-supported capital has no association with the imperialism that has guided capital for three centuries). Here I have in mind such dubious treasures as *The Hunt for Red October* (1990), *Patriot Games* (1992), or *Clear and Present Danger* (1994).

The recent films of Steven Spielberg are instructive as to the sanctioning of the violent image by official culture. The gory battle action that opens the much-ballyhooed *Saving Private Ryan* (1998), tacked onto a highly formulaic war film (Gabbard 2002) that makes the antiwar statements of late 1950s and early 1960s Hollywood seem absolutely radical (*Hell Is for Heroes* [1962], *The Young Lions* [1958], *The Victors* [1963], *Attack* [1956]), has as its project valorizing not so much the GI—although the film bows in that direction as it takes part in a strange and highly reactionary Oedipal drama playing out in millennial pop culture, courtesy of Tom Brokaw's *The Greatest Generation* and its spin-off industry—as a hazy, nostalgic, Norman Rockwellian image of pre-1960s America with the 1940s portrayed as an age when men and women knew their proper gender and economic roles.

Schindler's List (1993), a film that also helped shape a consideration of Spielberg as serious filmmaker, has less to say about the Holocaust than it does about notions of "evil" as central to the political-economic order that produced European fascism. The film is hardly about the suffering of the European Jews; the images of Auschwitz and the slave labor camp at Kraków are horrific filler providing the backdrop for the battle of the Super Aryans, Schindler (Liam Neeson) and Goeth (Ralph Fiennes). The interimperial rivalry that was World War II, and the political economy of Nazism, with its ideology of *untermensch* (embraced by the entire West), is here reduced to the struggle of a Rhett Butler–style high-minded mercenary and his comic book doppelgänger. Spielberg's *A.I.* (2001), a project he inherited from Stanley Kubrick about a technocratic future wherein humanity is threatened by cybernetics, seems to challenge notions of the Holocaust's sacredness and historical centrality that Spielberg pretended to extol (as self-appointed caretaker of

Holocaust representation and archivalism following *Schindler's List*). In fusing the Holocaust with a tired, typically mawkish Pinocchio narrative, humans sending cyborgs to an Auschwitz for robots replete with images of massed body parts replicating death camp footage, *A.I.* shows, under the cover of a puerile moral lesson, the dissolution by the commercial entertainment industry of serious discourse about the politics of mass murder.

Postmodern disaster films such as *Armageddon* (1998), *Deep Impact* (1998), and *Independence Day* (1996) use images of mass death in a fashion more cavalier than *Saving Private Ryan, Schindler's List,* or *A.I.,* but for similar ideological ends. Whereas disaster films of the 1970s (for example, *The Towering Inferno* and *Earthquake* [both 1974]) saw the post-Vietnam bourgeois order as fragile at best, perhaps irreparable, the disaster cycle of the 1990s, by contrast, assures the public that institutions such as the patriarchal family, religion, capitalism, and militarism are essential to national survival rather than part of the underlying contradictions of American life. *Independence Day* and its ilk are very blithe about the destruction (within single shots!) of whole populations, largely because they laud sacrificial violence in service of state power and the conservative social order reasserted in the 1980s and 1990s. *Armageddon* praises the technology developed through a century of U.S. imperialism and interimperial warfare, informing the viewer that the bloodbaths of the century provided the United States with the comforting resolve and know-how to strike at its celestial threat. The alien invaders of *Independence Day* are a version of the Other closely associated with peoples of the Middle East (the East being the dominant locus of the racial Other in the cinema of the 1980s and 1990s); at various junctures the film looks back nostalgically (as if the moment was eons ago) to the attack on the Persian Gulf, applauding the film's "action president" (Bill Pullman) modeled on George H. W. Bush. The graphicism of devastation depicted in *Independence Day* and *Deep Impact* colludes with the postmodern conceit that all human experience (or at least all experience worth writing criticism about) is mediated, an idea furthered by the presentation of the Gulf War as video game on the state-regimented corporate media. An apparent continuity exists between the 1970s disaster film and its successors in the 1990s, however. The flying or crushed bodies of *Earthquake* and *The Towering Inferno* are sanctioned violent images, often noted and criticized by the mainstream media to be sure (and thus perhaps "semisanctioned"); their sanctioning flows in part from their creation by the studio industry rather than the fringe cinema, but more importantly from their contextualization within narratives about heroics aimed at preserving, however futilely, American society.

Two films of 1960, Stanley Kubrick's *Spartacus* and John Wayne's *The Alamo,* serve as a useful instruction concerning acceptable renderings of violence in mass art. One cannot say that one film was accepted by official culture and the other entirely vilified; both films are historical epics, their content dealing with historical episodes (usually seen as far removed from public interest), the Roman slave revolt and the 1836 Texas Revolution respectively. Both films were beset with problems: *Spartacus* by conflicts between Kubrick, the nominal director, and actor/producer Kirk Douglas; *The Alamo* by phenomenally bad scripting and a wretched publicity campaign. Both films were intricately involved in the discourse about the Cold War. The radical aspirations of *Spartacus* are hard to miss. Aside from portraying a revolt long held up by the left as the originary popular struggle against oppression, producer Kirk Douglas hired blacklisted screenwriter Dalton Trumbo, giving him full screen credit, in an attempt to shatter the grip of the House Un-American Activities Committee and McCarthyism. *The Alamo* was John Wayne's long-term pet project and perhaps his defining statement. The film is one long rightist diatribe, written for Wayne by fellow zealot James Edward Grant. *The Alamo* was Wayne's attempt to castigate the "flabby" patriotism of Dwight D. Eisenhower and contained a warning (in the form of an anti-Jefferson tirade delivered by Laurence Harvey's William Barrett Travis) about voting for the Democrats (John F. Kennedy) in the 1960 election, which followed immediately the film's premiere. And aware of Douglas's *Spartacus* project and the hiring of Trumbo, Wayne and gossip columnist Hedda Hopper tried to squelch the film.

The two films provide a locus for understanding the presentation of violence in Cold War media culture. Aside from a few saber-to-the-gut shots, the violence of *The Alamo* is fairly stately and antiseptic (and with no relation to the historical record). As with *Saving Private Ryan* (which contains an allusion to the Alamo battle) forty years later, *The Alamo* believes in the efficacy of sacrificial slaughter for state purposes and the U.S. expansionist project. *Saving Private Ryan*, as with a good deal of neoconservative cultural production, must acknowledge the audience's cynical hesitation to believe in the "realism" of the image (and its exposure to the previous thirty years of cinema) by adding considerable blood and gore to its first reel, after which it devolves quickly into a generic war film celebrating the fulfillment of national destiny in world conflagration. By contrast, *Spartacus* shows (within the restrictions of the Production Code) the consequences of violence and its context within class struggle and ideological conflict. Arms are chopped off, people are burned to death, trampled, and crucified (many of the more violent images were cut, some later to be restored on laser disc and DVD). Above all, *Spartacus* ends badly, its hero tortured to death by crucifixion (causing rumblings from the Catholic Church, which felt only Jesus Christ should be portrayed as a crucifixion victim). Neoconservative works such as *Braveheart* (1995) incorporate gore insofar as it sanctifies sacrificial violence and national destiny. But no triumphal anthems are heard at the end of *Spartacus* as they are in *Braveheart*, no brandishing of national banners is seen. The film also suggests, especially with the lingering tracking shots across acres of dead slaves murdered by Crassus (Laurence Olivier) and his legions, that this narrative is about a people's revolt, with Spartacus (Kirk Douglas) mainly a catalyst, however charismatic. In this, *Spartacus* shares something with Eisenstein's *Strike* and *Battleship Potemkin* (both 1925). The film tends to reject the notion of patriarchal heroism basic to mainstream commercial cinema. At the least, *Spartacus* begins the tradition of the commercial cinema's "Marxist operas," continued with *Once Upon a Time in the West* (1969), *1900* (1976), and *Heaven's Gate* (1980), all of which not incidentally share an unflinching portrayal of the consequences of violence coupled with a critique of state and private interests whose perpetration of mass murder flows from their ambitions.

VIOLENCE UNSANCTIONED

It is important to note that the films and other media singled out for censorship or various forms of public assault are most often works that offer a critique of violence and its role in history and current civilization. John Hinckley's 1980 shooting of Ronald Reagan spurred heated discussion of Martin Scorsese's *Taxi Driver* (1976) and one of its stars, Jodie Foster, apparently subjects that enamored the disturbed young man. Few journalistic commentators noted any of the film's themes: the disaffected nature of the postmodern urban population; the failure of political institutions; a popular culture fixated on the cult of the gun; the failure of narratives central to U.S. history, folklore, and popular art, including the journey of rescue (the movie has long been contrasted to John Ford's *The Searchers* [1956]); and the bankruptcy in particular of the Last Stand of folklore, in which the male subject validates a divinely ordained "mission" with bloodletting and self-destruction. Perhaps precisely because these themes are at the heart of the film's narrative, it became the subject of so much disingenuous ham-handed "impact theory" obloquy.

Similarly, the mind-numbingly fatuous Senator Robert Dole fulminated in 1994 on the senate floor about a young murderer who said he was a "natural born killer"—this was by way of a slam at the Oliver Stone film of a year earlier. Whatever its sins, Stone's skewed and disorganized *Natural Born Killers* attempts a sardonic consideration of the mediascape, the waning of affect associated with postmodernity, and the bankruptcy of conventions associated with the road movie and prison film. One can argue that the film proposes the United States as a landscape haunted by genocide and other forms of violence, including rape and child abuse, which the mass media merely reflect and largely endorse as fodder for salacious discourse about "scandal" (as opposed to critical discourse on institutional assumptions about gender, sexuality, and the status of the human subject as object).

By far the most vilified form of violent representation is the horror genre, and in particular its "gorefest" subgenre. Films such as Tobe Hooper's *The Texas Chainsaw Massacre* (1974) and the zombie films of George Romero, all in the vanguard of the horror film's new wave of the 1970s, were immediately vilified by the mainstream press, then reduced to cult items (even with—perhaps because of—the canonization of *Massacre* and *Night of the Living Dead* [1968] by the Museum of Modern Art). Romero's zombie films have long been noted for the sense of a world careening into chaos, their portrayal of an apocalyptic epoch unfolding in America (Wood 1984) that is as much a reflection on the entirety of the American civilizing process as a response to the Vietnam/Watergate era (Sharrett 1984). The chief violation of the modern horror film is its vision of the disintegration of the bourgeois order combined with—and this is the real transgression of taboos—its portrayal of the person as an object subject to destruction, consumption, and putrefaction. At the most obvious level, Romero's zombie films ask, "Who are the real zombies?" by showcasing the dehumanized, brutalized conditions of the late-twentieth-century capitalist United States. The conclusion of *Night of the Living Dead* portrays, however unconsciously, not just the conditions of the civil rights and antiwar struggles, but also the history of racial genocide here and in Europe over the twentieth century. The final scene—of the rednecks throwing Ben's body on the fire with grappling hooks—references both American lynching practices and the Nazi Holocaust.

Romero's *Dawn of the Dead* (1978) and *Day of the Dead* (1985) make more explicit the objectification of the human being, a condition many have associated with such images as the piles of the dead under European fascism. The images brought into play by Romero in a way prevent us from viewing the holocaustal destruction of humanity as unique to political formations such as fascism, itself often removed from the real dynamics of international capitalism. By turning a shopping mall into a charnel house *(Dawn of the Dead)* where bodies are shot to pieces, ripped apart, exploded, and disposed of en masse as nuisance debris, Romero's satire gives the lie to the sanctity of human life so fervently proclaimed by capitalist culture and its supporting institutions. Romero's point is explicitly—all too explicitly—the capitalist idea that the human being is valuable only as a predator and consumer and that the body in consumer culture has the same status as all other consumable objects, an idea made overt by Holocaust imagery and narratives of the human subject becoming an industrial by-product. This notion of the body as organism runs against capitalism and its ideological system, which although in practice treating persons as little more than industrial by-product proceed to advance the idea of the human being as immortal and noble, an infinite "desiring machine" of consumer culture hardly along the lines of Deleuze's notion of a mere unchained libido. Of course, the presentation of gore, like the presentation of genitals and the sex act, may be allowed when they serve state interests (fomenting rage against the Other) or provide a "safety valve" for a highly repressed culture (for example, the introduction of hardcore porn into skin magazines such as *Penthouse*).

For asserting so bluntly the material exploitability of human life, the modern horror film became the subject of much anxiety about a "pornography of violence" overtaking American life (Schlesinger 1968). Such complaints first came into view with Arthur Penn's *Bonnie and Clyde* (1967), Sam Peckinpah's *The Wild Bunch* (1969), and the imported Italian westerns of Sergio Leone and others. All of these films, like the horror genre of the period, raised fundamental questions about the American civilizing process and its narratives of consolation. Penn's film makes gestures toward the notion of a misty, golden, half-remembered American past. Burnett Guffey's remarkable photography offers the America of *The Saturday Evening Post* side by side with images of the desiccation caused by the Great Depression, a view of an earlier America opposite to that of *Saving Private Ryan*. The violence of the film is associated with the logic of capital, as Clyde (Warren Beatty) wants to "be somebody," while his girlfriend, Bonnie (Faye Dunaway), follows along as worshipper and faithful chronicler of her man and his world, deluded by her lover's charms, then realizing that Clyde, for all his own delusions, is preferable to the hollow world around them. The irony, of course, is that Clyde, the journeying hero, is impotent, a vainglorious adventurer in a brutal and dying world. In any event, the film forecloses any sense of escape, freedom, and rebirth basic to the American narrative. The sudden brutality of the film's shocking conclusion underscores the finality of death and the futility and artifice of notions of immortality, even as embodied in art (Bonnie's ballads).

The Wild Bunch is more unrelenting than *Bonnie and Clyde*, and far less concerned with a sense of nostalgia for the American past. The film suggests that whatever virtues were once embodied in the American experiment have long since been betrayed and that those virtues may have been delusions. At the heart of the film is the conflict between the realities of life in an already declining, brutal American landscape and the attempt to preserve idealistic principles (the idea is capsulated early in the film, when the boss of the rail depot berates a clerk: "I don't care what you meant to do. It's what you did that I don't like"). The cataclysmic violence of the final massacre seems a kind of preamble to the twentieth-century world where capitalism, technocracy, and imperialism not only foreclose the possibility of any human community but also reduce the human subject to the kind of object status (piles of the dead) *Dawn of the Dead* and 1970s horror developed.

The forms of violent expression not sanctioned by the official culture are almost invariably those forms that run against the grain of dominant ideology, although not always with anything like a conscious political program. Some forms of expression—gory video games or certain rock/rap acts such as Eminem—speak rather authentically to the disaffected, fragmented nature of American life. Such expression might be termed "semisanctioned" because industries obviously wish to exploit alienation, especially that of the young (a highly vulnerable audience with a good deal of fluid "disposable income"). The violence of video games such as Resident Evil replicates—at a level often not too hyperbolic relative to the bloodletting consequent to the strategies of state power—real conditions of life in postindustrial America, with its cityscape half corporate citadel, half dying slum. Eminem and many rap/heavy metal/death metal/doom industrial acts represent an assault on capital from the right that is complemented by the feigned outrage of opportunistic politicians and parents' groups. These forms of cultural production and the tirades against them inoculate the standing political-economic system, protecting it from radical criticism. The apocalypticism of such art acknowledges the crisis of capital and in so doing acknowledges the extreme cynicism of a depoliticized mass audience, but suggests that the crisis is a result of human degeneracy (the voice of dominant discourse) and destiny (the voice of the artists), not of decisions made calmly and with extreme violence by institutions.

FIGHT CLUB AND THE NEOLIBERAL ORDER

The apocalypticism saturating postmodern cultural expression, and its limitations as social criticism, are well represented in David Fincher's *Fight Club* (1999). Like the horror films of the 1970s, the film posits an atmosphere of chaos, of bourgeois society at the brink, all with the sense of satire associated with the horror genre at its height. Like the horror film, and Fincher's earlier *Se7en* (1995), *Fight Club* immerses us in a decayed, malevolent world, but whereas the horror film has no nostalgia for the collapse of reason and established institutions, Fincher's work shows a strong element of melancholy for the twilight of Enlightenment values, and finds recourse, especially in *Fight Club*, in the nihilism of a resuscitated male group. To be sure, the cult of the male and the whole of phallocentric culture are the key focus of satiric derision, but it is instructive that the anxieties of the male, and his attempt to prove himself sentient through nihilist violence and predation, are seen as the only real issues for a neoliberal economic order that has caused havoc for the planet as a whole and for vast, overexploited populations living below subsistence (Giroux and Szeman 2002). One may argue that the bloody fistfights and assorted mayhem of the film poke fun precisely at the solipsistic inversion at the heart of upwardly mobile Generation X executives (such frustrations were basic to the postwar Organization Man, who made the western, with its dreams of a male utopia, a key postwar genre), and also at the entire male social construct as effectuated by bourgeois civilization and enforced by representation. At the film's conclusion, Jack/Tyler is able to join hands with Marla (Helena Bonham Carter) after he has destroyed his face and obliterated his macho ego ideal. The two reconcile the male and female principles; feminism triumphs as capitalism implodes. But the only political vision in sight is nihilism, the only thinker referenced Nietzsche, whose romantic individualism and misogyny have had great cachet for both late capitalism and the postmodern theory that supposedly critiques it. The neobarbarism that is *Fight Club*'s response to consumer capital has the logic and satiric aspect of *The Texas Chainsaw Massacre*. The difficulty here is that the fringe cinema indeed accomplished such a response almost thirty years ago. That the commercial cinema has gone no further, and even regressed, insofar as *Fight Club* seems preoccupied with the obsessions of the male, says much about the limitations of discourse about violence and the political-economic prerogatives that engender it.

GENOCIDE AS ABERRATION

Perhaps the distinctions we find in American culture between sanctioned and unsanctioned violence are related as much to notions of the violent act flowing from "sick" individuals (rather than institutions and institutional assumptions) as to the refusal of the role of the violent act as an efficacious instrument in support of ideological ambitions. A recent discussion of the My Lai massacre (in a book on the workings of massacre in history, no less) observes:

> While the potential for the enactment of a My Lai may lie in all of us, only exhausted, disoriented, and extremely frightened army units are likely to vent their pent up frustrations on a supposedly hostile population in this particular form of atrocity. (Levene and Roberts 1999, 19)

That contemporary historians writing about a very recent historical moment could display this kind of ignorance is rather appalling, but it is representative of the reassurances desired not only within academe but also within large sectors of mass culture about the relationship of genocidal violence to ideology. Noam Chomsky remarks that during the period that circumscribed My Lai, the U.S. military ran a series of devastating B-52 strikes code-named Operation WHEELER WALLAWA. These bombings specifically targeted villages, systematically annihilating the Vietnamese population (2002, 2). The continued anxieties about the attack on Southeast Asia, with the focus on the people of Vietnam as aggressors (the proliferation of MIA flags even twenty-seven years after the U.S. withdrawal), certainly do not originate in a frustrated, angry, miseducated populace alone. Ongoing state and private interests nourish such frustration, as the state fosters the image of itself threatened by the Other at the same time that the neoliberal capitalist order seeks new territories, markets, resources, and sources of cheap labor. That this savagery continues to be part of state policy in a land now replete with pieties about violence and its effects on children and others is merely one of the essential contradictions of life in capitalist America, one that, without the intervention of progressive politics, will be an element of the continued unraveling of the social contract and the increased barbarism of daily life.

9/11 AND THE WORLD FOREVER CHANGED

The bloody events of September 11, 2001 produced fairly uniform responses from state power and the media. We were repeatedly told that we now live in "a new historical era" and that "everything has changed." But what has changed? Certainly very little with regard to the distribution of wealth and power in the United States. Throughout much of this last century up to the present writing, 2 percent of the population has owned and administered 90 percent of the national wealth. The welfare state has been all but destroyed, with single mothers forced to work at meaningless jobs, since the production of wealth for others is the only "true" form of work. The violence of poverty, homelessness, and crime continue to run rampant under various political regimes as the society polarizes.

If everything has changed, not included in the diagnosis is the representation of violence by the media. *Time, Newsweek,* and other publications issued special editions filled with graphic "splash pages" of exploding buildings, people covered in dust and blood, and people jumping from windows—images that recall Andy Warhol's early 1960s "Death and Disaster" silk screens, that, according to Fredric Jameson (1989) and others, spell the waning of public affect as image and lived experience merge in commodity culture. The appetite for such images suggests that affect has indeed waned; witnesses at the World Trade Center remarked that the tragedy "looked like Armageddon" and was "worse than *The Towering Inferno.*" The collapse of public affect, however, does not militate against state policy because a huge military build-up and global policing by U.S. state power may provoke the ultimate conflagration that has always been the wish-dream of the American civilizing experience. The new cinema of violence will contain gore, but the gore of U.S. combat troops, acknowledging the sensibilities of the current audience while focusing solely on bolstering state interests and the demonization of those people and ideas seen as antithetical to those interests. In the early twenty-first century, the capitalist entertainment industry continues a project manifest at the nation's inception and essential to American conquest.

WORKS CITED

Chomsky, Noam. 1997. *Media Control: The Spectacular Achievements of Propaganda.* New York: Seven Stories Press.

———. 2002. *Understanding Power: The Indispensable Chomsky.* New York: The New Press.

Davis, Mike. 2001. *Late Victorian Holocausts: El Niño Famines and the Making of the Third World.* London: Verso.

Gabbard, Krin. 2002. "Saving Private Ryan Too Late." In Jon Lewis, ed., *The End of Cinema as We Know It.* New York: New York University Press, 131–38.

Giroux, Henry and Imre Szeman. 2002. "Ikea Boy Fights Back: *Fight Club,* Consumerism, and the Political Limits of Nineties Cinema." In Jon Lewis, ed., *The End of Cinema as We Know It.* New York: New York University Press, 95–104.

Jameson, Fredric. 1989. *Postmodernism, Or the Cultural Logic of Late Capitalism.* Durham: Duke University Press.

Levene, Mark and Penny Roberts. 1999. *The Massacre in History.* Oxford: Berghahn Books.

Rosa, Joseph G. 1964. *They Called Him Wild Bill: The Life and Adventures of James Butler Hickok.* Norman: University of Oklahoma Press.

Schlesinger, Arthur, Jr. 1968. *Violence: America in the Sixties.* New York: Signet.

Sharrett, Christopher. 1984. "The Idea of Apocalypse in *The Texas Chainsaw Massacre.*" In Barry Keith Grant, ed., *Planks of Reason: Essays on the Horror Film.* Lanham, MD: Scarecrow Press, 255–76.

Slotkin, Richard. 1985. *The Fatal Environment: The Myth of the Frontier in the Age of Industrialization, 1800–1890.* New York: Atheneum.

Wood, Robin. 1984. *Hollywood from Vietnam to Reagan.* New York: Columbia University Press.

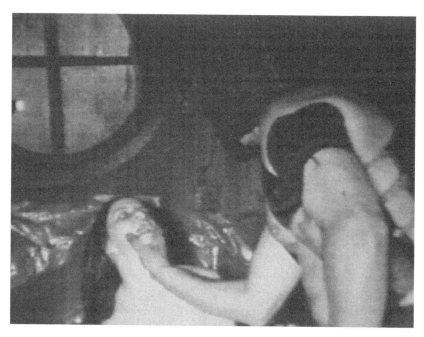

FIGURE 5. Pic-within-pic. What could be more depraved, Joel Schumacher would have us wonder in his *8MM* (Columbia, 1999), than "arranging the death of a teenage girl so that one can watch it being filmed?" Machine (Christopher Bauer, r.) "actually killing" Mary Anne Mathews (Jenny Powell, l.) for the viewer's pleasure—as depicted by Schumacher in what may be "the most pornophobic film ever made." (Frame enlargement)

CHAPTER FIVE

Bad, Worse, Worst:
8MM *and Hollywood's Bad Boys of Porn*

PETER LEHMAN

Hollywood does porn the way Debbie does Dallas—with an exuberant appetite. In fact, since the mid 1990s, Hollywood seemingly cannot get enough of films about porn and the porn industry. *The People vs. Larry Flynt* (Milos Forman, 1996), *Boogie Nights* (Paul Thomas Anderson, 1997), and *8MM* (Joel Schumacher, 1999) all deal with current porn ranging from *Hustler* magazine, to the golden age of 35mm theatrical porn and the rise of video porn, to snuff movies. *Strange Days* (1995) is a futuristic film that depicts a world with black market, virtual reality porn run amok. Not surprisingly, within this climate the Marquis de Sade, the original bad boy of porn, is the main character in *Quills* (2000). Nor is it surprising that this porn fervor has crossed over into television with such made-for-TV movies as Showtime's film about the Mitchell brothers, *Rated X* (2000), and Showtime's *Dirty Pictures* (2000), about the allegedly obscene, sexually controversial photographs of Robert Mapplethorpe. Even documentary is not immune. In 2001, *Pornstar: The Legend of Ron Jeremy* received a great deal of critical attention and made the art house circuits.

Something about a documentary on Jeremy playing the art house circuit (and even Jeremy himself who made personal appearances with the film in cities such as Tempe, Arizona) summarizes one of the many bizarre riddles with regard to this wave of fascination with porn: Why are people who (at least in polite society) shun porn in the name of art rushing to see and praise a documentary on an actor who works in a form they despise? If anyone thinks he knows the difference between art and pornography, it is the patron of the art cinema. Why does Ron Jeremy's name announcing a personal appearance on an art house marquee draw patrons who would run the other way if his appearance were tied in with one of his porn films? A local reviewer inadvertently pointed to this strange state of affairs when he praised *Pornstar,* faulting the movie however for concentrating on its charming central figure without representing the sleazy side of porn. But reviewers of documentaries about famous athletes, for example, do not demand inclusion of the sleazy side of professional sports. Nor do they presume that with the exception of the star of the film, all other athletes are sleazy. Why should Jeremy be such a startling exception with regard to the sleaze factor? All industries, including Hollywood (one is tempted to say, especially Hollywood), have their sleazy side. Why should we clamor to see porn's sleazy side with more zeal than, say, that of Hollywood or any other industry? When watching a documentary about Steven Spielberg, critics are unlikely to clamor for seeing the sleazy side of Hollywood. Why are porn's bad boys presumed to be worse, for example, than the CEOs of "respectable" (but obviously, in some way, sleazy) businesses?

Obviously, there is a fascination both in Hollywood and among moviegoers in general with what lies on the other side of that presumably clear-cut line between art and pornography or entertainment and pornography. But Jon Lewis (2000) reminds us that the line has not always been so clear-cut. A brief account of this history is vital to understanding what is happening in this recent spate of movies about the porn industry. Indeed, the title of Lewis's book, *Hollywood v. Hard Core,* would serve equally well for this chapter because all the films under consideration are in part the result of this adversarial relationship and how Hollywood represents porn cannot be separated from its actual historical encounter with that industry.

The rise of theatrical hard-core porn coincided with the new freedom in Hollywood that resulted from the end of the Hays Code and the adoption of a rating system that included X-rated movies by 1968. Precisely when Hollywood decided it was going to make sexually explicit films, it found itself in unexpected competition with the porn industry. Few people remember or know that for a brief period of time in the early 1970s porn films were being reviewed by *Variety,* among other publications, and that they were top-grossing films at the box office. As Lewis documents, porn films were regularly listed among the *Variety* top 50 box-office grossing films for the year in that time period and in 1972–1973, *Deep Throat, The Devil in Miss Jones,* and *Behind the Green Door* outgrossed on a per screen basis nearly all major studio releases (Lewis, 192). From a business point of view, Lewis argues that in 1972, hard-core porn might have seemed an attractive option for the film industry because the success of porn films would be easier to reproduce than that of quality studio films such as *The Godfather:* "When the studios accepted Valenti's argument that the hard-core business was best left to smaller, sleazier entrepreneurs, they began courting directors who seemed capable of producing quality pictures" (194–95). Lewis's characterization of Motion Picture Association of America President Jack Valenti's view of the porn industry as "sleazy" is important here because sleaziness is precisely what characterizes the porn industry in Hollywood films about porn. The "sleazy entrepreneurs" would become the "bad boys" of Hollywood porn films and the Milos Formans, Paul Thomas Andersons, and Joel Schumachers would become the quality directors telling good stories about these bad boys.

If the mainstream industry response to hard-core porn was to promote quality auteurs, the porn industry response was similar, and the early 1970s saw the golden age of porn auteurs such as Radley Metzger (also known as Henry Paris). Lewis argues that at this critical juncture the pendulum could have swung toward Hollywood going hard core just when the Nixon courts unexpectedly stepped in and in 1973 effectively ended the box-office reign of hard-core porn by making its theatrical exhibition illegal. Porn had gone from sleazy to criminal and Hollywood's main box-office competitor was gone, but, from my point of view, gone after the fact. In other words, quality Hollywood cinema had defined itself against hard-core porn, and that legacy, right down to the apparent aberration of a somewhat positive representation of the golden age of auteur porn in *Boogie Nights,* explains a significant aspect of how Hollywood would represent its former box-office enemy.

To have bad boys, of course, you have to have good boys. Joel Schumacher, director of such blockbusters as *Batman & Robin* (1997) and *Batman Forever* (1995) as well as such "serious" films as *Falling Down* (1993) is a perfect good boy candidate to tell a story about porn's bad boys, the sleazy criminals who make the kind of films he doesn't make. I begin here because in many ways this is the paint-by-numbers template of Hollywood's porn bad boys; and Schumacher's *8MM* is to my knowledge the most pornophobic film ever made. I then show how *The People vs. Larry Flynt* and *Boogie Nights* all contribute to a related, if somewhat more nuanced, discourse about these bad boys. My analysis here builds on a series of essays I published in *Jump Cut* on *The People vs. Larry Flynt, Boogie Nights,* and *8MM* (Lehman 1997, 1998, 2000). Those essays were close analyses of the individual films and Hollywood's assumptions about the porn industry. Here I want to shift the emphasis onto the bad boys represented in these films and their relationship to the good boys who make these films, and for that purpose I draw on Lewis's insightful analysis of the industrial relationship between Hollywood and porn.

8MM tells the story of Tom Welles (Nicolas Cage), a happily married private detective hired by Mrs. Christian (Myra Carter), the widow of a wealthy business tycoon. She has discovered a disturbing 8mm film hidden in a safe in her husband's office, and she seeks his opinion about it. After watching it, he tells her that it appears to be a snuff film but that such films are really faked and that no one is killed in their making. Nevertheless, he cannot guarantee that the girl in the film was not hurt or killed, and Mrs. Christian hires him to find out. Her motivation is clear: she is distressed by the knowledge that her 82-year-old husband, the father of her children, could have been aroused by such a pornographic film and, even worse, by the possibility that the film might be real. Welles adopts the guise of an investigator looking for a missing person and his investigation leads him to Janet Mathews (Catherine Keener) the mother of the girl, Mary Anne, in the 8mm film. He learns that Mary Anne left home with the intent of going to Los Angeles to become a film star. Welles follows the trail to L.A. and the porn underworld. Hiring as his guide Max California (Joaquin Phoenix), a clerk in a porn bookstore, Welles probes into the world of heavy bondage, s&m , and snuff in the hope of finding Mary Anne. His search leads him to Eddie Poole (James Gandolfini), a porn producer, and back to New York where he encounters Dino Velvet (Peter Stormare), a porn auteur who makes commissioned films and who he believes made Christian's snuff film. Welles learns that Mary Anne was indeed killed in the 8mm film—and that in the shadows a mysterious figure was watching—but then his true identity is discovered, and Welles is almost killed. He, however, manages to kill Velvet and escape. Becoming a vigilante (lest the point about Schumacher being a quality "auteur" be lost, Cage's character here bears strong comparison to the angry white male vigilante Michael Douglas plays in *Falling Down*), he hunts down and kills both the producer and star of Velvet's films. Having rid the world of the scum of the porn underworld, Welles returns home to his wife and daughter.

The film represents everyone from porn users to porn producers to porn makers to porn stars and with all due respect to Jack Valenti, the term *sleazy* does not begin to do justice to the depths of depravity and evil we see. The bad boys of porn are so bad in this film that to characterize them as sleazy would be a polite compliment. Max California, the bookstore clerk, is the exception who proves the rule. Max is really an out of work musician and not part of the porn world. To stress this, he is introduced reading a Truman Capote novel while working; the novel, however, is hidden behind the covers of a porn book. I will describe those despicable characters who really make and use porn in the order in which Welles encounters or learns about them.

When Welles goes to interview Eddie Poole, the porn mogul owner of Celebrity Films, he enters a dirty warehouse district. Celebrity Films is a seedy operation with an outer office crammed with would-be porn starlets and a messy inner office where we find a crude, cigar-chomping Poole, ill-groomed and shabbily dressed, sitting behind a desk. The disheveled appearance of the place and the man seem to reflect the man's soul, or lack thereof. He is much too busy to take any interest in a missing girl, asking if Welles has any idea how much "pussy" comes through his office every day. When Poole proves uncooperative, Welles sets up surveillance across the street where he witnesses, among other things, Poole receiving a blow job from one of the women hoping to get a part in one of his films. But this clichéd, sordid state of affairs is nothing in comparison to what follows.

Poole, it turns out, is in league with porn auteur Dino Velvet and participates in the planned murder of Welles. When Welles finally hunts Poole down near the end of the film, he discovers a man utterly devoid of humanity. Welles drags Poole to the snuff film's location, where Mary Anne was murdered. The depressing, abandoned, graffiti-covered building makes the offices of Celebrity Films look like Rodeo Drive. Poole reverts to disgusting language and behavior, callously talking about Mary Anne as someone who mattered to no one and whose death is of no importance. When Welles asks, "Why'd you watch?" Poole offhandedly replies, "I felt like it. I never saw anybody done before." When Welles ties Poole up and threatens to shoot him at point-blank range, Poole taunts Welles, saying he lacks the manliness to do it, and then begins to "tongue" the revolver barrel lewdly. Even as he prepares to die, his evil, depraved pornographic imagination rages. He is a total sociopath, feeling nothing for anyone, himself included, and this inhuman quality is fundamentally tied to his pornographic essence—this is a man who relishes giving a blow job to the gun that will kill him. Eventually Welles succumbs to temptation, shooting Poole execution style. Welles's contact with the porn world is turning him into a bad boy of sorts.

If Poole is the first porn "bad boy" we meet, Velvet is the second. Although assigning a clear hierarchy in the porn sweepstakes is difficult, he is a "worse boy." Velvet is represented as a decadent aesthete, a totally perverse "auteur." Max California dubs Velvet "the Jim Jarmusch of s&m," adding, "This guy I know, he thinks it's art." The reference to Jarmusch and art functions to alert the audience that just as some poor souls deceive themselves into believing that snuff films are fake, some deceive themselves into thinking that porn is just another form of art. Velvet himself seems to suffer from this delusion. When Welles poses as a patron interested in commissioning a film (further connotations of art), he tells Velvet that he is a big admirer of his work. Velvet, deluded as he is, asks which titles Welles likes best. The conversation mimics an auteurist analysis of Velvet's style and preoccupations.

The film that Welles commissions is shot in a New York warehouse. And as an independent, auteur filmmaker working in such a setting, Velvet conjures up the image of Andy Warhol and his "factory" where he shot films that became notoriously connected with the alternative sexual lifestyles of his "superstars." But if in the popular imagination Warhol seemed to the public like a perverse, mysterious figure inhabiting a sexual demimonde, by comparison with Velvet he appears to be a poster boy for healthy, normal living. At this "factory," Welles meets Machine (Christopher Bauer), the leather-masked star of Velvet's auteur creations. The scene is about to become crowded with several candidates for the title "worst boy," but let us grant Machine that dubious distinction for the moment. When Welles greets Machine on the empty set, he remarks, "I really like your work." Schumacher cannot get enough of what is for him the preposterous notion that the porn world could in any way resemble either the art world or Hollywood; it is a crazy, sick inversion of real "work," such as *8MM*, much as Velvet is a crazy, sick inversion of a real auteur such as Schumacher. Anyone stupid enough to believe that these films are "work" or that these people are artists is about to get a rude awakening from Schumacher.

At this point in the film, the other candidate for "worst boy" makes an appearance of sorts. But because he is dead, somebody else has to be his stand-in. Anthony Longdale (Anthony Heald), the lawyer for the late Mr. Christian, appears on the set of the film and reveals that he is in on everything. Mr. Christian wanted to secretly watch a snuff film being made, and he is the shadowy figure that was watching Mary Anne die. When Welles asks, "Why?" Longdale replies, "Because he could. He did it because he could. What other reason were you looking for?" Here Schumacher equates the evil of porn with pure abuse of power. Because everyone in this film who is remotely associated with porn is bad, we are not surprised that Longdale, the immoral lawyer who arranged all this, knows no bounds of evil himself and has now joined forces with Velvet and Machine to kill Welles.

What could be more depraved, Schumacher would have us wonder, than arranging the death of a teenage girl so that one can watch it being filmed? This, although there is not one documented instance of snuff pictures ever having been made, all the well-known "instances" in the history of porn having been frauds (Williams 1989). If in fact porn filmmakers shot films where they actually murdered teenage girls while clients watched the action, it would be as depraved as Schumacher makes out, but it is only within the twisted logic of *8MM* that this depravity exists, indeed, exists so matter-of-factly. If in the hysterical point of view the filmmaker adopts, arranging for snuff films is depraved, only accepting the commission to make such a film could be more reprehensible. Clearly, the film vacillates on its three candidates for "worst": Christian, the pillar of the community who commissions the evil; Velvet, the decadent "artist" who makes the film; or Machine, the monstrous actor who commits the actual murder in the film (these names are not subtle).

Max California is caught and also brought to the set. Welles, a handcuffed hostage, manages to upset Velvet by suggesting that Longdale has cheated him out of much of the money that Christian paid for the snuff film. Velvet shoots Longdale with a crossbow. Longdale, however, shoots Velvet, who falls to the ground saying, "Something's wrong. I'm supposed to have something more cinematic. Kill them, Machine. Kill them all." Velvet dies in his pathetic guise as a director, bemoaning that his death is not more "cinematic" while "directing" Machine. Machine slashes Max's throat, but both Machine and Poole escape from Welles, who has broken free and grabbed a gun.

After dispensing with Poole, as described earlier, Welles hunts down Machine, whose real name is George Anthony Higgins. Machine, wearing his mask, attacks and a brutal fight ensues. He tells Welles that the look on the face of his victims at the moment the knife goes in is the best part for him. Welles finally holds him at gunpoint and orders, "Take off the mask." As Machine identifies himself, we see a quite ordinary face with glasses. Reacting to Welles's deep need to understand, Machine says, "What'd you expect, a monster? My name's George. I don't have the answers. I wasn't beaten, molested, raped. I'm only what I am and that's all there is to it. . . . There's no mystery to the things I do. I do them because I like them, because I want to."

Here Machine echoes both Longdale's account of Mr. Christian's motivation and Poole's account of his own motivation; they all simply do it because they can, because they want to. Schumacher thus posits an unknowable, enigmatic evil in the heart of male pornography's bad boys. The fact that Machine and apparently the others were not beaten, molested, or raped may seem like a departure from clichés about porn but, in fact, it is just another variation. Rather than asserting some knowable social ill to be the cause of porn, this film posits some unknowable, "essential" evil within some men even if they have, like Christian, a loving, kind wife or, like George, a loving, devout mother. Indeed, in this version, porn is so evil that Welles's mounting need to know and learn who these people really are and why they do what they do is totally frustrated. The true answer he seeks to the mystery is simply that some men are so depraved that they do what they do. Any other answer would have been more bearable, made some sense, or have had an element of redemption to it. But Machine turns out to be just another guy. Longdale, Poole, Velvet, and Machine are all just essentially bad, and these bad boys come to characterize the porn world to which they are attracted and to which they belong.

Before offering explanations for this portrayal of the bad boys of porn in *8MM*, I want to relate it to the seemingly quite different bad boys of *The People vs. Larry Flynt* and *Boogie Nights*. The historical title character of Forman's film is quite literally a bad boy in the opening scene where we see him as a "white trash" boy selling moonshine. From this inauspicious beginning, it is a quick jump to a grown-up Flynt running a strip club and stumbling across the idea for *Hustler* magazine. Forman's Flynt (Woody Harrelson) is a bad boy in the sense that he is a crazy, out-of-control, belligerent, and obstinate man; he is not depraved as much as he is disturbed. Yet, throughout the film, Alan Isaacman (Edward Norton), Flynt's lawyer, stresses the distance between himself and Flynt; he protects Flynt's First Amendment rights, while distancing himself from everything Flynt says and does. Rather than making a case for the value of Flynt's work, both Isaacman and the film itself make a case solely for Flynt's right to do it. It is better, in other words, to live in a society with bad boys such as Flynt on the loose than to live in one in which such bad boys are silenced. What the bad boys have to say is beside the point.

Flynt's bad boy antics include constant courtroom disruptions such as showing up wearing a U.S. flag as a diaper and wearing a T-shirt with obscenities directed at the court. Early in the film, Flynt lets his appetites run unbridled (he has sex with all the dancers at his club), and he pushes the envelope of bad taste by doing such things as publishing nude photos of Jacqueline Onassis captured by voyeuristic photographers. After his paralysis, his bad boy status shifts to the legal and political arena where he relishes causing disruption and threatening to expose politicians' private lives. But he is also associated with drugs and casual morality throughout the film. He marries but is not monogamous, and his wife, Althea Leasure (Courtney Love), becomes a lifelong drug addict, eventually dying from AIDS. Flynt is a troublemaker in this film, and although certainly somewhat sleazy, he is never seen as fundamentally evil like those porn makers and users in *8MM*.

Boogie Nights is somewhat more complicated. For much of the film, it seems to represent porn filmmaker Jack Horner (Burt Reynolds) in a positive manner, as a good boy. The film begins in 1977 and Horner is represented as the type of hard-core auteur described by Jon Lewis as posing a true alternative and box-office threat to Hollywood in the early 1970s. Horner wants to make films with stories that are more than just sex scenes strung together. He is interested in photography, lighting, and editing, and he enjoys reading good reviews of his films. Far from being sleazy, perverse, or criminal, he is an attractive, caring figure. His cast and crew are like an extended, alternative family, and he is the father figure. The cast and crew hang out at his house where they eat, drink, and party; some of them even live there. Indeed, the entire porn scene seems devoid of bad boys or even bad girls for that matter. Everyone seems part of an open sexual culture; they are not evil, perverse, or even immoral—they simply lack sexual inhibition and enjoy an open sexual lifestyle. There are a few hints of trouble in paradise, such as when Horner's producer, Colonel James (Robert Ridgely) brings a young woman with him to a party and reacts callously when she overdoses. Although James appears to be a somewhat sleazy middle-aged man with a weakness for younger women, he is far from bad.

But all this changes as the film progresses. James gets arrested for having sex with underage children, a charge that leads to his conviction. Because he has been bankrolling Horner's productions and has been a part of his social life as well, suddenly the seemingly innocent world of auteur porn is tied to what our culture commonly considers the most heinous form of sexual perversion—child abuse. Soon thereafter, Horner himself is revealed as something of a bad boy. He coldly dismisses his main star, Dirk Diggler (Mark Wahlberg), from his family after Diggler gets jealous about the manner in which Horner has attached himself to a new, younger potential star. But business concerns, after all, rule Horner's family attachments. Similarly, he swears his allegiance to shooting porn on film for aesthetic purposes, but market pressures and changing industry standards force him to make video porn against his wishes (and with considerably lower-quality results in terms of the aesthetic aspect of the product). The first time we see Horner shooting video porn, it is in a car with Roller Girl (Heather Graham), one of his stars and part of his family. They pick up a guy on the street and engage in what is known in the trade as a pro/am video, a professional star teamed with a "real" person. But everything goes wrong. The young man recognizes Roller Girl from high school and he treats her crudely when they begin to have sex. She wants to call everything off and Horner quickly does. The young man is now angry and frustrated and he insults Roller Girl; and, as he exits the car, he insults Horner. Horner flies into a rage, lunges out of the car, and brutally beats the young man until he is restrained, at which point Roller Girl takes over, viciously kicking the prostrate man. Horner atavistically regresses with the deteriorating impact of video on the once-admirable porn film industry.

At the end of the film Horner redeems himself somewhat, but clearly no one can go back to the good old days: James is in prison, Diggler is a desperately broken man trying to reclaim a past glory, and Horner has revealed himself as a man who contains a seething rage beneath the surface. However, the film does maintain sympathy for its characters, even as they are revealed to be, in varying degrees, bad boys. Even the shot of James sitting beaten in prison, presumably because he is a known child abuser, is emotionally complex. Unlike Schumacher, who relishes presenting it as inhuman in *8MM*, Anderson represents perversion as all too human. Although to varying degrees these are all bad boys, Anderson does not hate or even fear them but, rather, feels something for them and the pornographic world of which they are a part.

Near the finale of *8MM*, Welles remarks to Max California, "These people we're dealing with, they're extremely disturbed." Although that may be the most redundant line in film history, all these bad boys of porn are in one way or another disturbed. How then do we explain these pervasive if widely varying depictions of the bad boys of porn? The answers lie in a complex nexus of issues including the relationship between Hollywood and the porn industry, technology, First Amendment rights, and dominant cultural fears about pornography. Comparing Dino Velvet to Jack Horner, the two porn auteurs represented in these films, is instructive. Schumacher can imagine the notion of porn authorship only as pure mockery and perverse decadence; in short, as the antithesis of true filmmaking auteurship such as his own. Velvet is the evil personification of the sleazy industry from which Hollywood has distanced itself and against which it has defined itself.

Anderson, on the other hand, begins his film in the late 1970s during the golden age of porn, an era for which, as he has openly acknowledged, he has great affection. He even casts porn stars Veronica Hart and Nina Hartley in his film. Jack Horner represents porn's auteur challenges to Hollywood's auteurs. By reverting to this period, Anderson is able to imagine porn within the context of Lewis's analysis of the early relationship between the two industries. Indeed, for Anderson, rather than Hollywood being the enemy of porn, video is the enemy. Anderson's dramatic (and historically distorted) characterization of the manner in which video and its attendant amateur forms ruined the aesthetics of 35mm, professional, theatrical porn is directly related to his notion of the bad boys of porn: the integrity of porn auteurs was destroyed by this easy, cheap form of production, and it is the producer who crassly announces the inevitability of video porn to Horner (symbolically on New Year's Eve minutes before ringing in 1980) who is in many ways the first bad boy in this film. Video drags Jack Horner down into the sordid street fight in which he engages. In an odd sense, Schumacher's vision of porn is not all that far from Anderson's: both posit a true auteur vision in relationship to a despicable enemy. The only difference is where they situate the good and where they draw the line between it and the bad. Some of the elements of *Boogie Nights* are as simplistic as those of *8MM*. Anderson, for example, can see video porn only as the ruin of the golden age of theatrical porn but in reality video porn brought its own auteurs such as John Stagliano and Ed Powers, and they in turn developed a "gonzo" porn aesthetics far removed from the manner in which the golden age auteurs modeled their aesthetics on the feature narrative film (Lehman 1999).

8MM and *Boogie Nights,* and to a lesser extent *The People vs. Larry Flynt,* point to yet another aspect of both the cultural context for fear of porn and the related manner in which Hollywood represents porn: technology. The history of pornography as we conceive it is tied to technology and its mass dissemination. When sexually explicit material was the province of the elite, upper classes it was thought of quite differently than when cheap printing and photography made it readily available to the masses and lower classes. The history of pornography is inextricably intertwined with the history of technology, including photography, film, video, and the Internet. *Strange Days* (1995) is an extreme illustration of the fearful manner in which this connection is commonly envisioned as making porn either more dangerously "realistic" and powerful or more dangerously readily available. In that film, virtual reality porn that the user can barely distinguish from lived experience includes snuff films.

Whereas *Strange Days* deals with a futuristic form of technological porn not yet available, both *8MM* and *Boogie Nights* strongly emphasize the relationship between pornography and outmoded forms of technology. In both of these films there is a displacement. *8MM* displaces the current fear of Internet porn so rampant in our society onto quaintly outdated 8mm film. I suspect that many young people seeing *8MM* have never actually seen either an 8mm camera or projector, let alone watched an 8mm film being projected; many may not even know to what the title refers. Similarly, many young people watching *Boogie Nights* have never seen a theatrical porn film, nor do they even know about the exhibition history of such films. For them, porn is synonymous with video and soon even that will be outmoded as a new generation associates it primarily with the Internet. On the surface, Schumacher and Anderson approach these technologies in nearly opposite ways: Anderson with nostalgia and Schumacher with repugnance. But each of them associates his bad boys with a porn/technology connection; the only difference is that Anderson displaces all his hatred onto video whereas Schumacher is more democratic in the manner in which he lumps everything together as part of one sewer.

The People vs. Larry Flynt fits in here as well. Although as we have seen Flynt is a bad boy from day one, he does not really become a *bad boy* until he expands into publishing. When he runs his *Hustler* strip club, he is not perceived as a special threat. Only when he turns to publishing and distributing his magazine to stores (it was originally conceived as a private newsletter) does he become really bad. The magazines are sold openly everywhere and threaten the entire community. This brings us to the First Amendment aspect of *The People vs. Larry Flynt*. As with the Schumacher/Anderson comparison, an opposition is apparent between Forman and Anderson. Whereas Anderson acknowledged to interviewers his love of golden age porn, Forman repeatedly mentioned that he had never looked at an issue of *Hustler* prior to making the film and that he had no interest in pornography. His sole interest was in the rights of pornographers to ply their presumably despicable trade in a free society. Here again, Forman plugs into a dominant cultural discourse about pornography: pornographers are bad but we must tolerate them for a larger good. Whereas Schumacher borders on hysteria about porn, Forman is more worried about what we lose if we rid society of these bad boys; whereas Schumacher invites us to revel in the vigilante justice that Welles employs in ridding society of the bad boys, Forman cautions that we must be careful not to violate their rights to be bad.

From whatever angle it sees them, Hollywood is stuck depicting pornographers as flagrant bad guys and the world of porn as an evil one that at best must be tolerated in the name of free speech and at worst eliminated because it destroys all those who come in contact with it. In all these films, after all, the lives of the pornographers and the lives of those they touch are threatened and destroyed. And all of these films share additional common ground. Forman, director of such "quality" films as *Amadeus* (1984), shares name standing with Schumacher as a recognizable Hollywood auteur. Anderson, in a related manner, gained that status with *Boogie Nights* and cemented it with *Magnolia* (1999), his next film. Indeed, his auteur status is clearly announced there with the Tom Cruise character who, like Dirk Diggler, builds his career and persona around the presumed power of the big dick. *The People vs. Larry Flynt, Boogie Nights,* and *8MM* are cautionary tales about bad boys told by good boys. Could it be otherwise, given the history of Hollywood in relation to porn? If the early 1970s had gone differently, Hollywood might have become the bad boys, rather than the good boys telling stories about the bad boys. Indeed the central irony here is that these and all Hollywood films about porn are almost by definition really about something else (social ills; First Amendment rights; a sign of the times such as the sex, drug, and materialistic excesses of the late 1970s and early 1980s). The reason is simple: Hollywood filmmakers cannot represent porn because if they do, they become indistinguishable from pornographers, which, as we know from Jack Valenti, is undesirable.

As Steven Spielberg reminded everyone with the opening of *Saving Private Ryan* (1998), the Hollywood war film is always trying to represent war more "realistically." But good realism is anathema to "good" representations of sleazy porn. Notice that none of the films I discussed attempt to represent porn in realist detail, not even *Boogie Nights.* If there's ever been a catch-22 this is it: once Hollywood drew a lasting, clear-cut line between its respectable product in opposition to the sleazy porn product in the 1970s, to represent that porn product realistically was to become indistinguishable from it. The good boys would have become the bad boys they so valiantly struggled to rise above.

WORKS CITED

Lehman, Peter. 1997. "Will the Real Larry Flynt Please Stand Up?: *The People vs. Larry Flynt," Jump Cut* 41, 21–26.

———. 1998. "Will the Real Dirk Diggler Please Stand Up?: *Boogie Nights," Jump Cut* 42, 32–38.

———. 1999. "Ed Powers and the Fantasy of Documenting Sex." In James Elias, Veronica Diehl Elias, Vern L. Bullough, Gwen Brewer, Jeffrey J. Douglas, and Will Jarvis, eds. *Porn 101: Eroticism, Pornography, and the First Amendment.* New York: Prometheus, 359–66.

————. 2000. "Will the Real Machine Please Stand Up?: *8MM*," *Jump Cut* 43, 16–20.

Lewis, Jon. 2000. *Hollywood v. Hard Core: How the Struggle Over Censorship Saved the Modern Film Industry*. New York: New York University Press.

Williams, Linda. 1989. *Hardcore: Power, Pleasure, and the 'Frenzy of the Visible.'* Berkeley: University of California Press.

FIGURE 6. Creative control: *The Truman Show* (Peter Weir, Paramount, 1998) "plays on anxieties that consumer utopia has co-opted autonomy, hyperrationalizing and numbing life . . . the corporation and the client are symbiotic but also parasitic and alienated, not to mention vacuous." Stage-managing the co-optation of autonomy is Christof (Ed Harris), who is directing the protagonist's everyday reality in a gargantuan television program of which he does not know that he is the star. (Frame enlargement)

CHAPTER SIX

Toxic Corps:
Rage against the Corporate State

KIRBY FARRELL

Ratio of businesses to military sites attacked by international terrorists between 1995 and 2001: 38:1. (Source: U.S. Dept. of State)
—*Harper*'s Index, December 2001

Almost from the moment of impact, the World Trade Center has come to
stand for all of the September 11 terrorist attacks. Given the Trade Center's
monumental image and the catastrophic death toll there, the logic behind
the substitution seems self-evident. The media's fixation on the horror of
the attack, the fortuitous video footage of the second plane's impact, and the
heroic rescue efforts kept world attention tightly framed. Disaster films such
as *The Towering Inferno* (1974) provided a ready model for the shock and
imply a preexisting undercurrent of concern. To a great extent the media
fixation was itself a response to the mythic status of the Trade Center in
world culture.

One way to get at this fixation is to recall Eric Harris and Dylan Klebold, the teenagers who ran amok in Columbine High School in Littleton,
Colorado, in 1999, killing thirteen people. In a video diary they told of their
dream of leveling their high school, then hijacking a plane and crashing it into
New York City. In their dream of civilization in flames, they echoed the 1993

93

bombing of the World Trade Center and prefigured the September 11, 2001 assault. In yet another version of the attack, on January 5, 2002, a teenage student pilot crashed a stolen Cessna into a bank skyscraper in Tampa, Florida, leaving a suicide note sympathizing with the September 11 terrorists.

For all their differences, these scenarios are grounded in the same buried trope of rage at the corporate state. Like the medieval image of St. George slaying the dragon, the trope finds transcendent meaning in the annihilation of a global enemy—the headquarters or powerhouse of the corporate state. The trope underlies consumer rights advocacy and antiglobalization protests, but it also serves specific groups as different as Al Qaeda terrorists and right-wing militias in the United States. Its relation to historical reality is bewilderingly equivocal. While the large-scale productivity associated with the corporate state has supported human populations at a level not seen since the disintegration of the Roman Empire—only in the last two centuries have Europeans ceased to fear famine—the environmental and social damage recorded in documentaries such as Michael Moore's *Roger and Me* (1989) and Deborah Chasnoff's *Deadly Deception* (1991) is atrocious, and the devastation wrought by fascist incarnations of the corporate state has been horrific.

The trope's lineage looks back to ancient parables such as Samson razing the Philistines' temple and David slaying Goliath. Jews, Christians, and Muslims have organized group identity around stories of resistance to the imperial oppression of Rome or crusaders. Religious psychology has readily demonized the oppressor, as in pitting the legendary St. George against the reptilian devil and infidels. In millennialist fantasies, victory over the empires of Antichrist and Satan is victory over death itself.

For movie audiences the trope has been as much a staple as popcorn. Early films relished spectacular ruin, from Nero's Rome to D. W. Griffith's Wagnerian Babylon, demolished in *Intolerance* (1916). In *Ecology of Fear* Mike Davis (1998) tallies up 138 novels and films that have dramatized the annihilation of Los Angeles, that epitome of Utopia and Sodom. Like ancient empires, Fritz Lang's futuristic city in *Metropolis* (1927) projects superhuman vitality, but it is embodied in the massive dynamo that energizes and eventually destroys the city. Where the ancient empire had a god-king, Metropolis is governed by a paternalistic captain of industry like Henry Ford, more gentleman-bureaucrat than depraved tyrant, and his power is dissociated—and euphemized—in a formidable dynamo. In demystifying Big Brother in *Nineteen Eighty-Four*, Orwell exposed the executive will as a tyrannizing fiction, the product of industrial propaganda. That in turn makes clear the force field of Oedipal ambivalence that conditions the ancient god-king and the bureaucratic machine as well.

What the trope leaves out is the dizzyingly equivocal nature of the corporate state. It is the golden goose of utopian plenty no less than the stran-

gling octopus nineteenth-century reformers despised. Even as it deploys pha-
lanxes of lawyers to protect its executive elite, it emphasizes contractual relationships between free agents. In consumer utopia the customer is always
right, even as in advertising culture the customer is a spreadsheet statistic to
be manipulated from cradle to prepaid grave. The economies of scale that
open the cornucopia also produce alienation and perilous susceptibility—
when Wall Street sneezes, markets everywhere shudder and employee retire-
ment savings vanish in the wind.

Anxiety understandably focuses on the corporate state's drive toward
monopoly. Orwell lambasted this totalizing mentality, but it lurks even in
banal, utopian-sounding MBA jargon such as "Total Quality Management."
Capitalism thrives on expansion and recognizes no natural limit. How much
is enough? The problem is our potential for predatory greed, but also the
mind-boggling scale of operations and the impersonal systems required to
manage them. When centralized government or the global entertainment
industry thoroughly penetrates remote markets, numbers alone cease to tell
the tale and local audiences may fret about a loss of identity and autonomy. In
effect, they fear the kidnapping or enslavement of their souls, rather like the
camera's capture of souls. Hence the movement toward worldwide devolution
at the end of the twentieth century, most shockingly in the breakup of the
Soviet empire.

King Kong (1933) defined the vertiginous scale of modernism by depicting the ancient folk hero as a gargantuan gorilla kidnapped out of nature and
killed by the corporate state's military technology atop the gargantuan Empire
State Building, the ancestral World Trade Center. Like the antiglobalization
movement, *King Kong* dramatizes the same brutality of urbanism and imperialism that was already making the Romans nostalgic about pastoralism in Vir-
gil's day. The film reimagines the trivial citizen as a magnificent beast, but it
also magnifies his feeling of helpless defiance and victimization. "Lord" of the
natural realm, the ape in chains epitomizes infantile innocence, seeking a
mother more than a mate in the beautiful but toylike Fay Wray. The consolation the film offers the sacrificial victim is the fantastic apparatus of global
celebrity and even martyrdom that terrorists grasp for. So strong is the aura of
victimization that audiences easily forget that in swiping at biplanes, King
Kong is also tacitly a warrior rebel.

King Kong debuted in 1933 when global depression had overtaken the
great business trusts and suffocated the promise of infinitely synergistic integration. Although New Deal remedies for the Great Depression emphasized
"firewalls" and regulatory oversight, they also spawned "socialistic" regulatory
mechanisms and massive power projects such as Hoover Dam and the Ten-
nessee Valley Authority that industrialized the last wilderness. Such com-
plexes anticipated the military-industrial state amassed to fight World War II,

whose apogee, horrific and tantalizing, proved to be the ultimate globalizing trope, nuclear energy. The atom split figuratively, too, into a utopian, inexhaustible power source and the demonic atom bomb. Revisited now in *The Atomic Cafe* (1982), Kevin Rafferty's documentary history, the childish arrogance and unreality of the first decades of the nuclear age is both laughable and chilling.

Like the Manhattan Project, war production entrained virtually all of the nation's institutions, from university physics laboratories to factories, and they have never fully decoupled. Policy may call for the "privatization" of government, but the drive toward integration and interpenetration has never let up. As "common markets" and "free trade zones" coalesce around the world, terminology has kept pace, with "multinational" and "meganational" now morphing into "metanational" entities. Where individual businesses once fought to the death to "make a killing" and mere nations savaged one another, a century of world wars has set the stage for the "clash of civilizations" Samuel Huntington foretells—although Huntington warns against the aggrandizement that propels the corporate state: "In the emerging world of ethnic conflict and civilizational clash, Western belief in the universality of Western culture suffers three problems: it is false, it is immoral, and it is dangerous" (1997, 310).

Although the West associates Islam with *jihad*, the humble corporation ("the customer is always right") has usually emulated military organization and the language of war. Conversely, the military has become increasingly corporatized, and its vast industrial base has become a "naturalized" part of the peacetime economy. Like the corporate state, the military is sharply ambivalent. In its peacekeeping missions, as in Bosnia, the military promotes the image of utopian benevolence. Playing on the Marshall Plan's vision for postwar Europe, films such as *The Mouse that Roared* (1959) joked about provoking a military confrontation with the United States that would bring consumer plenty to the Duchy of Grand Fenwick. The wish to be—and be blessed by—this corporate cargo cult colored perceptions of the Vietnam War and the antiterrorist campaign in Afghanistan in 2001. In response to the attack on the World Trade Center, President Bush called for Americans to wage an all-out military campaign, but also to shake off fear and "just go shopping."

Industrialism, military force, and empire have long been associated. The first factories may have been Roman slave workshops that produced standardized pots, lamps, and other goods. Today cartoons use the Roman galley slave to satirize dehumanizing industrial regimentation and imperial coercion. As a symbol, the galley itself combines all the features of the corporate state because it is a machine developed for trade and adapted for warfare, its personnel divided into an executive military elite and a body of robotic slaves. As Gabriel and Savage (1978) demonstrated in *Crisis in Command: Mismanagement in the Army*, under Defense Secretary (and former Ford executive) Robert McNamara, the U.S. Army nearly fell apart in Vietnam when corporatization degraded morale and led to an epidemic of assassinations ("fragging") by alienated soldiers. In 2002 the U.S. Marines sent out a recruiting flier presenting the soldier's job not as strategic killing in the crisis of war but as a corporate career. The flier invites prospects "to be a leader in today's global economy" and "Give yourself every advantage." Instead of celebrating old-style grit and patriotism, the flier promotes executive status and self-fulfillment through "training that is unmatched in the corporate world. Or anywhere else for that matter." It closes with a venerable advertising gimmick, the free offer: "A FREE Executive Pen is yours for the asking."

The proverbial origin of organized rage against the industrial order is of course the Luddite movement. Beginning in 1811, raiding parties of workmen destroyed textile machinery around England. Repression of the movement anticipated today's "war on terrorism" by construing it in military terms. The first personal injuries, for example, occurred when soldiers gunned down a party of Luddites in 1812, provoking the murder of a factory owner. Both sides conceived workmen in economic and cultural distress as an army led by a real or imaginary Ned Ludd—"General" or "King" Ludd. The governing classes crippled the movement through a campaign of hangings and transportation, although sporadic protests continued until 1816 and apparently subsided as living conditions improved.

In the course of the nineteenth century the industrial order engulfed traditional economies. Some early New England mills were paternalistic communities with utopian ambitions, attempting to supply all the needs of a captive workforce. Such family-scale enterprises were increasingly subsumed into larger factory systems and "trusts" whose unprecedented size, remote ownership, and political leverage defied accountability. In the twentieth century Henry Ford ran a paternalistic empire, but its scale led to a company police force, spies, and, during the Great Depression, Ford's open sympathy with Nazi labor policy.

Controlling labor through company housing and stores, using the military and the courts for enforcement, and focused on cheap labor and expansion, corporate power resembled colonial regimes. For all their differences, anticolonial uprisings in India, China, and the Philippines, and the wave of anarchist assassinations in the industrial world were attacks on the corporate state. Like the labor violence that Howard Zinn (1980) details in *The People's History of the United States*, they shared a common ground in the underlying trope of corporate oppression. Whether it was the British army using the Maxim gun to slaughter Africans, the U.S. Cavalry massacring Sioux civilians at Wounded Knee, as is shown in *Dances with Wolves* (1990), or soldiers murdering striking miners in Colorado, the basic characteristics of the trope of resistance appear in the victors' impersonal, disproportionate force and aggrandizement.

Film treatments of labor strife invariably rely on heroic models. John Sayles's sympathetic *Matewan* (1987), for example, frames a showdown with Pinkerton mercenaries in a lightly fictionalized coal-miners' strike as a triumph for the incorruptible local lawman, with echoes of Fred Zinnemann's *High Noon* (1952). In Mario Monicelli's *The Organizer* (1963), Martin Ritt's *Norma Rae* (1979), and Ken Loach's *Bread and Roses* (2001), labor organizers are sublimated warrior heroes. But the movies recognize that the core struggle is over morale. The problem is not just management's extraordinary command of incentives and intimidation, but the peculiar nature of corporate will. Corporations claim to be supremely rational systems, a faceless natural force, yet they also strive to project an intensely personal image as "Ma Bell" or "Colonel Sanders," or a tutelary spirit with the magical powers of angels (as in General Electric's slogan, "We bring good things to life"). This is the cognitive split that makes ideas about God or Satan powerful yet uncanny.

When angry employees personalize corporate will to deal with conflicts, the results are liable to be misdirected, deranged, or criminal. In the mid-nineteenth century Irish coal miners in Pennsylvania organized the secret Molly Maguires to intimidate oppressors—other miners as well as overseers. The group's brutality was explosively personal, yet it functioned strategically to protect the members' self-esteem and in turn the miners' morale. In this way the Molly Maguires' retaliation foreshadowed the rage of disaffected employees in the 1990s, many of them postal workers whose rampages came to be called "going postal."

Like soldiers facing death in combat, fired employees facing social death have sometimes gone berserk in the workplace, often with military-style weapons, and killed fellow workers as well as bosses. As in the Columbine High School carnage, workplace rampages usually involve some rational planning and cold rage. As in the Columbine killers' hijack plan, such rage tends to be self-intoxicating and drives toward spectacular violence that culminates in suicide (see Farrell 2000). Facing death, soldiers may run amok because they are trapped—enslaved—between the enemy and their own commanders and will be killed whether they advance or flee. Flinging aside armor and inhibition, they plunge into total risk, relying on the magic of superhuman luck and instinct (see Shay 1994, 77–97). Such a frenzy mimics the corporation in being at once machinelike and hyperpersonal, but it also confronts the corporation's euphemistic military order. As the corporation presents a larger-than-life image and subsumes individuals, so the killer pumps himself up for an apocalyptic reckoning that subsumes lives through murder and suicide.

In scheming to crash an airliner into New York, the Columbine High School killers looked to Hollywood to substantiate their grandiosity. "Directors will be fighting over this story," Dylan Klebold bragged in his video diary. The teenagers behaved as if their "story" was more important—more real—than real life. Their logic is the logic of the movies, advertising, and corporate image making. In his e-mail profile for his America Online account, for example, Harris allegedly whooped with exterminatory bravado, "Kill 'em AALL!!!!" (*Newsweek* [May 3, 1999], 27). The behavior is radically equivocal. His anger may be driven by a grievance against powerful "others." But it also substantiates his "immortal" story of global celebrity and mastery. As in other forms of hysteria, as the effort to sustain the fantasy becomes more extreme, the fury becomes increasingly adrenalized and physiologically compelling while the content becomes more abstract and unrealistic—more violently and glibly applied to its real-world target.

Dramatized onscreen in a movie theater, the global scale of the corporate state supports the globalized ideation and emotional flooding that give immortalizing narratives their conviction. To fuel that conviction, industrial entertainment promotes fantasies of warrior heroism, and in video games and movies such as *The Matrix* (1999) and the *Terminator* series (1984–2003), sympathetic underdogs battle against versions of the corporate state and commodified assembly-line enemies. Playing the aggrieved, solitary warrior, armed to the teeth, storming through an office building or an industrial plant to avenge an intolerable injury, the rampage killer plays a desperate Rambo. But then, the filmmakers scripted Rambo to engage the concerns of their audience, which makes the tragic causality a psychocultural feedback loop. Ordinary manufacturers may use similar fantasy materials, pumping up their product, as in a magazine ad captioned, "When the road bites back," which depicts a sleek Pontiac dashing through a landscape of giant circular saw blades with menacing teeth.

In its absurd extravagance the magazine ad is coolly competing against—and imitating—the armies of media images that inflate violence to arouse fantasies of warrior immortality. And just as industrial entertainment bids for attention with ever-more spectacular mayhem, so, as the *New York Times* database makes clear, many rampage killings have a strong copycat element, and some killers explicitly set out to wreak record-breaking havoc (Fessenden [April 8, 2000]). As products of a competitive culture—and workplace—rampage killers almost inescapably strive to outproduce rivals in

UNIVERSITY H.S. LIBRARY

a psychic economy where self-esteem is dangerously scarce and its loss equivalent to social death. Therefore the struggle for self-esteem is a matter of survival.

The range of movies that embody these dynamics is surprising. In *Kalifornia* (1993) an ex-con quits a dead-end job and takes out his rage on the road. He hitches along with two voyeuristic yuppies who are researching the sites of famous mass murders, and the filmmaker's ambition to discover a memorable spectacle in a numbed world becomes the motive energy in the story for the inevitable rampage. In Tony Scott's *True Romance* (1993) another working-class nobody triumphantly survives the berserk shoot-out that climaxes a drug deal, while a friend who has been aggressively seeking fame and fortune as a television actor dies.

Subtle variations on the rampage theme abound. In James Cameron's *Titanic* (1997), Jack Dawson wins a ticket to sail on the "unsinkable"—immortal—leviathan toward the entrepreneurial utopia of Gilded Age America. The film's Titanic is the consumer paradise of lore, but as the rebellious lovers seek hiding places, they discover a fiery workplace in the underworld below decks. The ship brilliantly evokes the corporate state and globalization, promising—or threatening—to triumph over time, space, and local differences. Its officers function as servants to a remote elite. But when Jack Dawson defies his despised rival, falling in love with the rival's fiancée, the ship's officers become a Praetorian guard and imprison the rebel—potentially fatally. In a complex twist, the film displaces the lovers' rage onto the iceberg, which could be said to run amok as the rival lovers do in the course of the sinking.

Titanic conjures up the juggernaut's potential for apocalyptic horror in allusions such as the familiar millennial formula a priest utters, "The first heaven and the first earth have passed away." The quasi-religious theme justifies Jack's grotesque death and gives lost love immortalizing significance. In effect, his beloved, the now elderly Rose, embraces this mystical renunciation of earthly values on the last day of her life when she produces an invaluable jewel the commercial salvagers have been seeking and throws it into the ocean. Like her first meeting with Jack, when she perches on the stern of the ship in despair, her final dream of glorious social and erotic fulfillment with Jack has suicidal coloration. Her dreaming death implies that an idealizing imagination of life matters more than life itself.

Yet all is not lost. Although *Titanic* violently repudiates a romantic consumer utopia, Rose and Jack turn out to have conceived a daughter, and at the end of her life Rose has been living with her in the utopia of a middle American, Midwestern suburb. In making Rose finally throw her cherished gem into the ocean, the film scorns the salvagers' acquisitiveness while discreetly leaving offstage the equally scorned suburban utopia it serves.

Nearly as euphemistic is *Schindler's List* (1993). Steven Spielberg's Nazis caricature the toxic characteristics of the corporate state, but the film presents Schindler as a remarkable, benign boss who rescues "his" workers from corporate death. The German war machine mass-produces land, cheap labor, and abundant loot, using terror as a management tool to wrest maximum productivity out of conquered people to feed German appetites. The film's Nazi officers behave like corporate executives or Gilded Age robber barons on the *Titanic*. In personal encounter, they bargain ruthlessly, commodifying all life. By mass producing death on the battlefield and in extermination camps, the Nazis strive to master death and buy a conviction of "pure" immortality. The death camps parody industrial processes at every step, manufacturing an illusion of superhuman control and purpose. Yet the Nazis' survival greed drives toward the soulless robotic necrophilia that is nightmarishly epitomized in the futuristic *Terminator* films.

As the affable impresario Schindler discovers, the monstrous futility of the Nazis' symbolic economy makes individual officers desperate for goods, pleasure, and at least a facsimile of companionship. Hence Schindler is able to develop a business plan that uses Hollywood theatricality and play to ransom some workers from the death factory. In the process Schindler becomes a redemptive "good" boss, able to reconcile movie audiences to the harsh realities of real-world managerial practices such as downsizing, exporting jobs, and union busting, which have degraded and disempowered labor outside the movie theater.

Schindler's List plays out a fantasy solution to the sort of conflicts memorably recorded in Michael Moore's struggle to confront General Motors executive Roger Smith in *Roger and Me*. Faced with slavery or death, his workers learn to love the boss. This is a love affair given a romantic treatment in Garry Marshall's *Pretty Woman* (1990), in which a mildly rebellious hooker (Julia Roberts) joins the corporate elite through marriage to her boss (Richard Gere), the fantasy knight who rescues her from social death at the film's close. Oliver Stone's *Wall Street* (1987) tries to disenchant the fantasy when a young protégé learns to love and then break with a boss (Michael Douglas) who promises to rescue him from nonentity but turns out to be just another cold, grasping Wall Street Ubermensch. Hidden in plain sight in all of these films is the cultural assumption that money is life, and infinite money is immortality achievable by sacrificing others.

The spell cast by these titans depends on mystification as well as persuasion. Like Schindler, tycoons such as J. P. Morgan have operated with the suave authority of a stage magician. The power of illusion is most striking when secret information makes a fortune for an insider such as Enron's former chief executive officer Kenneth Lay or Michael Milken, whose junk bond prestidigitation brought down his firm and sent him to prison. The theatrical analogy is more than ornamental. The star executive seems to give a corporation a mind and will that do not actually exist.

Historically corporations are enabling fictions that allow for wide sharing of risk, responsibility, and resources. At the same time they also dilute or diffuse agency and, in turn, responsibility. In some measure, that is, corporations are inherently mystifications. At the heart of most corporate violence—on and offscreen—is a struggle over accountability. The conflict is rooted in the difficulty of adapting law to business. As Russell Mokhiber (1988) succinctly puts it, "How can the corporation 'know' without a mind?" More specifically:

> *Mens rea* is a legal term used to identify the mental element in crime. If a harmful act is an accident, it is not a crime. The harmful act must be intended, the actor must possess the requisite *mens rea* for the act to be a crime. There is no crime without a mind at fault. Or, as Justice Holmes once said, "even a dog distinguishes between being stumbled over and being kicked." (23)

Structurally, corporations may elude legal accountability because command is distributed throughout an amorphous system that entangles bureaucracy, computer software, subsidiaries, regulators, and so on. When operations expand offshore, responsibility may disappear over the horizon. A chief executive may be a Napoleon when all is going well, but invisible when an investigation looms. This is the premise of *Roger and Me*, which documents General Motors' destruction of Flint, Michigan, and the panoply of defenses the corporation and its elite social milieu used to shield Chairman Roger Smith from accountability.

Whistle-blower films such as Mike Nichols's *Silkwood* (1983), James Bridges's *The China Syndrome* (1979), Steven Zaillian's *A Civil Action* (1998), and Steven Soderbergh's *Erin Brockovich* (2000) dramatize the same search. They identify the corporation's masked will with its toxic pollution. Behind a steel and glass façade the films find a mafialike mentality and ruthless greed for power. This, after all, is the subtext of "The Simpsons'" portrayal of the nuclear energy tycoon Mr. Burns, who could be taken as a bitter satire of the viciousness *Silkwood* exposes in Kerr-McGee's nuclear fuel operation.

When military-industrial secrecy hides that toxic pollution, as in General Electric's nuclear weapons production, it reduces community to the psychic wasteland Orwell described in *Nineteen Eighty-Four*. It is symptomatic that since World War Two the CIA ("the company") and Wall Street have been in many ways inseparable. Back and forth through the revolving door at the top have passed—among others—the Dulles brothers, Bill Casey, David Doherty, A. B. Buzzy Krongard, John Deutsch, Clark Clifford, and the elder George Bush. Films as different as *Rambo: First Blood* (1982) and *Three Kings* (1999) insinuate that the U.S. military operates as a mercenary force in the service of corporate masters and spooks.

The other source of managerial magic is the media, personified in Orson Welles's Hearst-like newspaper baron and grand fabulist Charles Foster Kane but in today's world a vast story factory controlled almost entirely by four multinational corporations. General Electric, whose weapons plant in Hanford, Washington spewed nuclear pollution for miles downwind, for example, owns NBC television. Just as the public relations industry mystifies the business world, media increasingly shapes elections and controls access to the corridors of power. As media ownership consolidates, news increasingly becomes an industrial product designed if not packaged by the corporate state.

As detective and courtroom dramas, whistle-blower films share the popular suspicion that a criminal mentality rules the nation from an unseen executive armchair. This is the premise of classic American westerns and detective fiction such as Dashiell Hammett's *Red Harvest* (1937) in which citizens fight to expose a corrupt political "machine" or to "clean up" a corrupt city. In whistle-blower films the protagonists are struggling to break Big Brother's spell and overcome their own compulsion to hero worship. Finally this is a crisis of belief that more often than not opens toward religious themes and the doomsday atmospherics of *Blade Runner* (1982), *RoboCop* (1987), *Strange Days* (1995), and *Johnny Mnemonic* (1995), and beyond them to the apocalyptic, postnuclear wasteland of the *Terminator* sagas.

Islamists justified the World Trade Center atrocity as a battle against Satan, while the U.S. president called for a "crusade" against cosmic "evil." And in one photograph of the smoke surging out of the stricken towers some people imagined they could see the face of Satan (*Discover* 2001). Although to Americans the apparition presumably represented the terrorists, the trade towers also had a sinister, demonic aspect in their overwhelming and entrapping immensity. As in the Tower of Babel story, gigantism arouses anxieties rooted in our terror of helplessness and death. The same anxieties may have been at work in the Islamists' rage at the World Trade Center as an instance of architectural imperialism. Its architect, Minoru Yamasaki, a favorite of the Saudi royal family, merged modernism with Islamic designs. He gave the towers Islamic arches and, in the eyes of some Middle Eastern designers, treated "the entire façade as a giant 'mashrabiya,' the tracery that fills the windows of mosques" (Kerr 2001). One critic theorizes that Osama Bin Laden must have seen how Yamasaki had clothed the World Trade Center, a monument to Western capitalism, in the raiment of Islamic spirituality. . . . [To] someone who wants to purify Islam from commercialism, Yamasaki's implicit Mosque to Commerce would be anathema. To Bin Laden, the World Trade Center was probably not only an international landmark but also a false idol. (Kerr)

In his overview of the Vietnam War, H. Bruce Franklin (2000) links Americans' fear and mistrust of the government to its deceit in managing the war. By implication, the war gave new authority and scope to the trope I have been describing. It took massive protests and media criticism, the Pentagon papers, shaken morale in the military, and economic stress to stop the war machine. We can see the trope at work in the widely reported self-immolation of Buddhist monks and U.S. protesters. But it is also possible to see in those horrific sacrifices a reminder that the trope is not—and cannot be—identical to historical reality.

In the real world, after all, the corporate state is never as monolithic as we imagine. Corporations and social forces clash like dinosaurs or incoherent weather fronts all the time. What is more, ordinary people are as richly implicated in the juggernaut as bees in a hive. In this perspective the corporate state is an enabling fiction that makes thinkable an unprecedented storm of forces tenuously harnessed by the high-strung human animal. In the post-Soviet world the emergence of feudal or ganglike concentrations of power—so-called "mafias"—revealed that communist state power had never been as concentrated as ideology had prescribed. Like Coppola's *Godfather* saga (1972–1990) in the United States, post-Soviet "mafias" remind us that in the end the search for accountability leads to particular people, groups, and histories.

Corporate structures dilute responsibility and mask some of our ugliest motives while increasing our capacity to inflict harm. One tentative source of reassurance that imaginations can learn to manage this relentless transformation might be the Renaissance, which Lynn White Jr. calls "the most psychically disturbed era in European history" (1974, 26). He holds that the era's abnormal anxiety "rose from an ever increasing velocity of cultural change compounded by a series of fearful disasters," and that "this spiritual trauma was healed by the emergence, in the minds of ordinary people, of an absolutely novel and relaxed attitude toward change" (26). Among other things, that attitude included a new acceptance of the theatricality and fluidity of identity and a vastly expanded horizon or scale in human operations. That said, we cannot deny that those changes in scale have if anything increased, pushing living systems toward the increasingly precarious equilibrium best symbolized by the Union of Concerned Scientists' "doomsday clock."

Despite the information revolution and a wealth of databases, we are hard pressed to see ourselves clearly in the whirlwind of recent history. To cope with our creaturely dread, as Ernest Becker (1975) would say, we still feed a predatory greed for life by sacrificing others, masking our rage for survival. And as Elias Canetti (1962) understood, the crowd magnifies not only the puny individual will, but also the capacity for violent self-deception. The Nazis terrify us in part because even with their sometimes laughably crude techniques they were able to galvanize gargantuan crowds, epidemic lies, and monstrous aggression.

Organizational history is a story of increasing powers of negotiation, hypocrisy, and euphemism: of ingenious compromises with truth that can hold conflicting, even vicious, motives in equilibrium; and no less adroit lies that book human suffering in the profits column of a spreadsheet and call it business (for a morally robust critique of euphemism as a weapon, see Stein 1998, chap. 6). In the popular mind the corporate state is a theater of illusion somewhere between an escapist theme park and a Nuremberg rally. The image makers counter by frankly celebrating the "cool" illusion: Goliath now winks at David and joins him at the video control stick slaying giants; by studying youth culture, marketers can package and sell the latest style of authentic hip-hop rage while it's still hot; the military-industrial state calls its drive to militarize space and project force anywhere in the world a "strategic defense initiative" against upstart "rogue nations."

Equivocal by nature, industrial entertainment fitfully labors to keep up with corporate usurpation of cultural life. *The Matrix* shrewdly projects the conceptual prison of global image making, although the film itself never ventures beyond rude melodrama. *RoboCop* scorns the corporation that has privatized and co-opted Detroit's governance, for example, yet it makes the silver-haired chief executive a model of grandfatherly innocence and unaware of the "rebellious" junior executive who is supposedly the criminal mastermind behind the city's torment. The film celebrates its bionic hero, but without facing up to the desolate enslavement of RoboCop's infantile, programmed "mind." In his moment of triumph, the hyperspecialized, dehumanized Robo-Cop, once a family man named Murphy, is now a caricature of the villainous corporation he has defeated, the more disturbing because he is unquestionably both victim and hero.

If you watch *RoboCop* critically—if your critical curiosity has you joining me in this reading—you are free to ask the haunted question the film makes possible but never confronts: What kind of animals are we? If we escaped from our controllers, who or what would we want to be? To get Socratic about it, what self should we be trying to know?

In Peter Weir's *The Truman Show* (1998) an Everyman (Jim Carrey) discovers that his humdrum life is in fact an elaborately staged "reality TV" show monitored from every angle for an invisible mass audience. The film plays on anxieties that consumer utopia has co-opted autonomy, hyperrationalizing and numbing life so that comforts become an epidemic of—as the sociologists quip—affluenza. In such a psychic economy the corporation and the client are symbiotic but also parasitic and alienated, not to mention vacuous. The film may be dumbed-down Pirandello, but it too raises the haunted question: What kind of animals are we? Projecting fantastic versions of ourselves on a screen, we are tacitly exploring that question, opening imagination to exhilaration and vertigo. Radical historical change presses us to question the emerging corporate state as another form of human identity. In the movies, it would seem, we are working out our consternation at the shockingly ambiguous face we are beginning to recognize in the mirror.

WORKS CITED

Becker, Ernest. 1975. *Escape from Evil.* New York: Free Press.

Canetti, Elias. 1962. *Crowds and Power.* New York: Continuum.

Davis, Mike. 1998. *Ecology of Fear: Los Angeles and the Imagination of Disaster.* New York: Metropolitan Books.

Farrell, Kirby. 2000. "The Berserk Style in American Culture," *Cultural Critique* 46 (Fall), 179–209.

Fessenden, Ford. 2000. "They Threaten, Seethe, and Unhinge, Then Kill in Quantity: Rampage Killers/A Statistical Report," *New York Times* (April 8).

Franklin, H. Bruce. 2000. *Vietnam and Other American Fantasies.* Amherst: University of Massachusetts Press.

Gabriel, Richard A. and Paul L. Savage. 1978. *Crisis in Command: Mismanagement in the Army.* New York: Hill and Wang.

Huntington, Samuel. 1997. *The Clash of Civilizations and the Rethinking of World Order.* New York: Touchstone.

Kerr, Laurie. 2001. "The Mosque to Commerce," *Slate* (December 31). www.slate.com.

Mokhiber, Russell. 1988. *Corporate Crime and Violence.* San Francisco: Sierra Club Books.

Shay, Jonathan. 1994. *Achilles in Vietnam.* New York: Atheneum.

Stein, Howard F. 1998. *Euphemism, Spin, and the Crisis in Organizational Life.* Westport, CT: Quorum Books.

White, Lynn, Jr. 1974. "Death and the Devil." In Robert Kinsman, ed., *The Darker Vision of the Renaissance.* Berkeley: University of California Press, 25–46.

Zinn, Howard. 1980. *A People's History of the United States.* New York: Harper & Row.

FIGURE 7. Utopian possibilities need to be reclaimed against an "utterly privatized notion of resistance." Enid (Thora Birch, r.) and her friend Rebecca (Scarlett Johansson), come across an older man sitting at a bus stop that has been closed for years in Terry Zwigoff's *Ghost World* (Jersey Shore/United Artists, 2001). Enid tells him the bus route has been cancelled, but he tells her to leave him alone. (Frame enlargement)

CHAPTER SEVEN

The Ghost World *of Neoliberalism:* *Abandoning the Abandoned Generation*

HENRY A. GIROUX

> If you want to maim the future of any society, you simply maim
> the children.
> —Ngugi Wa Thiong'O, *Moving the Centre*

MURDERING THE SOCIAL

Every society creates images and visions of those forces that threaten its identity (Bauman 1998, 73). In the aftermath of September 11, 2001, the most pressing danger facing the United States appears to come from Muslims, Arab Americans, and other alleged "terrorists." But the foremost danger facing the United States predates the terrorist attacks on the Pentagon and the World Trade Center and, in fact, provides a crucial continuity bridging the past and the present. That danger constitutes nothing less than the devaluing of the social and the growing irrelevance of a democratic future that such a devaluing implies. Not only can our thoughts of the future harbor impulses and a horizon of expectations that often challenge and exceed the narrow conceits of a society dominated by market relations and the transformation of the citizen into a consumer, but they also prefigure those social bonds that invoke a responsibility to others, especially young people. Underlying a refusal of the future is a notion of the social world bereft of ethics, social justice, and any viable notion of democratic public culture (Binde 2000).

109

Prior to the events of September 11, democracy was defined largely through the relations and values of the market. Labor was seen increasingly as an obstacle to productivity, and citizenship was being rewritten so as to strip it of any critical substance. Emptied of any social content, the public was reduced to a phantom sphere largely dominated by the vocabulary of the private. Politics for the most part turned inward, as the language of community, public action, and citizen participation were redefined as matters of privatized choice and individualized desire. Such changes can be traced to two major events that have recast both the nature of politics and the relevance of the social.

First, power has become increasingly detached from politics. As power travels beyond national boundaries, it is largely disconnected from any moral obligations and accountability to its employees, the young, the aged, the local community, and the larger social order. In the age of neoliberal globalization, as Manuel Castells (1998) and others have observed, power extends across, around, and over territorial boundaries disrupting the neat correspondence between the sovereignty of the nation-state and the space of the political. Power is now more extraterritorial, increasingly escaping from the reach of political institutions such as the nation-state and extending beyond the reach of the average citizen (see Castells; Beck 2000; and Bauman 1999). As Zygmunt Bauman points out, one consequence of globalization is that politics is more place based whereas power defies the traditional regulations and governance imposed by nation-states:

> Our dependencies are now truly global, our actions however are, as before, local. The powers which shape the conditions under which we confront our problems are beyond the reach of all the agencies invented by modern democracy in the two centuries of its history. As Manuel Castells put it—real power, the extraterritorial global power, flows, but politics, confined now as in the past to the framework of nation-states, stays as before attached to the ground. (2001, 149)

As power distances itself from traditional modes of politics, nation-states have lost much of their capacity to control and regulate powerful corporations, except to become their security service and watchdogs for them and for the wealthy. The state under such circumstances does not disappear as much as it is reconstructed largely as a repressive force for providing a modicum of safety for the rich and middle classes while increasing its focus on disciplining those populations and groups that pose a threat to the dominant social order (see, among the many sources in which this issue is taken up in detail, Aronowitz 2001; Parenti 1999; and Garland 2001).

Under the auspices of neoliberal policies, identities based on stable work disappear as the success of new technologies and productive forces is judged by "the replacement and elimination of labor" (Bauman 1998, 65). In the current neoliberal economy, labor has become a constraint on profits not only because of the emergence of new labor-saving technologies but also because much less labor is needed to produce huge volumes of goods; and even if it is needed, corporations can simply relocate to capitalize on the availability of cheap labor.

Secondly, as globalization saps the ability of either the state or individuals to influence the modalities of power, politics, and ideology, collective action seems improbable and politics turns inward. Individuals assume the burden of their own fate, even though the forces that largely shape their destiny are beyond the scope of individual behavior. Under such circumstances, all problems are defined as self-made, reduced to matters of character and individual initiative or its lack. The result is that personal worries and private troubles are disconnected from public issues and social problems. The political economy of insecurity now becomes endemic to everyday life for millions and is generally understood in relation to a depoliticized notion of citizenship largely defined as the right to consume rather than the enabling quality of individuals to shape the basic economic and political structures of their society. As the vast majority of citizens becomes detached from public forums that nourish social critique, agency not only becomes a mockery of itself, it is replaced by market-based choices in which private satisfactions replace social responsibilities and, as Ulrich Beck suggests, biographic solutions become a substitute for systemic change (1992, 137). In a world marked by deregulated markets, downsizing, and growing unemployment, the uncertainty and insecurity that individuals experience appear to be matched by retreat from, if not indifference to, a politics of collective struggle and social transformation (Bauman 1999).

As the state is hollowed out and public services are either cut or turned over to the forces of privatization, security is decoupled from freedom, and freedom is reduced to a matter of individual resources and choices. Moreover, as many centralized forces are ceded to the market (with the exception of those state forces that provide policing or military functions), the public treasury is emptied and nearly all of the "public infrastructure—roads, water systems, schools, powerplants, bridges, hospitals, broadcast frequencies—that provide the country with a foundation for its common enterprise" fall into disrepair (Lapham 2001, 10). Lacking a critical vocabulary as well as those non-commodified public spaces necessary for young people and adults to defend the institutions that are crucial to a democracy, the American public finds it more and more difficult to acknowledge and understand how the growth of individual freedom, defined largely through the discourse of consumerism, coincides with the growth of collective impotence (Bauman 1999, 2).

As the call to prioritize self-reliance and private considerations in the place of collective struggles came to assume the importance of an unquestionable form of common sense; as the citizen's right to interfere was replaced by the individual's liberty from interference; as all references to the social safety net for the relatively powerless—the poor, the disabled, young people, and the aged—were disparaged; as government came to seem wasteful, capitalism democratic, and history nothing but a summation of market forces (Lapham, 8), so also the growing inequalities between the rich and the poor, persistent racism, violence against women, the collapse of social housing, the breakdown of public health, and the crisis of public education were increasingly erased from the inventory of public concerns. The connection between education and democracy was broken, and the importance of viewing young people as an obligation to the future was downplayed. The welfare of society's most vulnerable citizens—the young and the poor—was no longer a focus of social investment but a matter of social containment.

The terrible events of September 11 opened a new possibility for engaging the relationship among youth, society, and the future. In many ways, the September 11 actions pointed to the importance of providing crucial public services—to save lives, to put out fires, to assist decimated families, and to offer some modicum of protection against further terrorist actions. But the reliance on and celebration of public services and public life itself seemed short-lived as the Bush administration seized upon the insecurities and fears of the populace to expand the policing and military powers of the state through a series of antiterrorist Acts that compromised some of the basic freedoms the Bill of Rights provides. At the same time, Bush and his supporters pushed through political legislation that drained projected public surpluses by offering tax breaks—approximating $1.3 trillion—for the wealthy and major corporations. Tax cuts that mostly benefit the top 1 percent of the population at a time when "the financial wealth of the top 1 percent of households now exceeds the combined wealth of the bottom 95 percent" (Gates 2000, xxxvii) do more than undermine any pretense to democratic values. Such welfare schemes for the rich also blatantly exhibit the ruthlessness of a society that, on the one hand, allows one American, Bill Gates, to amass "more wealth than the combined net worth of the poorest 45 percent of American households" (Henwood 1999, 12) and, on the other, refuses to provide adequate health care to 14 million children. It is difficult to understand how democratic values are deepened and expanded in a society in which, according to the U.S. Bureau of Labor statistics, the typical American now works 350 hours—almost nine full weeks—more per year than the typical European. Under such conditions, parents are not only working longer, but they are also spending 40 percent less time with their children than they did forty years ago (Handy 1998, 17). While it is too early to see how this tension between democratic values and market interests will be played out in the larger society, it is crucial to recognize that young people more than any other group will bear the burden and the consequences of this struggle as it bears down on their everyday lives. Clearly, these are poor conditions under which they must learn to assume the mantle of leadership necessary to shape the future they will inherit.

Youth, indeed, have become a target of disciplinary control, surveillance, and punishment, especially on the streets and in the public schools. Monitored, regulated, and disciplined, youth are increasingly viewed as depraved rather than deprived, troubling rather than troubled. For instance, in the last decade, schools have passed harsh zero-tolerance laws, established dress codes, regulated hair color, imposed drug testing, banned certain forms of music, and now monitor many of the movements and much of the behavior of students (Giroux 2001). Young people are viewed as either a threat to society or too infantile to protect themselves from being corrupted. Adult society refuses to view young people as responsible citizens with a sense of independence and agency—yet they are treated as adults when they commit allegedly irresponsible acts. The contradiction speaks to more than generational conflict or even hypocrisy; it registers an all-out assault on youth that has emerged since the 1980s. Cultural studies theorist Lawrence Grossberg writes in the following terms about the chilling contradictions that mark what he calls the "war" on youth:

> In most states in the United States, at 16 today, you cannot get your ears pierced without the permission of your parents. You cannot get a tattoo, and you cannot buy cigarettes. In fact, people under 16 cannot go to the Mall of America in Minnesota (the largest shopping mall in the country) after 6 P.M. on Friday or Saturday without a parent. But, you can be tried and jailed as an adult, and more and more kids are. And in a growing number of states, you can be put to death as a penalty. Think of that—you can't get your ears pierced, but you can be put to death. (2001, 117)

Social guarantees are now provided for only the most privileged youth, and those less fortunate, such as poor inner-city kids, are offered inspirational tales if not by Hollywood then by conservative luminaries such as William Bennett, about the virtues of self-reliance, competition, picking oneself up by the bootstraps, and reaching deep down into one's character to embolden oneself with the virtues needed to survive in a world increasingly wedded to the ruthless tenets of social Darwinism. When self-reliance doesn't work in a world of endemic uncertainty and universal struggle, a ballooning prison-industrial complex offers a different alternative to the current youth "problem." As their behavior is increasingly criminalized, youth are suspended or expelled from schools and incarcerated in record numbers, even though crimes by youth have been declining sharply in the last decade. It is not surprising that in a society that largely constructs others as failures, youth marginalized by class and color either vanish from the agenda of public concerns or invoke the wrath of an increasingly repressive state that sees them as a threat to the social order. This war against youth, as Grossberg rightly argues, "is a war against youth's ability to embody the very necessity of commitment to a future and to a particular future insofar as it entails certain kinds of political and economic visions of the [democratic] American dream" (133).

GHOST WORLD: YOUTH IN THE AGE OF CYNICISM

The continuity that bridges a pre- and post-September 11 social reality resides in the relationship between a depoliticized public sphere and the current attack on youth. These related crises are best exemplified in various representations of youth that shape the contemporary political landscape of American culture. How a society understands its youth is partly determined by how it represents them. Popular representations, in particular, constitute a cultural politics that shapes, mediates, and legitimates how adult society views youth and what it expects from them. Such representations, produced and distributed through mass media sites such as television, video, music, film, publishing, and theater, function as a form of public pedagogy actively attempting to define youth through the ideological filters of a society that is increasingly hostile to young people. All of these sites make competing claims on youth and their relation to the social order. At worst, they engage in a politics of representation, whether offered up in Hollywood films, television dramas, magazines, or popular advertisements that construct youth in terms that largely serve to demonize, sexualize, or commodify them—to reduce their sense of agency to the consumerist requirements of supply and demand. Most Hollywood images not only resonate with larger public discourses that contribute to a moral panic about youth, but they also help to legitimate policies aimed at both containing and punishing young people, especially those who are marginalized by virtue of class, gender, race, and sexual orientation. At best, such representations define youth in complex ways that not only capture the problems, issues, and values that bear down on them, but also illustrate how varied youth in diverse circumstances attempt to negotiate the contradictions of a larger social order.

The following examines an exemplary independent film, *Ghost World* (2001), as part of a broader attempt to engage critically the question of how popular representations of youth signal a particular crisis—but do so through a discourse of privatization that fails to locate youth and the problems they face within social and political geographies. *Ghost World* is a particularly interesting film because it is sympathetic to the plight of alienated, downwardly mobile teenage girls and goes to great lengths to let the principal characters speak in a way that gives meaning and affect to their sense of despair, their ennui, and their resistance to the adult world. This attempt at "authenticity" has won praise from critics and viewers alike, and makes the film all the more important to analyze as a form of public pedagogy that provides a unique opportunity to take up the troubled dynamic between teenage resistance and the privatization of the social.

Loosely adapted from an underground comic book by Daniel Clowes and directed by Terry Zwigoff, who also directed the 1995 documentary *Crumb*, *Ghost World* presents a portrait of two teenage malcontents, Enid (Thora Birch) and Rebecca (Scarlett Johansson), whose adolescent angst and resentment informs both their resistance to a phony middle-class world and their attempts to adjust to it without losing their self-ascribed marginal status. Best friends since elementary school, the lonely, sardonic Enid and Rebecca, her slightly more conventional companion, negotiate the complex territory between high school graduation and the plunge into adulthood. *Ghost World* also chronicles the story of their increasingly strained friendship.

In the opening scene of the film, which takes place during their high school graduation ceremony, Enid and Rebecca are clearly out of sync with the boorish world of dominant school culture and the deadness of American suburbia it reflects—a world embodied by testosterone-driven surferlike athletic drones, obsequious academic climbers, and pom-pom–waving cheerleaders just waiting to become soccer moms. They snarl through a graduation speech by a classmate in a head brace and wheelchair that begins with the cliché: "High school is like the training wheels for the bicycle that is life." While listening to the speech, Enid whispers, "I liked her so much better when she was an alcoholic and drug addict. She gets in one stupid car crash and suddenly she's Little Miss Perfect." When their classmates throw their caps in the air and cheer, Enid and Rebecca respond accordingly by giving their fellow students a middle finger, and to bring the point home, Enid throws her cap on the ground, stomps on it, and shouts, "What a bunch of retards." Rebecca nods in approval, making clear their shared and active refusal to buy into a world filled with what Enid calls "creeps, losers, and weirdos."

When we meet the adults who touch Enid's life, they seem to give legitimacy to her presumption that most adults are either phonies or losers. Her timid dad (Bob Balaban) fits into the latter category. Living with him in a small apartment in Los Angeles, Enid seems to be in pain every time he approaches. Not only does he call her "pumpkin" and mutter imperceptibly practically every time he opens his mouth, but he is also about to ask his corny girlfriend Maxine (Teri Garr), who tries to befriend Enid by involving her in the exciting world of computer retailing, to move in with them. Needless to say, Enid despises her.

The other adult Enid has to endure is a gushy, purple-clad performance artist/teacher named Roberta (Illeana Douglas), who is a comically drawn mix between a hippie leftover from the 1960s and a recruit from the take-no-prisoners and I-am-always-right-and-righteous strand of feminism. Enid is forced to take Roberta's lame art class during the summer to graduate officially, and she sits in class rolling her eyes every time Roberta speaks. Roberta operates on the pedagogical assumption that the only way to reach her students is to relate to their lives, speak in terms they understand, and help them to "find themselves." The problem is, Roberta confuses her own ideological interests with her students' and rather than listen to them, she simply rewards those students who feed back to her what she wants to hear. From day one in class, this art teacher rubs Enid the wrong way so she passes time by adding to her repertoire of violent comic-book drawings, which she eventually shows Roberta. Roberta soon displays some interest in Enid and even helps her to get an art school scholarship. But her convictions soon dissipate when she receives a lot of flak from the school and community for showing a piece of Enid's work—a representation of a racist ad called "Coon Chicken"—at an art exhibition ironically titled "Neighborhood and Community: Art and Dialogue." As a result of school and community indignation over Enid's artwork, which was, after all, an attempt to foster real dialogue about the community's racist history, Roberta withdraws the art school scholarship and joins the rest of the adult creeps and hypocrites who seem to inhabit Enid's life.

These adults seem to fuel Enid's desire to ridicule and inflict pain on every adult she and Rebecca come across. With high school behind them, Enid and Rebecca hang out in mock 1950s diners and record stores. At first, their friendship is fueled by their mutual disdain for everyone around them. "Like totally losers," Enid scoffs and Rebecca fully agrees. Biting sarcasm is interlaced with Enid's comiclike portraits of the various adults they encounter along the way. Nobody appears to escape their sardonic looks, commentaries, and visual escapades. When not ridiculing people and indulging their unlimited capacity for scorn, Enid and Rebecca embark on their shared dream of renting an apartment together and putting their lives in order. Somewhat bored, they set up a meeting with a hapless schmuck—Seymour (Steve Buscemi)—whom they discovered in the personal ad section of the local newspaper. Seymour was using an ad to solicit a woman he briefly met in an airport. Enid and Rebecca respond to the ad and set up a meeting in a diner, wait for him to show up, then watch him drink milkshakes as he waits for a woman who never appears.

As the summer unfolds, a strain develops between the two girls as Rebecca moves into high gear by getting a job working in a local Starbuckslike emporium, earnestly starts looking for an apartment, and uses her free time to spend money in typical consumerlike fashion on cheap wares for her new place. Nonetheless, Enid resists what appears to be her only option, disinclined to adapt to an adult world she loathes. She is put off by the colorless neighborhood in which Rebecca tries to find an apartment, has no interests in shopping for mall goods to clutter the apartment, and just can't seem to bring herself to look for a job in the corporate world that sickens her. The one job she does get is a short-lived stint at a local multiplex. But unable to prod customers into buying oversized drinks or to suggest that the movies they are watching are worth the effort, she is soon fired. Rebecca disapproves of Enid's inability to move forward, and Enid is confused by Rebecca's easy adaptation to a world they both despised while in high school.

Their relationship is further strained when Enid's life takes an unexpected turn when she meets Seymour, the victim of her personal-ad prank. While hunting for an apartment together, Enid and Rebecca come across him at a garage sale, where he is selling some of his vintage 78 rpm collection of blues records out of milk crates. Rebecca finds the fortysomething Seymour gross and admits to Enid that she has "a total boner" for some wholesome-looking young, blond guy who likes to listen to reggae. But Enid is intrigued by Seymour's sad-sack looks, his commitment to old blues music and various collections of Americana, his intelligence, his isolation, and his utterly alienated life. Before long, Enid begins to see him less as a pathetic, middle-aged geek than as a poster boy for permanent rebellion. Things soon begin to click between them, especially after Seymour gives Enid his 1931 recording of Skip James's "Devil Got My Woman." Enid decides she is going to be a matchmaker for Seymour, but each attempt institutes a series of inevitable disasters. Seymour sees himself as a bad candidate for a relationship with another woman, telling Enid, "I don't want someone who shares my interests. I hate my interests." This makes Seymour all the more odd—a mixture of unapologetic loneliness and refreshing honesty, and hence all the more attractive to Enid, who tells Rebecca, "He's the exact opposite of all the things I hate." Each "date" disaster seems to feed their own relationship as they spend more and more time with each other. Enid tells Seymour, "Only stupid people have healthy relationships." And Seymour, sharing her own sense of alienation and cynicism counters, "That's the spirit." Unfortunately for Enid, Seymour does meet up with the personal ad girl, Dana (Stacy Travis), and the relationship between Seymour and Enid begins to sour. Seymour's new girlfriend represents everything Enid despises. Dana and Seymour go shopping together and she buys him stone-washed jeans in an attempt to transform him into a prototype for an Eddie Bauer ad. She works as a real-estate agent and seems utterly attached to a world far too normal and far too removed from the self-deprecation, misery, and disdain that keeps Enid alert to everything that is phony and empty in middle-class suburban life. Moreover, Seymour seems attracted to his new girlfriend's utterly bourgeois lifestyle, although she sees his music and art collection as so much junk, compromising Enid's view of him as an oddball resister. Enid wages a desperate campaign to win Seymour back and rekindle her friendship with Rebecca, but to no avail. In the end she boards a bus during the middle of the night and leaves both Los Angeles and her adolescence behind her.

Ghost World is an important film about youth, friendship, alienation, and survival. Many commentators named it as one of the top ten films of 2001, if not the best film yet produced about youth. And one critic for *USA Today* actually named it as the best film of the year (Clark 2001). Some critics labeled it as the filmic equivalent of *Catcher in the Rye*. Most celebrated the film for its dead-end irony, its hilarious dialogue, and its honest portrayal of the posturing and superiority befitting youth who drape themselves in the cloak of rebellion. Unlike many other youth films of the past decade—for example *Kids* (1995), *American Beauty* (1999), or *American Pie* (1999)—*Ghost World* refuses to trade in caricatures, stereotypes, or degrading representations of youth. Moreover, *Ghost World* rejects the traditional Hollywood narrative that chronicles teenage rebellion as part of a rite of passage toward a deeper understanding of what it means to join adult society. Instead, the film focuses on the dark side of teenage alienation, exploring the fractures, cracks, and chasms that locate teenagers in a space fraught with resentment, scorn, and critical insight. *Ghost World* gently and movingly attempts to explore in uncondescending terms the pain of broken relationships, the justifiable teenage fear of being trapped in an adult world that offers few rewards and even less fulfillment, and the difficulty of choosing an identity that is critical of such a world yet not so removed as to become marginalized or irrelevant. Moreover, this film rightly appealed to critics who celebrated its refusal to offer a predictable Disney-like solution to the problems teenagers face and its ability to capture, with depth and empathy, the tensions and ambiguities that shape the lives of many teenagers on the margins of a throwaway culture. Underlying almost all of the reviews I have read of this film is an affirmation, if not a romanticizing, of an alleged kind of "authenticity" as the ultimate arbiter of the film's worth. *Ghost World* arguably may be, as many critics suggest, one of the most important youth films of the decade—its importance stemming in part from its attempt to address how marginalized youth attempt to negotiate, if not resist, a political and social landscape that offers them few hopes and even fewer opportunities to see beyond its ideological boundaries.

At the same time, *Ghost World* is notable for its complicity with a dominant discourse that, in spite of its emphasis on youth resistance among teenage girls, too easily functions pedagogically to depoliticize rebellion by displacing the social as a crucial political concept that could provide a sense of what it might mean to struggle individually and collectively for a more just and democratic future. The most important pedagogical issues that hold this film together appear to resonate with a much broader set of discourses and values that increasingly celebrate and romanticize individualized youth rebellion while denying young people "any significant place within the collective geography of life in the United States" (Grossberg 2001, 112–13). Irony, pathos, rebellion, and gritty dialogue may help to capture the spirit of teenage girls who "talk back," but depictions in terms of these elements remain utterly privatized and ineffectual unless they are situated in relation to broader social, economic, and political forces—the crisis of labor, political agency, democracy, and the meaning of the future itself.

While *Ghost World* is certainly not a comforting depiction of youth for the middle class, it also does nothing to link the current war being waged against youth with any of the political, economic, and cultural realities that for the last twenty years smoothed the sailing waters of yuppie greed and spectacle. Nor does it address the poverty of public discourse about youth and the breakdown of civic culture in American life during the same period. Unwilling to do justice to the urgent crisis that youth face in the United States, or to the complex of violence, meanings, and practices that shape children's lives, *Ghost World* ignores the possibility of any pedagogy of resistance that might disrupt and challenge conventional narratives of marginalized youth in ways that exceed its own ideological limits. Enid may live in a world of existential angst, but her anger seems to be so diffuse that it is meaningless. Why does she display so little understanding of an economic order in which the future for young people such as herself seems to offer nothing more than the promise of fast food jobs and low-skilled labor? Why do so few commentators on the film in the national media point out that both Enid and Rebecca seem to define their sense of agency exclusively around consuming, whether it be housewares or bohemian artifacts? As Cynthia Peters points out in a different context:

> Somehow, when young adulthood should be an ample universe of growth and discovery—one that gives kids the chance to learn, contribute, experiment, envision, and carve out a meaningful role in the world—it is instead shrunk into the pinpoint activity of buying and selling. We treat kids contemptuously by herding them into de-skilled, meaningless, low-wage jobs and by taking them seriously only insofar as they might divulge to marketers how they plan on spending their on-average $84 per week. (2001, 2)

Why is it that audiences watching this film are never given a clue that Enid and Rebecca live in a society that bears down particularly hard on the lives of young people? Why do so few critics take note of the fact that Enid and Rebecca's world is a society in which the wealthiest nation on earth allows one third of its children to live in poverty, or of the fact that they inhabit a society that invests more in building prisons for young people than in institutions of higher learning? Consider the statistics: one in six children in the United States—12.1 million—still live in poverty. Nearly 11 million children are without health insurance, 90 percent of whom have working parents. One in eight children never graduates from high school and "children under 18 are the fastest growing and largest portion of the population of homeless in America, with an average age of 9 years old" (Children's Defense Fund; see also Grossberg, 114–15). By contrast, the experience "crisis" for Enid and Rebecca is shown over and over as a personal, individualized affair.

Ghost World hammers home the lesson that in a world of high youth unemployment, poverty, incarceration rates, and a disintegrating urban education system, youth have only themselves to rely on and only themselves to blame if they fail. Against the constant reminders of a society that tells youth it neither particularly needs them nor wants them, youth are offered only right-wing homilies about relying on their own resources and cunning. In the context of this rhetoric of nomadic subjectivity and privatized resistance, the dystopian notion that there are no alternatives to the present order reinforces the message that young people should avoid at all costs the prospect of organizing collectively to address the social, political, and economic basis of individually suffered problems.

Resistance in this film rarely touches on the possibility for recovering the ideals of a democratic social order or a robust form of collective intervention. So *Ghost World* is defined less by what it says than by what it omits. This absence is precisely what is necessary for engaging *Ghost World* within a broader set of historical and political contexts. And though *Ghost World* lampoons the middle-class mores of a market-driven society, it ends up replicating rather than challenging the privatized utopias and excessively individualistic values it sets out to critique—a position that both undercuts its progressive implications and begs for more analysis. Resistance as presented in *Ghost World* points approvingly to how insightful and nuanced young people can be about the phoniness and emptiness of adult society, but it refuses to expand and deepen this notion of resistance to see it in terms of the obligations of critical citizenship, the power of collective struggle, or the necessary translation of private troubles into larger public considerations. This film has a historical, political, and social void that not only isolates and privatizes teenage resistance within the narrow confines of an art-film sensibility, but also fails to address the role that adults play in creating many of the problems that young girls like Enid and Rebecca face on a daily basis. Adults are not simply boorish or phonies, for example, they also pass legislation that denies children the most fundamental and basic services. Adults commit 75 percent of the murders of youth in the United States; they also sexually abuse somewhere between 400,000 and 500,000 young people every year. Talking back to adults through clever irony and sarcasm points to neither understanding nor challenging the attacks often waged on young people by adult society.

Enid may strike a blow for a hip teenage aesthetic with her black fingernail polish, excessive makeup, and de rigueur combat boots, but these are only the trappings of resistance, without any political substance. The narrative gives Enid and her companion few if any insights about a society marked by massive youth unemployment, the commercialization and sexualization of kids, the increasing incarceration of young people—especially those marginalized by virtue of their class and color—and the collapse of health care, decent public education, drug programs, and job training for teenagers. These are the problems that real youth face, and it is hard to believe that Enid and Rebecca can appear oblivious to them as they get caught in the very dynamics such issues produce.

But around the relevance of the future for Enid, and by implication for marginalized youth, the film and many of its critics seem to waver badly. Throughout the story, Enid comes across an older man sitting on a bench at a bus stop that has been closed down for quite some time. He seems to be there at all hours of the day. One day Enid tells him the bus route has been cancelled and that he is wasting his time, but he simply snarls at her and tells her to leave him alone. But near the end of the film while Enid is approaching the stop, a bus mysteriously arrives and the man boards it and is never seen again. In part, this symbolizes in rather dramatic form the notion that possibility exists within the realm of the impossible; that as bleak as the future might seem, there is hope. This scene is all the more poignant because in the last scene of the film, Enid is seen boarding that same mysterious, cancelled bus, uncertain of where she is going or what she is going to face in the future. Making the possible out of the impossible surely opens up the issue of how the future is being shaped for children as we enter the twenty-first century. But with no analysis grounded in the brutal social realities with which she must live, *Ghost World* romanticizes Enid's contempt and offers no sense of how she might find her way without being subject to oppressive practices.

It is hard to imagine that Enid will hold on to her critical intelligence and biting wit without eventually succumbing to cynicism, and this is where the film reveals its most egregious shortcoming. It resonates too intimately with a major aim of neoliberalism, which is to "make politics disappear by, in part, producing cynicism in the population" (Grossberg, 127–28). Cynicism does more than confirm irony as the last resort of the defeated; it also substitutes resignation and angst for any viable notion of resistance, politics, and social transformation. It is precisely on these terms that *Ghost World* both indicts and reflects the very society it attempts to portray through the eyes of alienated teenage girls.

As a symbolic register of contemporary culture, *Ghost World* points to crucial problems without fully engaging them and by never adequately attending to "questions of politics, power, and public consciousness" (Dirlik 2003, 7) it displaces political issues to the realm of aesthetics and depoliticized forms of transgression. This is not to suggest that the film does not offer any real pleasures in its depiction of teenage rebellion. On the contrary, its richly textured script of sensory experience and comic pleasure is woven into the girls' speech, punkish style, and offhand body language. If pleasure and knowledge intersect in this film in a way that allows students to make a real affective investment in Enid's and Rebecca's lives, all the more reason to connect the pleasures of entertainment that the film provides with the "learned pleasure of [critical] analysis" (Miles 1996, 14). *Ghost World* both shapes and bears witness to the ethical and political dilemmas that animate the broader social landscape that structures teenage life. If youth are viewed as a threat to the larger social order, raising pedagogical questions about how *Ghost World* works in diverse ways not only to challenge, but also to reinforce, this perception becomes necessary. Making the pedagogical more political in this instance serves not only to locate *Ghost World* within a representational politics that bridges the gap between private and public discourses, but also to offer students the space "to break the continuity and consensus of common sense" (Olson and Worsham 1999, 11) and to resist forms of authority that deny the value of political agency, the importance of the social, and the possibility of social change. Maybe the value of this film resides not only in what it says, but also in the discussions it might provoke about what it ignores. When read against itself, *Ghost World* offers a rich pedagogical terrain for critically engaging the limits of an utterly privatized notion of resistance and for reclaiming utopian possibilities by reasserting the inseparable connection between private troubles and public discontents, between social transformation and democratic struggles, between political agency and public life.

WORKS CITED

Aronowitz, Stanley. 2001. "Globalization and the State." In *The Last Good Job in America*. Lanham, MD: Rowman and Littlefield, 159–75.

Bauman, Zygmunt. 1998. *Work, Consumerism and the New Poor*. Philadelphia: Open University Press.

———. 1999. *In Search of Politics*. Stanford: Stanford University Press.

———. 2001. *The Individualized Society*. London: Polity Press.

Beck, Ulrich. 2000. *What Is Globalization?* London: Polity Press.

———. 1992. *Risk Society*. Trans M. Ritter. Thousand Oaks: Sage.

Binde, John. 2000. "Toward an Ethic of the Future," *Public Culture* 12:1, 51–72.

Castells, Manuel. 1998. *The Information Age: Economy, Society, and Culture*. 3 vols. Malden, MA: Blackwell.

Children's Defense Fund. http//www.childrensdefense.org/factsfigures_moments.htm.

Clark, Mike. 2001. "'Ghost World' Charms, 'Freddy' Fizzles," *USA Today* (December 28), 13D.

Dirlik, Arif. 2003. "Literature/Identity: Transnationalism, Narrative and Representation," *Review of Education/Pedagogy/Cultural Studies* 24:3, 209–34.

Garland, David. 2001. *The Culture of Control*. Chicago: University of Chicago Press.

Gates, Jeff. 2000. *Democracy at Risk*. Cambridge: Perseus.

Giroux, Henry A. 2001. *Stealing Innocence: Corporate Culture's War on Children*. New York: Palgrave.

Grossberg, Lawrence. 2001. "Why Does Neo-Liberalism Hate Kids? The War on Youth and the Culture of Politics," *The Review of Education/Pedagogy/Cultural Studies* 23:2, 111–36.

Guinier, Lani and Anna Deavere Smith. 2002. "Rethinking Power, Rethinking Theater," *Theater* 31:3 (Winter), 31–45.

Handy, Charles. 1998. *The Hungry Spirit*. New York: Broadway.

Henwood, Doug. 1999. "Debts Everywhere," *The Nation* (July 19), 12.

Lapham, Lewis H. 2001. "Res publica," *Harper's Magazine* (December), 9–11.

Miles, Margaret. 1996. *Seeing and Believing: Religion and Values in the Movies*. Boston: Beacon Press.

Olson, Gary and Lynn Worsham. 1999. "Staging the Politics of Difference: Homi Bhabha's Critical Literacy," *JAC* 18:3, 11.

Parenti, Christian. 1999. *Lockdown America: Police and Prisons in the Age of Crisis*. London: Verso Press.

Peters, Cynthia. 2001. "Treating Teens Contemptuously: The Retail Squeeze." (August 4). Available at owner-znetcommentary@tao.ca.

Wa Thiong' O, Ngugi. 1993. *Moving the Centre: The Struggle for Cultural Freedom*. London: James Currey.

PART **II**

Auteurs of Negativity,
Icons of Darkness

FIGURE 8. Jean Cocteau (1889–1963), a model in many ways for the *artiste* of the twentieth century. His allegiances and friendships "were often only matters of convenience or self-advancement, to be broken off on a whim," yet "everywhere Cocteau appeared he charmed his audiences into imagining that his affections and attentions were directed to them alone." (Collection Wheeler Winston Dixon)

CHAPTER EIGHT

"How Will I Get My Opium?": Jean Cocteau and the Treachery of Friendship

WHEELER WINSTON DIXON

"Étonnez-moi!"
—Diaghilev to Cocteau

When World War II erupted in Europe, Jean Cocteau was aghast. "How will I get my opium?" was the poet's first response, and he added, "I've been assassinated by the Fifth Column" (Steegmuller 1970, 436–37). The *Fifth Column* reference related to not the German advance but advance proofs of a venomous attack on Cocteau by Claude Mauriac, which was to be published in the June 1940 issue of *La Nouvelle Revue Française*. "Mauriac must be arrested!" Cocteau demanded as the Nazi tanks rolled into Paris. As Francis Steegmuller, Cocteau's most perceptive biographer, notes, "There could be no question as to order of importance between overwhelming private betrayal and mere public catastrophe" (437).

More than most mortals, Jean Cocteau created his public persona through an elaborate series of alliances, "political" friendships, and strategic campaigns designed solely to enhance and perpetuate his reputation as a Renaissance artist. Gossip was his preferred mode of social discourse, either about himself or others, calculated to be either flattering or devastating as the occasion required. One of his most frequently revived theatre pieces, "La Voix humaine," was inspired by a couple quarreling on the telephone. Cocteau overheard their heated conversation ("They kept losing the connection, hanging up, and trying again. Georges kept groaning, 'Hello Hello!' into a dead mouthpiece" [Steegmuller, 402]), and transformed it into a one-act monologue in which a young woman tries to recapture her ex-lover's attentions with a final, desperate telephone call. Not only is the woman unsuccessful, but as their conversation grows more heated, she becomes aware that her ex-lover's new romantic interest is silently listening in on an extension, at her apartment, where the two are already carrying on their affair.

The brutality of this exhausting scenario (which has been performed by Anna Magnani, Ingrid Bergman, Liv Ullman, and others on stage and screen, and recorded in Francis Poulenc's operatic version by Carole Farley and Jessye Norman) is exponentially heightened by the fact that Cocteau felt no compunction in using two strangers' private telephone conversation as the basis for his play. This intrusion into the personal lives of others (made even bolder by Cocteau's divulging the actual identity of the quarreling lovers in a letter to Max Jacob) crystallizes within the confines of a single work the lengths to which Cocteau was willing to go in his search for new material (Steegmuller, 402). How else could he find enough material to create an endless succession of plays, novels, poems, films, murals, sculptures, and librettos? Because Jean Cocteau is in many ways a model for the twentieth century *artiste*, his apparently perfidious working style may shed light on the creative problems encountered by others working in the arts, most notably, perhaps, filmmakers, for whom the real world is a direct substance of transformation.

Cocteau mined his own life, particularly his childhood and adolescence, for semiautobiographical works such as *Les Enfants terribles* (1950), and the formidable figure of the actor Jean Marais's mother reportedly served as the basis for the maternal monster in Cocteau's *Les Parents terribles* (1948). Even when composing scenarios for others, as in his brilliant script for Robert Bresson's film *Les Dames du Bois de Boulogne* (1945), Cocteau's favorite themes (the myth of Orpheus and Eurydice, the "eternal return" of the poet, and the essential mystery of true self-knowledge) are evident in the webs of deceit, betrayal, and malicious gossip that comprise the story.

A firmly held personal belief of Cocteau's was that no one's word could truly be trusted in life. Essential information would always be withheld in conversation as a matter of course, for possible later use either in self-defense or as a weapon. The withholding was clearly his own preferred strategy, at any rate. In the opening moments of *Les Dames du Bois de Boulogne*, for example, Hélène (Maria Casares, who would become one of Cocteau's favorite actresses) and her fiancé Jean (Paul Bernard) discover that they no longer love each other, but have been afraid to admit it. Hélène speaks first of the end of their affair, but then, to her utter astonishment, Jean agrees with her assessment and praises her for her honesty. Pretending to accept what has now become an insulting situation for her, Hélène plots an elaborate and successful campaign to trap Jean into an arranged marriage with Agnès (Elina Labourdette), who is, unknown to him, a prostitute. As soon as the marriage has been performed, Hélène springs the surprise on Jean at the wedding reception. He is nearly incoherent with shock. "How can someone be capable of such viciousness?" he wonders aloud. Are those we trust the most really our truest enemies? How might the continuing possibility of betrayal, and the defenses one builds against it, work to facilitate the creative life of an important filmmaker? Will our friends *always* betray us?

For Cocteau, the answer was always yes. Despite a series of lasting romantic relationships (with Raymond Radiguet, Jean Desbordes, and most famously, Jean Marais), and despite the numerous acts of kindness and generosity by others that enabled him to live a relatively lavish life, Cocteau remained constantly on guard, suspicious of the motives of others, aware that what others gave as "lasting friendships" could be withdrawn at a moment's notice. Nor was he mistaken in this assumption, because he knew himself. In the high profile, evanescent world in which Cocteau lived and worked, most of his "friendships" were in fact strategic alliances for his personal benefit, or in some cases the mutual benefit of both parties.

An interesting exception is Jean Marais. Marais wanted above all else to be a movie star—not just an actor, but a matinee idol. In Cocteau, he sensed that he had found his ideal scenarist and director. Yet after making his debut as a filmmaker in 1930 with *Le Sang d'un poète* (which was not actually released to the public until 1932), Cocteau essentially abandoned the cinema for a fifteen-year addiction to opium. In part, his retreat into drugs was a response to the untimely death of his first great love, the poet and novelist Raymond Radiguet, who after a brief and meteoric career died of typhoid on December 12, 1923 (Steegmuller, 314). At first, Cocteau's opium addiction was not crippling; the drug made life more tolerable. By the mid-1930s, however, when Cocteau had taken up with Jean Desbordes, his use of opium had escalated to the point where he was incapable of any serious work. It was Jean Marais, then, who answered Cocteau's cry, "How will I get my opium?" by suggesting that he kick the habit altogether and concentrate on a return to the screen (Steegmuller, 440). After writing the dialogue for Serge de Poligny's *Le Baron fantôme* in 1942, in addition to serving as offscreen narrator and making one brief onscreen appearance in the film (where he crumbles to dust before the viewer's eyes), Cocteau plunged into a modern-day adaptation of the story of Tristan and Isolde, *L'Éternel retour,* directed by Jean Delannoy in 1943. In the leading role of Patrice, a role Cocteau had tailored specifically for the actor, Jean Marais became an overnight romantic idol. Intoxicated by his renewed celebrity, Cocteau's drug use tapered off and then ceased altogether, allowing the artist to create his masterpiece *La Belle et la bête* (1946), as well as the films of his plays *L'Aigle à deux têtes* (1947) and *Les Parents terribles,* and what many feel is his crowning achievement, *Orphée* (1949). None of this would have been possible without the intervention of Marais. Of all of Cocteau's relationships, Marais remained (even after their love affair ended) one of Cocteau's staunchest champions and defenders. But Cocteau's other friendships and allegiances were often only matters of convenience or self-advancement, to be broken off on a whim.

How could it be otherwise in such a fiercely competitive social and artistic milieu where inspiration was very often fleeting, fragile, and intermingled with other inspirations? As a self-declared spokesman and honorary member of "Les Six"—a group of composers including Francis Poulenc, Darius Milhaud, Louis Durey, Germaine Tailleferre, Arthur Honegger and Georges Auric, with Erik Satie as spiritual father—Cocteau was intimately involved in the world of contemporary French music, which abutted the worlds of painting and ballet. As Arthur King Peters notes, Cocteau's colleagues and rivals included Misia Sert, Serge de Diaghilev, Igor Stravinsky, André Gide, Jean Hugo, Pablo Picasso, Max Jacob, Christian Bérand, Man Ray, Coco Chanel, Guillaume Apollinaire, and Colette—and these were only his most celebrated associates (1986, 28). Each of these individuals routinely sought to claim his or her own share of the spotlight, and running feuds and scandals were commonplace. Cocteau's relationship with Stravinsky began promisingly when the composer considered scoring the music for a ballet based on a Cocteau scenario, entitled *David*. It was Diaghilev who had put Cocteau on the project, and for a time things progressed smoothly. However, in typical fashion, Cocteau boasted of the impending collaboration with Stravinsky to his coterie of admirers and simultaneously developed an infatuation for Waslaw Nijinsky, the premier dancer of Diaghilev's company. That was too much for Diaghilev. He artfully intervened, convincing Stravinsky to drop *David* and work on a new ballet, *The Nightingale,* instead. Cocteau, demonstrating the tenacity that was the guiding spirit of his career, absorbed the rebuff with icy aplomb and set about revising the scenario into the ballet *Parade* with music by Erik Satie (Peters, 42).

Cocteau was not one to let the matter rest there, however. He went so far as to publish a pamphlet in 1918, *Le Coq et l'arlequin,* in which he stated that "the theatre corrupts everything, even a Stravinsky." This manifesto he dedicated to the composer Georges Auric, who would later write the scores for several Cocteau films, including *Le Sang d'un poète* (Peters, 42). Stravinsky was outraged and declared their friendship finished. Yet, in a characteristically quixotic gesture, Cocteau kept in touch with the composer by letter, and sent him inscribed copies of his books. Eventually, some measure of equanimity was restored, and Stravinsky and Cocteau finally collaborated on a single project, the oratorio *Oedipus Rex* (Peters, 43). Stravinsky remained suspicious and jealous of Cocteau to the end of his life. Cocteau suffered a massive heart attack in April 1963, shortly before his death, and Stravinsky's assistant, Robert Craft, noted that when Stravinsky was asked to record a get-well message for the artist he violently refused to do so, even though Picasso and Georges Braque had already participated in the project. At lunch the same day, Stravinsky told his assembled guests that "Cocteau can't die without making publicity out of it," and expressed great irritation at the outpouring of public feeling for Cocteau's precarious health (Brown 1968, 409). However, when Cocteau finally did die, Stravinsky was genuinely moved and broke down in tears (Steegmuller, 496). This paradoxical love/hate relationship can serve, in many respects, as a template for Cocteau's interaction with his other collaborators. During periods of work, his friendships flourished; when a task was completed, he was capable of dropping a former associate "without a backward glance," as François Mauriac noted of his own experiences with Cocteau (Peters, 43).

All of Cocteau's interactions with others were based on this scale of utilitarianism; yet it is also true that in circumstances where others faltered, Cocteau was capable of displaying considerable moral courage. During the Nazi Occupation of France, despite his initial desperation and with Marais's support, Cocteau decided to stay and work in Paris while many of his contemporaries fled to safer climes. By the fall of 1940, Cocteau and Marais were able to stage a revival of the play *Les Parents terribles,* only to have the performance interrupted by stink bombs hurled by "Vichyite hooligans [who] climbed onto the stage cursing Cocteau and Marais" (Peters, 139). In this decidedly hostile climate, Cocteau nevertheless managed to navigate a curious course between collaboration with the enemy and cooperation with the Résistance. While under the Nazi Occupation he created a prodigious amount of work between 1940 and 1944—"five plays, two films, and a monologue, while publishing two books and numerous articles" (Peters, 140)—he was still able to avoid prosecution as a collaborator when the war ended.

Cocteau artfully survived by balancing his attentions to the Nazis (gracing numerous social functions, including the opening of an exhibition of sculptures by Arno Becker, whom Hitler admired immensely) with acts that placated the Résistance; in one instance he was "severely beaten up near the Champs-Elysées by a group of LVF (French militia) for not saluting a procession of French and Nazi flags" (Peters, 141). As with all his other affairs, Cocteau's prolificity during the Occupation was assisted by the intervention of powerful allies, especially Florence Gould, who held a regular Thursday salon where French artists and, surprisingly, some German officials would meet and discuss literature and the arts. Luckily for Cocteau, one of the salon's regular participants was Lieutenant Gerhard Heller, who had been given control of the press under the Nazis. Predisposed to appreciate French culture, Heller's relationship with Cocteau and other members of the Gould Salon facilitated their continued productivity as artists.

When the Vichy regime collapsed, Cocteau discovered that he had managed to remain in the good graces of both the victors and the vanquished, and continued with his work uninterrupted (Peters, 139). In effectively executing this precarious balancing act, Cocteau avoided the self-exile that plagued Jean Renoir, who eventually landed in the United States; André Gide, who went to North Africa; and Malraux and Sartre, who vacated Paris for the relative safety of the French Riviera (Peters, 139). Perhaps such a delicate act of social negotiation would have been impossible for these artists, but for Cocteau, to whom strategic flattery was instinctive, life in France under the Nazis was inconvenient, but little worse.

The same skill and mercuriality that ensured Cocteau's survival during the Occupation of France stood him in good stead in his relations with the press. During the round-the-world publicity launch of *La Belle et la bête*, Cocteau wrote numerous paeans to his own film, each designed to appeal to the viewers in a different country. In the United States, "the land of Edgar Allan Poe," Cocteau predicted that his film would find a receptive audience because "childhood is fresher . . . and better preserved in men's spirits than in France . . ."; for the film's premiere in Czechoslovakia, Cocteau sent a recorded announcement that expressed "my great sadness at not being in Prague . . . [to let you know] how warmly I desired our meeting and how reluctantly I have to forego it because of my work." In Belgium, Cocteau hoped that his "dear Belgian friends" would find the film to their liking; in Shanghai, Cocteau declared that "if I had not been born in France, China would be my homeland" (Cocteau 1994, 142–45).

Everywhere Cocteau appeared he charmed his audiences into imagining that his affections and attentions were directed to them alone. Indeed, many have argued that Cocteau was often so caught up in his own publicity machine that his feigned sincerity was, paradoxically, genuine by default. As a poet extremely sensitive to inspiration from all directions and wholly taken over by it once it struck him, he could be forgiven for what other, more linear, thinkers might call "changes of mind." In fact, he may well have believed everything he said at the moment he said it. One could persuasively argue that Cocteau invented the modern global publicity blitz for independently produced motion pictures because, as he noted in the late 1940s, "a book can wait. A play can flop. But a film must appeal to its audience" (Cocteau 1994, 140). With this brief statement, he reveals himself as an astute businessman as well as an artist. Cocteau was always a salesman—of himself, of his image as an artist, and of the products he created, no matter the medium he employed. Each new novel, each play, each fresco required "presentation" to the public and also Cocteau's personal mediation as the creator of the specta-cle he presented. And each creative moment required wholesale belief and conviction from Cocteau, regardless of the trivial contradictions in which he might later seem to be trapped.

Cocteau's career as a filmmaker was incandescent but relatively brief if one sets aside his apprenticeship on *Le Sang d'un poète*. As a director, he made only six features over which he exercised complete creative control: *Le Sang d'un poète, La Belle et la bête, L'Aigle à deux têtes, Les Parents terribles, Orphée,* and *Le Testament d'Orphée* (1960). His innumerable contributions to the films of others as a scenarist or narrator, in addition to his personal "experimental" films in 16mm (*Coriolan* [1950] and *La Villa Santo-Sospir* [1952]), constitute an entirely different body of work. Cocteau also encouraged directors such as Jean Delannoy (for *L'Éternel retour*), Pierre Billon (*Ruy Blas* [1947]), and Jean-Pierre Melville *(Les Enfants terribles)* to direct adaptations of his own works, and he contributed dialogue or brief prefaces to other films he cham-pioned, such as Jean-Isidore Isou's highly idiosyncratic work, *Traité de bave et d'éternité* (1950).

All of Cocteau's alliances, friendships, and social acquaintanceships were designed for maximum personal benefit to the artist. There had to be an advantage, a tangible objective for a truly satisfactory relationship. This is not surprising in someone who was intensely aware of the necessity of "connec-tions" within the art world, and who, under the tutelage of Étienne de Beau-mont, Anna de Noailles, Lucien Daudet, and perhaps most importantly, Édouard de Max, became the "poet of the salons" while still in his teens. Yet disliking Cocteau is impossible, no matter how opportunistic his dealings with others may appear at first glance, because although he always took care of his own interests first he did not hesitate to use his influence and negotiat-ing skills to assist others whose work he believed in. In 1953, in the south of France, events occurred to produce a case in point.

When Cocteau was elected president of the jury at the Cannes Film Festival, he conspired, with the unwitting aid of fellow juror "Edgar" G. Robinson (as Cocteau persisted in calling the actor), to award the first prize to Henri-Georges Clouzot's *Le Salaire de la peur* (1953). Cocteau set his plans in motion on January 23, 1953, after Clouzot arranged a clandestine screen-ing of the film for his benefit. As Cocteau recounts in his diary on that date:

> Dinner last night with Clouzot. He takes me to see his film *[Le Salaire de la peur]*. We are alone in the dark theater. Magnificent film. . . . He didn't want to show the film at the Festival, but he will, because I am presiding. (Cocteau 1990, 9)

When the film was finally screened in competition, Cocteau went to great lengths to disassociate himself from the affair he was orchestrating. Again in his diaries, he notes that:

> Tonight we saw *[Le Salaire de la peur]*, hiding Clouzot in the projectionist's booth and then in my hotel room. The film produced a considerable effect. In order not to seem to be conspiring, we went back downstairs through the kitchen. And the Clouzots could get to their car without being seen. (1990, 84)

Even when the *Herald Tribune* published an article accusing *Le Salaire de la peur* of "being a Communist film and insulting to America" (Cocteau 1990, 91), Cocteau loyally held his ground and refused to be swayed by public opinion, while for his part Robinson, the victim of a smear campaign by the House Un-American Activities Committee at the time, carefully kept out of the controversy. On April 18, Cocteau notes that "Clouzot lunched with the American delegation. Things are working out . . . ," but notes in the same entry that "people are saying that the prizes were awarded in advance. Nothing less true. Except for one or two films, I haven't a clue which will win a majority of votes" (1990, 92–93). A few days later, the Grand Prix of the Cannes Film Festival was awarded to Henri-Georges Clouzot and *Le Salaire de la peur,* just as Cocteau had planned.

But we must ask, is there anything really *wrong* with this? Cocteau's taste, as always, remains impeccable; *Le Salaire de la peur* is a remarkable film, still revived today and still considered one of the classics of world cinema. Judging from Cocteau's diary entries during the festival, the competing films were very poor, and because Cocteau felt that *Le Salaire de la peur* was "a thousand miles above all the others in the race" (1990, 82), it is with some justification that he felt compelled to make certain of Clouzot's victory. Without his help, that victory was hardly guaranteed. While fellow juror Robinson was in total accord with Cocteau's judgment (the two men hit it off from the start, when Robinson commented, much to Cocteau's amusement, "I've always played thieves and criminals, and now I'm a judge" [Cocteau 1990, 79]), Fritz Lang was on the jury as well and was surprisingly unsympathetic toward the film. "I had supposed [him] cleverer than that," Cocteau notes disdainfully (1990, 82). Clearly, Lang's interference had to be circumvented, and in such a situation a little extra help was obviously both required and appropriate.

If all of Cocteau's affairs were a series of checks and balances, of strategic alliances where benefits and risks were carefully weighed and measured, who should be surprised that this same logic pervaded the scenarios of the films he had a hand in? *La Belle et la bête* is, on the surface, a film that dwells in the realm of fantasy, based on the fairy tale by Madame Leprince de Beaumont. Behind the trappings of a children's fable, however, Cocteau uses the story of Belle (Josette Day) and the Beast (Jean Marais) to create a (somewhat

self-justifying) parable on the virtue of blind faith when all material considerations oppose it. Consider Belle's triumph over adversity through love. Her
two sisters, Félicie (Mila Parély) and Adelaide (Nane Germon), are veritable
monsters who treat Belle as if she were the family servant rather than their
equal. Belle's father (Marcel André) is powerless to stop Félicie and Adelaide's
exploitation of Belle, even as his business is driven into ruin by his daughters'
extravagance. In the triple role of Avenant, the Beast, and, in the film's final
moments, the Prince, Jean Marais is able to portray a gallery of conflicting
postures and emotions: as Avenant he is weak and indecisive, although filled
with false bravado; as the Beast, he inhabits his role so thoroughly that one
identifies immediately with his unending suffering. The Prince, a figure who
might have stepped off a wedding cake, is the mute repository of feminine
desire. As the Prince joins hands with Belle in the film's final sequence, the
two drift toward heaven in an exquisite matte sequence, caught in the rapture
of an all-encompassing love. By contrast, the petty squabbling of Avenant,
Félicie, and Adelaide seems paltry and ineffective, as if Cocteau deemed the
threat that they pose to Belle's happiness and the Beast's redemption nothing
but a distracting blind to brush through in the quest for ultimate glory.

    Once Belle decides to take her father's place in the Beast's castle, with
its magical candelabra arms and fireplace ornaments that exhale plumes of
smoke through human mouths, the audience senses that whatever obstacles
might be put in the couple's path, love will win the day. Because Cocteau
believed in the reality of evil, he concomitantly held that truth and beauty
were equally concrete and not abstract concepts. As Susan Hayward noted,
"Two essential motifs, fidelity to a pledge on the one hand [Belle's promise to
return to the castle and remain there] and marriage on the other [the fairy tale
betrothal to the Prince at the film's end]" are the central belief systems present in *La Belle et la bête* (1990, 127). The wicked sisters in Cocteau's film are
not so much characters as situations; they remain in stasis because their view
of events is both narrow and flawed. Belle's generosity of spirit leads ultimately not only to the Beast's release from the curse that has entrapped him,
but also to her own "happily ever after" romance. After all, as Cocteau notes
in the written prologue to the film, the action of *La Belle et la bête* takes place
"once upon a time." Should it not, then, have a conclusion equally fitting to
its temporal and phantasmal origins?

    A conflict both more serious and more conventionally situated is the
focus of *Les Parents terribles*, which Cocteau directed from his own screenplay.
Michel (Jean Marais) is young and in love with Madeleine (Josette Day),
unaware that she is also his father Georges's (Marcel André) mistress. The situation is further complicated by the fact that Michel's mother, Yvonne
(Yvonne de Bray), is pathologically possessive of her son and opposes any talk
of marriage, exclaiming, "He's just a child." Michel is determined to wed

Madeleine, however, and Yvonne is pushed to extreme measures to prevent the couple from wedding. Both Georges (a hopelessly impractical inventor) and Yvonne (who does nothing but smoke cigarettes and take drugs) are dependent on Michel's aunt, Léo (Gabrielle Dorziat), for their meager existence. Léo had once been engaged to Georges, but had stepped aside so that Yvonne and Georges could marry. Now, the two prevail upon Léo to put a stop to Michel and Madeleine's budding relationship.

Through a complex series of lies and machinations, Léo manages to estrange the couple, but at the last moment she cannot deny Michel and Madeleine the happiness she herself sacrificed when she gave up Georges. The young lovers are reunited, but Léo has reckoned without the pathological jealousy of Yvonne, who takes a massive overdose of drugs and dies in her bed as the stricken assemblage looks on helplessly. The intricate turns and twists of this film, together with its immaculately hermetic camerawork and claustrophobic mise-en-scène make *Les Parents terribles* equally effective as a satire of Parisian mores or as stark tragedy. Yvonne de Bray's performance is rivetingly self-absorbed; she is interested only in keeping her son, her fading beauty, and various intoxicants within her grasp. Cocteau displays genuine sympathy for Yvonne's misguided affections, as well as for Léo's near-disastrous meddling in Michel and Madeleine's affairs. Léo, ever practical, at first strives to keep the spectacularly dysfunctional ménage together, but realizes just in time that although she, Yvonne, and Georges are condemned to a twilight existence, Michel and Madeleine should be given a chance to escape. As the couple's reunion is effected, we see Yvonne gradually move away from the others, disappearing into the ever-present shadows of the gloomy apartment, convinced that Michel has abandoned her. Yvonne's final deathbed scene severely undercuts the couple's promised happiness, saving the film from the burden of a conventional heterotopic scene of domestic closure and demonstrating that in every "happy ending" there are disappointed suitors, even if, as in this case, the suitor is the groom-to-be's own *maman*.

Although he did not direct *Les Enfants terribles,* Cocteau's cooperation with director Jean-Pierre Melville was complete, and he even directed an afternoon of filming when Melville was indisposed. Charting the incestuous hothouse relationship of brother and sister Paul (Édouard Dermithe) and Elisabeth (Nicole Stéphane) in an apartment every bit as cramped as the spatial terrain of *Les Parents terribles,* Melville's film was an enormous hit with disaffected, postwar Parisian youth, even as it outraged moral censors of the period. When Paul is injured in a snowball fight with school bully Dargelos (played, oddly enough, by a young woman, Renée Cosima), he is forced to stay in his apartment as a virtual invalid under the care of his sister, Elisabeth. Their morbidly close relationship is threatened when Elisabeth brings home a friend, Agathe (Renée Cosima again), to whom Paul becomes increasingly attracted.

As usual in Cocteau's films, matters soon become even more complex: Paul's friend Gérard (Jacques Bernard) is smitten with Elisabeth, but Elisabeth suddenly decides to marry rich playboy Michael (Melvyn Martin), who dies in an automobile accident shortly after their marriage, leaving her a very wealthy widow. When Paul's devotion to Agathe increases, Elisabeth is threatened and contrives through a series of letters to drive the lovers apart. Shattered, Paul takes a fatal dose of poison, and in the film's final shot, Elisabeth, unable to live with her treachery, kills herself with a gunshot to the head as the camera swoops toward heaven above her.

In its portrait of alienated and disaffected youth, *Les Enfants terribles* anticipates the drug culture of the 1960s, and prefigures such films as Nicholas Roeg and Donald Cammell's *Performance* (1970), in which Mick Jagger presides over a similarly decadent household whose participants engage in casual sex, drug use, and, in the film's climax, ritualistic murder (again with a bullet to the head). Elisabeth's betrayal of Paul and Agathe is her own undoing, and her unnatural attachment to her brother provides us with a younger image of Yvonne, besotted with her son Michel in *Les Parents terribles*.

While *Les Enfants terribles* is not, in the strictest sense of the word, a Cocteau film, his stamp on the finished film is unmistakable. Darker than *Les Parents terribles*, *Les Enfants terribles* manages to conflate incest, suicide, drugging, and social isolation into one explosive construct. The protagonists live in a world devoid of adult supervision, except for an old family servant and a doctor who visits the apartment occasionally to treat Paul. Left alone under the cruel and willful domination of Elisabeth, the adolescents in *Les Enfants terribles* seek amusement through self-destruction. The adult world is meaningless to Elisabeth and Paul; its authority is bankrupt and counterfeit. But, as in all of Cocteau's work, idleness breeds danger, and what starts as play acting becomes deadly business. The protagonists of *Les Enfants terribles* have it all—time, money, and the ability to make of their lives whatever they wish. But as Cocteau demonstrates, we are ultimately ruled by our emotions rather than our rational selves. The risk in all relationships is that one may go too far, with potentially fatal consequences. The twin deaths of Elisabeth and Paul reflect perfectly their inseparability in life; where one goes, the other must follow. From some journeys there is no return, as Cocteau knows.

In 1949 Cocteau completed his most famous and perhaps most accessible film, *Orphée*, with Jean Marais and Marie Déa in the lead roles. The real star of the film, however, is Maria Casares, who played the diabolically manipulative Hélène in *Les Dames du Bois de Boulogne* five years earlier. As the Princess, bringer of death, coming and going through mirrors and driving through the countryside attended by leather-jacketed motorcycle punks who first run down her intended victims and then assist her in spiriting them off to the realm of death, Casares gives the performance of her career, one she would reprise in Cocteau's last film, *Le Testament d'Orphée*. Unlike Hélène in *Les Dames*, Casares is both sympathetic and hypnotic as the figure of Death, coping with the clumsiness of her assistant Cégeste (Édouard Dermithe) and matching wits with Heurtebise (François Périer), who hopes to aid Orpheus in his quest to reclaim Eurydice from the bowels of Hell. Casares's Princess is not so much evil as terminally bored and utterly alone, a functionary who answers to a higher tribunal and must carry out her orders without question.

In the beginning of *Orphée*, a writer (Roger Blin) in a sidewalk café advises Orphée to take care; he is too popular, and his fame has inspired jealousy among his colleagues. Orphée dismisses this warning, but events prove that it is more than justified. Romantically obsessed with Orphée, the Princess watches him while he sleeps and plots to steal him from Eurydice. Orphée himself is going through a crisis in his career as a poet, doubting his own powers and abilities even as he approaches the height of his fame. Everywhere, his enemies converge on him, led by the vindictive Aglaonice (Juliet Greco), who with some justification accuses Orphée of plagiarism. To lure him to her side, the Princess has arranged to broadcast a series of enigmatic messages through Orphée's car radio, fragments of poetry that he copies down frantically, convinced that his own muse has failed him. Now he is under attack from two fronts: his rivals want to destroy his reputation, and the Princess seeks to destroy his seemingly idyllic marriage. As Arthur King Peters notes, at least one aspect of *Orphée*'s fictive plot was based on the public's perception of Cocteau's own oeuvre, which was losing favor with a new generation of poets:

> In one scene in the film, at the entrance to the Café des Poètes, Dermithe/Cégeste comes in as Marais/Orphée goes out. They pause, and Cégeste (Segistus) mutters scornfully at Orphée. That instant on screen . . . portrays [Cocteau's] awareness that by 1949 he was being rejected by the young public, the new generation of Saint-Germain-des-Prés. (1986, 172–73)

Once again Cocteau confounded his critics. Completed in 1950, the film won the Prix International de la Critique at the 1950 Venice Film Festival (Steegmuller, 483). Its dazzling special effects, especially the Princess's numerous entrances and exits through mirrors, have been copied in such films as *The Matrix* (1999), in which the Wachowski brothers appropriate the liquid intensity of Cocteau's imagery in a triumph of technology over imagination. Indeed, the influence of *Orphée* is so pervasive that it became the model for an entire generation of experimental films in its wake, including Kenneth Anger's *The Inauguration of the Pleasure Dome* (1954), which Cocteau himself described as "a highly ingenious Chinese torment" (as quoted in *Canyon Cinema* 1988, 4) and *Scorpio Rising* (1963), which fuses Cocteau's death-messenger motorcyclists with a soundtrack of 1960s rock and roll. In addition, MTV in its formative years ripped off many of *Orphée*'s stylistic conceits, in videos for now-forgotten bands such as Missing Persons and A Flock of Seagulls. Indeed, one of the dangers of Cocteau's influence is that it is so pervasive, providing a ready-made grab bag of tricks for the neophyte to dip into. But the triumph of *Orphée* crowned Cocteau's international reputation as a filmmaker, and after it, except for a few brief films in 16mm, he was content to let the medium rest.

Cocteau's last film, *Le Testament d'Orphée*, is a gentle remake of *Blood of a Poet*, a catalogue of recurring themes and iconic obsessions that dominated Cocteau's work in film, poetry, novels, and paintings from 1930 onward. *Le Testament d'Orphée* is also notable for the appearance of many of Cocteau's friends and associates, willing now to forget the breaks and reconciliations of the past and participate in one more project with the aging master. In addition to Maria Casares reprising her role as the Princess from *Orphée*, and Édouard Dermithe again appearing as Cégeste, Jean Marais, Charles Aznavour, Brigitte Bardot, Pablo Picasso, Serge Lifar, Roger Vadim, and Yul Brynner performed brief cameos in the film, participating "not because they are famous, but because they are my friends," as Cocteau advises the viewer on the film's soundtrack.

In addition to providing the narration for *Le Testament d'Orphée*, Cocteau, for the first and last time, appears as the star of his own film, playing himself in a series of picaresque adventures that unfold before the viewer as the visions of a hypnotic, if undeniably self-indulgent, daydreamer. François Truffaut contributed to the film's production costs, as did Cocteau's most important patron, Francine Weisweiller, who had assisted him financially as far back as *Les Enfants terribles*, when Jean-Pierre Melville ran into financial difficulty during the last days of filming. By the time *Le Testament d'Orphée* was being shot, Cocteau and Dermithe were living in Madame Weisweiller's luxurious home at the Villa Santo Sospir on a more or less permanent basis.

Even this relationship, however, was not without its difficulties. After years of patronage, Madame Weisweiller and Cocteau quarreled, and Cocteau and Dermithe were evicted from Santo Sospir. Cocteau initially found shelter in Jean Marais's villa outside Paris for a time in the spring of 1960, before moving permanently to Milly-la-forêt, where he decorated a tiny chapel, Saint-Blaise-des-Simples, as his final resting place (Brown, 407). As always, Marais remained the one friend that Cocteau could truly count on to come to his aid, no matter the circumstance. Just before his death, Madame Weisweiller arrived in Milly in the early part of October 1963, hoping for a reconciliation, but this was not to be. "You bring death with you!" Cocteau exclaimed on seeing her (Brown, 409). On Thursday, October 11, 1963, Jean Cocteau died, but even in death, his critics would not be silenced. "I'm amazed that he could do something as natural, as simple, as undevised as dying," carped François Mauriac, proving that Cocteau's controversial self-performativity would remain a point of contention, lasting to the present day. And yet Cocteau's work has transcended the jibes of his erstwhile associates, remaining a living and vital repository of images and ideas that continue to influence contemporary cineastes.

In the summer of 1994, I visited Cocteau's grave at Milly-la-forêt, where his body is interred in the floor of a small chapel underneath a slab of stone on which are engraved the words, "Je reste avec vous." A bust of Cocteau by the Nazi artist Arno Becker rests on a pedestal in the rear of the small enclosure. As a final Coctelian touch, a continual tape loop of Cocteau's voice speaks directly to the visitor, admonishing us to "only pretend to weep, since poets only pretend to die." In death as in life, Cocteau remains acutely conscious of his audience, a tangible presence whom death can mediate, but not obliterate. In an interview near the end of his life, he stated flatly, "I believe sexuality is the basis of all friendship" (Fifield 1964, 37), adding of his books, plays, and films that "the work of every creator is autobiography, even if he does not know it or wish it, even if his work is 'abstract.' It is why you cannot redo your work" (Fifield, 32).

Cocteau's work exists as an extension of his life and his many relationships, illuminating not only the cruel, calculating machinations he himself was capable of, but also the triumph of his visions over the vicissitudes of gossip, scandal, and the envy of his peers. As an artist, Cocteau was capable of both generosity (he would regularly make drawings for friends who were short on funds, specifically so they could sell them to pay their debts; Klaus Kinski was such a recipient) and brutality (when people were no longer of use to Cocteau, personally or professionally, they were disposed of forthwith). Yet Cocteau's best work transcends conventional moral boundaries and constraints, and his faults are those of any highly egotistical creative artist, who instinctively feels the clock running out and moves to accomplish all that is possible before death calls a halt to the labor. There is no need for Cocteau's work, or his life, to be "redone." His "autobiography," flaws and all, remains alive and intact, a reminder of our mendacity, our human complexity, and our ongoing potential for both harm and good.

WORKS CITED

Armes, Roy. 1985. *French Cinema*. New York: Oxford University Press.

Bazin, André. 1981. *French Cinema of the Occupation and Resistance: The Birth of a Critical Aesthetic*. Trans. Stanley Hochman. New York: Frederick Ungar.

Brown, Frederick. 1968. *An Impersonation of Angels: A Biography of Jean Cocteau*. New York: Viking.

Canyon Cinema. 1988. *Canyon Cinema Catalogue No. 6*. San Francisco: Canyon Cinema.

Cocteau, Jean. 1968. *Opium*. Trans. Margaret Crosland and Sinclair Road. London: Peter Owen.

———. 1972. *Beauty and the Beast: Diary of a Film*. Trans. Ronald Duncan. New York: Dover.

———. 1987. *Past Tense: The Cocteau Diaries*, Vol. I. Trans. Richard Howard. San Diego: Harcourt, Brace, Jovanovich.

———. 1990. *Past Tense: The Cocteau Diaries*, Vol. II. Trans. Richard Howard. London: Metheun.

———. 1991. *Souvenir Portraits: Paris in the Belle Epoque*. Trans. Jesse Browner. London: Robson.

———. 1994. *The Art of Cinema*. Ed. André Bernard and Claude Gauteur. Trans. Robin Buss. London: Marion Boyars.

Crosland, Margaret. 1956. *Jean Cocteau*. New York: Knopf.

Evans, Arthur B. 1977. *Jean Cocteau and His Films of Orphic Identity*. Philadelphia: Art Alliance Press.

Fifield, William. 1964. "Jean Cocteau: An Interview," *The Paris Review* 32, 12–37.

Fraigneau, André. 1961. *Cocteau*. Trans. Donald Lehmkuhl. New York: Grove.

———. 1972. *Cocteau on the Film: Conversations with Jean Cocteau*. Trans. Vera Traill. New York: Dover.

Harvey, Stephen. 1984. "The Mask in the Mirror: The Movies of Jean Cocteau." In Alexandra Anderson and Carol Saltus, eds., *Jean Cocteau and the French Scene*. New York: Abbeville, 185–207.

Hayward, Susan. 1990. "Gender Politics: Cocteau's Belle is not that Bête." In Susan Hayward and Ginette Vincendeau, eds., *French Films: Texts and Contexts*. London: Routledge, 127–36.

Johnson, Douglas and Madeleine Johnson. 1987. *The Age of Illusion: Art and Politics in France 1918–1940*. New York: Rizzoli.

Peters, Arthur King. 1986. *Jean Cocteau and His World*. New York: Venome.

Sadoul, Georges. 1953. *French Film*. London: Falcon Press.

Steegmuller, Francis. 1970. *Cocteau: A Biography*. Boston: Little, Brown.

FIGURE 9. Russ Meyer "brought sexploitation into the mainstream," moving it "out of the male-only grindhouse circuit and into first-class theaters." Indeed, until the release of his *Beyond the Valley of the Dolls* (20th Century Fox, 1970), in which Edy Williams plays porn star Ashley St. Ives, Meyer's films were "understood in relation to the framework of the stag film." (Frame enlargement)

CHAPTER NINE

The Sweeter the Kitten
the Sharper the Claws:
Russ Meyer's Bad Girls

KRISTEN HATCH

BOSOMANIA

Russ Meyer holds a distinctive place in the pantheon of American film auteurs. In the wake of loosening censorship laws, he helped to transform exploitation film and to pave the way for the eruption of hard-core film pornography in the 1970s. His films are landmarks in exploitation filmmaking. In *The Immoral Mr. Teas* (1959) he adapted techniques developed for photographing centerfolds for *Playboy* and other men's magazines to a grindhouse narrative, which was a radical departure from the documentaries and nudist films of the decade. In *Lorna* (1964) he introduced art-house aesthetics to sexploitation. And with *Vixen!* (1968) he brought sexploitation into the mainstream, breaking out of the male-only grind-house circuit and into first-class theaters.

Meyer brought a distinctive vision to exploitation audiences. He often wrote, edited, and produced his films, in addition to directing them, and his crew usually consisted of a handful of friends he had met during his service in World War II. The resulting films were tremendously profitable. Shot with a miniscule budget, *The Immoral Mr. Teas*, for example, brought in a 40-to-1 return. According to the *Los Angeles Times*, the only previous film to beat that profit ratio was *Gone with the Wind* (1939) (Prelutsky). *Vixen!* earned a large enough profit on its $70,000 investment to attract the attention of Richard Selznick at Fox, who hired the exploiter to direct *Beyond the Valley of the Dolls* (1970) for the studio, thus marking Meyer's entry into mainstream Hollywood. Nearly half a century after the release of *The Immoral Mr. Teas,* Meyer's films continue to attract audiences. During the 1970s, he developed an underground following that included the director John Waters, who cited *Faster, Pussycat! Kill! Kill!* (1965) as the best film ever made. And Meyer was quick to recognize the marketing possibilities of video technology, releasing his films on VHS under the blanket title "Bosomania." In 1994 his films were rereleased in theaters, introducing his body of work to a new generation of filmgoers. As a result, whereas most exploitation films are all but forgotten, Meyer's continue to circulate in the popular imagination. Today, his films are enthusiastically embraced by feminists. Linda Perry, of the band 4 Non-Blondes, describes his oeuvre as having inspired her own filmmaking efforts (Wilson 1996). In her presentation of video clips, "All Girl Action: A History of Lesbian Erotica" (1990), Susie Bright extols the pleasures of *Vixen!* for lesbian audiences. A women's bar in New York has been named for *Faster, Pussycat!* And feminist film critic B. Ruby Rich has published her own celebration of that film in the *Village Voice,* praising it as "a model that's been appropriated by dykes in search of some shit-kicking history and who find just the tonic in this band of frenzied femmes whose approach to men lies half way between Sharon Stone and Hothead Paisan" (1995, n.p.).

Meyer's signature—as distinctive as Hitchcock's icy blondes or Griffith's child-women—is the casting of large-breasted women in his leading roles, as the title "Bosomania" implies. They are viciously bitchy, flouting nearly every rule invented by man. Given both Meyer's formative role in the evolution of American sexploitation film and his surprising popularity with contemporary feminists, it is worth asking what the sexual politics of these bad women might be.

Roger Ebert has divided Russ Meyer's film career into three stages: The first he describes as the "nudie cuties"—*The Immoral Mr. Teas, Eve and the Handyman* (1961), *Wild Gals of the Naked West!* (1962), and *Heavenly Bodies!* (1963)—comedies characterized by only the skimpiest of narratives and nonsynchronous sound. The second group he terms Meyer's "drive-in Steinbeck" films—*Lorna, Mudhoney* (1965), *Motor Psycho* (1965), and *Faster, Pussycat! Kill! Kill!*—consisting of black-and-white melodramas. The third comprises Meyer's sexual melodramas: *Common Law Cabin* (1967); *Vixen!; Finders Keepers, Lovers Weepers!* (1968); and *Cherry, Harry, and Raquel!* (1969). David Frasier adds a fourth period to the list: the "parody satires": *Beyond the Valley of the Dolls, Supervixens* (1975), *Up!* (1976), and *Beneath the Valley of the Ultra-vixens* (1979) (1990, 4). It is the women who emerge in the films of the middle periods—from *Lorna* to *Cherry, Harry, and Raquel!*—who best represent Meyer's vision of busty excess. The earlier films are little more than extended dirty jokes of the sort found between the pages of *Playboy*, and the later films, following Meyer's work at Fox, are self-conscious reworkings of his previous films. Therefore, this chapter focuses on the middle films to understand how these bad women function in the context of Meyer's oeuvre.

At the time of their release, far from being embraced by feminists, Meyer's films were picketed by women who objected to his representation of female sexuality. Bearing placards with such slogans as "Sex is Beautiful, Exploitation is Ugly" (Frasier, 45–46), feminists objected to Meyer's fantasies of female voracity. Although the protests were relatively mild (Meyer himself complained that he would like to have seen even more objections because controversy helps sell tickets), they do point to an important aspect of Meyer's films: they were produced within the context of a rapidly changing social structure, in which the very definition of gender roles was being challenged. These changes contained a not-so-subtle threat to masculinity and, by extension, to a social order that rested on male authority.

LEAVE IT TO CLEAVAGE

In Meyer's films, masculine authority does not occupy the same incorruptible position that it does in classical Hollywood. In his view, American society has become ineffective, impotent in its attempts to contain the burgeoning of violence and sexuality of the postwar years. His films offer a critique of the now-defunct principles of moral authority that once held American society in place, but now they expose it to the chaos of unbridled desire. With moral authority gendered male and unbridled sexuality gendered female, Meyer's films seek a middle ground, a happy medium between plenitude and lack.

Many of Meyer's films are directly inspired by those of the Hollywood studios, functioning as a commentary on the dominant film industry and exposing the repressed elements that lay just beneath the surface of the country's legitimate film dramas. *Cherry, Harry, and Raquel!*, for instance, is clearly inspired by the Hollywood western. The film's villain is a faceless Indian, known only as Apache (John Milo), who threatens the white townspeople by riding circles around them in his Jeep. In the film's final sequence, Harry (Charles Napier), the town's sheriff, dukes it out with Apache in hand-to-hand combat. Meyer underscores the homoeroticism of this and every other Hollywood fight sequence by intercutting the fight between Harry and Apache with the lovemaking of Cherry (Linda Ashton) and Raquel (Larissa Ely). Likewise, *Good Morning . . . and Goodbye!* (1967) and *Common Law Cabin* make explicit the incestuous underpinnings of the family melodrama, and *Finders Keepers, Lovers Weepers!* exposes the lie of the iconic hooker with a heart of gold.

Faster, Pussycat!, too, was indirectly inspired by Hollywood. Meyer's film was conceived as a follow-up to *Motor Psycho*. Both feature a trio of rebels wreaking havoc on small-town America, although whereas in *Motor Psycho* the gang was composed of three male bikers, *Faster, Pussycat!*'s rebels are a gang of women in sports cars. Both bear more than a passing resemblance to Laszlo Benedek's *The Wild One* (1954), which starred Marlon Brando as a rebel biker. And, as with Meyer's other send-offs of Hollywood, *Motor Psycho* contains its own critique of the values espoused in Hollywood film. Meyer's film quotes *The Wild One* in a sequence in which the motorcycle gang, astride their bikes, threateningly encircles a woman walking across a street. However, whereas in the Hollywood imagination, the threat of rape leads to an erotic struggle between a good girl and Brando's bad boy, Meyer rejects the romantic image of the rebel tamed by feminine innocence. Instead, he makes the violence of rape explicit; the woman who has been raped is last seen, bruised and bloody, in the back of an ambulance.

But Meyer does more than merely expose the mythology of mainstream Hollywood. His films also expose the problems inherent in the very ideology on which classical Hollywood is built. Hollywood films such as *The Wild One* might suggest the failure of masculine authority, but they do so only to reinforce its centrality in maintaining social order. Meyer's films, by contrast, reflect an ambivalence toward the traditional authority figures that classical Hollywood had helped to reinforce, showing masculine social authority to be in a state of disarray.

Motor Psycho and *Faster, Pussycat!* blame the chaos introduced by their wheeled outlaws on a failure on the part of male authority figures, and this failure is indirectly linked to women's sexual aggression. In *Motor Psycho,* men are not able to protect their wives from the band of lunatic bikers. Three times, husbands prove incapable of protecting their wives from the gang. The film begins with a couple enjoying a day off by the side of the river. The wife (Arshalouis Airazian) tries to get her husband's (Steve Masters) attention, but he prefers to fish. With her husband ignoring her, she settles for sunbathing. At this point the biker gang happens on the scene, knocks out the husband, and rapes the wife. The second rape occurs while a veterinarian (George Costello) is at work, leaving his wife (Holle K. Winters) home alone. And the third occurs when a husband and wife (Coleman Francis and Haji) suffer a flat tire on the side of the road. The husband is an older man, a veteran of World War I. He is no match for the Vietnam veteran (Stephen Oliver) who ruthlessly shoots both him and his wife.

As in *The Wild One,* the violence in *Motor Psycho* escalates because of the complicity of the criminal justice system. However, whereas the earlier film had attacked the pacifism of a sheriff who was equally concerned with the rights of bikers and townsfolk, the latter is critical of a justice system that does not recognize rape as a crime of violence. After the veterinarian's wife is raped, the sheriff (Russ Meyer) refuses to regard her attack as a legitimate crime, claiming instead that "nothing happened to her that a woman ain't built for." Thus it is the failure of the U.S. criminal justice system and the men responsible for its execution that forces the veterinarian to turn to vigilante justice.

In *Faster, Pussycat!*, the police are notably absent. Rather, here the corruption of the family structure is portrayed as contributing to the chaos engendered by these bad girls. The film has transformed the family-owned farm from an idyllic remnant of the past to a horrifying image of contemporary society. The film's trio of bad girls is mirrored by a family of men—a father and two sons—living on a run-down ranch in the desert. The father (Stuart Lancaster), known only as "old man," is confined to a wheelchair from which he dominates his sons, one of whom is an imbecilic muscle man. The old man is a misogynist, blaming women in general for his paralysis. In exacting his revenge on womankind, he encourages his imbecilic son (Dennis Busch), known only as the Vegetable, to bring women to the farm where they are raped and murdered. The horror of this all-male family is captured in a sequence in which the characters sit together around the table, evoking a familiar scene of family harmony. As they consume their meal, Linda (Sue Bernard), whom Varla (Tura Satana), the gang's leader, has kidnapped, tries to make the family understand her plight. But everyone ignores her hysterical screams for help, gorging on chicken and whiskey and flirting with one another across the table. (This sequence bears a striking resemblance to one in *The Texas Chainsaw Massacre* [1974], in which a hysterical woman begs for mercy at the dinner table, surrounded by a cannibalistic family of men who ignore her pleas for help as they enjoy their meal.)

This concern that the patriarchal structures that once kept American society in check are no longer capable of maintaining order is reflected in his other films as well. Within Meyer's oeuvre, the traditional signs of patriarchal order—religion, law, and the family—are consistently shown to be ineffective. In both *Lorna* and *Mudhoney,* a preacher threatens fire and brimstone as retribution for sexual pleasure. Whereas in *Lorna* the dissatisfied wife (Lorna Maitland) is killed for the sin of seeking sexual pleasure outside of marriage (Meyer later expressed a desire to remake the film, without the death of its title character), in *Mudhoney* the preacher (Frank Bolger) is exposed as having instigated the film's violence, condemning a good couple as sinners because they are not married and promoting a cruel husband's violence because his claims on his wife are legitimated by the church.

Furthermore, the patriarchal family structure is shown to be perverted. In *Good Morning . . . and Goodbye!* and *Common Law Cabin,* fathers struggle to overcome incestuous desires for their daughters. The horror of *Faster, Pussy-cat!*'s all-male family is equaled by a family of women in *Mudhoney.* The cackling crone of a mother (Princess Livingston) plays both mother and madam to her buxom daughters, one of whom, like Vegetable the innocent imbecile, is an innocent mute (Rena Horton, whose heavy accent made muteness a necessity). And, whereas the patriarchal family structure is based on an economic system whereby men earn wages and women tend the home, Meyer's representation of characters engaged in various forms of sex work precludes this neat division of labor. *Mudhoney*'s is not the only cathouse in Meyer's collection of films. In *Finders Keepers, Lovers Weepers!,* Paul runs a topless bar and frequents a bordello run by a scheming madam. In *Cherry, Harry, and Raquel!,* Cherry is a prostitute and Raquel is a nurse who doesn't hesitate to indulge her patients' every whim. In *Common Law Cabin,* as in *Faster, Pussycat!* and *Finders Keepers, Lovers Weepers!,* women work as erotic dancers.

Clearly, then, Meyer's films endorse the dominant power structure no more than they do the chaos of its overthrow. In the end, his films suggest ambivalence, dissatisfaction with existing social structures combined with anxiety over the loss of a stable social order. Meyer exists outside the mainstream, yet is able to look to the dominant culture only as a reference point, unable to imagine a viable alternative. It is best to remember that Meyer's films existed on the fringes of Hollywood films, at once in their shadow and outside their purview, unbounded by the strict rules of the Production Code or, after 1968, the restrictions imposed by a studio demanding an R rating. (When Meyer actually did make studio films, beginning with *Beyond the Valley of the Dolls,* they were rated X, by virtue, Meyer later claimed, of his reputation as an exploiteer.) Indeed, he refused to make hard-core pornography, although he recognized that the mainstreaming of porn spelled the end of his particular film niche.

Given Meyer's ambivalence toward existing power structures, his bad girls take on a new meaning. Bad women are nothing new to the screen. Since the silent period, Hollywood has portrayed an array of vamps, women characterized by excessive and destructive desires. However, within the context of Meyer's ambivalence toward social structures, these bad girls no longer represent a feminine force that must be brought under the control of patriarchal society. Rather, at their best they offer a peek into a world of pleasure, unrestricted by the mindless dictates of a corrupt society. In Meyer's world, masculine authority has been eroded not only in the public realms of law and commerce but in the private sphere of the bedroom as well.

Both *Faster, Pussycat!* and *Motor Psycho* end with the formation of a new couple. In *Faster, Pussycat!,* Kirk (Paul Trinka), the elder brother, vanquishes Varla with the help of the kidnapped Linda, and in *Motor Psycho,* the veterinarian teams with Ruby, the wife of the old-timer, to bring down the biker gang. Ruby is a former prostitute, a Cajun who married the older man to escape Louisiana. Unlike the veterinarian's wife, she is able to stand up for herself, knifing her would-be assailant in the back as he attempts to rape her. Both couples represent the reconciliation of straight society and its outcasts. This attempted reconciliation between a corrupt order and the chaos of its overthrow is repeated in several films in which swingers are coupled with squares. And, for the most part, in Meyer's universe, the female half of the couple is the one who swings. *Vixen!*, for example, portrays a happily married couple in which a swinging wife (Erica Gavin) is married to an incurably square husband (Garth Pillsbury) who remains faithful and completely blind to his wife's multiple couplings.

However, even as this image of the sexually insatiable woman promises an abundance of sexual pleasures, it serves as a reminder of the loss of male authority. Sexuality, in Meyer's world, functions as a sign for social roles in general. This tension between abundance and scarcity, plentitude and lack is at the center of Meyer's oeuvre.

VORACIOUS, VARIETARIAN VIRAGOS

Concomitant with the deterioration of masculine authority that Meyer explores is the radical redefinition of femininity in U.S. society during the 1960s. The films of his middle period were produced parallel to the nascence of second-wave feminism. Women were beginning to redefine their roles in society, to demand a part in shaping the social order. Meyer expresses the anxieties that attended the demise of patriarchal institutions in American society through the depiction of sexually voracious women who contest the once-assured masculine dominance in sexual and political relations. During the 1960s, women began to demand parity in the bedroom as well as the boardroom.

In their survey of the impact of the sexual revolution on the social construction of female sexuality, *Re-Making Love*, Barbara Ehrenreich, Elizabeth Hess, and Gloria Jacobs (1986) demonstrate how a Freudian understanding of female frigidity, which was the dominant model for understanding female sexuality in the 1950s, was displaced by new understandings of women's pleasure. Beginning with Alfred Kinsey, sex researchers were discovering that, far from being frigid, women were capable of multiple orgasms. According to Ehrenreich, Hess, and Jacobs, the popular media did not begin to speak of a sexual revolution until 1966, when Masters and Johnson's *The Human Sexual Response* and Jacqueline Susann's novel *Valley of the Dolls* became best-sellers. However, the elements that would contribute to this transformation were already in place in the 1950s. Alfred Kinsey's *Sexual Behavior in the Human*

Female was published in 1953, introducing the female orgasm to American consciousness. Also, during the postwar years, young unmarried men and women moved in increasing numbers to the cities, and the same set of circumstances that contributed to the development of gay subcultures in these centers—the relative anonymity of city life, young working people's increased independence from family, and the consequent decline of patriarchal control over sexual and social behavior—permitted the development of new sexual practices for straight men and women, including, by the 1960s, increased premarital sex for both. The result was a dramatic shift in the popular understanding of normative sexuality for women, at least urban women. No longer were women expected to submit passively to active male sexuality. Rather, they were to begin to pursue their own orgasms (Ehrenreich, Hess, and Jacobs, 40–43). Thus male sexual authority, as well as social authority, was effectively challenged.

Meyer's films were produced in the midst of this transformation in the construction of female sexuality and were increasingly concerned with understanding its implications for men. On the one hand, the new image of feminine pleasure played into fantasies of sexual plentitude that have long characterized pornography. But on the other hand, changing norms of feminine sexuality threatened the conditions of male sexuality. No longer was sex predicated on a man's pleasure. Suddenly, women were understood to have needs as well. Meyer's films simultaneously celebrate the new image of normative female sexuality and struggle to come to terms with its consequences for men.

Faster, Pussycat! explicitly links the film's carnage to changes in the construction of American femininity. The film's parody of a square-up has an off-screen narrator intoning a warning to the spectator that a "new breed" of women has emerged. These women, according to the narrator, may be "your secretary, your doctor's receptionist, a dancer at a go-go bar." Women are definable, then, by occupation, rather than through the agency of their familial relations. Furthermore, their access to technology undoes their reliance on men. Racing across the desert in cars built for speed, the film's three rapacious go-go dancers are at the height of ecstasy, completely self-contained. With their cars they are able to compete on an equal footing with men, not only beating them at speed racing, but also murdering them. The film also suggests that the influx of immigrants who have flocked to the cities from overseas is responsible for this transformation of American womanhood. Varla, whose face is described by one *Variety* reviewer as "mystic oriental" (Murf 1966) uses karate to kill a man with her bare hands, while her lover, Rosie (Haji), is portrayed as a belligerent Italian immigrant. Conversely, the square couple—Tommy and Linda—whom the trio harass in the desert, are unmarked, nondescript, all-American.

Faster, Pussycat! is unusual among Meyer's films in its portrayal of female criminality run rampant. However, most of his women break the rules of civilized society in pursuit of their voracious appetites. No Meyer heroine is faithful to her husband. In *Lorna,* the film's lusty wife conspires with her new lover in her husband's murder, regretting her decision only at the last minute. In *Common Law Cabin,* Sheila (Alaina Capri) deliberately taunts her husband into a show of his strength—although she knows his weak heart will kill him—so that she can enjoy the company of other men. And in *Vixen!,* Vixen (Erica Gavin) seduces every man and woman within her purview, including her brother (John Evans).

Sexual frustration plays a major role in Meyer's films, which are constantly searching for the middle ground between plentitude and scarcity. And for the most part, it is the women who are burdened with an insatiable sexual appetite. Meyer's women are characterized by a voracious desire for pleasure, a desire that, when it meets with restrictions, has a tendency to erupt into glorious bitchiness. (*Faster, Pussycat!* is unique among Meyer's films in its depiction of women who substitute violence for sex.) Lorna takes out her sexual frustration by neglecting her domestic chores, refusing to make her husband breakfast because he has been unable to satisfy her sexually. By contrast, when she discovers sexual ecstasy with an escaped convict, she dotes on him in the kitchen. Likewise, Alaina Capri's characters in *Good Morning . . . and Goodbye!* and *Common Law Cabin* are shrewish because they are unsatisfied in the bedroom.

If this unremitting bitchiness is an expression of sexual frustration, however, the women as embodiments are signs of sexual plentitude. The abundance of breasts, which are the hallmark of Meyer's body of work, connotes sexual desire; it is as though the breasts had become a sign of the women's sexual appetite. A slippage has occurred here. Breasts are generally a sign of women's desirability, a visually erotic part of the female body, evidenced by the fact that they are consumed *en masse* in topless bars. Although breasts certainly are erogenous zones, they rarely function as the center of women's sexual pleasure. To a certain degree, Meyer has relocated women's sexual pleasure from the vagina to the breasts. The filmmaker repeatedly voiced his refusal to enter the domain of hard-core films by filming genitalia or unsimulated sex. Although his later movies do include long shots of women's pubic area, even here women's breasts persist as a sign not only of women's desirability but also of their capacity for sexual pleasure. The large breasts of Meyer's heroines, rather than representing the audience's desire for more—bigger breasts and more of them for the viewer to consume—are representative of their bearers' desire for more: more sex. Thus, even as the large breasts of Meyer's heroines offer the promise of plentitude, they contain the threat of scarcity, functioning as a sign of their bearers' endlessly unfulfilled sexual desire.

Furthermore, these fantasies of abundance produced anxieties of impotence that are reflected in extradiegetic attempts to come to terms with the changes in female sexuality explored in Meyer's films. *Vixen!* marked a break-through for Meyer; it was released into general theaters where, presumably, both men and women would view it. Reviewers described seeing women in the audience for the film, and Meyer himself promoted the fantasy of actress Erica Gavin's being consumed by women as well as men.

However, the changes in female sexuality the women's presence in the theater suggested gave rise to equal parts pleasure and anxiety. As though to reassert the centrality of the male organ as the sole measure of sexual pleasure, several critics referred to Meyer's ability (or lack thereof) to rate on the "peter-meter." It seems that the possibility of sex without a penis was of particular concern; men's magazines in particular worked to contain the threat of lesbian pleasure. A *Penthouse* pictorial focusing on the lesbian sequence in *Vixen!* reassures readers that they are observing only a temporary dalliance: "Varietarian and voratious, Vixen takes full advantage of companion's momentary pique with stronger sex and perpetrates lusty bedroom bijinx" (Finborough n.d.). And an article in a 1969 issue of *True* "describes the shooting of the film's lesbian lovemaking scene and its traumatic effect on actress Erica Gavin" (Frasier 1990, 102).

SQUARE-JAWED AND SLACK-JAWED

Meyer's films pose sexual frustration as a significant problem, the resolution of which is central to the films' narratives. What is striking is that they should pose sexual frustration as a problem for women, given that the films were interpreted to have been made for male audiences in search of sexual thrills. Until the release of *Beyond the Valley of the Dolls,* Meyer's films were understood in relation to the framework of the stag film. Indeed, before *Vixen!* trespassed into general theaters in 1969, they played in theaters that were virtually off-limits to women. *Vixen!* was widely seen as a stag film. Complaining of its release to legitimate theaters, one reviewer pleaded for keeping Meyer's brand of soft-core a male-only phenomenon, describing it as a film of "stag dimension":

> the kind that played in off-Hollywood houses for off-Hollywood clientele . . . a picture that is clearly a vehicle for the voyeurs and a film made expressly to titillate the prurient senses. It is the kind of film that should be screened in the men's room with corresponding obscenities on the walls. (Edwards 1969, n.p.)

It is not surprising that Meyer's films should be concerned with the problem of sexual frustration and the search for sexual fulfillment, given that they were playing to what reviewers referred to as "slack-jawed" audiences or the "trench coat" crowd. According to the *Wall Street Journal,* "all the women costumed in plunging, bulging or bursting necklines could appeal only to 'the slack-jawed trade.' . . . [Meyer] admits that he deliberately appeals to 'the pant-and-drool crowd'" (Lovelady 1968, n.p.). What is surprising is that this search for sexual plenitude should be articulated so consistently through female characters.

In *Men, Women, and Chainsaws,* Carol Clover (1992) considers the genre of the slasher film and comes to the surprising conclusion that in these films, produced for and consumed largely by adolescent boys, the spectator is encouraged to identify with a female victim, the "final girl," who survives the slaughter. According to Clover, this identificatory position permits the spectator to engage in the character's abject terror, a position associated with femininity, not with manliness. Thus, although the genre itself is defined as masculine, identification with a female figure is necessary if the audience is to indulge in the pleasures of horror without threatening a gender system that attributes fear to femininity.

A similar set of identificatory processes is at work in Meyer's films, particularly *Vixen!* Here, however, rather than indulging in the pleasures of terror, which are gendered feminine, the spectator enters with the expectation of sexual pleasure. In posing sexual frustration—of all things—as a significant problem for the female character, Meyer's films simultaneously address the audience's fear of sexual scarcity while offering the illusion of sexual plenitude and disavowing anxieties about sexual frustration.

Throughout his early career, reviewers repeatedly complained of a disjunction in Meyer's films between his technical virtuosity and the ineptitude of his scripts and actresses. An unnamed director at Warner Bros. complained to the *Wall Street Journal,* "A lot of people are just plain confused by Russ Meyer, me included. . . . Everything he shoots is filled with all those incredibly overdeveloped babes prancing around without their clothes, right in the middle of what is some powerful drama and brilliant use of the camera. You just don't know how to react to that incongruity" (Lovelady). In fact, the tension between these two aspects of his films is at the center of their meaning.

Such responses miss the joke of Meyer's films. Even as he offers the viewer "more" in terms of narrative, he exposes that "more" as a fabrication, not the truth of female sexuality but a fantasy reflecting male desire. In casting women on the basis of their anatomy rather than their acting talent, he creates films in which verisimilitude is only precariously maintained, particularly the verisimilitude of the female characters. This is reinforced in the over-the-top scripts in which the characters spout lines that even trained actors would be challenged to make believable.

In contrast, Meyer offers the viewer physical thrills not through characterization but through his adept use of the medium. His camera work heightens the beauty of his busty women as well as the landscapes in which they cavort. His editing, combined with the musical scores, heightens the visceral pleasures of his films. Eric Schaeffer argues that exploitation films are organized around the necessity of spectacle, rather than narrative, in contradistinction to mainstream Hollywood. This "reliance on spectacle as an organizing principle forged their squalid style and resulted in an experience for the spectator that can best be described as delirium . . . [there was] no compelling need for them to be 'good'" (1999, 43). Meyer's technical skill brought the delirium of his filmic spectacles to new heights, thus further highlighting the films' shortcomings in terms of narrative and character development.

The newfound appreciation of Meyer's films on the part of feminists reflects changes in feminist politics since the 1960s and 1970s. Whereas feminism was once dominated by a rhetoric of abuse in which male sexual fantasies were read as built on the subordination of women, the advent of queer theory has opened up feminism to the possibilities of women's own sexual pleasures. And if Meyer's films ultimately connote scarcity for male audiences, they suggest plentitude for women, who are not as concerned with the mysteries of their own desires and more than ready, by now, to satisfy them fully.

WORKS CITED

Anonymous. 1999. "The Bitch List: More than a Few of Our Favorite Things," *Bitch: Feminist Response to Pop Culture* 3: 1 (April 30), 35.

Clover, Carol J. 1992. *Men, Women, and Chain Saws: Gender in the Modern Horror Film*. Princeton, NJ: Princeton University Press.

Edwards, Nadine. 1969. "Russ Meyer's *Vixen* Strictly Stag Film," *Hollywood Citizen News* (May 5). *Vixen!* production file, Margaret Herrick Library, Academy of Motion Picture Arts and Sciences, Beverly Hills.

Ehrenreich, Barbara, Elizabeth Hess, and Gloria Jacobs. 1986. *Re-Making Love: The Feminization of Sex*. New York: Doubleday Anchor.

Finborough, Roger. n.d. "The Nudes: Part VI," *Penthouse*. Russ Meyer biography file, Margaret Herrick Library, Academy of Motion Picture Arts and Sciences, Beverly Hills.

Frasier, David K. 1990. *Russ Meyer: The Life and Films*. Jefferson, NC: McFarland & Co.

Kinsey, Alfred et al. 1953. *Sexual Behavior in the Human Female*. Philadelphia: Saunders.

Lovelady, Steven M. 1968. "King Leer: Top Nudie Film-maker Russ Meyer Struggles to Outshock Big Studios," *Wall Street Journal* (April 24). Russ Meyer biography file, Margaret Herrick Library, Academy of Motion Picture Arts and Sciences, Beverly Hills.

Masters, William H. and Virginia E. Johnson. 1966. *Human Sexual Response*. Boston: Little, Brown.

Muller, Eddie and Daniel Faris. 1996. *Grindhouse: The Forbidden World of 'Adults Only' Cinema*. New York: St. Martin's Griffin.

Murf. 1966. "Faster, Pussycat! Kill! Kill!," *Variety* (February 7). *Faster, Pussycat! Kill! Kill!* production file, Margaret Herrick Library, Academy of Motion Picture Arts and Sciences, Beverly Hills.

Prelutsky, Burt. 1969. "King Leer," *Los Angeles Times West* (June 8). Russ Meyer biography file, Margaret Herrick Library, Academy of Motion Picture Arts and Sciences, Beverly Hills.

Rich, B. Ruby. 1995. "What's New Pussycat?," *Village Voice* (January 17). *Faster, Pussycat! Kill! Kill!* production file, Margaret Herrick Library, Academy of Motion Picture Arts and Sciences, Beverly Hills.

Schaefer, Eric. 1999. *"Bold! Daring! Shocking! True!": A History of Exploitation Films, 1919–1959*. Durham, NC: Duke University Press.

Susann, Jacqueline. 1966. *Valley of the Dolls: A Novel*. New York: B. Geis Associates.

Thomas, Kevin. n.d. "King of the Nudies in Biggest Film Caper Yet." Russ Meyer biography file, Margaret Herrick Library, Academy of Motion Picture Arts and Sciences, Beverly Hills.

Verrill, Addison. 1976. "Preposterous Sex Dimensions, and Russ Meyer's Hang-ups," *Variety* (November 10). Russ Meyer biography file, Margaret Herrick Library, Academy of Motion Picture Arts and Sciences, Beverly Hills.

Wilson, Ra Nae. 1996. "Linda Perry: Struggling to the Top," *ROCKRGRL* 11 (November 30), 8.

Williams, Linda. 1989. *Hard Core: Power, Pleasure, and the 'Frenzy of the Visible.'* Berkeley: University of California Press.

FIGURE 10. Eric Portman (1903–1969) as Lieutenant Hirth in *Forty-Ninth Parallel* (Michael Powell, Ortus/Columbia, 1941). "Portman so impressed his more eminent costars with the intensity of his performance that they began a campaign to give him costar billing." The director notes that the performance exuded religious fanatacism. (Frame enlargement)

CHAPTER TEN

Wanted for Murder:
The Strange Case of Eric Portman

TONY WILLIAMS

In part because they were able to transport lucrative star careers to Holly-wood, a significant number of British actors have become well known in con-temporary cinema, particularly as villains. George Sanders, Peter Cushing, Donald Pleasence, James Mason, Anthony Hopkins, Ian McKellen, Alan Rickman, Richard E. Grant, Tim Roth, and Gary Oldman are but a small number of the legion of "bad Brits" who recognizably, even delightfully, inhabit the modern screen. As many again actors of lesser repute—meticu-lously trained and brilliant in their method—have filled the screen with per-formances that grip viewers, among them Robert Hardy, Alan Badel, Ernest Clark, Peter Copley, Bernard Miles, Niall MacGinnis, and Ray McAnally. But only some of these actors established careers as rich and strange as the subject of this chapter.

Although largely forgotten today, the name of Eric Portman (1903–1969) figured prominently in 1940s and 1950s British cinema. Ken-neth Tynan (1950) once pointed out that, unlike a contemporary screen actor such as Jack Hawkins, Portman could elicit respect from both the theatrical

I wish to thank Steve Crook, David Del Valle, Alan Kibble, Richard Pope, and Chris Rolph for the many insights they have provided me with for this piece.

and cinematic worlds rather than just one. In this respect, he resembled Laurence Olivier. But, although having a more prolific screen career, Portman never reached the heights of this eminent figure. Instead, he played a variety of leading and subordinate character roles throughout his career. Despite the excellent quality of his performances, he never achieved the star status associated with actors such as Olivier or Vivien Leigh who made successful, celebrated crossovers from theater to film. This Yorkshire-born actor of second generation Italian descent (Rolph 2001) would always gain good notices by his accomplished acting in whatever capacity he performed, and his character roles toward the end of his career resembled the type of quality performances Margaret Leighton often brought to memorable productions such as John Ford's *7 Women* (1966) or Joseph Losey's *The Go-Between* (1970) and forgettable ones such as *Zee and Co.*, *Lady Caroline Lamb* (both 1972), *A Bequest to the Nation* (1973), and *From Beyond the Grave* (1973). Like Portman, Leighton was also associated both personally and professionally with the playwright Terence Rattigan and she starred opposite Portman in the London and New York stage productions of Rattigan's *Separate Tables*.

Portman's theatrical stature reached its height with dual portrayals in that play: the disgraced, violently abrasive former Labour politician-turned-journalist John Malcolm and the pathetic Major Pollock. The play opened in London on September 22, 1954, and on Broadway on October 25, 1956, with Portman repeating his acclaimed performance. This latter run probably led to the actor's U.S. television appearances in "A Double Life" on "The Alcoa Hour" (1957), "The Hero" episode of "Alfred Hitchcock Presents" and "The Pedigree Sheet" episode of "The Naked City" (both 1960), as well as his playing Dr. Manette in "A Tale of Two Cities" (1958) and Fagin in "Oliver Twist" (1959). Portman had earlier created the role of that archetypal symbol of British repression and thwarted personality, Arthur Crocker-Harris in *The Browning Version*, as well as Arthur Gosport in *Harlequinade*. These plays formed the basis of Terence Rattigan's double-header, *Playbill*, which opened at London's Phoenix Theatre in 1948. Portman also played Sydney Carton in a 1951 BBC radio production of *A Tale of Two Cities*, based on a 1935 collaborative theatrical adaptation by Rattigan and John Gielgud, which was never performed at the time (Darlow 2000, 95–98, 115 n.7).

However, the actor was no stranger to Hollywood. He had previously appeared in the Errol Flynn–Warner Bros. swashbuckler *The Prince and the Pauper* (1937) in a heavily disguised character role as the First Lord. But, in his own words, he "walked out on Hollywood" seeking a "range of characters that prevents one from becoming stale and mannered" (McFarlane 1997, 456). A few years later, Michael Powell cast him in the leading role of the Nazi submarine commander Lieutenant Hirth in *Forty-Ninth Parallel* (1941), as Yorkshire copilot Tom Earnshaw in *One of Our Aircraft Is Missing* (1942) and, most significantly, as the aberrant "Glueman" Thomas Colpepper JP in *A Canterbury Tale* (1944). During the late 1940s, Portman appeared in a succession of British films noir leading the *Picturegoer Annual* of 1949 to remark that the actor "seems doomed to play sinister, psychopathic characters" (Macnab 2000, 174). Another contemporary *Picturegoer* review of Portman's performance in *The Spider and the Fly* (1949) found defining the exact nature of the actor's star persona difficult. "He remains one of the problem figures of British pictures, regularly doing work of distinction in them, never quite belonging to them" (McFarlane, 455).

Despite Portman's role in *The Colditz Story* (1955) as the gentlemanly Colonel Richmond, who congratulates his fellow officer British P.O.W.s on the number of escapes from the notorious German prison camp and anticipates more "home runs," the most recent reference to this actor occurs in Raymond Durgnat's taxonomic "Some Lines of Inquiry into Post-War British Crimes" in the two-paragraph section, "Middle-Class Noir II: The Portman Murders" (1997, 92–93). Noting Portman's diversity of roles up to 1945, Durgnat comments that films such as *Wanted for Murder* (1946), *Dear Murderer* (1947), and *Daybreak* (1947) exhibit confusion by evoking "crimes passionnels, in evolving sexual jealousy, but they smack even more strongly of offended vanity (egomania), or cold pathology, which are hardly 'passionate,' in the usual sense of loving attachment to an individual" (92). The key to Portman's obsessional acting persona during this period may lie in certain British cultural codes of behavior that evoke a "return of the repressed" performative response, the peculiarly mannered British coldness that Durgnat would find "pathological." Although Robert Murphy (1992, 186–87) suggests that Portman's character in *A Canterbury Tale* may have influenced his relatively prolific sinister roles in the "morbid burrowings" of postwar British cinematic film noir, he limits his analysis to a particular period rather than considering other broader explanations.

Portman's professional and personal relationship with Terence Rattigan may provide more fulsome illumination. Although Portman achieved cinematic and theatrical acclaim long before his association with Rattigan, he achieved his most distinctive fame as a result of his performances in the playwright's work. Long neglected as "old school" in the post–*Look Back in Anger* Angry Young Man theatrical revolution, Rattigan's plays are now gaining long-overdue recognition for their insights about the dangerous behavioral aspects of British middle-class society. Sir Peter Hall recognized this in his 1979 diaries:

> Perhaps any homosexual dramatist who, during a time of secrecy and blackmail, presented his own emotional life in his work as if he were a woman, suffered

some terrible disability. . . . I think the problem with Rattigan was that even if he had the opportunity for frankness, his whole repressed class background, the stiff upper lip of Harrow, would have made it impossible for him. Deception and restraint are at the heart of that kind of Englishman. I suppose it's at the heart of men, heterosexual as I am. (Darlow, 474)

Darlow also comments that "it is the deception and restraint which Sir Peter Hall finds at the heart of himself as much as at the heart of Rattigan that gives the plays their enduring resonance with English audiences" (474). But the same may be said of the emotionalism and intensity at the heart of many of Portman's interesting performances. Several of these qualify him as an auteur of negativity and an icon of darkness, especially if we place Portman within the specific cultural context of repressive British social life. Whether we see the "actor as auteur," as Patrick McGilligan (1982) saw James Cagney, or recall Richard Dyer's (1979) concept of stars embodying the cultural contradictions of a particular era, the fact remains that Portman often exhibits an intense form of authorship situated within certain social and historical parameters.

Both Rattigan and Portman were homosexual, a fact that has led several critics to accuse the playwright of committing a form of dramatic transvestism by conceiving his female characters as disguised gays. Indeed, Rattigan's original conception of Major Pollock's offense was not touching up females in the darkened auditorium of the cinema but homosexual importuning. When *Separate Tables* moved to New York, the playwright wished to restore his original version but Portman finally talked him out of it. According to Darlow (who superbly depicts the dark, repressive nature of 1950s British society well before the legalization of homosexuality in the 1960s), Portman refused to play the Major as a homosexual because he "regarded his sexuality as an entirely private matter between himself and those closest to him" (323). Ironically, it would not be until the actor's last screen appearance in *Deadfall* (1968) that he came out of the closet performatively. Rattigan believed that the hotel guests' final acceptance of the Major in the play would be more affirmative if they recognized a character very different from themselves. However, American impresario Bob Whitehead argued that by changing the nature of the Major's offense, Rattigan would diminish the universality of the message about man's inhumanity to man and make the play much smaller in scope.

Rattigan stated in the *New York Times* that he wanted to avoid a thesis drama. But both he and Portman were entirely aware of the other implications of a play they collaborated on under the guise of a plea for the understanding of everyone. Portman's comments in *The Stage* are instructive here:

I believe that Rattigan is helping to open up fresh paths for the treatment on the stage of all sorts of topics and emotions that, so far, have not been allowed in our theatre. But, like any expert and intelligent man of the theatre who wishes to command an audience, he never chooses the wrong psychological moment or goes beyond the capacity of his audience's understanding. (Young 1986, 136)

None of Portman's films noir opens the possibility of treating "all sorts of topics and emotions that, so far, have not been allowed." They are more attuned to the destructive aspects of human personality resulting from a social conditioning that stifles any opportunity for personal development and ultimate salvation. In many ways, the Portman star persona resembles Robin Wood's analysis of Alfred Hitchcock's gallery of "murderous gays" in terms of its invitation to understand the "aberrant" activities of such individuals as the result of a repressively patriarchal culture based on homophobia, misogyny, and the fear of bisexuality. Several of Portman's performances demonstrate a neurotic obsessiveness. This may result from a personal expression of dramatic authorship involving a reaction to a strictly regimented society. As Wood points out, "Neurosis, by definition, damages the psyche, stunting its free growth, its blossoming; yet, it must also be read as an instinctual rebellion against the sexual and generic regulation of our culture" (1986, 355).

Although elements of neurotic obsessiveness appear in some of Portman's early British screen performances such as *Hyde Park Corner* (1935), the Rattigan connection seems very important to the star persona of Eric Portman, a factor Kenneth Tynan noted concerning the actor's roles in *Harlequinade* and *Separate Tables*. "I wasn't mad about 'Harlequinade' but I said that in 'The Browning Version,' Mr. Portman had Rattigan 'right behind him'—i.e. supporting his talents to the hilt" (Tynan, 1994, 313). Tynan had earlier commented in *Playbill* about Portman's association with "the vampirical school of acting. . . . A vampirical actor is one who sucks the blood from every scene he plays in as soon as he appears, and makes it seem cold, contrived, and dissected" (1950, 107). This is an interesting recognition of both Portman's formal style of acting and its dangerous overtones in his noir appearances. Apparently playwright and actor knew each other long before they began working together. Darlow (2000, 150) mentions that Portman recommended Jack Watling for the role of a young Royal Air Force bomber pilot in Rattigan's 1942 play *Flare Path*. Ironically, Rattigan offered the role of Sir Robert Morton in *The Browning Version* to Portman in 1946 who, like John Gielgud, turned it down. Both playwright and actor were very much associated with the British theatrical gay mafia associated with Hugh "Binkie"

Beaumont, which drew unwelcome Cold War homophobic attention from many in the 1950s (Darlow, 321). We must remember that J. Edgar Hoover and the C.I.A. were incensed about British blindness toward the spying activities of gay diplomat Guy Burgess who defected to Moscow with Donald Maclean during the early part of the decade.

Although Portman had appeared in several British films during the 1930s—*Abdul the Damned, Maria Marten, or The Murder in the Red Barn* (both 1935), *Hearts of Humanity, The Crimes of Stephen Hawke, The Cardinal* (all 1936), *The Singing Marine,* and *Moonlight Sonata* (both 1937)—it was not until his leading performance as Lieutenant Hirth in *Forty-Ninth Parallel* that he attracted attention, holding his own against cinematic and theatrical heavyweights such as Laurence Olivier, Leslie Howard, Raymond Massey, and Anton Walbrook. His career then grew in significance until he began to be associated with certain roles in the British film noir movement of the 1940s. This association was not entirely exclusive because the actor varied his roles during wartime and afterward. Portman's Charlie Forbes in *Millions Like Us* (1943), a working-class Yorkshire foreman intelligently skeptical of the "People's War" egalitarian philosophy, represents one of his best performances as a level-headed character, a part he initially protested against by returning to his home town of Halifax and getting drunk (McFarlane, 225). This character not only represented the actor's Yorkshire roots but also embodied a variation of the Yorkshire foreman role he had played in the theatrical production of *Jeannie.* Seeing that play, Michael Powell noted characteristics that would also typify the actor's later screen roles even if they were not used to portray sympathetic characters. "Eric Portman was particularly good at showing, without words, the inner workings of this simple, intelligent, and practical man" (1986, 358). His roles as Yorkshire copilot Tom Earnshaw, sailor James Hobson, District Commissioner Randall, and barrister Sir John Dearing in *One of Our Aircraft Is Missing, We Dive at Dawn* (1943), *Men of Two Worlds* (1946), and *The Blind Goddess* (1948) are also distinctive. But his most intense and (creatively neurotic) wartime and postwar roles occur in *Forty-Ninth Parallel, A Canterbury Tale, Great Day* (1945), *Wanted for Murder, The Mark of Cain* (1947), *Dear Murderer, Daybreak, Corridor of Mirrors* (1948), and *The Spider and the Fly,* all of which were made within a short period and represent his most significant work within the decade.

Portman's characters represent versions of a neurotic personality trapped within social conventions and unable to break away entirely. Reaction to such restraints results in obsessional and violent patterns of behavior in many ways linked with Rattigan's dramatic explorations of individual repression within the context of a rigidly British class culture hostile toward any behavioral challenge to the status quo. The Rattigan influence may not be a direct one on Portman as an auteur of negativity. But, insofar as the work of both playwright and actor reflect certain personally destructive aspects of British culture—involving the repression of ideologically unacceptable forms of human desire—their association appears highly significant.

Despite occasional references in Kenneth Tynan's reviews and the conflicting opinions of those who worked with him such as Betty Box, George Cole, Dulcie Gray, and Bill Owen (McFarlane, 86, 133, 173, 448), no biography has ever been published about Eric Portman. The diaries of British *Carry On* comedian Kenneth Williams contain a few scattered references. His December 8, 1969 entry mentions the actor's death and the fact that he "had been kind to me" (1994, 363), while his March 20, 1982 references refer to the death of Alan Badel whom Williams comments on as being "much in the same tradition as Eric Portman—both superb romantic actors, yet both capable of an extraordinary tour de force and character ability" (650). According to Steve Crook, potential biographers stumbled on the fact that nobody who knew Portman personally had a good word to say about him. Kieren Tunney's report about a meeting between a drunken and abusive Portman and the legendary Tallulah Bankhead is one such appalling example (1972, 183–208).

Eric Portman won the role of Lieutenant Hirth in *Forty-Ninth Parallel* because Michael Powell's favorite actor Esmond Knight had joined the Royal Navy, although with regard to star quality he was "comparatively unknown" (Powell 1986, 358) at the time. Despite personal difficulties with Powell's directing, Portman so impressed his more eminent costars with the intensity of his performance that they began a campaign to give him costar billing. According to Powell, Portman's performance as Lieutenant Hirth exhibited overtones of religious fanaticism especially when "he poured out his long Hitler tirades with the conviction and sincerity of an acolyte serving an archbishop" (359). Emeric Pressburger and Rodney Ackland's screenplay certainly depicts a character who is not only obsessively sincere in his beliefs but also one who may suffer repressed feelings of male insecurity. This appears several times in the film, not only in the frequent arguments over leadership and strategy that Hirth has with Raymond Lovell's Lieutenant Kuhnecker (who has preceded him in the Nazi party) but also in his asceticism and "deep religious sincerity" (359). Powell also mentions that this quality is "quite frightening," ironically anticipating the description that Portman's Commodore Wolfgang Schrepke (a mellower and older version of Hirth) would use against the puritanical Cold War warrior played by Richard Widmark in the closing scenes of *The Bedford Incident* (1965). Despite Hirth's *ubermensch* persona, Portman's acting often seems to suggest that much more lies beneath the authoritarian surface. Although battling Powell throughout the entire production, Portman became impressed by Pressburger's dialogue and eventually became the director's "greatest trumpeter"

(38) during postproduction. Portman reprised his fanatical Nazi role in Lance Comfort's *Squadron Leader X* (1942) for which Pressburger wrote the original story (Macdonald 1994, 196).

Eventually, Portman began liking working with Powell so much that he accepted the low-key role of Tom Earnshaw in *One of Our Aircraft Is Missing* despite its not having "any opportunity for his genius." Had he won the leading role in *The Life and Death of Colonel Blimp* (1943), the film would have been much darker than it finally became particularly in terms of the morbid obsessiveness the actor could have brought to Candy's *Vertigo*-like search for the eternal woman (Macdonald, 219), a trait that also appears in *Corridor of Mirrors*. Macdonald notes that Portman "brought the same crusading intensity to the part of Colpepper [in *A Canterbury Tale*] as he had to Hirth in *Forty-Ninth Parallel*" (238). Ironically Roger Livesey, who played the title role in *The Life and Death of Colonel Blimp*, had refused the role (Powell 1986, 440), which led to Portman's "extraordinarily perceptive performance" (441). Although Powell could retain none of the sentimentality Livesey might have given to Colpepper, he gained in other ways with the darker persona of Portman. "His Colpepper had the head of a medieval ascetic, which could quite easily have been torn out of a monkish manuscript" (441). When Powell later remembers the actors he worked with he describes Roger Livesey as a "Christian soldier" and Portman as "a devil" (Powell 1992, 477).

Portman's performance as Colpepper is complex and extraordinary in many ways. As a celibate bachelor living at home with his mother, he is a figure of order by day in his capacity as magistrate and a dark symbol of disorder at night in his other persona as the Glueman. This mysterious figure uses the cover of darkness to pour glue over women's hair to protect his audiences of bored servicemen attending his local history lectures from temptation by the "weaker sex." Not only does Colpepper symbolically resemble a serial killer in his methods but the character also anticipates those dark creative monsters in Powell's other films such as *The Red Shoes* (1948) and *Peeping Tom* (1960). Macdonald also notes that the photographer Mark Lewis (Karlheinz Böhm) of *Peeping Tom* "bears a passing resemblance . . . to Emeric's earlier 'mass-murderer pot-boiler,' *Wanted for Murder*" (382). Also coscripted by Rodney Ackland, this 1946 production casts Portman as another celibate bachelor living with his mother, but now engaged in the more deadly creative act of murdering his female victims. Portman's character in *Wanted,* along with Hirth, Colpepper, Lermontov in *The Red Shoes* (Anton Walbrook), and Mark Lewis are "all celibate males who devote themselves exclusively to their artistic goals by dominating others" (Williams 2000, 67). *Wanted for Murder* is significant because it casts Portman as a serial killer who has no control over his actions due to the genes left to him by his hangman father. The role represents an extension of Portman's earlier performance as Edward Chester in *Hyde Park Corner*, a neurotic character also doomed by an ancestral curse.

Portman's involvement in British film noir has certain historical associations. Postwar British society exhibited several dislocating social tensions, most notably associated with the problems of returning servicemen adjusting to civilian life and the disturbing activities of serial killers such as Neville Heath and John George Haigh. Many of these characters "used dubious wartime heroic identities for their murderous activities" (Williams, 113). Several of Portman's maladjusted male characters in postwar cinema are really symbolic scapegoat figures for a syndrome of male trauma that remained deliberately denied for many years (Williams 1999, 267–68, n23). This began with Portman's role as Captain Ellis in *Great Day*. His disturbed World War I veteran hero cannot settle down to civilian life and resents his more active wife and daughter who symbolize the temporarily significant roles of women in this era. Ellis is a traumatically suicidal character who exhibits a masochistic desire to be caught and punished, as revealed by his risk-taking theft in an English pub where he has no chance of succeeding (not unlike the real-life activities of Heath and Haigh). Other Portman characters represent significant variations on this traumatically disturbed male phenomenon. *Dear Murderer, Daybreak, Corridor of Mirrors*, and *The Mark of Cain* all present Portman as "a victimized male suffering from traumatic insecurity leading to murderous activities. . . . Despite the different nature of these films, it is hard not to see in them indirect allusions to suspicions of returning veterans concerning both the new independent roles and fidelity of wives while they were away in battle" (Williams 1999, 259).

Furthermore, because Portman's intended victim in *Dear Murderer* and *Daybreak* is Maxwell Reed, it is hard not to see dark elements of repressed homoerotic desire in the relationship between the two men. Portman's dominating attitude toward his murder victim played by Dennis Price in the opening sequence of *Dear Murderer* contains more emotionally seductive overtones than later scenes between him and Greta Gynt in the rest of the film. The same feature occurs in the homosocial relationship between Portman's policeman and Guy Rolfe's thief in Robert Hamer's *The Spider and the Fly*. Although inheritance and property figure strongly in *The Mark of Cain* as they do in *Blanche Fury* (1947), Durgnat notes the irony behind Portman's activities in the former film. "To win Sally Gray, he poisons his manly brother (Guy Rolfe), and this time frames her, inadvertently, but gets sussed out by another virile admirer (Dermot Walsh). In *Corridor of Mirrors*, he's also goaded by his possessive housekeeper (and malignant mother-figure?) Barbara Mullen" (1997, 92–93). Durgnat's last comment certainly notes the quasi-Hitchcockian associations that also surround Portman's performances in *A Canterbury Tale* and *Wanted for Murder*. Both disturbed characters, still living with their mothers, anticipate Norman Bates.

These inflections are significant enough. But fascinating links are found between the behavioral traits of Rattigan's characters and Portman's dark cinematic incarnations. Both are equally products and victims of the same crippled and rigid social structures in British society, although Portman's characters express more aberrant and darker overtones. For example, although he did not play in the stage production of Rattigan's *The Deep Blue Sea* (1952), he did appear in the role of Miller in the 1955 film version. Formerly a doctor, Miller has been struck off the register for some offense, the nature of which is never disclosed in either the stage or film version. Based on the suicide of Rattigan's former lover Kenneth Morgan, *The Deep Blue Sea* in first draft was a homosexual version, which contains the reference that Miller's professional ostracism resulted from his sexual preferences. "Some people are born different to others and it's no good pretending that that makes them wicked and striking them off registers just because of that" (Darlow, 279). However, Portman's acting in the film version and his unsentimental sympathy toward the plight of Vivien Leigh's abandoned character Hester contain subtle resonances that speak for themselves. For Bertram A. Young, the implications are quite clear that "Rattigan meant [Miller] to be a homosexual" (1986, 110).

The recently published uncensored version of Kenneth Tynan's diaries contains an interesting entry that sheds light on the roots of the obsessional aspects of Eric Portman as person and performer. Tynan mentions knowing "this ferocious, self-loathing, sporadically brilliant actor in the fifties" (Lahr 2001, 241) when he began working on a biography he never completed. One evening Tynan and his first wife visited the actor in his Chelsea apartment where he lived alone with his Irish valet. As in Tunney's account of the Tallulah Bankhead incident, the evening began well until Portman confided that he was not only born in the same town as the late 1940s mass murderer and necrophiliac John Reginald Christie, but also knew him as a boy. After providing Tynan with this revealing anecdote, Portman became paranoid and accused the critic of being responsible for the recent arrest of John Gielgud for importuning and planning "to do the same to me" (241). The actor then became violent and *pounced* toward the Tynans forcing them to seek refuge in his bedroom. Portman's Irish valet later smuggled the Tynans out and apologized for his master's behavior. "He's always like that. Every weekend we go down to his cottage in Cornwall. He gets tight and the first thing he does is smash every mirror in the house. I have to replace them every Monday morning. Good-night, sir" (242).

This anecdote is interesting for several reasons. Not only does it shed light on the paranoia felt by a homosexual living within a repressive British society of the type depicted in Basil Dearden's *Victim* (1961) long before reform of the homosexual laws, but it also reveals an actor flirting with a dark example of the "outsider" figure he often portrayed in British film noir. Portman never lived to play John Reginald Christie on screen. Richard Attenborough performed this role in *10 Rillington Place* (1971) three years after Portman's death. We should also remember that John Gielgud's arrest for indecency was no isolated incident but the result of a British witch-hunt against prominent gays in society (Croall 2001, 382–87). Like Dirk Bogarde's character in *Victim,* Portman must also have feared blackmail. Significantly, Portman's Cornwall cottage was also the place the actor felt free enough to engage in his "illegal" activities with trusted acquaintances. Tynan's reference also explains many things about the actor's fascination in playing tormented, obsessional characters during his noir period. These characters not only represent a psychotic obsessiveness within the actor's "self-loathing" persona but also represent a dark incarnation of similar outlaw figures in postwar British society who murderously reacted against rigid social and gender constraints in ways similar to Robin Wood's definition of Hitchcock's "murderous gays."

Portman's later screen roles were sparse. But as well as his climactic performance in *Deadfall, The Naked Edge* (1961), *Freud* (1962), *West 11* (1963), and *The Whisperers* (1966) are worthy of mention as depicting aspects of Portman's cinematic dark persona. His Jeremy Clay in *The Naked Edge* represents a darker version of both Dr. Miller from *The Deep Blue Sea* (1955) and Colpepper in *A Canterbury Tale.* Confronted by Gary Cooper's Radcliffe, Clay refers to the fact that he is a disbarred lawyer and "intellectual Peeping Tom." In many ways, Clay also embodies Graham Greene's "Greeneland" concept of the seedy aspects of a destructive British culture because in addition to being an unsuccessful thief and murderer he is also a lover and distributor of pornography. Like Miller, his professional disgrace resulted in the downwardly mobile status of "handyman" stealing bottles of whisky to indulge his taste for "more exotic vices." About to fake Mrs. Radcliffe's suicide during the climactic scenes of the film, he acts obsessively like a high priest at a sacrificial ritual, uttering lines that evoke the fanaticism and repressed sexuality of his Hirth and Colpepper characters. "Oh Lord! I wonder if women get naked when they kill themselves this way." These lines also evoke a prayer to a dark deity embodying Clay's obsessional desires.

As Dr. Theodore Meynart in John Huston's *Freud,* Portman's opening appearance as an authoritarian professional fully confident of his medical conservatism offers contrasts with his last scene in the film, which sees him dying, conscious of the fact that his whole career and opposition to the theories of the young Freud were all based on lies. An additional poignancy of this scene lies in the tragic picture of a man who knows that his entire life has been based on deliberate repression resulting in tragic waste. This role represents the first of the failed father figure roles he would develop in both *The Whisperers* and *Deadfall.* In *West 11,* Portman portrays a more manipulative and sinister version of the false military persona adopted by Major Pollock in *Separate Tables.*

His Captain Richard Dyce embodies a composite of both Pollock and the violent persona of the Malcolm character in the first part of Rattigan's play. Mysteriously dependent on another dominant mother figure, Aunt Mildred
(Marie Ney), dominating the "whining and snivelling moron" Jacko (Peter
Reynolds) possibly in some sexually ambiguous manner, and using and abus-
ing women such as Diana Dors's Georgia, Dyce enlists the services of failed
"angry young man" and emotional leper Joe (Alfred Lynch) to murder Aunt
Mildred for her money. Despite Dyce's "officer and a gentleman" persona,
Portman's character is a sadistic and dangerous manipulator. In *The Whisper-
ers* he plays Archie, the wastrel husband of Edith Evans. Having abandoned
both wife and son years before, he now reluctantly returns to their dilapidated
apartment. The character reflects the dark side of the Yorkshireman persona
Portman had previously used in films such as *One of Our Aircraft Is Missing,
We Dive at Dawn, Millions Like Us, His Excellency* (1952), and *The Good Companions* (1957). In *Whisperers*, it is clear that in choosing Archie, Edith
Evans's character had married beneath her social status. Indeed, as Archie
exploits the pathetic figure of a middle-aged prostitute (Claire Kelly) and
takes the money and runs away from a criminal gang, he also embodies a dark
working-class version of his Clay and Dysart characters from *The Naked Edge*
and *West 11*. Having worked with Portman on stage as early as 1931, Edith
Evans was very familiar with the actor's private life and requested Bryan
Forbes "to add a line to indicate that she married slightly beneath her" (Forbes
1977, 256). Both actors admired each other professionally. But Portman also
confessed to Forbes "with more bluntness . . . that there were aspects of her
offstage personality that grated on him." He then requested that the director
"somehow insert an extra line which would indicate she married a much
younger man" (256). This request uncannily echoes some of Portman's noir
performances where he is clearly dominated by an older mother figure. Forbes
succinctly comments that, "I kept both confidences to myself, duly made the
amendments and neither of them ever referred to it again" (256).

According to Darlow (274), Bryan Forbes had read the first (that is,
homosexual) draft of *The Deep Blue Sea* and knew both Portman and Rattigan. It is not surprising, then, that the actor gave his last great performances
in films Forbes directed. *Deadfall* represents his cinematic swan song. Written and directed by Forbes, this complicated and often-pretentious film gave
Portman one of his most challenging roles. Portraying the openly homosexual Richard Moreau, Portman lives in an ambiguous relationship with his
much younger wife, Fe (Giovanna Ralli). Moreau is a dark father figure expert
at "playing games with other people." Michael Caine's Henry Clarke becomes
the latest in a long line of young protégés Moreau has used and abused
throughout most of his career as a professional thief. Henry cannot understand why Fe has remained with her older husband for more than six years

when she knows he is homosexual. Ultimately he discovers that Fe is actually Moreau's daughter, a fact of which she is ignorant and the revelation of which produces the climax of the film. A close-up on her face registers both her understanding why she has a close personal bond with him and can never leave him and a suggestion of actual incest in their relationship. The film ends with Henry shot during a robbery attempt and Moreau committing suicide as he looks at a photo of the wartime lover he betrayed, as well as with Moreau's last lover (yet another substitute for his betrayed lover) waiting outside the churchyard as the police lead Fe away for questioning. Moreau's obsessionally destructive repetitive-compulsive tendencies finally end but not without the physical and spiritual desolation of those closest to him.

Deadfall is Portman's last screen testament to his significant acting roles as an auteur of negativity and icon of darkness within British cinema. As John Caughie (1981) notes, authorship is a complex process resulting from many factors, involving cultural, social, industrial, and historical issues, as well as personal ones. Portman's particular form of screen authorship owes much to the formative role played by a particular repressive British culture—one understood at the same time by Terence Rattigan in many of his plays—as well as to aspects of personality and social context now lost to us. If his obsessional and distinctive type of acting is attractive today, we should remember its origins in a social structure that thwarted "different" personal expression. The same cultural repressions that gave rise to Eric Portman's dark performances also brought about the alcoholism that, unleashing the destructive demons in this talented figure's soul, ultimately led to his death.

Although Eric Portman shares with many other actors a career centered on the performance of "evil," onstage and onscreen, his is in some ways an especially illuminating case. Because in many of his films he portrayed neurotically disturbed characters who had associations with the dark side of his own character, and because his performances often exhibit "intense" tendencies that can be seen as both creative and destructive—his stage, film, and television performances revealing the former tendency while certain significant factors we know about his personal life graphically illustrating the latter—examining his work makes it possible to see with new light how the device of "Othering" helped audiences classify and appreciate his work. Much of our filmgoing "experience" of evil may work in much the same way. "Othering" often ignores relevant social and cultural factors existing within the dark side of many societies, which can shed significant light on why people behave as they do, in and out of character. In Portman's fascinating case, it helps to remember that the actor belonged to a particularly repressive phase of early-twentieth-century British society in which many types of behavior now acceptable were regarded as both taboo and criminal. Portman was a product of a particular social structure that deemed lifestyles such as his "evil" and "nefarious." This tension between the actor's own personality and a society condemning it as illegal may explain the particular roots of the performances he delivered throughout his brilliant career.

WORKS CITED

Caughie, John. 1981. *Theories of Authorship.* London: British Film Institute Publishing.

Croall, Jonathan. 2000. *Gielgud: A Theatrical Life 1904–2000.* London: Methuen.

Darlow, Michael. 2000. *Terence Rattigan: The Man and His Work.* London: Quartet Books.

Durgnat, Raymond. 1997. "Some Lines of Inquiry into Post-War British Crimes." In Robert Murphy, ed. *The British Cinema Book.* London: British Film Institute Publishing, 90–103.

Dyer, Richard. 1979. *Stars.* London: British Film Institute Publishing.

Forbes, Bryan. 1977. *Dame Edith Evans.* Boston: Little, Brown.

Lahr, John, ed. 2001. *The Diaries of Kenneth Tynan.* London: Bloomsbury.

Macdonald, Kevin. 1994. *Emeric Pressburger: The Life and Death of a Screenwriter.* London: Faber and Faber.

Macnab, Geoffrey. 2000. *Searching for Stars: Rethinking British Cinema.* London: Cassell.

McFarlane, Brian. 1997. *An Autobiography of British Cinema: As Told by the Filmmakers and Actors Who Made It.* London: Methuen.

McGilligan, Patrick. 1982. *James Cagney: The Actor as Auteur.* San Diego: A.S. Barnes.

Murphy, Robert. 1992. *Realism and Tinsel: Cinema and Society in Britian 1939–1949.* London: Routledge.

Powell, Michael. 1986. *A Life in Movies.* New York: Alfred A. Knopf.

———. 1992. *Million Dollar Movie.* London: Heinemann.

Rolph, Chris. 2001. Personal e-mail communication (October 9).

Tunney, Kieren. 1972. *Tallulah—Darling of the Gods.* London: Secker & Warburg.

Tynan, Kenneth. 1950. *He that Plays the King.* New York: Longman's Green and Company.

———. 1994. *Letters,* ed. Kathleen Tynan. New York: Random House.

Williams, Kenneth. 1994. *The Kenneth Williams Diaries,* ed. Russell Davies. London: Harper Collins.

Williams, Tony. 1999. "British Film Noir." In Alain Silver and James Ursini, eds. *Film Noir Reader 2.* New York: Limelight Editions, 243–70.

————. 2000. *Structures of Desire: British Cinema 1939–1955*. Albany: State University of New York Press.

Wood, Robin. 1986. *Hitchcock's Films Revisited*. New York: Columbia University Press.

Young, Bertram A. 1986. *The Rattigan Version: Sir Terence Rattigan and the Theatre of Character*. London: Hamish Hamilton.

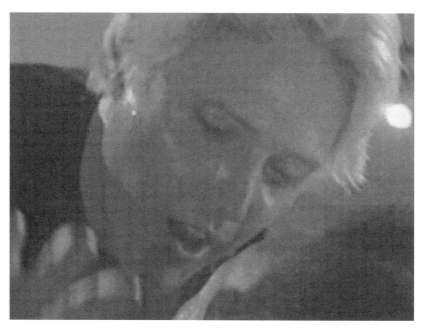

FIGURE 11. Producers of James Bond films, "ever aware of the need to address a global market with their British-produced product . . . have been careful to craft for Bond antagonists who present a threat to all governments whether democratic or communist. Max Zorin (Christopher Walken) intimately unsheathing his malevolence in *A View to a Kill* (John Glen, United Artists, 1985). (Frame enlargement)

CHAPTER ELEVEN

The Arch Archenemies of James Bond

STEVEN WOODWARD

> Bond told the story in simple terms, with good men and bad men,
> like an adventure story out of a book.
> —Ian Fleming, *Dr. No*

> What do you believe in? The preservation of capital?
> —Renard (Robert Carlyle) in *The World Is Not Enough*

A hero takes shape only in relation to his enemies. In the case of the James
Bond films, these enemies, whether incarnated as Ernst Stavro Blofeld,
Emilio Largo, Auric Goldfinger, Hugo Drax, Elliot Carver, Mr. Big, Franz
Sanchez, General Georgi Koskov, Karl Stromberg, or under some other suggestive name, seem intent on total global domination through the disruption
of national boundaries and governments, the manipulation of the global economy, or the utter extinction of humanity as we know it. The depiction of villainy in Bond films differs somewhat from that in creator Ian Fleming's novels, where James Bond's patriotic feelings, sense of decency, and restrained
heterosexual appetite play against criminal barbarity, communist deceit, colonial corruption, and rampant sexual perversion.

To be sure, the first Bond film, *Dr. No* (1962), used Fleming's polarities
while significantly enlarging Bond's sexual appetite. But as the film series has
progressed to the present time (through twenty-two films and six incarnations
of Bond: Sean Connery, David Niven, George Lazenby, Roger Moore, Timothy Dalton, and Pierce Brosnan), the moral, political, and sexual landscapes

of our culture have become hazier, the distinction between dignity and depravity less easy to make in everyday life. As Rick Lyman recently observed in the *New York Times*, "When it comes to choosing villains for big popcorn movies—a task that used to be as easy as 'Where did we put those Nazi uniforms?'—it is becoming more and more difficult to take a step without treading on someone's tender toes" (2002). If in response the scriptwriters have gradually reduced the most politically incorrect markers (such as, for example, the use of Harlem as a setting for a massive drug deal in *Live and Let Die* [1973]), they nevertheless seem to have found the means to keep intact the sexual coding and Oedipal drama of Fleming's narratives, primarily through the self-conscious irony embodied in Bond himself. James Bond's masculinity, in other words, is no longer for men only. As Toby Miller has observed, "Masculinity is no longer the exclusive province of men, either as spectators, consumers, or agents of power. And Bond was an unlikely harbinger of this trend" (2001, 245).

Although the Bond stories always attempt to anchor their narratives in historical specifics, they are, as Romano Calisi notes, more akin to romance or fairy tale in their use of a character typology: "James Bond does not exist, his Antagonist really does not exist, their characters do not exist in contour. There only exists a rhythmic succession of type-situations—which are significant socially and culturally" (1966, 83). Both Bond and his adversary have been carefully maintained as symbols rather than as individuals, symbols that take their meaning from their relationship with each other rather than from any iconic or indexical ground of truth. So it is that even in the novels, which have often been criticized for their jingoism, the exact content of Bond's ideals, encapsulated in his Englishness, remains, as Kingsley Amis noted, vague: "The England for which Bond is prepared to die, like the reasons why he's prepared to die for it, is largely taken for granted" (1965, 95). Amis identifies the result of Fleming's motives and methods as a particular "ethical frame of reference":

> Some things are regarded as good: loyalty, fortitude, a sense of responsibility, a readiness to regard one's safety, even one's life, as less important than the major interests of one's organization and one's country. Other things are regarded as bad: tyranny, readiness to inflict pain on the weak or helpless, the unscrupulous pursuit of money or power. (85)

These ideals, however, can be summarized more or less in one conception for Fleming: Englishness.

The producers of the films, ever aware of the need to address a global market with their British-produced product, have had to downplay the novels' use of Englishness as a moral anchor. Many of the actors they chose, perhaps unconsciously, for Bond were not English (a Scot, an Australian, a Welshman, an Irishman), as Anthony Lane has recently commented: "It was tempting fate to put a staunch, purebred Brit in a bunch of movies that were themselves, to a surreal degree, about the staunchness of British conduct" (2002, 80). More obviously, the producers have been careful to craft for Bond antagonists who present a threat to all governments whether democratic or communist (the numerous attempts at extortion by SPECTRE [Special Executive for Counterintelligence, Terrorism, Revenge and Extortion]; Elliot Carver's [Jonathan Pryce] global media empire in *Tomorrow Never Dies* [1997]), to families (the murder of Melina Havelock's parents [Jack Hedley and Toby Robbins] in *For Your Eyes Only* [1981]), to widely accepted public institutions (Goldfinger's attempts to corner and revalue the U.S. gold supply) and, indeed, to the very idea of romantic love (the rape and murder of Felix Leiter's bride [Pamela Barnes] on her wedding night in *Licence to Kill* [1989]). Certainly, the films take advantage of current international events for their staging: the action of the early films takes place against a backdrop of Cold War conflict, that of the later films against scenes of more recent international conflict and tension—for example, the terrorist arms bazaar where everything from automatic weapons to F-18 fighters is for sale in the precredit sequence of *Tomorrow Never Dies*. But such conflicts rarely generate the main antagonist for Bond himself. Bond's former personal enemy has now been shaped into a universal one, a nameless, faceless source of fear that is explicitly given a name and a face by screenwriters who, in the words of Neal Purvis, a cowriter of *Die Another Day* (2002), "come in with ideas, things we've found in science magazines, on the Internet, interesting weapons and what's happening in technology. Then we try to find a journey for Bond to go through" (Yarborough 2000). One archvillain who emerges as a serious adversary for Bond is media mega-mogul Elliot Carver, a demonic hybrid of Bill Gates and Rupert Murdoch and a clear example of how the Bond narratives are constructed from the fusion of appropriate social and political details with a conventional romance structure.

From *Dr. No* to *The World Is Not Enough* (1999), the romantic journey has involved both exotic migration—a passage from West to East and back again—and a vertical quest, a descent below the surface of the postcard reality of these exotic destinations. Indeed, Michael Denning sees the surfacy touristic aspect of the stories as a device for titillating the audience as consumers, solving the problem that all tourists face in their search for authentic experience of place: how can one believe in the authenticity of the tourist experience when one is conscious of being part of the mass spectacle that is tourism? As Denning observes, "This dilemma—to be superior to the 'tourists' while at once recognizing one's kinship with them—is what is solved by Bond, the ideal tourist" (1992, 221). (Bond's discovery of the authentic place, his special insight, often depends on a distinctively characterized "man on the spot," a sort of cicerone who guides him in his journey.) Often, too, this discovery involves a literal descent: into the Byzantine reservoirs below modern-day Istanbul in *From Russia with Love* (1963); beneath a volcano's lake in the Japanese archipelago in *You Only Live Twice* (1967) or a mountain lake in Cuba in *GoldenEye* (1995); through the tunnels and caverns below a mountainous island in *The Man with the Golden Gun* (1974); frequently, under the sea in *Dr. No, Thunderball* (1965), *The Spy Who Loved Me* (1977), *For Your Eyes Only*, and *The World Is Not Enough*. Certainly, this descent may allow the audience a consumer pleasure: the paradox of a vicarious experience of authenticity. But it is also symbolic, resulting in the discovery of a villain who lurks beneath a surface, hiding beneath the appearance of respectability.

What defines these villains is that they are deceitful: they bear the marks of success, but they have acquired such marks through nefarious means. In *A View to a Kill* (1985), for example, Zorin (Christopher Walken) uses a remote-control radio device to inject racehorses with a steroid that enables them to win and secure him his fortune. Bond, on the other hand, comes by his successes "honestly," which is to say, as a result of "proper" indoctrination by "bona fide" agencies of the state. The real mark of such villains as Zorin, apart from their cold-bloodedness, is their imposture: they operate under a veil of secrecy, cloaking their real intentions behind the fronts of legitimate business operations or high-tech industries with swank logos—Drax Industries (a builder of space shuttles for the U.S. government) and Zorin Industries (a gold-mining enterprise), to name two.

In the politically bipolar Cold War world, the early Bond films posited the idea of a third position, a sinister alternative to communism and capitalism, a conspiracy that would undermine the rules of the game as the superpowers were playing it: SPECTRE. Thus, where the novels maintained an element of contemporary political and social reference, the films discovered and exploited a fantastic and surreal dimension that, because of its generality, continues to encompass the most irrational and indefinite of public anxieties: "The conspiracy, if it involved the Russians, was a third party, either Red China or Spectre, taking advantage of the Cold War fears that divide the Soviet Union and the West" (Price 1992, 30). The game of international politics has particular rules, but the villains in the Bond films defy such rules: they are liars, thieves, and cheats who attempt either to subvert or to destroy the system. SPECTRE is one name for a conspiracy of global proportions, and even when SPECTRE disappeared from the films (after *Diamonds Are Forever* [1971]) they continued to exploit the notion of conspiracy, of a concealed enemy.

Bond's enemies have consistently been crafted as powerful, wealthy organizations, headed by a criminal mastermind and capable of building labyrinthine secret laboratories, missile silos, ships, and spacecraft. In this respect, they are akin to national governments. However, within these organizations the individual is subsumed into a collective directed by a single-minded autocrat. This picture of evil as rationalized, technologized, brilliantly organized and managed, and inspired by the megalomania of a single individual must have recalled, for early viewers of the films in Europe, the regime of Nazi Germany. For North Americans, the deceitfulness of this enemy and the homogenizing demands of its organization may have reflected a particular fear of communism but continue today to reflect a more generalized fear, of an unknown enemy that burrows like a mole within the democratic system, able to hide itself precisely because of the freedoms central to that system (and hence still of great relevance). Thus, the films do not simply champion an English-derived code of decency (that Bond represents) over a depraved, rationalized amorality, but, more crucially, celebrate individual freedom and desire over collective enslavement. Bond's job is to expose the hollowness of the villain's project at every level: his romantic allure converts the villain's women; his cultural knowledge exposes the villain's ignorance; his incisive probing of false corporate fronts reveals a malicious hierarchy of bullying; his courage defeats the villain's cool passions. Interestingly, this picture of the enemy and the narrative pattern it engenders has not changed much in the four decades of production of Bond films, although the plots have shifted to reflect the anxieties viewers feel at any particular moment about the likely face of such an insidious enemy—orientalized, latinized, arabicized, homoeroticized, and so on.

In Fleming's novels, the Soviet Union was the most recurrent sponsor of the villains that Bond battles. There was also a smattering of other villainous organizations, including the Syndicate and Castro, and many of Fleming's villains were self-employed (for a chart of the villains in Fleming's Bond texts, see Amis, 156–59). SPECTRE made a relatively late appearance, in *Thunderball*, and was not Fleming's idea at all. The idea of an international band of terrorists had been floated as early as 1959, at preliminary meetings between Fleming and several others—Ivar Bryce, Kevin McClory, and Ernest Cuneo—interested in adapting Bond to the screen (Price, 23). But the films' producers, Harry Saltzman and Albert R. "Cubby" Broccoli, decided from the start that SPECTRE and the recurring conflict between Bond and this organization would allow for spectacular images (fantastic set designs in particular), an international appeal for the films, and the definition of a personal motivation for Bond's action that would give some depth to his screen persona. Furthermore, because SPECTRE (something of a 1960s harbinger of the contemporary multinational corporation) is an organization devoted to extortion from all national governments regardless of ideology and because the possession of a large nuclear arsenal is more likely to make a nation a victim of SPECTRE, it does not seem ludicrous that Great Britain, a relatively small power in nuclear terms, and its agent, 007, could assume a crucial role in facing and defeating this enemy.

One of the most remarkable things about the films is the degree to which they insist on the superior ability of the British to locate and expunge evil. The Americans may have the kind of firepower that is crucial in dealing with military threat, but far less obsessed with bipolar militaristic thinking, the British have a keener insight into this apolitical evil, which is, after all, an even greater threat to the world. The trope of U.S. and Soviet belligerence proves counterproductive to uncovering the villains' insidious plots in Bond films. For example, in *You Only Live Twice*, a U.S. spaceship is snatched from space by an "intruder missile," and U.S. diplomats are quick to accuse the Soviets of making "a blatant attempt to gain complete and absolute control of space itself for military purposes." But the British occupy a third table at this tense meeting, positioned between the two antagonists, and the British representative (Robin Bailey) calmly asserts:

> We don't agree. Her Majesty's government is not convinced that this intruder missile originated from Soviet Russia. A tracking station in Singapore reported faint echoes of this craft coming down in the Sea of Japan area. Might I suggest, gentlemen, that this is where you should concentrate your intelligence forces. The Prime Minister has asked me to assure you that this is what *we* propose to do. As a matter of fact, our man in Hong Kong is working on it now.

The next shot shows Bond in bed with a Chinese woman. By implication, the concentration of intelligence that Bond represents is more or less synonymous with his heterosexual enthusiasm. The import of this equation will soon become clear: we will discover that although Bond is a representative of all legitimate governments in his battle with the villain's organization, he is the champion of heterosexual masculine desire in his battle with the villain himself.

The recurrence of SPECTRE as the enemy—in *From Russia with Love, Thunderball, You Only Live Twice, On Her Majesty's Secret Service* (1969), and *Diamonds Are Forever*—also allowed for the development of a personal conflict between Bond and the paragon of evil, Ernst Stavro Blofeld, a conflict motivated not just by previous violent encounters but by Blofeld and Irma Bunt's murder of Bond's wife, Tracy, at the end of *Secret Service*. Even when SPECTRE itself vanished, reconfigured into other organizations, the conflict between Bond and his villain continued to make use of these two dimensions of the political and the personal.

The producers had to make a considerable effort to define SPECTRE from the outset as the most dangerous threat both to the world and to Bond himself. Although *Thunderball* was to have been the first of the novels transposed to film, legal complications forced the producers to undertake *Dr. No* instead (see Chapman 2000, 73–74). And in scripting that film, they transformed Dr. No from a Soviet agent to a member of SPECTRE. Similar revisions were made to *You Only Live Twice* and *Diamonds Are Forever*, so that, throughout the Connery years (1962–1971), SPECTRE appears and reappears at intervals, but is never defeated. Blofeld died in the novel *You Only Live Twice*. But the films' producers insisted on his survival and reappearance—in performances or vocalizations by Eric Pohlmann, Anthony Dawson,

Joseph Wiseman, Donald Pleasence, Telly Savalas, and Charles Gray—until, in the pretitle sequence of *For Your Eyes Only*, Roger Moore's Bond scoops up a wheelchair-bound Blofeld (John Hollis) with a helicopter runner and drops him down a massive industrial chimney.

This comic disposal of a long-term adversary by no means signaled the end of the battle between Bond and the evil organization headed by a mega-lomaniac villain. Indeed, even the non-Blofeld villains are megalomaniacs, although their motives range from pure criminal glee to misanthropy. Auric Goldfinger (Gert Frobe) is typical of the first. He orates to an assembly of mobsters in the high-tech boardroom of his Kentucky ranch: "Man has climbed Mount Everest, gone to the bottom of the ocean; he has fired rockets at the moon, split the atom, achieved miracles in every field of human endeavor, except crime." Hugo Drax (Michel Lonsdale) in *Moonraker* (1979) is the ultimate narcissistic misanthrope, planning to wipe out all humanity on Earth before recreating it in his own image. Drax pontificates at length to a captive audience, the carefully selected couples who populate his space station:

> First, there was a dream. Now there is reality. Here, in the untainted cradle of the heavens will be created a new super-race, a race of perfect physical specimens. You have been selected as its progenitors. . . . Your offspring will return to Earth and shape it in their image. You have all served in other capacities in my terrestrial empire. Your seed, like yourselves, will pay deference to the ultimate dynasty, which I alone have created. From their first day on Earth, they will be able to look up and know that there is law and order in the heavens.

Frequently, the two impulses of criminality and misanthropy are united, as in the case of Max Zorin in *A View to a Kill* or Elektra King (Sophie Marceau) in *The World Is Not Enough*.

But perhaps the stated motives for villainy are irrelevant. What matters most is that the villain appear to be a figure of power and authority who is at the same time corrupt and perverse. For as numerous critics have pointed out, the romance narratives of the Bond films enact an Oedipal drama through which sexual and political threads are fused (see, for instance, Bennett and Woollacott 1987, chap. 4). The conventional romance structure is easily summarized. A gentleman warrior, armed by his paternal masters with potent or magical weapons, sets off into strange lands and does battle with fantastic and monstrous enemies (the first of the Bond films, *Dr. No*, even includes a mock dragon). Inevitably Bond encounters maidens along the way, many of them in collusion with the enemy, but there is always one who, if not innocent, is at least pure in purpose. It is she who provides the ultimate love-object for our hero, and the union of Bond and this "lady" conventionally provides the comic (in two senses) ending to the Bond film. To convert this romance into Oedipal terms, Bond is the son of a benevolent father figure, M (though recently, as we shall see below, M has been played by a stoical woman), who subverts the son's rebellious energies by "licensing" him to confront and destroy a father-impostor. The conflict between Bond and this villain involves the exposure of the villain's corruption—that is, his lack of merit—and of his sexual impotence. Bond's successful completion of the mission is marked by the coincidence between his destruction of the father-impostor and his exogamous union with the girl, while the legitimate father typically looks on from a great distance with grudging approval.

This Oedipal element of the films was more or less lifted intact from the books. In these, the father-impostor is made monstrous, both physically and mentally. Take, for example, Dr. No, a "bizarre, gliding figure" that "looked like a giant venomous worm wrapped in grey tin-foil, and Bond would not have been surprised to see the rest of it trailing slimily along the carpet behind" (Fleming 1960, 127). The character is allowed a full chapter, "Pandora's Box," to describe his history and explain the evolution of his villainous project to his captive, Bond. He outlines his genealogy, describing himself as "the only son of a German Methodist missionary and a Chinese girl of good family" (133) and explaining the source of his malice in psychoanalytic terms as righteous indignation for the lack of his parents' love: "I changed my name to Julius No—the Julius after my father and the No for my rejection of him and of all authority" (134). Not surprisingly, such psychoanalytical observations were generally absent from the Bond films, if still implicit in their visual codings and narrative repetitions, and were revived only for the parodic *Austin Powers: International Man of Mystery* (1997) where Dr. Evil (Mike Myers), obviously echoing Blofeld, confesses the sexual abuses of his childhood in group therapy with his son (Seth Green). Such psychosexual revelations could hardly be made in the real Bond films without destroying the potency of the suppressed Oedipal narrative I have described.

The "extreme physical grotesqueness" that as Amis observed of Fleming's novels "is . . . a *sine qua non* in Bond's enemies" (64) was more or less eschewed by the filmmakers, who have given us instead "malformed egomaniacs in tight collars" (Lane, 79). Certainly, Blofeld's various incarnations in the films are marked by physical eccentricity, and Bond's mission involves uncovering the lair in which Blofeld hides it. But as the series has progressed, the villain has come out into the open, has become more or less indistinguishable in physical terms from common humanity. Grotesqueness has sometimes been displaced onto the villain's henchman, as in the case of Zao (Rick Yune) in *Die Another Day,* whose face is pocked with diamonds, or Jaws (Richard Kiel), the steel-toothed giant in *The Spy Who Loved Me* who returned in *Moonraker* only to be converted to Bond's cause at that film's end as a result of his infatuation with a diminutive, pigtailed "girl." Although the presence of such henchmen is a sure sign of Bond's proximity to the villain, the nexus of evil has generally proven much more difficult to locate after the demise of Blofeld. Indeed, in the very film in which Bond finally disposes of this archenemy, *For Your Eyes Only*, he is caught in a blood feud between two former resistance fighters, now smugglers, Kristatos (Julian Glover) and Columbo (Topol), unsure as to which of them is the real villain.

Fortunately, if physicality is no longer a reliable mark by means of which the enemy can be divined, Bond can expose him through another test. As Andrea Barbato noted of Fleming's narratives, Bond's "success perhaps really derives from being a real man, with common passions and appetites which all [readers] share" (1966, 135). Those "common passions and appetites" are clearly heterosexual, as Fleming himself professed: "[My thrillers] are written for warm-blooded heterosexuals in railway trains, airplanes or beds" (1963, 14). Not surprisingly, the films have fully exploited the spectacular and voyeuristic possibilities of this sexual dimension, if not starting in the pretitle sequence, then in the title sequence itself and the sassy theme song that inevitably accompanies it. In those distinctive title sequences (most attributable to Maurice Binder), silhouettes of naked girls dancing or performing acrobatics or pointing guns are combined with key images from the films. In *GoldenEye*, for example, these girls drive sledgehammers against statues of Lenin and Stalin, helping signify an end to the Cold War conflict that had provided the backdrop to Bond films for so long and the emergence of the new, more sinister adversary that is global capitalism.

If Bond is the "real man" then clearly the villain must not be, and the imposture of the villain, his impotence, has been coded in two ways. Sometimes the villain is suggested to be asexual or homosexual. In *Diamonds Are Forever*, Blofeld (Charles Gray) has taken over the penthouse suite of Texan Willard Whyte (Jimmy Dean), and lives there with a man who is literally a mirror image of himself, a clone. Furthermore, his henchmen, Mr. Kidd (Putter Smith) and Mr. Wint (Bruce Glover), and his henchwomen, Bambi (Lola Larson) and Thumper (Trina Parks), seem homosexual, displaced images of Blofeld's own predilections. The villains in other films show little sexual interest in women, even when they have captured one of Bond's confederate girls—Dr. No (Joseph Wiseman) with Honey Ryder (Ursula Andress); Scaramanga (Christopher Lee) with Mary Goodnight (Britt Ekland); Stromberg (Curt Jurgens) with Anya Amasova (Barbara Bach).

More frequently, however, Bond proves the villain's impotence by seducing the villain's girl, thus symbolically castrating him. As Furio Colombo observed, Bond is involved in two games simultaneously: "how to approach, recognize, mislead, uncover and liquidate the enemy. . . . And how to take, defend and hold on to the girl, who serves excellently as a symbol of the stake in the game, as a measure of the wickedness and scant charms of the enemy" (1966, 87).

Goldfinger (1964) offers a particularly clear example of the connection between the two games. Bond's (Sean Connery) first contact with Goldfinger involves seducing Jill Masterson (Shirley Eaton), a girl whom Goldfinger pays to help him cheat at cards. As a result of this seduction, Goldfinger loses his mastery both of the card game and the girl. But he takes his revenge: first, by painting the girl gold and thus "converting" her from sex object to fetish object; and secondly, by attempting to castrate Bond with his giant laser. But Goldfinger's grandiose posturing cannot prevent his ultimate failure in "Operation Grand Slam," which comes as a direct result of his inability to seduce Pussy Galore (Honor Blackman). Goldfinger has convinced Pussy to kill the 60,000 U.S. troops stationed outside Fort Knox with "Delta nerve gas," but he is presumably able to persuade her only because she has rejected her position in the field of patriarchal romance in favor of lesbian pleasures with the other female pilots of her Flying Circus (a Freudian pun for a lesbian orgy?). As the mission approaches, Goldfinger makes a hopelessly paternalistic attempt to woo Pussy, the failure of which is followed closely by Bond's tussle with her in the hay. After an exchange of judo throws with Bond, Pussy is finally mastered. We later discover that after this corrective sexual encounter, Pussy has informed Washington about Goldfinger's plan and has replaced the nerve gas with a harmless substitute. Later, Bond quips to his C.I.A. buddy Felix Leiter (Cec Linder) about Pussy's change of heart: "I must have appealed to her maternal instinct."

The Oedipal nature of Bond's relationship with the legitimate paternal authority M represents and the displacement of their father-son aggression onto the agent-villain conflict also explains the numerous repetitions of image and narrative motif in the films. Indeed, the institutional structure of "British Intelligence" is often mirrored in the villain's organization: M's authority is matched by the villain's; Q's technological obsession and fanciful weaponry, essentially an extension of a boyish interest in train sets, is matched by the villain's elaborate arsenal; Miss Moneypenny's prim Oedipal attractiveness (as reassuring mother-lover) is displaced by the villain's beautiful but deceitful henchwomen. In terms of the narrative, Bond's interview with M in his office is often counterposed with a similar interview with the villain. And both M's office and Q's laboratory demand comparison with the villain's lair: the stern leathery warmth of the office and the collegial fun of the laboratory are converted into the rock and steel of the lair where the villain's uniformed faceless employees move in synchronization with the machines of calculated destruction. Designer Ken Adam consciously gave these lairs (in *Dr. No, Goldfinger, Thunderball, You Only Live Twice, Diamonds Are Forever, The Spy Who Loved Me*, and *Moonraker*) a distinctively modernist style: "Adam eschewed any notion of conventional realism and enjoyed creating a visual world which is as distinctive in its own way as the cinema of German Expressionism" (Chapman 2000, 61). The comparison seems apt: for instance, the subvolcanic silo of *You Only Live Twice* seems to replicate the underground factories of Lang's *Metropolis* (1927).

On occasion, Bond has to do battle with a mirror image of himself, a "son" who has not been licensed by the father. Scaramanga in *The Man with the Golden Gun* is the most obvious example. His estrangement from the "family fold" and resulting sexual ambivalence is marked on his body with a third nipple. Scaramanga, like Bond, kills for a living, but for the "wrong" reasons: his golden gun is symbolic of the coincidence of the act of killing with the acquisition of wealth. While Bond (Roger Moore) is given a license to kill by his superiors, Scaramanga takes orders for killings from anyone who can pay his price: one million dollars. He is Bond's evil twin, and the film's conclusion involves a descent into a cavern and a hall of mirrors, symbols of the unconscious and the confrontation with self.

The evil twin has come to be increasingly indistinguishable from Bond himself, most obviously in *GoldenEye*. Here, Bond (Pierce Brosnan) does battle with a mysterious adversary known as Janus, who turns out to be Alec Trevalyan, the former 006 (Sean Bean). Trevalyan has learnt that loyalties are a liability: his parents were Cossacks who fought against Stalin, and then sought refuge with the British, but were betrayed by them and sent back to Stalin. As a Cossack, Trevalyan has an uncanny insight into the provisional nature of morality and its shifting currents. In a scrap yard of broken statues of Lenin and Stalin, Trevalyan asks the questions that must be in the mind of many viewers in the post-Soviet era: "Did you ever ask why? Why we toppled all those dictators, undermined all those regimes? Only to come home: 'Good job. Well done. But sorry, old boy, everything you risked your life and limb for has changed.'" If we think of the enemy as the Russians, then indeed we may be dismayed to find the political landscape has changed. An enemy should remain an enemy. Trevalyan also diminishes Bond's own loyalties: "James Bond, Her Majesty's loyal terrier, defender of the so-called faith."

Bond's self-evident moral superiority, his "faith," unquestioned at the genesis of the series in the 1960s, has become ever more problematic in light of the self-questioning ethos of post–Cold War politics. In the early films, the bipolar political thinking of the Cold War underwrote a corresponding bipolar morality and sexuality. With that conflict over and the power of national governments waning with the rise of international corporate capitalism, what Bond stands for as a British secret agent might seem less clear. Rather than simply eliding this problem by reasserting some gross moral framework, the scriptwriters have decided to encounter it directly by bluntly challenging Bond's motives and values or by rendering those motives in entirely ironic terms. So, in *Die Another Day*, Jinx (Halle Berry), agent of the NSA, wryly iterates the goal she shares with Bond: "World peace, universal love, and a chance to get at that guy with the expensive acne."

At the same time, M has changed sex—Judi Dench has taken over the role formerly played by such paternal actors as Bernard Lee and Robert Brown—unsettling the Oedipal dynamics of the narratives. In *Tomorrow Never Dies*, M's authority is challenged by Admiral Roebuck (Geoffrey Palmer): "With all due respect, M, sometimes I don't think you have the balls for this job." Indeed, M's feminine sympathies have already proven to be a liability. In *The World Is Not Enough*, her decision to become personally involved in Bond's mission, after the murder of her friend Sir Robert King (David Calder), results in her humiliating imprisonment by King's daughter, Elektra. And with the familiar and familial roles of British intelligence disrupted, Bond has trouble orienting himself and is surprised to discover that Elektra, the woman he has been protecting, is the ultimate villain. In her showdown with Bond on an island in the Bosphorus, Elektra straps Bond into a contraption that will eventually break his neck, but will produce a spontaneous erection from him before that, an erection she plans to use. Certainly, such purposive (even masculine) females have appeared throughout the series—Rosa Klebb (Lotte Lenya) in *From Russia with Love*, May Day (Grace Jones) in *A View to a Kill*, and Xenia Onatopp (Famke Janssen) in *GoldenEye*. But with Elektra King, a woman who plans not to avenge her father but to take over his reign, the gender coding of the central conflict in the Bond romance has perhaps finally been toppled.

Despite this gender confusion, we can be sure that one convention of the Bond films will remain: Bond will always be English and the villain will invariably not be. He may imitate the accent or even transform himself into the epitome of Oxbridge suavity—the North Korean Colonel Moon (Will Yun Lee) is genetically morphed into billionaire entrepreneur Gustav Graves (Toby Stephens) in *Die Another Day*—so that the Queen will be tricked into receiving him. But ultimately, Bond will expose the masquerade. Rather peculiarly, this seemingly outmoded element of Fleming's narratives may well be the key to the films' continuing success. By being the agent of a former imperial power that has seen the error (and era) of its ways and unleashed the subjugated and colonized people of its global empire, the representative of a disinterested "British Intelligence," Bond is perhaps the ultimate ironic hero, whose success can be celebrated by every member of the audience. By standing for nothing in particular, except the defeat of a megalomaniac unlicensed emperor, the filmic James Bond, and the monarchical England for which he stands, becomes a kind of nothing, a hollow agency for the new globalized utterly postimperial world. And Pierce Brosnan—"a creature of immaculate exterior and no core," according to Anthony Lane—is the perfect man for the part (81). The Bond villain, however—surrounded by beautiful women who do not love him, comfortable with wealth although obsessed with its acquisition, connoisseur of food and wine although ascetic to a fault—is the true, perhaps insoluble, mystery at the heart of the narrative, the Being whose personality fills the vacuum that is James Bond with what seems like a dose of character.

WORKS CITED

Amis, Kingsley. 1965. *The James Bond Dossier*. London: Jonathan Cape.

Barbato, Andrea. 1966. "The Credible and the Incredible in the Films of 007." In Oreste Del Buono and Umberto Eco, eds., *The Bond Affair*. Trans. R. A. Downie. London: Macdonald, 133–45.

Bennett, Tony and Janet Woollacott. 1987. *Bond and Beyond: The Political Career of a Popular Hero*. Houndmills: Macmillan.

Calisi, Romano. 1966. "Myth and History in the Epic of James Bond." In Oreste Del Buono and Umberto Eco, eds., *The Bond Affair*. Trans. R. A. Downie. London: Macdonald, 76–85.

Chapman, James. 2000. *Licence to Thrill: A Cultural History of the James Bond Films*. New York: Columbia University Press.

Colombo, Furio. 1966. "Bond's Women." In Oreste Del Buono and Umberto Eco, eds., *The Bond Affair*. Trans. R. A. Downie. London: Macdonald, 86–102.

Denning, Michael. 1992. "Licensed to Look: James Bond and the Heroism of Consumption." Rpt. in *Contemporary Marxist Literary Criticism*, edited by Francis Mulhern. London: Longman.

Fleming, Ian. 1960. *Dr. No*. London: Pan.

Fleming, Ian. 1963. "How to Write a Thriller," *Books and Bookmen* 8.8 (May), 14–19.

Lane, Anthony. 2002. "Mondo Bond: Forty Years of 007," *The New Yorker* (4 November), 78–82.

Lyman, Rick. 2002. "Suddenly, It's Easier to Find a Hero Than a Villain," *New York Times* (December 22), 4:2.

Miller, Toby. 2001. "James Bond's Penis." In Peter Lehman, ed., *Masculinity: Bodies, Movies, Culture*. New York: Routledge, 243–56.

Price, Thomas J. 1992. "The Changing Image of the Soviets in the Bond Saga: From Bond-Villains to 'Acceptable Role Partners,'" *Journal of Popular Culture* 26.1 (Summer), 17–37.

Yarborough. 2002. "Production Newsflash 12 / A Sitdown with the Writers." *Bond 20 Website*. 27 March. <http://www.jamesbond.com/bond20/newsflash/newsflash_12.php> 22 April 2002.

FIGURE 12. Yellow Peril: a Chinese master criminal with a heritage of European violence and a good Western education. Boris Karloff in the title role in *The Mask of Fu Manchu* (Charles Brabin, MGM, 1932), a character with "enduring global appeal." (Frame enlargement)

CHAPTER TWELVE

From Fu Manchu to
M. Butterfly *and* Irma Vep:
Cinematic Incarnations
of Chinese Villainy

GINA MARCHETTI

The emergence of the cinema in the late nineteenth century occurred at a
time when European and American imperial conquests and colonial ambitions in Asia were at their height (Marchetti 2001a, 2001b). Perhaps more
than any other country in Asia, China had a particular hold over the popular
imagination globally. All of the major (and many of the minor) powers in
Europe held concessions there. The French, for example, had their own territory in Shanghai, and the other world powers shared the "international district." In 1900 the Boxer Rebellion in China galvanized the West with grue-
some tales of butchered Americans and Europeans reported in the press and
recreated through the magic of the new motion pictures.

Concomitant with European and American colonialism in China,
the Chinese ventured out in record numbers as gold prospectors in California, Canada, Alaska, and elsewhere; as indentured laborers throughout
the British Empire, including Africa, the Caribbean, and Southeast Asia;
and as merchants throughout Europe and the Americas. In 1882 the
United States passed the Chinese Exclusion Act, and similar laws and

restrictions followed in Canada and Australia. With the dual need to legit-
imize colonial rule abroad and control the immigration of the Chinese
domestically, newspaper accounts, political tracts, and fiction involving the
Yellow Peril grew exponentially.

The Chinese screen villain emerged from within this environment of
colonial expansion and domestic xenophobic exclusion. For example, the Yellow Peril became inextricably linked to Sax Rohmer's creation Fu Manchu, a
Western-educated, Chinese master criminal, through a series of novels beginning in 1913 and quickly taken up by magazines, radio shows, motion pictures, and later television. With origins in the United Kingdom, Fu Manchu
clearly represents British ambivalence about the consequences of imperial
conquest and the opening of global routes for the exchange of people and
goods. The character symbolizes the fear of colonial hybridity produced from
Western education and European violence (his family fell victim to the sup-
pression of the Boxers), which gives him the motivation and the ability to
threaten white supremacy.

This vision of Asian evil quickly struck a responsive chord in Hollywood, and the first U.S. film portrayal of the character appeared in 1929 in an
early sound film, *The Mysterious Dr. Fu Manchu,* starring Warner Oland, who
made a career of these "yellow face" roles, most notably as Charlie Chan. In
fact, Oland serves as a link between the characters of Fu Manchu and Charlie Chan, and it is not surprising that historian Gary Y. Okihiro should see
the "model minority" Chan as an ideological continuation of the yellow peril
Fu Manchu:

> Both were steeped in Orientalism which they learned from the West, and they
> challenged and threatened white supremacy, and galvanized and attested to
> European superiority. They operated from within the white homeland, within
> the colonial enclaves of Chinatowns and Hawaii, and hated and envied the
> West. In the end, Fu Manchu and Charlie Chan, yellow peril and model
> minority, personified the cunning, sensuality, and mysticism of a feminine Asia
> (the body) and the intellect, logic, and science of a masculine Europe (the
> mind). (1994, 145)

In a similar way, the "dragon lady" and the "lotus blossom" form two
halves of one coin in the popular Western imagination. Seductive and exotic,
the former must be forced into submission, while the latter innately recognizes Western superiority and freely acquiesces to the will of her white mas-
ter/lover. However, both represent equally taboo desires that must be contained, and their inevitable deaths symbolize the vanquishing of those desires
in the name of white "civilization." *The Mask of Fu Manchu* (1932), with Boris
Karloff as the eponymous villain, features a particularly campy performance by
Myrna Loy as Fu Manchu's equally dastardly "dragon lady" daughter who has

a taste for white men, and in fact Hollywood history brims with films featuring memorable Chinese villains, male and female, including *The Red Lantern* (1919), *55 Days at Peking* (1963), *The Tong Man* (1919), *The Hatchet Man* (1932), *Old San Francisco* (1927), *Narcotic* (1934), *The Bitter Tea of General Yen* (1933), *The General Died at Dawn* (1936) *Shanghai Express* (1932), *The Shanghai Gesture* (1941), *The Shanghai Story* (1954), *Barricade* (1939), *7 Women* (1966), *The Left Hand of God* (1955), *Blood Alley* (1955), *Yangtse Incident* (1957), *Satan Never Sleeps* (1962), and *Big Trouble in Little China* (1986), among many others.

Although some of the Yellow Peril rhetoric was toned down as the United States drew closer to its Chinese allies in the years before World War II, Fu Manchu has had enduring global appeal with notable yellow face incarnations by Henry Brandon, Christopher Lee, and Peter Sellers. As Sheng-Mei Ma (2000) notes in *The Deathly Embrace: Orientalism and Asian American Identity*, the figure of Fu Manchu continues to influence other popular cultural villains from Ming the Merciless (Charles Middleton) in the Flash Gordon serials to Khan (Ricardo Montalban) and General Chang (Christopher Plummer) in the *Star Trek* films.

With the establishment of the People's Republic in 1949, the Yellow Peril became linked in Western cinema with the Red Menace. On the eve of the United States' involvement in the Vietnam War, for example, John Frankenheimer created one of the more bizarre intersections of American liberalism and anticommunist hysteria in *The Manchurian Candidate* (1962). The film follows an elaborate political assassination plot initiated through brainwashing a group of prisoners of war in Korea. Khigh Dhiegh (who played a similar character, Wo Fat, on the television series "Hawaii Five-O") portrays the particularly sinister Dr. Yen Lo, who takes delight in mentally torturing his captives, controlling their thoughts, and forcing them to murder. An ideal consumer, he takes time out from his heinous deeds to buy designer presents for his wife at Macy's while continuing the plot in the United States. As an updated Fu Manchu, Yen Lo may be the ideal embodiment of the Yellow Peril, but he does not appear to buy into the anticapitalist stance of Red China and seems to take the bite out of the Red Scare. The fact that the mother of one of the soldiers (played by a demonic Angela Lansbury) turns out to be the real villain of the piece serves to weaken both the Yellow Peril and Red Menace aspects of the film's plot, but Yen Lo still manages some chilling brainwashing sequences under menacing portraits of Stalin and Mao Tse-tung.

In fact, the Yellow Peril/Red Menace combination of the Cold War continues to endure in contemporary figurations of Red China. After the expansive media coverage of the uprising in Tian'anmen Square in May–June 1989 and the speculation surrounding Hong Kong's return to

China in 1997, Hollywood intensified its use of the Red Menace formula in films such as the Richard Gere vehicle *Red Corner* (1997) and several films made to support the Dalai Lama's bid for Tibetan autonomy from the People's Republic, for example, Jean-Jacques Annaud's *Seven Years in Tibet* (1997) and Martin Scorsese's *Kundun* (1997). As China and the Chinese diaspora hold an increasingly prominent place within the global cinematic imagination through the work of China's Fifth and Sixth Generations, Hong Kong's and Taiwan's New Wave, and the enormous success of Hong Kong's popular cinema worldwide, the Chinese villain has taken on a new dimension within the American and European imagination. Although the links to the "yellow peril" fantasies of the nineteenth and twentieth centuries may seem strained today, the fact that the qualities associated with Fu Manchu still evoke a response and insinuate themselves into films as diverse as David Cronenberg's *M. Butterfly* (1993) and Olivier Assayas's *Irma Vep* (1996) merits closer scrutiny.

And although evil, slime, infamy, and villainy may not immediately be associated with the rather pathetic figure of Song Liling in *M. Butterfly* or with the popular film icon Maggie Cheung who plays herself in *Irma Vep*, the racist slime associated with Fu Manchu still clings to these characters. They function as hazy figures associated with darkness, illicit sexual desire, and duplicity. However, rather than uncritically representing an Orientalist vision of the "other" as essentially evil, these characters embody a postcolonial crisis in the Western psyche. In these films, the realization begins to dawn that the evil "other" actually reflects the fantasies of the Western male heterosexual self. Thus, Song Liling and Maggie Cheung incarnate a crisis in the West's capacity to define evil because of this failure to continue to know the Asian "other" as unequivocally "bad," and, as a consequence, to be assured that the Western self epitomizes virtue, light, cleanliness, and good.

FU MANCHU, MAGGIE CHEUNG, AND SONG LILING

Although they seem to be worlds apart, *M. Butterfly* and *Irma Vep* actually share some strikingly similar characteristics. Using a screenplay written by David Henry Hwang who brought the tale to the New York stage, *M. Butterfly* is based on the "true," if incredible, story of Bernard Boursicot/René Gallimard (Jeremy Irons), a French diplomatic functionary stationed in the People's Republic of China during the 1960s, who falls in love with a male Chinese spy/Peking opera diva, Shi Pei-Pu/Song Liling (John Lone), believing him to be a woman. *Irma Vep* (an anagram for "vampire") deals with an ill-conceived and ill-fated attempt by a fictional, aging French New Wave director, René Vidal (Jean-Pierre Léaud), to remake a classic French silent serial about the Parisian underworld with Hong Kong film star Maggie Cheung in the title role.

Both narratives revolve around Chinese thespians playing a titular role. These Chinese performers try diligently to recreate late-nineteenth/early-twentieth-century European fictions (Puccini's *Madama Butterfly* [1904] and Louis Feuillade's *Les Vampires* [1915], respectively). Both films deal with a particularly French approach to Asia (see Said 1993). Puccini's opera, for example, had its original incarnation as Pierre Loti's *Madame Chrysanthème* (1887) eventually known to Puccini through David Belasco's play based on John Luther Long's 1896 story that took up Loti's tale in an English-language version. Boursicot and Shi's actual romance follows *Butterfly* so closely, in fact, that Shi eventually connives with his government handler to produce a biracial baby as "their son."

Both films feature a Frenchman's fascination with a Chinese performer and a liaison that at first energizes and later debilitates the Western man—this relationship, in each film, serving as an allegory for the state of European culture and civilization vis-à-vis the "Orient." Thus, both films link a crisis in Western masculinity with a crisis in colonial authority and Western epistemology because the Western man can never seem to get a grip on his attraction to, desire for, and inability to control the Chinese woman and, by extension, all she embodies as the female, nonwhite, Asian Other. He can never quite figure out how to "know" this elusive Chinese figure, how to fix his own identity in relation to that alterity. At one point in *Irma Vep,* José Murano (Lou Castel), a director brought in to save the failing remake of the silent serial *Les Vampires,* cannot understand Vidal's choice to cast a Hong Kong actress as the French archcriminal Irma Vep. Exasperated he exclaims, "*Les Vampires* isn't Fu Manchu, right?" Actually, as Edward W. Said notes, Europe has set itself against "the Orient as a sort of surrogate or underground self" (1979, 3), and it may not be stretching the point too thin to see a connection between the villainy of Vep and the fiendishness of Fu Manchu. Like all villains, these characters represent secret, taboo desire, unstated envy, and a projected lust for power, violence, wealth, and control.

Fu Manchu, Song, and Maggie all stand firmly outside the norms of white heterosexuality, representing homoeroticism, transvestitism, lesbianism, and bondage and, like many other screen villains, linking evil with queer desire. Incubi and succubi having plagued the Western imagination for centuries, the association of the seductive Asian villain with the alluring vampire comes as expected. Although the combination of a goatee, silken robes, and lengthy fingernails made Fu Manchu an object of questionable desire, Maggie's Westernized pants and black latex bodysuits help her strike a sinister pose as a demonic mistress of bondage. Song's sleek body and husky voice are coupled with waist-length hair and white, diaphanous robes that suggest the fragile butterfly and the dangerously seductive ghost of the Chinese imagination, where white is associated with the crypt and long, unbraided hair is a sure visual clue for a supernatural seductress in search of an unsuspecting human victim.

If Gallimard and Vidal fall for Song and Maggie Cheung, they also fall precipitously within the precincts of European society. Although bolstered at first by their associations with these Chinese performers, the two men quickly lose everything as they become more deeply involved with the objects of their obsessions. As the Cultural Revolution and U.S. losses in Vietnam disprove his analysis of a passive Asia, Gallimard, already passing sensitive information to Song about U.S. troop movements in Vietnam, loses favor and is shipped back to France. Pursued by Song, he again passes government secrets until his espionage comes to the attention of the authorities, and he and Song are put on trial.

Similarly, Vidal's muse turns into a Medusa when he does not see the magic he expected during the first screening of dailies featuring Maggie Cheung. His creative energies wane; when last seen in the film, he has been drugged to calm his nerves—literally struck dumb—and he falls back in a stupor as if petrified. Although Maggie loses her role in the film-within-the-film, she goes on to New York to meet with Ridley Scott and Los Angeles to meet with her American agent and, presumably, to satisfy in Hollywood the fantasies she only promised to fulfill in France. "Vampire-like" Maggie moves on untouched by Vidal's obsession, just as Song moves on at the end of *M. Butterfly* as a plane carries him back to China while Gallimard commits suicide in prison (see Chow 1998; Ciecko and Lu 1999; De Lauretis 1999).

MASKS AND SCREENS

Villainy has long been linked to masquerade and theatricality—the seductive as well as the dangerous qualities of the mask (Butler 1990, 1993; Holmlund 2002). Because one of the principal hallmarks of villainy is disguise, the connection between masquerade and deviant, evil, or criminal behavior has been long-standing. Just as Fu Manchu is a master of disguise, Song Liling and Maggie Cheung, as performers, are associated with masks and the many negative attributes that have been connected with the theatrical profession for centuries, including treachery, deceit, duplicity, guile, and fraud.

As Marjorie Garber (1992a) notes, Shi/Song does not hold a unique place in the annals of world espionage. Rather, treasonous transvestite actor-spies actually appear with some regularity in global history. Certainly, the glamour and scandal of the great transvestite theatrical traditions of Peking Opera, Japanese Kabuki, and the Elizabethan stage open themselves up to various permutations of this theme. In fact, Shi Pei-Pu claims that Boursicot mistook him for a woman because he saw photographs of the performer playing a woman in the opera, *The Story of the Butterfly,* in which a girl pretends to be a boy to get an education. Rather than seeing a man playing a woman playing a boy, Boursicot preferred to believe the fantasy Shi concocted that he, indeed, was a woman raised as a son to avoid the wrath of his father who already had a household full of daughters. Shi, of course, recognized the importance of hiding any hint of homosexuality behind whatever mask might be available, no matter how improbable. As Joyce Wadler notes in her interview with Shi, "Shi was both captivated and frightened by the female roles. 'The men who played those roles would begin to think of themselves as feminine,' Shi explains. 'It was sad because in China, homosexuality was frowned upon. I had two professors who fell in love: later, the one who was the 'lady' was beaten to death'" (1988, n.p.).

On the screen, Fu Manchu, Cheung, and Song are all adept at playing roles to further their own ends, and all seem to relish the roles they play. Song seems more than a little disingenuous, for example, when he claims that looking at fashion and glamour magazines to portray a more convincing woman in order to elicit secrets from Gallimard is a sacrifice he must make to further the goals of the Cultural Revolution. His government contact remains less than convinced. Clearly, Song enjoys "being a girl," like Nancy Kwan in *Flower Drum Song* (1961), as much as he relishes the double deception of playing it "straight" for Comrade Chin and playing the Butterfly for Gallimard. Thus, the mask reveals—as much as it hides—the motives of the villain.

Rather than hiding the "truth" of identity, the mask serves the more important function of creating the villain. Even the ostensibly benign Maggie becomes associated with criminality and deception when she puts on her latex mask and takes on the persona of Irma Vep, the master thief and head of the "Vampires," a gang that steals only at night under the cloak of darkness. In one scene, for example, Maggie puts on her latex costume, cases the corridors in her hotel, follows a maid into a room where a naked woman (Arsinée Khanjian) is on the phone with her absent lover, steals some jewelry, and sneaks up to the roof to dispose of the ill-gotten goods. Here, the mask seems to take her over, and the reasons for her behavior (acting challenge, rehearsal, research, impulse, intoxication, and so forth) are secondary to her embodiment of the underworld figure she has been brought to Paris to play. Thus, Cheung takes on the role designed for her and becomes the criminal she has agreed to play.

In keeping with the theatrical themes in *M. Butterfly* and *Irma Vep*, the screen, like the mask, takes on a particular significance. In *M. Butterfly*, the image of the Butterfly is projected onto the body of Song, and, after the artifice is revealed with the bare body of the performer, the image turns back on Gallimard who takes on the role himself, as he should, because the Butterfly is a figment of the white European imagination. Gallimard returns obsessively to Puccini's opera that Marina Heung has described as "a foundational narrative of East/West relations, having shaped the Western construction of 'the Orient' as a sexualized, and sexually compliant, space that is ripe for conquest and rule" (1997, 160). *M. Butterfly* never lets it be forgotten that the Butterfly is a projection of desire, a screen that hides what is behind the projected image.

In *Irma Vep*, Vidal decides to project the Asian woman—"mysterious, beautiful, very strong"—onto his "modern" Irma, Maggie Cheung, after a screening of Johnny To's Hong Kong action fantasy *The Heroic Trio* (1992) in the former French colonial outpost of Marrakech. Thus, Vidal's conception of Maggie as the master thief is filtered through a projection of the product of a British colony, Hong Kong, in a former French colony, Morocco, onto the body of a Chinese woman who must somehow embody mystery, beauty, strength, and modernity on a French movie screen torn apart by a postmodern crisis in representation where past images can only be re-presented and only the postcolonial margin holds out hope for shoring up European civilization. Vidal tries to fit his vision of the Asian Irma Vep into a cinematic history weighed down by Feuillade's silent film serial conception of underworld chaos during World War I as well as by his own generation's failed efforts to merge the cinematic with the political. This failed impulse is represented by a clip from a film by the SLON group (Société de Lancement des Oeuvres Nouvelles/Society for the Launching of New Works), formed by Chris Marker in the mid-1960s to empower workers by enabling them to make their own motion pictures (Erickson 1996). *M. Butterfly* also takes up the failure of the Left globally in its depiction of the Cultural Revolution as destructive, chaotic, and irrational. Instead of pointing to an unrealized potential for a complete political transformation, it uses the spectacle of the demonstrations in Beijing and Paris to point to the threatening chaos that lies behind the docile mask of a "feminine" China. Although Assayas may have more sympathy for the ambitions of the Left in the 1960s than does Cronenberg, the failure of the liberatory qualities of modernism points to the postmodern crisis of Western epistemology and bourgeois representation taken up in each film.

In *Irma Vep*, in addition to dealing with the weight of the history of Western cinema, Vidal must also negotiate Hong Kong screen culture's reception in Europe. In an interview with a journalist (Antoine Basler), Maggie hears an action fan's projection of the absolute wonder of working with Jackie Chan and John Woo. Obsessed with Hong Kong action, the critic is unable to grasp that the joy of working with Chan lies in the feeling of being protected as a star, not in doing death-defying stunts; or that Woo does not thrill Maggie as a director because his films revolve around men. As Grace An notes, "This scene becomes less an interview of Maggie Cheung and uses her facial image instead as a platform, a screen onto which French self-deprecation about its own cinema projects itself" (2000, 407).

Ultimately, *Irma Vep* refers to Assayas's own vision of Maggie as a projected image and locus of erotic fantasy because he made the film, in part, to court his leading lady, whom he later married. His constantly moving super-16 camera links the film to cinema vérité and the French documentary tradition of Chris Marker, whereas his penchant for blindingly overexposed shots, ambient noise, and the youth culture of the Parisian streets places him squarely within the French New Wave. If Léaud could be François Truffaut's alter ego (in the Antoine Doinel films), he could also play Assayas's double. However, having been a critic for *Cahiers du cinéma* and a Hong Kong film "fan boy" like the character played by Basler, Assayas cannot help but see himself as the "enemy" of the French New Wave tradition as well. Eventually the director confronts his own obsessions with the Chinese actress and with the difficulty of depicting her without projecting a Western fantasy onto her. Vidal, exasperated, says, "I am interested in you. You are more important than the character. But in the end, there is nothing for you to act." Assayas seems to agree as (through Vidal) he transforms Maggie into "pure" film by scratching and optically printing the footage with light—exposed by scraped emulsion—bursting out from the eye sockets of the faces on the screen. Whether Maggie's encounter with the avant-garde has reinvigorated or destroyed French cinema is hard to say, but the romantic link to criminality, through the French industrial rock version of the "Ballad of Bonnie and Clyde" playing over the end credits, keeps her image within the realm of the scandalous and the iniquitous, even as it helped to launch Olivier Assayas's career as an international auteur.

Although it had been a New York stage sensation, *M. Butterfly* did not dramatically add to David Cronenberg's critical cache. In some respects, this fact-based rumination on East-West politics is out of keeping with the rest of an oeuvre that favors horror and science fiction. However, the film's "typical" white male imploding when confronted by his own sexuality and assailed by those different from him resonates with other Cronenberg characters— Jeremy Irons in *Dead Ringers* (1988), for instance: sexually obsessed, mad, and unable to apprehend the reality behind the surface mask of existence. Cronenberg's other horror films involve horrific and grotesque transformations of the body, the uncertainty of the identity and intent of others, and one's own body becoming the enemy. Imagining sex as horrific and reproduction as grotesque, Irons's seemingly straight white man seduced by a cunning Chinese transvestite is, for Cronenberg, a horror story indeed.

John Lone's inability to play a woman convincingly was seen as a major flaw (Ebert 1993; Corliss 1993). Actually, his Song is more than a blank screen for the projection of Gallimard's fantasies, and the insistent image of the unconvincing transvestite becomes an important part of the ideological operation of the film. Throughout his career, Lone has embodied a catalogue of Hollywood Asian types, including the Yellow Peril gangster Joey Tai in Michael Cimino's *Year of the Dragon* (1985) and Shiwan Khan in *The Shadow* (1994). Even when performing racially unmarked roles—Bertram Stone in Alan Rudolph's *The Moderns* (1988)—Lone has made his career primarily as a villain. In *M. Butterfly*, playing off this career, he stresses the sinister side of Song. Often "feminized" in many of his roles, Lone has always played male characters, and, given his star status, would inevitably have difficulty "fooling" the audience about his gender. He is particularly well suited to the role of a Peking Opera performer, having trained in Chinese opera as a child and being able to bring a stylized physicality to the characterization. As Pu Yi in Bertolucci's *The Last Emperor* (1987), for example, he had incorporated all the dramatic pomp and regal movements of stage emperors, occupying what Rey Chow has called a "feminized space" under Bertolucci's Western male gaze; Lone builds on this association of China with femininity in *M. Butterfly* (Chow 1991; Suner 1998).

Lone is less the flamboyant diva of B. D. Wong's interpretation of the role and more the Cold Warrior in the "gray flannel" skirt. Often, he looks drab in his blue Mao suits, trench coats, and dusty Chinese reeducation camp garb. Indeed, Lone's Song is a decidedly macho transvestite (more akin to Tim Curry's Frank N. Furter in *The Rocky Horror Picture Show* [1975] than to *The Crying Game*'s [1992] Dil [Jaye Davidson] to whom Song has been compared [Rodney 1993]). Song's control in the bedroom scenes is particularly telling: Gallimard may initiate a kiss, but Song places his head in his lover's crotch, forcefully stops his groping, and manages to produce ecstasy by rubbing his buttocks on the seated man's genitalia.

Although it may be entertaining at first to see the Westerner duped by his own imperialist fictions, the relationship takes on an added poignancy as it progresses and Song, increasingly weary of the sham, longs to come out of the closet. Indeed, Song comes most fully into focus when the film's emphasis shifts from East-West politics to sexual politics. Imprisoned together in a police van, Gallimard and Song sit on opposite sides of the screen, framed by wire fencing and engulfed by the grayness of their nearly identical suits and the drab interior of the vehicle. Rather than gloat over his ability to "butterfly" the naïve Gallimard, Lone reads Song's lines as a plea for affection. Confident at first, Song states, "You still adore me, don't you? You still want me—even in a suit and a tie." However, as Gallimard tries to escape from Song's advances, the increasingly desperate Song disrobes and asks to be loved and accepted as a man, pleading, "It was always me. Tell me you adore me." Gallimard, however, white "imperialist devil" to the end, dashes any illusion of genuine love beyond race, nation, and gender: "You show me your true self and what I love is the lie." The broken Song sobs on the empty seat Gallimard had occupied. All of Song's deceptive, but also defensive, masks have been stripped away. The masquerade of femininity has been taken from him, and he can no longer hide behind the Bamboo Curtain of the self-sacrificing comrade. Only his desire for love remains, a queer trace of a postcolonial encounter.

Because neither Maggie nor Song seems to fit into the villain's skin completely they must ultimately remain unconvincing (see Bannerman 2000). Although Maggie manages to be a naughty thief and to miss her work call in the morning, she remains the affable defender of Vidal. Even though he is a spy, Song—like Fu Manchu and Yen Lo—has a taste for Western "decadence" and a decidedly bourgeois lifestyle, and his heart does not seem to be in the role of Red Chinese espionage agent. Unlike Fu Manchu, Maggie and Song have trouble being bad, and this marks the greatest crisis for Western epistemology in these films. If the Orient can no longer function as the "underground self," then the projected fantasy of imperial ambition, colonial conquest, and patriarchal privilege loses its screen in the Other and must ricochet back onto the white male. Underscored by Song and Maggie, then, and by Olivier Assayas and David Cronenberg who screen them, is a Western crisis in masculinity, in sexual identity, and in representation. Ours to consider here, too, is an even more pressing crisis: the West's inability to know itself in relation to the Other, to see itself with respect to Asia, to accept itself in terms of its deepest desire.

WORKS CITED

An, Grace. 2000. "Par-Asian Screen Women and Film Identities: *Irma Vep,*" *Sites* 4:2 (Fall), 398–415.

Bannerman, J. 2000. Review of *M. Butterfly. http://www.stomptokyo.com/otf/Butter-fly/Butterfly.htm*

Butler, Judith. 1990. *Gender Trouble: Feminism and the Subversion of Identity.* New York: Routledge.

———. 1993. *Bodies that Matter: On the Discursive Limits of "Sex."* New York: Routledge.

Chow, Rey. 1991. *Woman and Chinese Modernity: The Politics of Reading between West and East*. Minneapolis: University of Minnesota Press.

———. 1998. *Ethics after Idealism: Theory-Culture-Ethnicity-Reading*. Bloomington: Indiana University Press.

Ciecko, Anne T., and Sheldon H. Lu. 1999. "*The Heroic Trio:* Anita Mui, Maggie Cheung, Michelle Yeoh—Self-Reflexivity and the Globalization of the Hong Kong Action Heroine," *Postscript* 19:1 (Fall), 70–86.

Corliss, Richard. 1993. Review of *M. Butterfly, Time* 142: 4 (October 4), 85.

De Lauretis, Teresa. 1999. "Popular Culture, Public and Private Fantasies: Femininity and Fetishism in David Cronenberg's *M. Butterfly*," *Signs: Journal of Women in Culture and Society* 24:2, 303–34.

Ebert, Roger. 1993. Review of *M. Butterfly*. *Chicago Sun-Times* (October 8). *http://www.suntimes.com/ebert/ebert_reviews/1993/10/882758.html*

Erickson, Steve. 1996. "Making Connections between the Cinema, Politics and Real Life: An Interview with Olivier Assayas," *Cineaste* 22:4, 6–9. *http://home.earthlink.net/~steevee/Assayas.html*

Garber, Marjorie. 1992. *Vested Interests: Cross-Dressing and Cultural Anxiety*. New York: Routledge/Harper Collins.

Heung, Marina. 1997. "The Family Romance of Orientalism: From *Madame Butterfly* to *Indochine*." In Matthew Bernstein and Gaylyn Studlar, eds., *Visions of the East: Orientalism in Film*. New Brunswick, NJ: Rutgers University Press, 160.

Holmlund, Chris. 2002. *Impossible Bodies: Femininity and Masculinity at the Movies*. London: Routledge.

Ma, Sheng-Mei. 2000. *The Deathly Embrace: Orientalism and Asian American Identity*. Minneapolis: University of Minnesota Press.

Marchetti, Gina. 2001a. "America's Asia: Hollywood's Construction, Deconstruction, and Reconstruction of the 'Orient.'" In Roger Garcia, ed., *Out of the Shadows: Asians in American Cinema*. Milan: Edizioni Olivares, produced in conjunction with the 54th Locarno International Film Festival, 37–57.

———. 2001b. "Du péril jaune à la menace rouge" and "Les acteurs asiatiques, du déni au défi." In Charles Tesson, Claudine Paquot, and Roger Garcia, eds., *L'Asie à Hollywood*. Trans. Stéphane Roques. Paris: *Cahiers du cinéma*, in conjunction with the 54th Locarno International Film Festival, 12–33, 34–47.

Okihiro, Gary Y. 1994. *Margins and Mainstreams: Asians in American History and Culture*. Seattle: University of Washington Press.

Rodney, Chris, ed. 1993. *Cronenberg on Cronenberg*. London: Faber and Faber.

Said, Edward W. 1979. *Orientalism*. New York: Random House.

———. 1993. *Culture and Imperialism*. New York: Vintage.

Suner, Asuman. 1998. "Postmodern Double Cross: Reading David Cronenberg's *M. Butterfly* as a Horror Story," *Cinema Journal* 37:2 (Winter), 49–64.

Wadler, Joyce. 1988. "For the First Time, the Real-Life Models for Broadway's *M. Butterfly* Tell of Their Very Strange Romance," *People* 30: 6 (August 8), 88ff. *http://www.cwrl.utexas.edu/~contests-am/hwang/realstory.html*

FIGURE 13. Gobby (Mel Ferrer) with his painting of a "resourcefully resilient figure whose sins are unstoppable" in the coda to Nicholas Ray's *Born to Be Bad* (RKO, 1950). On the canvas at least, Christabel (Joan Fontaine), "a perfect embodiment of the notion of the scheming adventuress," has increasing value "since the scandals of her trajectory will obviously continue and give her a marketable reputation." (Frame enlargement)

CHAPTER THIRTEEN

On the Bad Goodness of Born to Be Bad: Auteurism, Evaluation, and Nicholas Ray's Outsider Cinema

DANA POLAN

What makes a movie bad? When does badness happen? What happens when it does?

Cinephiles—including auteurists—have long held a special key to cinematic enjoyment: the films that are the most fun to watch are often those deemed least in conformity to conventional conceptions of quality. For example, a well-known secret of cinephilia is that the films most deemed bad by tastemakers are often good viewing experiences. Take, for instance, Leonard Maltin's vastly popular *Movies on TV* and *Movie &Video Guide*. Anyone who uses these volumes, with their reduction of film evaluation to rankings that go from "Bomb" to four stars, quickly learns a trick: anything rated "Bomb" has a good chance of being a lot more enjoyable than anything given one-and-a-half stars or, even worse, two-and-a-half stars. Bombs have the possibility, at least, to come off as excessive, extravagant, and outlandish in their blend of pretension and failure, whereas the midrange rankings tend to indicate films that are dull, affectless, unengaging, and forgettable in their uninspiring anonymity. An interesting reversal, then: that which is all the more striking in its "badness" offers a less bad experience than that which is better made. It would seem that there are multiple ways in which badness (and goodness) operate as evaluative forces.

In the cinema (and obviously beyond it), the concept of badness covers at least two ideas. On the one hand, there is the notion of *moral* badness. In this perspective, the cinema is interrogated for the ethics of its representations and their imputed effects; some films will be seen to have unethical and improper themes or characters or situations or whatever, and this will lead to moral critique and even condemnation. There is in this moral perspective on film an understanding of badness as that which reaches beyond the content of the film itself to have a potentially contagious, deleterious effect on spectators (or on some classes of spectators, as in cases of moral panic around what children should or should not see). On the other hand, there is a notion of *aesthetic* badness. Here, cinema is judged for artistic quality: some films will be seen to offer unsuccessful style and will be found to be bereft of beauty or related values. Such films look, feel, and are . . . bad.

As different as these understandings of badness are, they are sometimes conjoined so that an ostensibly immoral film is also declared to be one that is thereby lacking in artistry. Some will even make the assumption that an immoral work must of necessity be lacking in aesthetic value. For instance, when it came out in 1967, *Bonnie & Clyde* was subject to much criticism that seemed to assume that the film's concern with, and perhaps valorization of, a criminal life somehow had an intimate connection to what the critics perceived as the film's supposed aesthetic failures (for example, moral condemnations of the film would sometimes single out Michael J. Pollard's acting style, deemed to be cretinous).

Obviously, there is no transcendental guarantee to attributions of moral and aesthetic badness (or goodness, for that matter). Examples of the moral and the artistic, as well as the very notion of what these terms refer to, are fully historical. We have only to look at the changing reputation of *Bonnie & Clyde* from sleazy exploitation to a classic of cinema to see one immediate case of the revision of values (this is a case, moreover, where the change occurs almost instantaneously in 1967 as some originally condemnatory critics go back to the film and begin to appreciate what they now see as positive values).

Auteurism would be one of those conditions that enable a revision of prior aesthetic categories. In auteurism, precisely those films that a mass public or a certain criticism has condemned as rough, raunchy, unpolished, or schlocky—in other words, as aesthetically "bad"—now often receive valorization: think, for example, of the auteurist defenses of Sam Fuller, a cinematic primitive whose films become for the auteurist a site of value to the extent that they depart from the tedium of standard Hollywood fare. In auteurism, what others take to be bad is now assumed to be good in a special way. Thus, to take another example, whereas mainstream criticism would judge Howard Hawks's *Red Line 7000* (1965) to be an aesthetically uninteresting work that shows the falling off of talent in an aging director, for Hawksian auteurists it is a masterpiece, an autumnal work that enables radiant reflection on the whole of a career.

To be sure, auteurism engages in its own practices of aesthetic inclusion and exclusion and has its own pit of badness to which certain works can be consigned: for example, works by nonauteurs, works by auteurs over which they were putatively unable to have sufficient control, works that auteurs made before they discovered their authorial voice, and so on.

In several respects, *Born to Be Bad,* a film directed by Nicholas Ray in 1950, is a useful case for the examination of what constitutes badness. In the postwar moment of transition from older American moral practices to potentially new ones, the film is situated on the cusp of a clash of ethical positions. The film acknowledges how moral stabilities can mutate, and it describes in detail one embodiment of moral badness in the character fully defined by the film's title. As morality itself is shown in the film to be changing, its mutation is available as a means for staging the castigation and exorcism of the immoral insofar as the mutation is from one moral system to another and must therefore exclude positions (such as that of immorality) that hover between. Despite the badness of its central figure and despite the exploitation-like nature of its title (which, at first, could seem very 1950s in its evocation of sleazy confessional literature or sensationalist pulp novel covers and titles), *Born to Be Bad* encloses badness within an aesthetic frame of good taste, of the well-made Hollywood film. Indeed, the potentially schlocky title plays itself out onscreen against lush romantic music (piano and strings) and not the strident brass we might expect from the "shock" nature of that title. From the start, *Born to Be Bad* signals that it is not going to be as morally or artistically *bad* as all that.

And yet, ironically, it is the very conformity of *Born to Be Bad* to a model of good taste in which there is condemnation of the perfidy of its central character that has led auteurists to declare the film *aesthetically* bad. The conjunction of the film's good morality and its stylistic conformity as one more ordinary work of the studio system mean that it is not granted auteurist merit. By falling into Hollywood anonymity, the film falls outside of auteurist appreciation. Nick Ray auteurists particularly valorize rebelliousness and outsider conditions—that of characters but also that of a visual look that vibrantly brushes against the limits of Hollywood stylistic modes and substitutes for narrative ordinariness an energy, an excitement, the boiling over of a passion (or of "Hot Blood," to cite the title of another Ray film). That the evil figure of *Born to Be Bad* is accorded little admiration by the film's narrative is only one mark of the film's failure to fit auteurist parameters. Another is that the bad figure in the film is not bad in any complex, conflicted fashion—unlike archetypal Ray good-bad figures such as Jim Stark in *Rebel Without a Cause* (1955) or Johnny Guitar—and this lack of ambiguity in character portrayal can only disappoint the Ray auteurist.

My goal here is not to save *Born to Be Bad* for auteurism. I tend to agree with those who contend this film can be inscribed within dominant authorial concerns only with difficulty. But the film is interesting precisely because it shows the pressures of conformity to the dominant system in action. If, in a classic Nick Ray film such as *Rebel*, the end-of-story bow to conformity (Dad promises to be strong for Jim Stark) is inadequate to marshal in all the emotion, passion, and violence of mind and body that have preceded it, *Born to Be Bad* is strongly enclosed by processes of containment: the containment within Hollywood norms of its anonymous style; the containment of its central character's ethical badness by the moral structures and strictures in the film's narrative universe; the containment of a rather ordinary Hollywood film within the evaluative precepts of an auteurism that celebrates the aesthetics of bad boys.

Born to Be Bad* chronicles a segment in the life of Christabel (Joan Fontaine), a perfect embodiment of the notion of the scheming adventuress. An orphan, Christabel has been sent by her Uncle John to live in the big city with his office assistant, Donna (Joan Leslie), and through diligence and dedication to learn to rise through the ranks of the world of work. But Christabel has no intention of playing by the rules and waiting patiently for meager advancement. Through careful plotting, she manages to win and eventually marry Donna's millionaire boyfriend Curtis (Zachary Scott) while continuing a passionate affair with a vibrant, manly novelist, Nick (Robert Ryan). Christabel appears to get her expected comeuppance when, while her aunt is dying, she sneaks off to see Nick and her affair (and her callousness about her aunt) is found out, leading Nick to dump her and Curtis to return to Donna. In the penultimate scene, Curtis takes Donna up in his private plane, and the ride is imaged as a moment of transcendence in which the couple can be freed from the evils of a dangerous world (that is, from Christabel, as the figure who intruded into their romantic bliss). Interestingly, however, for Christabel there is no ultimate punishment. A coda shows an artist, Gobby (Mel Ferrer), a hanger-on who is admired by everyone in the film (from Christabel to those she tries to exploit), making a profit from a painting that he did of Christabel and that promises to rise in value since the scandals of her trajectory will obviously continue and give her a marketable reputation.

This coda is interesting in two ways. First, it suggests that Christabel's badness is not fully contained by the narrative's imposition of a moral lesson: for all the setback that Christabel experiences when Curtis and Nick reject her, she is revealed ultimately to be a resourcefully resilient figure whose sins are unstoppable. Interestingly, this nonending ending—Christabel as a force that will continue to sow badness—might appear to contradict the opening of the film. The very fact that Christabel at the beginning of the narrative has lived so long with her aunt and uncle without them having noticed that she was "born" to be bad implies that such badness was in fact not her fate, but something that grew in her as opportunity presented itself (perhaps in the transition from small town to big city with all its possibilities for advancement). Yet, the fact that at the end it is indicated that Christabel will continue on with her plots and machinations after both Curtis and Nick chastise her suggests that badness, if not her fate from birth, has now become her destiny, the thing that will define her (the portrait is at once the image of her and the sign of the value produced by her sins).

But there's a second way in which the coda is important and this has less to do with Christabel than with Gobby. That is, what we learn in seeing Gobby display the portrait with its new price is not only that Christabel is continuing her career of scandal but also that Gobby intends always to be there, following that career and making as much money from it as he can. In fact, Gobby is shown throughout the film to be a veritable social parasite whose existence depends on his ability to profit from the more productive figures around him (and even Christabel is productive of valuable scandal). This depiction of the artist as crass entrepreneur is important because it signals the film's complicated negotiation of moral positions. In other historical contexts and even in other cultural representations of the moment, we might have imagined such hucksterism to be an object of condemnation (as it is in Frederic Wakeman's *The Hucksters* [1947] from just after the war), but *Born to Be Bad* participates in an increasing postwar valorization of unbridled entrepreneurial spirit, one that extends additionally to its depiction of the big capitalist Curtis as a lovable figure of reason besieged by the machinations of an evil woman. Masculine acquisitive spirit is treated kindly, gently. Indeed, in the historical moment of what Betty Friedan will start to research in the early 1950s as the "Feminine Mystique," the masculinist *Born to Be Bad* requires a positive version of profiteering all the better to castigate and then cast out its improper, immoral, bad feminine version. Gobby's explicit moneygrubbing is deemed part of an acceptable postwar world: the film witnesses a social shift from an older morality that condemns greed and self-interest to one that justifies it as long as it does not originate in a feminine figure who would be better off supporting the entrepreneurial ventures of a man (as it is implied Donna does).

And just as it excuses male entrepreneurialism while condemning feminine ambition in the realm of financial self-aggrandizement, *Born to Be Bad* also endorses other forms of male behavior that only a few years earlier might have met with moral condemnation. If Curtis represents a world of monetary well-being to which both Gobby and Christabel aspire—with admittedly contrasting gendered ethical valences granted to them by the film—very different from this way of life governed by money is the world that Nick represents. Nick is depicted as a raw, even carnal, force; he knows what he wants, which includes a passionate relationship with Christabel. He is a man without guile, a primal fount of will and frank-speaking drive. (*Mea culpa:* when in 1986, in the days before the widespread use of VCRs for film research, I commented on this aspect of *Born to Be Bad,* I misquoted Nick's description of the relationship. At that time, I indicated that he calls it a "sex thing," whereas he in fact qualifies it as a "sex attraction," a phrase that, in keeping with Hays Office regulations, is a little less explicit about the relationship's consummation [see Polan 1996, 292].)

Nick is a writer whose published work is said to derive from his war experience, and *Born to Be Bad* clearly derives his portrait both from the prewar Hemingway model and from the postwar Mailer model. Where there is something a bit unmasculine according to the film's terms in the painter-artist Gobby, a nonsexual figure whose only passion is to take the scraps that fall down to him from the rich people he sycophantically attaches himself to, Nick is represented as fully masculinized according to norms of earthy virility. Lustiness is increasingly given positive moral tones in the postwar moment (we might note that in 1952 Ray himself made a film with the revealing title *The Lusty Men*).

The postwar period embodies, then, a mutation in everyday morality around both financial aggrandizement and sexuality. More and more, a hunger for money and a hunger for sexual pleasure are openly expressed and approved. With the bemused representation of Gobby that offers no condemnation of his moneygrubbing and, even more, with the portrayal of the bland capitalist Curtis, the film valorizes men who ambitiously set out after profit and live a life of privilege far above the masses (the metaphor of Curtis in his airplane). In Nick, by contrast, the film celebrates a new physicalized vibrancy to romance, embodied in a forthright physicality that brooks no connivance or pussyfooting around the fundamental things men and women should do with each other.

But Christabel is excluded from both revisions of morality. As what readers of romance fiction have come to term the "scheming adventuress," Christabel is doubly out of place for the morality of the moment: women are not granted the right to show the entrepreneurial spirit, which would mark their refusal of the dutiful sexualized role of domestic partner, homemaker, and fertile producer of future baby boomers. Significantly, the narrative's castigation of Christabel is accompanied by a stylistic distance from her, and in the film's timorous visual style with respect to Christabel, its hesitation to approach her, we can begin to see some of the reasons for the auteurist refusal to see it as anything more than aesthetically bad.

There's a stylistic sobriety to *Born to Be Bad*, and this can explain much of the auteurist disdain for it. Whereas some directors are lauded in auteurism for their unassuming professionalism (the straightforward action cinema of a Howard Hawks, for example), a recurrent auteurist admiration also exists for directors of excess—directors in whose films suddenly something wild, something vibrant and violent erupts out of the calm of classical style. This is the orbit of directors such as Robert Aldrich or Sam Fuller or Nick Ray or perhaps Anthony Mann (the revenge westerns in which a man is pushed to want in obsessive fashion an extreme retribution for ills done to him). In their acclaimed films, these directors chronicle people (usually men) teetering between obedience and rebellion and frequently exploding into virulent outbursts of rage and railing against the world in which they find themselves. The energetic display of such figures is frequently mirrored in a filmic style that becomes baroque, grandiose, strange, or just downright wacky and wild in its depiction of its losers and loners. (Take, for instance, the opening of Aldrich's *Kiss Me Deadly* [1955]: credits crawling the wrong way up the screen, the headlights of a fast car penetrating forcefully into the night before it, the quiet and melodious strains of Nat King Cole estranged by a young woman's panting that is supposed to indicate terror but actually sounds all too aroused and orgasmic.)

At the beginning of this chapter I noted the seeming paradox by which those films the critical establishment deems terrible are often redeemed in cult fashion. We might call this the Maltin syndrome (for what it's worth, *Born to Be Bad* gets his dreaded two-and-a-half-star rating). But why does such a paradoxical situation exist? Why does popular criticism so frequently conflict in judgment with the taste of those who adore film?

I think we can find one way to deal with the apparent paradox and at the same time more clearly understand the reception of *Born to Be Bad:* by reviewing the distinction between an aesthetic notion of badness and a moral one. The idea of moral badness brings with it an emphasis on effect. That is, it matters that certain things are morally "bad" because of the potential *effect* of this "badness" on certain individuals (for example, children or others who are morally vulnerable). In such a perspective, a typical question to ask of the film would be, what harm can Christabel's adventuring bring and to whom? Whereas aesthetic judgment—a different kind of judgment than moral judgment—can remain fixed on the thing itself (there is, indeed, a whole tradition of philosophy of art that posits value can be decided in terms of internal qualities of art objects without reference to impact on audiences), imagining a theory of morality that would not deal with *effect,* with subjects' investments in moral and immoral objects and the effects such objects have for those subjects, is much more difficult. Moral criticism is always about response—effect, affect, and impact. It is about things done to those who receive the work of art to good or bad ends. Note, for instance, how our language about the beneficence of moral art resonates with a vocabulary that is physical and implies not only spiritual values but corporeal ones. Bad art and good art do things to us. For instance, morally good art, we say, is "uplifting," and in this expression is implied a notion of the very physical act of raising one's being to a new dimension. Likewise, we sometimes talk of good art as "moving," using, again, a vocabulary of transport to do so. From this point of view, and speaking morally, *Born to Be Bad* does not "move" us; it is not "uplifting." It is, perhaps, "degrading."

But when we begin to think aesthetically, two very different notions of badness can be elaborated and contrasted. First, it can be claimed that even though art may move us, "bad" art moves us in the wrong way: emotionally, not aesthetically; in terms of feeling, not form. In one tradition of aesthetics, good art should be altogether above the physical, the affective, and the effective. Indeed, the philosophical tradition of aesthetics that I alluded to earlier, that wants to look at artistic objecthood independent from subjective effect, can at times go as far as to contend that response to art is utterly irrelevant to artistic value (the famous "affective fallacy"). Either art is to be judged without reference to its effect—and is deemed "good" when it can be so judged—or else art that appeals to affect and effect (sentimental art, an art of emotional content) is to be proclaimed as inferior, fallen art. Here the aesthetic is divorced from subjective impact, from emotional affect, and from physical effect. From such a perspective, what would be with *Born to Be Bad*, then, is either that (1) one cannot speak of it *without* getting involved in the deleterious effects of Christabel's actions on other characters and on the audience (without being forced to abandon an aesthetic critical stance for a moral one), or that (2) as art it is only a profoundly sentimental and emotional film, thus, of the *boue*.

But there is a second position that judges art in terms, precisely, of effect. Curiously, however, this is a position that can unite a moralizing approach to art and a trash, cult, or even auteurist aesthetics that finds enjoyment in the bad. If moralizing criticism valorizes works that move us to a "better" place, the discourse of the bad-as-good also valorizes works that work on us, that do things to us, such as excite us, energize us, touch us in ways that seem raw, searing, and corporeal. Hence, the quite strong emphasis, in laudatory writing on trash or notoriously bad cinema, on a vocabulary of the intensely sensory and of the tactile (note how even the subtitle for this volume of essays on filmic badness associates "Infamy, Darkness, Evil, *and* Slime" so that moral issues immediately, naturally, logically, and necessarily slide into sensations that are viscous and visceral). In such a perspective as this, a failed work of art will be not so much one that moves us in the wrong way (although auteurism did have as one of its targets the ostensibly cheap emotionalism in the liberal moralism in the 1950s cinema of directors such as Fred Zinnemann) as one that does not move us at all. This "unifying" perspective would allow for us to think of *Born to Be Bad* as a failed film *precisely because* it has no affect, no effect.

To the extent that the popular press dealt with *Born to Be Bad* at all (and a few reviews were written over the years), it generally saw the film as a slight and even boring mechanical work with little engagement of any sort. Even though its aesthetic decisions and values can seem eccentric in terms of mass taste, auteurist esotericism is related to popular criticism in the sense that both want works that "engage" the spectator. Indeed, at times we find an overlap, such as when auteurism applauds the 1940s films of Howard Hawks for their highly professionalized classicism. What is being promoted in such a case is a mastery of rules of a "Golden Age" of Hollywood films: for both auteurism and popular criticism, the very perfection of the system is itself seen to be a moving experience (and in this respect, auteurism and popular reflection on this "Golden Age" after the fact is always tinged with a high dosage of nostalgia). By the 1950s, however, auteurism increasingly tended to valorize not the followers of rules but those who bent them, filmmakers who made the easy professionalism of classical Hollywood a source for explosive excess.

In this respect, there can be no place for a film like *Born to Be Bad,* regardless of its treatment of the morality of its characters, because it offers little visceral thrill, little that moves the spectator. Ironically, as I write this chapter, the University of California at Berkeley is announcing a conference on trash cinema with the title "Born to Be Bad." It is easy to imagine that Ray's film would have little or no place in such a venue: just as the film's title plays out against romantic music, the film tries for a high-class respectability that turns its back on exploitation cinema. It is not "bad" in a usefully trashy way.

The treatment of morality in *Born to Be Bad* is linked to a treatment of gender. In an early English-language critical study of Nicholas Ray, Michael Wilmington had suggested that the failure of certain Ray films came when they concentrated exclusively on one gender or the other. Wilmington contrasts Ray in this respect to Robert Aldrich where violent, visceral energy comes from focus on only one gender at a time:

> Aldrich is famous for his excesses and grotesque exaggeration: he makes all-male pictures *(The Dirty Dozen, Attack!)* and all-female pictures *(Whatever Happened to Baby Jane?, Sister George),* which after a while begin to seem perverse reflections of each other, the physical violence of the male world balancing the emotional savagery of the female world, and both of them—fierce and chaotic—kept rigorously apart. Ray, on the other hand, very often links these two "separate" worlds in a single film. This mixture of male and female "domains" is expressed, eerily, as an *intrusion.* . . . Intrusion is, perhaps, the most vital element of Ray's universe, and his ideal in this period is a surface harmony which contains, but also reveals, conflicts and tensions. His failures are usually the films in which there is little or no mixture: the two women's films [i.e., *A Woman's Secret* and *Born to Be Bad*] and *Flying Leathernecks.* Paradoxically, the best moments in *Born to Be Bad* are the most vicious ones. (1973, 52)

This is an intriguing analysis but I think it strongly needs to be nuanced. For example, it does not explain the power of late, masculine homosocial films such as *Bitter Victory* (1957) or *Wind Across the Everglades* (1958). Moreover, for our purposes, it must be said that even when Ray films figure the intersecting worlds of the two genders, each is given a different valence. Although emphasizing rebels, resisters, outsiders, marginal figures, wanderers, and so on is central to Ray's cinema, these tend to be male characters exclusively and the female figure is reduced to the role of inspiring—sustaining support of—the man in his rebelliousness (for example, the unbearable Hope Lange in *The*

True Story of Jesse James [1957]). True, Judy (Natalie Wood) is arrested along with Jim (James Dean) and Plato (Sal Mineo) in *Rebel Without a Cause* but quickly Judy is revealed to be no real rebel, just a lost girl looking for love and serving as veritable chattel to be exchanged between men (she goes from Buzz to Jim in just a few scenes). With the primary exception of *In a Lonely Place* (1950), Ray's films spiritualize femininity as a force that tames men who are "on dangerous ground" (to quote the title of a Ray film where, in accordance with a widespread mythology, a woman's physical handicap—in this case, blindness— is equated with her powers to inspire and uplift a confused masculinity). *In a Lonely Place* matters in Ray's oeuvre because it counterbalances the stereotype of woman's capacity for moral amelioration of man with a powerful image of a strong, self-willed woman who resists her stereotypical role (but who is no less conflicted about her actions than the typical Ray male figure).

Even if, per Michael Wilmington, Ray's best films mix male and female worlds, these films essentialize femininity to juxtapose it with a fractured, lost, confused masculinity. Furthermore, the films find visual and visceral correlates for this tortured masculinity in violent actions (for example, Jim pounding on the desk in *Rebel Without a Cause*) and in vibrant nonclassical mise-en-scène (for instance, the canted angles in the same film). This fascination with troubled masculinity has as its complement the relative lack of interest—in the films and in the spectators watching the films—in depiction of pure, unambiguous evil. Ray's films are not about a badness "out there," the badness of an irremediable Other that heroes oppose with unambiguous purity of purpose. This, perhaps more than the lack of women, explains the unimportance of *Flying Leathernecks* (1951), which finally is little more than a typical us-versus-them war picture (with a hero who is tortured and rebellious emerging from that condition to fulfill his bellicose function). Likewise, *55 Days at Peking* (1963) ultimately turns any struggle of characters with their own internal demons into the more externalized battle with a faceless, orientalized enemy.

Similar to these simplistic us/them Manichean action films, *Born to Be Bad* is a film about a purity of binary values—good and bad—rather than any chaos or confusion within and between them. The men are secure in their identities: Curtis the upright millionaire, Gobby the charming artist-parasite, Nick the virile writer. The women are secure—and secured—in theirs: Donna the simpering and always-faithful fiancée and Christabel the never-hesitating, scheming adventuress. Ironically, *Born to Be Bad* resembles less the films of tortured souls that Ray and others (including Aldrich) would create out of the chaos of the 1950s than it does the bug-eyed monster science-fiction film of the period with its cold and hygienic us/them morality. In both cases, badness is embodied in a pure and unambiguous force of menace, and that fixed identity finds its correlate in a dry, functional, often uninspired cinematic style— often, a zero degree of style. (Few excessive science-fiction films exist other than those in low-budget cinema; likewise, few science-fiction auteurs exist: instead, we get the invisible nonstyle of a Robert Wise or a Jack Arnold or the competent professionalism of a Christian Nyby.)

As in *Born to Be Bad*, in science fiction of the 1950s the camera often stays at a distance from the action, all the better to capture the duel of pure good and evil. Such sober distance also shows up in the relative paucity of point-of-view shots: because the good guys have no depth, insofar as they exist just to fight the monsters, we have no need to enter their psychology or even their viewpoint (except when a monster attacks—hence, the first-person sensationalism of 3-D science fiction). In similar fashion, the style of *Born to Be Bad* stays at a distance from its narrative world: this is also an antiseptic work that is not about psychology and complex and conflicted emotion.

For the critical establishment, the result can only be badness of the least interesting sort. Would there be a way to redeem *Born to Be Bad?* Probably not, nor need we hope for its redemption. But studying the film can be instructive. On the one hand, the film serves as a useful symptom of shifts in postwar American morality. This does not make the film "good": any number of films and other cultural works could serve as especially revelatory symptoms of the age. (Indeed, one of the lessons of my book on the period, *Power and Paranoia* [Polan 1996], is that we need a large sampling to draw strong relations between cultural production and social moment. In this respect, any single work is of relative unimportance.) On the other hand, the failure of *Born to Be Bad* to find a place within aesthetic systems of valuation—such as that of auteurism—instructs us as much about the functioning of those systems as about the value (or lack thereof) of this one film. Perhaps it would be useful for critical theory to move outside the framework that assumes we must condemn or else redeem films, in order to look at why we need to evaluate in the first place, why the practice of evaluation has been centrally equated with the project of film study. Indeed, the primary concern of this chapter has been a metacritical one: not a judgment about the badness or goodness of *Born to Be Bad* but a foundational critique of the very procedures by which we distinguish good and bad yet also blur them (for example, the good bad film, the merely bad bad film). No film is "born to be bad": it finds its value only within a user community that takes for itself the right to judge and to decide cinematic fate.

WORKS CITED

Polan, Dana. 1996. *Power and Paranoia: History, Narrative, and the American Cinema, 1940–1950.* New York: Columbia University Press.

Wilmington, Michael. 1973. "Nicholas Ray: The Years at RKO (Part One)," *The Velvet Light Trap* 10 (Fall), 46–53.

FIGURE 14. In *The Birds* (1963), a mother (Doreen Lang) accuses Melanie Daniels ('Tippi' Hedren) of causing the bird attacks. "In a shot framed from Hedren's perspective, the hysterical woman screams right into the camera (symbolically, right at us, right at Hitchcock), 'I think you're *evil!*'"—perhaps "the only occasion . . . when a Hitchcock character utters the word *evil*." (Frame enlargement)

CHAPTER FOURTEEN

The Villain in Hitchcock:
"Does He Look Like a 'Wrong One' to You?"

WILLIAM ROTHMAN

Numerous observers have noted that Hitchcock's villains are often the most interesting characters in their films—the most charming, and, strangely, even the most sympathetic. Hitchcock often seems to *identify*—however exactly we understand this term—at least as much with his villains as with his protagonists (although the matter is complicated by his equally strong identification with his female characters).

Within Hitchcock films, the villain represents, at one level, a recurring character type or set of types, like the girl-on-the-threshold-of-womanhood, as I call her in *Hitchcock—The Murderous Gaze* (1982) or the policeman who uses his official powers for his own private ends. Most often, Hitchcock's villains possess the *sang-froid* of the gamesman, who treats matters of life and death as merely aesthetic matters. Just think of the moment in *The 39 Steps* (1935) when Richard Hannay (Robert Donat) tells the Professor (Godfrey Tearle) that he has been warned to be on the lookout for a diabolical mastermind missing the top joint of his little finger, and the Professor, with a grin that invites an appreciative grin in return, holds up his own hand to disclose that he is that villainous character. Not only villains, among Hitchcock characters, have such a sense of style, however. When at the end of *Frenzy* (1972) the Inspector (Alec McCowen) catches the murderer with his pants down, as it were, he speaks the wonderful line, "Mr. Rusk, you're not wearing your tie," with exactly the same understated relish that we hear in James Mason's voice, at the end of *North by Northwest* (1959), when Vandamm, now in custody, says to the Professor (Leo G. Carroll), who has just had a marksman shoot Vandamm's lieutenant, Leonard (Martin Landau), "Not very sporting, using real bullets."

With his cockney upbringing, Hitchcock no doubt found satisfaction in embracing the honorable, time-honored tradition of associating villainy with the manners of the English upper class. (But compare *Frenzy,* with its unapologetically working-class villain.) The effeteness projected by this style also gives many Hitchcock villains a hint of homosexuality. This enhances our sense, in several Hitchcock films, most notably *Strangers on a Train* (1951), that the bond between protagonist and villain is deeper than the relationship either has, or desires, with whatever woman whose affections are ostensibly at issue. There are other Hitchcock films, however, in which the villain loves a woman, or at least passionately desires her. We see this in *Notorious* (1946), for example; hence Hitchcock's remark to Truffaut that Sebastian's (Claude Rains) love for Alicia (Ingrid Bergman) is deeper than Devlin's (Cary Grant). We see it in *North by Northwest,* as well. When Leonard informs Vandamm that Eve Kendall (Eva Marie Saint) has betrayed him, Vandamm loses his composure and slugs him. In *Murder!* (1930) we see Handel Fane (Esme Percy) momentarily lose control when Sir John (Herbert Marshall) has him audition for the killer's role in his new play, revealing beyond a shadow of a doubt that, despite his disciplined efforts to keep his feelings hidden, he is as seething with emotion as the "bloke what twitches" in *Young and Innocent* (1937). Such cases are illustrations of Hitchcock's oft-repeated dictum that we are fated to kill what we most love. These are crimes of passion, not profit. And the tormented villains who commit them are what I call "Wrong Ones."

Hitchcock's "Wrong Ones," such as Handel Fane in *Murder!,* the "bloke what twitches" in *Young and Innocent,* Uncle Charles (Joseph Cotten) in *Shadow of a Doubt* (1943), Bruno (Robert Walker) in *Strangers on a Train,* or, most famously, Norman Bates (Anthony Perkins) in *Psycho* (1960), are unfit for love. Condemned from childhood to a life outside the human circle, their form of life is solitary, and sexuality remains a closed book to them. Perhaps Hitchcock, too, is a Wrong One, his films imply—at least rhetorically—even as they call on us to acknowledge that we may be Wrong Ones as well.

In *The 39 Steps,* by contrast, we never see a crack in the villain's façade that is wide enough to reveal what inner turmoil, if any, lies beneath—except, perhaps, when his wife (Helen Haye) knocks on the door to call him to lunch at just the moment when he is waiting to see how Hannay will react to his theatrical master stroke of unmasking himself by showing his hand. As the villainous Professor goes to unlock the door, he casts Hannay a look of frustration, as if he expects his intended victim to share his impatience with his wife's untimely interruption. By presenting us with this look, Hitchcock invites us to speculate that the Professor's work as a spy is his one area of self-assertion in a sexless marriage. Alone in his study, the Professor can escape from his wife and from the confines of domesticity, and, like Hitchcock storyboarding his films, he can absorb himself in his dream or fantasy of authoring the world. The interpretation invited, then, is that the Professor's traitorous schemes are displacements of his wish to murder his wife, perhaps a wish to do violence to all women (which would explain his relentless designs on Annabella Smith [Lucie Mannheim]). Viewed this way, the Professor, like a number of other Hitchcock villains, becomes an Avenger figure, a descendant of the original villainous "Wrong One" in *The Lodger* (1926). In the case of the Professor, however, this interpretation remains speculative, precisely because we never see his *sang-froid* decisively break down. Hitchcock chooses to leave unresolved whether the Professor is really a "Wrong One," tormented by emotions he struggles to control, or a heartless monster like the shipwrecked Nazi (Walter Slezak) in *Lifeboat* (1944) or Eric Mathis (Ivan Triesault), the most murderous of the Nazi conspirators in *Notorious*, who quite simply have no feelings to hurt.

In this context, the singularity of *Vertigo*'s (1958) Gavin Elster (Tom Helmore), who may otherwise strike us as one of Hitchcock's least memorable villains, stands out. Gavin Elster seems no more a soul in torment, no more a "Wrong One" gripped by powerful emotions he struggles to control, than do Hitchcock's cold-blooded Nazis. Yet no heartless Nazi would be capable of transforming Judy Barton into the Madeleine (Kim Novak) who makes Scottie (James Stewart) and us (and no doubt Hitchcock, whose art effects a comparable metamorphosis when it creates the figures of Judy and Madeleine out of the "stuff" of Kim Novak) fall in love with her. How could Gavin Elster *not* fall in love with this beautiful creation? And yet he ditches her, leaving her only the necklace that ultimately seals her fate. What motivates Gavin Elster, then? Profit? Hardly. The wish to commit a perfect murder, like John Dall in *Rope* (1948)? No. Somehow, we sense that his specific intent is to transform Scottie's darkest nightmare into reality by performing a gesture that is perfect in its cruelty. What motive, intelligible in human terms, could he possibly have for singling out Scottie and making him suffer like Job? None, it would seem. Perhaps that is the point. At the end of *Stage Fright* (1950), the Richard Todd character realizes that if he kills again, this time with no discernible motive, a jury would take that as proof that he was mad, hence not guilty by reason of insanity of the murder he has already committed and for which he would otherwise be hanged. It is as if Gavin Elster has no other motive than to prove—to Scottie? to himself? to us?—not that he is mad, but that a cruel divinity holds sway over this madhouse of a world. We might also say that Gavin Elster has no motive other than to enable *Vertigo,* Hitchcock's perfect work of art, to be created. Without Gavin Elster, *Vertigo* would have no plot. In his cruelty, he is not an agent of the Devil, like the villain in a nineteenth-century theatrical melodrama. He is an agent of the film's author, Alfred Hitchcock.

In Hitchcock's films, villains are not the only ones who perform acts of cruelty, of course. No one could be crueler than the detectives who interrogate Manny Balestrero (Henry Fonda) early in *The Wrong Man* (1956). (When one of the detectives says to him, "This looks bad for you, Manny, it really looks bad for you," he is being so cruel, and his cruelty is so gratuitous, that I have always found this line—in a perverse way, of course—to be one of the most hilarious in all of Hitchcock.) When the surviving Americans in *Lifeboat* realize that they have let the villainous Nazi outsmart them, they exact cruel vengeance, brutally beating the German before tossing him overboard to his death. In *Rear Window* (1954), there is an unmistakable element of cruelty in Jeff's (James Stewart) relentless efforts to prove that Lars Thorwald (Raymond Burr) murdered his wife (Jeff seems to feel no human sympathy for the dead woman, or for the desperation that may have driven Thorwald to commit the crime). In *Notorious,* Cary Grant is crueler to Ingrid Bergman than Claude Rains, the villain, ever dreams of being, and Grant is no less cruel to Eva Marie Saint in *North by Northwest,* especially in the celebrated art auction sequence. In *Vertigo,* Scottie is as cruel to Midge (Barbara Bel Geddes) as he is to Judy ("It can't matter to you," indeed!). It isn't a capacity for cruelty, then, that distinguishes Hitchcock's villains from his other characters—or from Hitchcock. In *Sabotage* (1936), Hitchcock cruelly traps Sylvia Sidney, the film's protagonist, in a marriage as frightful as Margaret's in *The 39 Steps;* calls on her to affirm her innocence by killing her husband, the film's villain; and plays for suspense—for kicks, we might say—the violent death of her likable young brother, not to mention his cute puppy, compelling us to recognize that the author's capacity for cruelty—to his characters, to us—equals that of his most villainous characters.

When in *The 39 Steps* the Professor holds up his hand and Hitchcock cuts to a close shot from Hannay's point of view, the Professor presents to Hannay a view meant to shock and rivet him. "When describing what happens in a film," I wrote in *The Murderous Gaze,* "we frequently find ourselves identifying with the camera, saying, for example, 'Now we see . . .' But the agency that presents us with *this* view cannot be thought of as 'we.' The view imposes itself on us, disrupting and compelling our attention. It is Hitchcock, as it were, showing us his hand" (1982, 144).

The Hitchcock villain, master of the art of murder, is also—as *Vertigo* declares with exceptional clarity—an allegorical stand-in for Hitchcock himself, the master of "the art of pure cinema." That Hitchcock's art has a murderous aspect is a—or *the*—quintessentially Hitchcockian idea. *Sabotage* suggests, specifically, that Hitchcock's art is the murderous work of a saboteur—in today's parlance, a terrorist. Is Hitchcock, then, in George W. Bush's immortal phrase, an *evil doer?* Donald Spoto's biography of Hitchcock maliciously spread the impression—based on remarkably little evidence—that in his personal life as well as in his role as author he was so cruel it would be accurate to call him "evil."

How villainous is Hitchcock? Is he really evil? For that matter, how villainous are Hitchcock's villains? Are *they* evil?

In *The Birds* (1963), a mother (Doreen Lang) accuses Melanie Daniels ('Tippi' Hedren) of causing the bird attacks. In a shot framed from Hedren's perspective, the hysterical woman screams right into the camera (symbolically, right at us, right at Hitchcock), "I think you're *evil!*" I stand to be corrected, of course, but this is the only occasion I can think of when a Hitchcock character utters the word *evil*. One reason the moment is so startling is that evil is a concept alien to the Hitchcock worldview. In nineteenth-century theatrical melodramas, as I have said, villains are exemplars of pure evil, where evil is understood as an occult, supernatural force in eternal opposition to the forces of good. If villains are agents of the devil, in effect, the Hitchcock characters I have been calling "villains" are not true villains. Hence it is an ironic moment when, in *Blackmail* (1929), the Artist (Cyril Ritchard), having lured Alice (Anny Ondra) up to his atelier, waits for her to finish dressing, and Hitchcock contrives for there to be a shadow on Ritchard's face that momentarily makes him appear to have the pencil mustache of a stock stage villain.

Film massively appropriated nineteenth-century theatrical melodrama, even as it fundamentally transformed it. As I argued in "Virtue and Villainy in the Face of the Camera" (1988), Griffith's films, which owe everything to theatrical melodrama, also undermine it by bringing to the fore encounters between the camera and its human subjects, encounters for which theatrical melodrama knows no equivalent. They place the viewer in intimate relationships, unavailable to theater audiences, with human beings who inhabit the world, creatures of flesh and blood, not agents of supernatural forces.

In theatrical melodramas of the nineteenth century, Peter Brooks argues in *The Melodramatic Imagination,* the nightmare struggle for the liberation of virtue is won when goodness is publicly recognized in a "movement of astonishment," and evil—with its own lesser power to astonish—is driven out. They are dramas of recognition in which acts that Brooks calls "self-nomination" play an essential role. "The villain at some point always bursts forth in a statement of his evil nature and intentions" (1976, 37), just as the heroine announces her moral purity. In films, however, characters do not have the authority to declare their moral identity, for they are always also subjects of the camera. They do not, and cannot, know themselves the way the camera enables us to know them.

When Professor Jordan holds up his hand in *The 39 Steps,* the view Hitchcock presents to viewers, which is meant to shock and rivet us, matches the view the Professor presents to Hannay. The shot of Jordan's hand, viewed from Hannay's perspective, links Hitchcock with the villain (both are authors of views). And it links us with the villain's intended victim (Hannay is a viewer, just as we are). Like Hannay, we are compelled to recognize that a diabolical mastermind has set a trap for us.

At the same time Jordan unmasks himself to Hannay, Hitchcock unmasks himself to us, in other words. Indeed, Hitchcock's gesture not only declares its affinity with Jordan's, it trumps it. Through the gesture of showing his hand, the Professor opens Hannay's eyes to the fact that he has been Jordan's unwitting pawn. But by presenting us with a view that *contains* the view Jordan presents to Hannay, Hitchcock opens our eyes to the fact that Jordan is *his* unwitting pawn, as surely as Hannay is. Jordan, too, is subject to Hitchcock's camera. Professor Jordan claims authorship of this moment, but he is trapped, like Hannay, within a world whose real author is Hitchcock.

In passages such as this, Hitchcock declares the camera to be an instrument of villainy by asserting a link between a villain's gesture and a gesture of the camera. In other passages, he has the camera assume the villain's point of view, or frames a villain staring into the depths of the frame in a way that makes of him a veritable stand-in for the camera. In these cases, it is the camera's passive aspect, not its agency, that is associated with villainy. Hence they are akin to the Hitchcock passages that portray guilty acts of viewing. When Norman Bates views Marion Crane (Janet Leigh) through his secret peephole, this is not an example of a villain's self-nomination, as in theatrical melodramas. This villain is "nominated" by the camera, which links his villainy to his—and our—act of viewing.

Another strategy Hitchcock employs to declare the camera's villainous aspect is exemplified by the ending of *Psycho.* When Norman Bates/Tony Perkins raises his gaze directly to the camera and grins, he presents himself to be viewed. Like the Professor when he shows his hand, he authors a view. But the view whose authorship he claims is a view of *him.* And it is presented *to us.* That is, it is a view framed by Hitchcock's camera. Presenting this view is a gesture by the camera and the camera's subject at once. Their gestures are not only linked; they are one and the same. At this moment, Hitchcock and Norman/Perkins appear to be conspirators of such intimate complicity that a distinction can hardly be drawn between them. In effect, I argue in "Virtue and Villainy," the film's author has become one with his camera's human subject. "Norman/Perkins has become a mask for Hitchcock, one of Hitchcock's stuffed birds. In turn, the grinning Norman/Perkins has been impressed indelibly on our idea of who Hitchcock is" (1988, 76).

There is one last strategy I would like to consider. It is exemplified by the passage in *The Lodger* that begins with a shot of the lodger (Ivor Novello) staring directly at the camera, a knowing look on his face, as if he were a villain in complicity with it. That we cannot tell where he is, or whom he is looking at, invites us to imagine that he is the serial killer known as the Avenger in the presence of his next victim. The next shot, from his point of view, of Daisy, his landlord's daughter, modeling a high fashion dress, retroactively places him in the audience at a fashion show. For a moment, we are relieved. This man no longer seems to be the villainous Avenger, but only an innocent spectator who takes pleasure in viewing Daisy, exactly as we do in viewing him viewing her. Then it strikes us that perhaps the lodger is the Avenger after all. Perhaps this viewer is not innocent. Perhaps no viewer is.

This sequence initially seems to unmask the lodger as a villain. Then it seems to assert his innocence. Ultimately, it turns out to be ambiguous. The sequence does not declare that he is guilty. Nor does it declare him innocent. Rather, it compels us to recognize that we do not know his real intentions. For all we know (Hitchcock is saying), this subject of the camera—any subject of the camera—may be capable of murder, whether he knows it or not. In the face of the camera, the lodger is a human being, as we are. But to be human is to be capable of villainy.

The grueling sequence in *Frenzy* in which the fruit-vendor Rusk (Barry Foster) rapes and murders Brenda Blaney (Barbara Leigh-Hunt), the former wife of his friend Richard Blaney (Jon Finch), the film's protagonist, is in a sense the inverse of the *Lodger* passage. When Rusk visits Brenda in her office—she runs a matrimonial agency—she coldly informs him that on the basis of the information in his file, her agency cannot service a man with his repulsive sexual appetites. Finally he discloses to her that he is not there because he wants her to fix him up with someone. He wants *her*. She is "his type of woman." Repelled by him, she becomes more and more frightened as he seems increasingly to lose control. Soon he begins to rape her. When he comes too quickly, he seems so possessed by frustration and rage that his voice becomes strangely slurred, as if he were in the grip of an epileptic fit, and (to borrow a phrase from Norman Bates) he is transformed into a "raving thing." At this point, Brenda knows that he is going to strangle her. But she believes that her killer is a pathetic, sick man driven mad by his sexual impotence. We believe this, too, until Rusk goes over to the dead woman's desk and stands there for a moment with his back to the camera. Still turned away from the camera, he picks up a half-eaten apple and takes a hearty bite. Then he puts the remainder in his pocket and, with a jaunty bounce to his step, walks coolly out of the office. From the moment he takes the bite out of the apple, he no longer seems like a tormented "Wrong One." Now he has the insouciant air of a cold-blooded villain with no regard for human frailties—not an Adam, but an evil Serpent. Which is his true face, then? Which is a mask? We cannot know the answer to this question because Rusk never unmasks himself. Nor does Hitchcock unmask him. At the moment Rusk bites into the apple, his face is hidden from the camera, or, rather, the camera hides his face from us.

When Norman Bates/Tony Perkins fixes the camera in his gaze, by contrast, a villain appears to be unmasking himself with the camera's complicity. But then "mother's" mummified face is momentarily superimposed over (surfaces from within?) this man's living face.

Hitchcock's extraordinary gesture declares that whoever or whatever we take Norman Bates/Tony Perkins to be—male or female? alive or dead? son or mother? murderer or victim? creation or creator?—this is a human being, a creature of flesh and blood.

In *The Murderous Gaze,* I interpret this composite figure, this being possessed by death, as emblematic of the condition of all human beings on film. Villainy is integral to Hitchcock's vision, but it emerges from, and expresses, a perfectly human wish to escape from the real conditions of human existence:

> The camera fixes its human subjects, possesses their life. They are reborn on the screen, creatures of the film's author and of ourselves. But life is not fully breathed back into them. They are immortal but they are always already dead. The beings projected on the screen are condemned to a condition of death-in-life that may be a dream of triumphing over death, holding death forever at bay. But . . . the world of a film is not a private island where we may escape the conditions of our existence. At the heart of every film is a truth we already know: we have been born into the world and we are fated to die. (1982, 341)

In theatrical melodramas, villains are not human beings; they are exemplars of pure evil, understood as an eternal, supernatural force. Their moral identities are fixed. Hence, they are capable of knowing—and thus "nominating"—themselves. They have the authority to declare their own evil. Human beings, creatures of flesh and blood, do not possess such power. Our identities are never fixed. Always in the process of becoming, we never fully know ourselves.

The subjects of the camera are human beings, not agents of occult forces. Characters in films are always mysteries to themselves. (It is no accident that film and psychoanalysis grew up together.) Only the camera can nominate a villain, and it can do so only by nominating itself. When human beings perform villainous acts, as they often do, the camera is implicated—the film's author is implicated, we are implicated—in their villainy.

No filmmaker has had a deeper understanding of these principles than Hitchcock. His cinema is a sustained, profound meditation on their implications.

WORKS CITED

Brooks, Peter. 1976. *The Melodramatic Imagination.* New Haven, CT: Yale University Press.

Rothman, William. 1982. *Hitchcock—The Murderous Gaze.* Cambridge, MA: Harvard University Press.

———. 1988. "Virtue and Villany in the Face of the Camera." In *The "I" of the Camera: Essays in Film History, Criticism and Aesthetics.* New York: Cambridge University Press.

Spoto, Donald. 1983. *The Dark Side of Genius: The Life of Alfred Hitchcock.* Boston: Little, Brown.

PART III

The Charisma of Villainy

FIGURE 15. Irena Dubrovna (Simone Simon) in *Cat People* (Jacques Tourneur, RKO, 1942): her efforts to become a modern American wife are haunted by the memory of a suppressed female cultural history. In the end, she shares "the common fate of pathetic or dangerous homosexuals in literature, theatre, and films," invoking a "medieval evil," the queer possibilities of which fascinated American viewers. (Frame enlargement)

CHAPTER FIFTEEN

The "Evil Medieval": Gender, Sexuality, Miscegenation, and Assimilation in Cat People

ALEXANDER DOTY

AND

PATRICIA CLARE INGHAM

As temporal categories go, "modernity" usually stakes a claim to progressive social mores, technological progress, and political enlightenment. As popularly the opposite of *modernity,* the *medieval*—especially when used as an adjective—tends to register the complete absence of tolerance, lawful order, progress, or enlightenment. To describe an activity, belief, or political regime as *medieval* is more often than not to place it outside contemporary civilized culture, caught in an apparently "primitive" time beyond the reach of progress. According to this traditional view, medieval times were evil days now replaced by the enlightened virtues of progress.

And yet, as Carolyn Dinshaw has recently argued, the "medieval" can also be deployed to critique the ideologies of modern power, particularly those that police sexuality. In her fresh rereading of Foucault's later work, Dinshaw suggests that Foucault's complex use of the "medieval" embeds a twofold history. On the one hand, "medieval" techniques of the self (specifically, the confessional) constitute an early version of what will eventually become a modern regularized regime of repression; yet, for Foucault, the "medieval" also recalls a time outside the modern regulation of unitary normative sexuality, a time of polymorphous, and multiple, erotic surfaces. This second "medieval," Dinshaw argues, is the one Foucault "most deeply desires": "a time whose lack of unified sexuality is preferable to the present with its 'fictitious unity' of normative sexuality, a time whose sexual disaggregation is not to be feared but can for the future offer a creative, even liberatory, potential" (1999, 205). Figured in this way, the medieval signals a potential space for alternatives to contemporary gender and sexual normativity. Pleasures policed by the modern state may have been less efficiently suppressed, and less easily defined, even in the premodern confessional. What modernity marks as "outlaw" may emerge, once we "get medieval," as the multiply ambiguous, the indeterminate, the "queer."

Cat People (1942) offers a view of this ambiguous, indeterminate "queerness" as a phenomenon with a powerful medieval history. The film alludes to a twelfth-century sisterhood, the Cat Women of Serbia, who, through their dalliance with the Mamaluks, contest the traditional, Christian, patriarchal rule of King John. These Cat Women encode the queer space Dinshaw describes as Foucault's "second" medieval: lacking a clearly defined sexuality, they (and their descendants) offer "a liberatory potential" beyond the confines of heterosexual patriarchy. Yet at first glance, the film seems invested in a vision of the "evil medieval," staged both through the central icon of the film (a statue of King John of Serbia) and the unfolding of narrative events. Set in 1940s New York City, the story focuses on the difficult assimilation of Serbian émigrée Irena Dubrovna (Simone Simon), a woman who seeks to escape what she understands to be the savagery of her cultural history. Rooted in a legend of the medieval Serbian "good" King John, this history tells of his heroic reconquest of Irena's village from the "evil" Mamaluks and the reestablishment there of Christian law and order. Irena hopes that her assimilation to modern U.S. culture through her marriage to Oliver Reed (Kent Smith), a self-proclaimed "good ol' Americano," will effect her escape from this horrifying medieval past. But her efforts to take on the role of modern American wife remain haunted by the twelfth-century history of the Cat People, "the wisest and most wicked" followers of the Mamaluks who escaped "good" King John's sword.

Among other things, Cat People deploys this trope of the "evil medieval" as an unconscious marker of American history. As E. Ann Kaplan suggests, Cat People is "America's 'dream' about its own 'dark places'" (1997, 120). And these dark places are connected with the so-called Dark Ages. The film displaces twentieth-century issues of sexuality, gender, race, and ethnicity onto medieval times through a conservative official history that identifies King John as its patriarchal cultural hero. Yet despite this apparent conservatism, the film also invites attention to a competing version of medieval history, an alternative story that foregrounds the oppression of the Cat People, a queer culture driven into the hills. This is a culture that embraces multiculturalism and nonnormative gender and sexuality. From the view of that cultural history, King John is no hero, but a victimizer, and the once-oppressed Cat People survive into the twentieth century as a queer force to be reckoned with.

KING JOHN VS. THE CAT WOMEN:
COMPETING ACCOUNTS OF HISTORY

The official version of medieval Serbian history in *Cat People* centers around the statue of a triumphant, conquering King John that Irena keeps in her apartment just as, she will tell Oliver, "perhaps you have a picture of George Washington or Abraham Lincoln." The king sits astride a horse, raising aloft a sword on which is skewered a large pantherlike cat. Irena will tell King John's history to the film's two representatives of straight white, American male culture: her boyfriend, soon-to-be-husband, Oliver, and her psychoanalyst, the predatory Dr. Judd (Tom Conway). In response to Oliver's initial questions about the statue, the desperate-to-be-assimilated Irena tells an "official story" of dark foreigners, the Mamaluks, who invaded her Serbian village in the twelfth century. At first, the people of the village had been "good and worshipped God in a true Christian way," but eventually the Mamaluk influence—which presumably included exogamous relations between Mamaluks and Christians—made the people change. When King John arrived, so Irena tells Oliver, "he found dreadful things. People bowed down to Satan and said their masses to him; they had become witches and were evil." The Christian, and in this account good, King John kills the evil ones, ridding the village of Mamaluk influences. The "wisest and most wicked" escape King John's wrath and flee into the hills. Irena concludes: "The wicked ones, their legend haunts the village in which I was born."

Yet, even as Irena offers the official version of Serbian history, visual cues trouble her account. Whereas Irena and Oliver initially share the left side of the screen, as soon as she begins her story the statue is positioned between them, separating instead of uniting them in a shared connection to heroic national liberators (King John, Washington, Lincoln). Furthermore, when Irena tells Oliver that the cat on King John's sword is "not really a cat," but a representation of "the evil ways into which [her] village had once fallen," she turns her back on him and moves across the room, signaling a subconscious discomfort with the official version of history she narrates. She is now positioned as a small figure in the background of a shot in which the statue and Oliver's silhouetted arm loom in the foreground. At this point there is a shot/reverse shot series in which a shot of Oliver next to King John's statue alternates with one of Irena positioned in front of the fireplace. Over the fire-place hangs a painting, the bottom half of which contains a man's legs and feet beside two small black cats. With Irena positioned in front of the painting, the man's feet appear to be standing directly on her head. The two black cats peer out from beside her face. This frame juxtaposes the image of a man tow-ering over Irena with the faces of the cat couple alongside her. This picture and Irena's position vis-à-vis the picture, as well as the shot/reverse shot edit-ing between Irena/the cat painting and Oliver/King John's statue, suggest the contested spaces of her history.

On the one hand, Irena's story of the Serbian "George Washington" attempts to flatten out racial, cultural, ethnic, religious, and sexual hetero-geneity into a fantasy of historic and cultural homogeneity, a history of male conquest as national liberation from the perverse "evil" of Mamaluks and witches/Cat People. However the mise-en-scène and editing described above emphasize Irena's separation, disjunction, and alienation from (and perhaps even oppression by) Oliver, King John, and the official patriarchal positions that they represent. Thus, Irena's position visually signals a subconscious ambivalence—hers and the film's—about the story she tells. Verbal hints of that ambivalence also emerge occasionally, most notably when Irena describes the putatively evil Cat People who fled to the hills as the "most wicked" but also as the "wisest." Earlier Irena tells Oliver that, although she finds a lion's roar from the nearby zoo "soothing and natural," she finds the panther's cry disturbing, "like a woman screaming." Viewed in the context of the scene's visual disjunctions and juxtapositions, such moments raise if only in a tenta-tive manner here questions about the legendary past Irena narrates. What if the "wisest and most wicked" who fled to the Serbian hills are evoked by the panther who screams like a woman? Might Irena be disturbed by the panther's cry because it reminds her of a female cultural history suppressed through offi-cial accounts of "good King John"? Might there be another version of medieval Serbian history, one in which King John and other national "libera-tors" like him turn out to be the oppressors of those screaming women, the witchy Cat People who fled to the hills?

This alternative account of a considerably richer women's history embedded in the official patriarchal narrative of the Cat People remains, for the time being, evoked mainly by the open expressions of the two cats that sit at the feet of the patriarch in the painting over Irena's head. Among other things, this cat couple represents patriarchy's view of the queer matriarchal collective history that Irena is attempting to transcend through her marriage to Oliver. Besides their largely dominant cultural connections with "the fem-inine" (catty, cat fight), within the logic of the film cats are gendered femi-nine. The film's very title, *Cat People,* seems to be a misnomer. *Cat Women* would be more accurate, since it appears that those people who escaped into the hills were—if not initially, then finally—a group of women who "mated" and then killed the men with whom they had sex. As Irena eventually tells Dr. Judd, her own father "died in some mysterious accident in the forest before [her] birth." Dr. Judd also discovers that the Cat Women, including Irena, turn into panthers and kill men who engage them sexually.

As it turns out, however, even if it were changed to *Cat Women*, the film's title would be wrong. These women turn into panthers, not house cats, when they become jealous, angry, or passionate. Unlike cats who are coded as feminine, panthers are more queerly coded in the film, figured simultaneously as masculine and feminine. The male zookeeper refers to the black panther as "he." But when Irena, drawn to the animal, listens to it from her apartment window, she says it sounds "like a woman screaming." On the one hand, the film's narrative, through its male characters (Judd, Oliver) and the men who made the film (Val Lewton, Jacques Tourneur, DeWitt Bodeen), uses a slew of cat associations (the film's title, the cats in the picture, references to "Cat People") to position Irena and her Serbian sisters within the conventionally feminine and domestic. On the other hand, the film makes us vividly aware of the more accurate connection between Irena (and her sisters) and the gender indeterminate and wild panther. The difference between the pantherlike Cat Women and the house cat is in fact emphasized at one point when Irena scares a kitten that Oliver gives her as a pet. King John, Oliver, Dr. Judd, and other men would like to reduce the queer threat of the panther-women by representing them as house cats. But the film does not fully allow for this possibility. Recall, for one thing, that the animal on King John's sword is too small to be a panther, but too large to be a cat.

Irena's queerly gendered sisterhood—with queer sexuality added to the mix—is further explored at the moment of her legal assimilation into American domesticity: the scene of Irena and Oliver's wedding dinner held at the Serbian restaurant, the Belgrade. Oliver's work colleagues and friends, a group of American ship designers and builders, comprise the party guests. Two men note, and draw our attention to, a mysterious woman seated at a table across the room. The Commodore remarks to Carver, "Look at that woman; isn't she something?" To which Carver casually replies, "Looks like a cat." Even from the back, this female figure seems strange. While she is impeccably dressed and beautifully draped with furs, she also wears a small bow perched on the top of her head, framing her face as if with animal ears. Her image is striking, even startling. In the next few shots, the woman directs her own gaze at someone in the wedding party. She rises and moves over to stand in front of Irena who is at the center of the table flanked by Oliver and his colleague Alice (Jane Randolph). In a close-up, the woman addresses Irena: "Moia Sestra? Moia Sestra?" The subsequent two-shot has Irena looking disturbed as she sits beside a puzzled Alice. "What did she say?" Alice asks. "She greeted me," Irena replies, "she called me sister."

One understanding of this scene is that it reinforces the official history that Irena seems to want to believe. That is, the foreign woman is a wicked, queer cat person who threatens Irena's married life with Oliver and the newly acquired U.S. citizenship that comes with her wedding. A descendant of those medieval Cat Women, this woman has potentially devastating supernatural powers and is to be shunned. Interrupting Irena's wedding dinner and calling her "sister," she seems to draw Irena away from normative heterosexuality. After all, the stranger is dining alone and her gaze is engaged only by Irena (or possibly by the sight of Irena sitting with Alice). The cat woman's appearance, therefore, opens up queer possibilities for Irena that are potentially, but not necessarily, lesbian ones. From the point of view of those who believe in the heroism and power of King John, these queer possibilities constitute the threat of an atavistic return to medieval wickedness. On the other hand, in light of the alternative history to which the scene with Irena and the painting with the cat couple alludes, the Serbian woman's address evokes a different interpretation of history as it invokes a different community. She clearly recognizes Irena as a kindred spirit. Although Irena anxiously insists that the woman's address is a misrecognition (and refuses to return it), the film implies that they are linked, however much Irena may wish to disavow it. The shared history earlier evoked in the image of the two black cats is here claimed to be a sisterhood. Furthermore, while Irena seems disturbed by her encounter with the Serbian woman, the foreigner is represented as intriguing and sympathetic, rather than as dark and sinister. Blond and tall, she is self-possessed, wealthy, glamorous, and graceful. If, as the narrative implies, this woman is a descendant of, and an emblem for, the Cat People, the film seems only half-hearted in representing her as a noirish femme fatale. Her invitation to Irena, moreover, suggests rather explicitly that the alternative Serbian past involves a potentially positive bond between women that is in opposition to the American heterosexual marriage contract.

Such a bond is suggested by alternating shots of Alice and Irena sitting together with shots of the Cat Woman. Indeed, although the scene begins by focusing on the heterosexual couple as the center of the wedding table, the appearance of the Cat Woman marks a shift. The narrative is recentered, if only temporarily, around Alice, Irena, and the cat woman. As Kim Newman says of this woman in her monograph on *Cat People*, "It's tempting to wonder about her story" (1999, 31). While she clearly longs to make connections with her sisters, all indications are that this well-heeled, single, queer female is thriving.

"THEY ARE IN ME": FROM SUPPRESSED
COLLECTIVE HISTORY TO INDIVIDUAL NEUROSIS

Oliver's rejoinder following the scene in the Serbian restaurant is a joking suggestion that Irena needs therapy: "She looks like a cat so she must be one of the Cat People, one of King John's pets. Oh, Irena, you crazy kid!" Oliver's words trivialize Irena's acknowledgment of a powerful collective (if also suppressed) view of her Serbian past. According to Oliver's joke, Irena is no woman, but a "crazy kid"; and the Cat People she fears as threatening and fascinating are nothing more than the harmless "pets" of the patriarch. Yet Oliver quickly turns serious, realizing the implications of Irena's concerns for their marital, specifically sexual, future. Confronting Irena's increasing unwillingness to consummate their marriage, Oliver asks Alice to recommend a psychoanalyst. In doing so, Oliver pressures Irena to jettison her narration of a collective history, a story that has the power to trouble the patriarchal myth of the national hero. In place of attention to the oppressions and suppressions that constitute her cultural history, Irena is encouraged to view her troubles as a case of individual psychic repression and submit to the analyst's couch. In place of wrestling with two competing versions of cultural history (King John's and the Cat Women's), Irena becomes subject to a reenactment of King John's power: Dr. Judd is a powerful man who purports to "liberate" her from her repressed demons. The dream sequence in the midst of Irena's psychoanalytic treatment displays her subconscious identification of Dr. Judd with King John—an identification that seems more ominous than reassuring. Dr. Judd's incipient sinister, predatory character (already suggested by Alice's derision of his overly suave hand-kissing manner) becomes clearer throughout Irena's analysis. Irena's nightmarish image of Dr. Judd as King John reminds us of the suppressed collective story of King John's oppression of Irena's matrilineal ancestors.

Thus, and despite the fact that psychoanalysis might assist in the project of recalling repressed and contested histories, the film sets out to supplant collective memory with individual neurosis. In the view of Oliver and Dr. Judd, Irena's story is not a tale of cultural oppression but one of sexual repression. Although psychoanalysis is ultimately shown here to be worse than useless, the narrative result of Irena's sessions with Dr. Judd, by and large, does not recommend the recovery of collective history. Instead of moving to history as a means to ameliorate Irena's distress, the narrative finally moves to biological determinism, emphasizing the impossibility of Irena's domestication and the immutability of an evil Serbian inheritance that, as a Panther Woman, she cannot escape.

But why does the film ultimately jettison the opposition of collective history to individual neurosis in favor of a clear assertion of Irena's biological, atavistic panther essence? And why does Irena, once clearly victimized by her predatory psychoanalyst, come finally to stand for the immutability of biology rather than the victimization of the culturally oppressed? Irena's death at the end of the film resolves none of the issues the film explicitly or implicitly raises about collective history and individual neurosis. The film's shift to biological essentialism alludes instead to issues that occupy or preoccupy the film's own narrative unconscious: the inescapability of an ethnic and racial past. Whereas on the manifest level the film links Irena's problems to her dark Serbian female essence, these associations gesture toward a latent concern with issues of race that "good ol' Americanos" like Oliver have successfully repressed from their own collective and individual memories. Issues of race mixing are raised repetitively and in odd places in the film. The most dramatically odd and seemingly trivial scene takes place at Sally Lunn's, a restaurant near Oliver's office. While in the Serbian restaurant the specter of gender and sexual queerness stalks Irena, in this American café the specter of race mixing intrudes on Oliver.

"DON'T NOBODY LIKE CHICKEN GUMBO?": QUEER RACE/ETHNICITY AND THE SPECTER OF MISCEGENATION

Following another unsuccessful attempt at conversation with a still-troubled Irena, Oliver goes to the office to avoid a quarrel. After a tough night at work, he heads off to Sally Lunn's where he "disconsolately orders some American comfort food, apple pie and a cup of coffee" (Newman 1999, 40). He is served by Minnie (Theresa Harris), a young black waitress dressed in attire reminiscent of a nineteenth-century Creole servant complete with headscarf and apron. Minnie is the seemingly successfully assimilated black woman employed as a server. She is represented as a "good" domesticated black, but one who is trying to get Oliver to change his order from apple pie to gumbo. When Oliver refuses, she retorts, "My goodness, don't nobody like chicken gumbo?" Clearly her white, middle-class New York customers want nothing to do with Creole gumbo served by a light-skinned black woman. On the face of things, there seems no particular reason either for Minnie's presence in this film or for her Creole coding. Also, why disturb the "normal, American" order of apple pie and coffee by drawing attention to something that suggests American cuisine might also be represented by a hybrid dish derived from a long history of consolidating multiple ethnicities?

Minnie's relatively benign presence alludes to an American history much more controversial than films at the time could treat openly. On its manifest level, the film wants to present America as clear, uncomplicated, and direct: a nation of white shipbuilders and devoted apple pie–eating husbands. Oliver and Alice are both blond, bland, and usually filmed in brightly lit surroundings. However, Minnie's presence as a waitress in the well-lit, white-populated American café and her desire to serve up some gumbo suggest an alternative to an all-white America. Minnie with her mixed American racial ancestry and cuisine can readily be connected to dark, Serbian Irena and her mixed Mamaluk-Christian heritage, the latter of which is marked as "evil" in the official history Irena relates. No wonder Oliver and the other restaurant patrons reject Minnie's offer of gumbo—and no wonder the narrative contrives to have Irena's dark "problem" prevent her from having sex with Oliver.

E. Ann Kaplan has similarly read *Cat People* as unconsciously preoccupied with race, and she situates those concerns in part through the film's duplication of Nazi Aryan ideologies. Through its images of foreignness and blackness, Kaplan argues, the film "manages to link the realities of violent Nazi racism against blacks as well as Jews with unconscious guilt at America's own dehumanizing and violent slavery system" (1997, 121–22). Kaplan also links, as she puts it, "the dark continent of the psyche and the dark continent of Serbia" (117). Yet she assumes an automatic equivalency between Serbia and Africa, asserting that Serbia "references Africa" because King John is vaguely "identified with the East" (117). Yet, the Mamaluks, not King John, are coded as the eastern "other." Moreover, the film takes significant pains to position these dark "others" as medieval as well as evil, with their descendants (the Cat Woman in the restaurant, Irena) coded as atavistic returns to an archaic disorder that should be surmounted through white, American "progress."

The temporal moves that the film makes could be said to displace WASP American concerns over mixed ethnic and racial bodies like Minnie's onto Irena and "the medieval." Kaplan finds that the "invisible or marginalized" figure of black women such as Minnie is "doubly displaced, first through the body of a white woman, and then through that of the black leopard *[sic]*" (117). But there is also a temporal displacement that moves us from foreign Irena as a Panther Woman in 1942 America to the Cat Women of medieval Serbia. Finally, only such folk as Irena's Cat Women are explicitly abhorred for the suggestions of their apparent racial and ethnic "corruption." Trafficking with the Mamaluks (a complicated ethnic category during the Middle Ages identified with the Seljuk Turks and the Islamic East more generally), the Cat Women turned from their "good Christian ways." Although the film's manifest concern is with ethnic mixing coded as an atavistic evil that is distant in both time and place, it clearly harbors a latent anxiety about the very category of "good ol' [white] Americano" that Oliver claims and that he unwittingly reinforces by his rejecting the gumbo and reaffirming his desire for apple pie. It is ironic, then, that Oliver's "good ol' Americano" self-nomination is itself hybrid, formed from a mixture of English and Spanish.

The troubled and troubling past of U.S. race relations is also evoked through the image of the black panther, caged for an American zoo. Although it points toward Irena and her "evil" medievalisms, Kaplan notes that the caged panther also alludes to America's history of slavery, when individuals who had been judged to come from apparently primitive cultures were caged and chained, kept under lock and key (122). With her associative links to the "dangerous" panther, Minnie's saucy service offers a challenging reminder that American identity comprises chicken gumbo as well as apple pie. Minnie's domesticated Creole presence alongside the image of the caged black panther cuts two ways. On the one hand, Minnie and the black panther can be read as the contrast between a "good" assimilated racial/ethnic "other" and its rebellious opposite. On the other hand, they suggest the potentially dangerous and disruptive return of a repressed American history of miscegenation often forced on black women. It is this latter threat that the film displaces upon a distant "evil" medieval European past.

CONCLUSIONS: "SHE NEVER LIED TO US"

In *The Women Who Knew Too Much*, Tania Modleski notes the "complex and contradictory" relationship of women to patriarchy: neither entirely complicit, nor fully resistant (1988, 116–17). The same might be said of Irena's position at the end of *Cat People*. The double-edged nature of Irena's position vis-à-vis patriarchy emerges forcefully in the film's final encounter between her and Oliver. The scene follows Irena's last session with Dr. Judd in which he tells her to forget "the mad legends of [her] birthplace" and "lead a normal life." She returns home seemingly determined to embrace her marriage and assimilate into American patriarchy. At this point, with "spectacularly bad timing" (Newman 1999, 55), Oliver confesses his love for Alice, informing Irena that it would be better for them to divorce. Stunned, Irena drops to the sofa murmuring inconsolably, "There's nothing you can say, there's only silence. . . . I love silence. . . . I love loneliness" (56). Irena's sadness seems to indicate the disappointment of her failed marriage, and thus suggests at first glance her complicit desire to be normalized, ruled by a patriarchal American husband. Yet signs of Irena's resistance remain: the eeriness of her whispered avowal that she loves silence and loneliness, especially in the context of Oliver's rejection, positions desires such as Irena's fundamental response to heterosexual marriage. Loneliness and silence constitute a beloved refuge from the bland forthrightness that marriage to a "good ol' Americano" seemed to promise. Furthermore, Irena's apparent resolve to forget the "mad legends" of her cats and her insistence that she is "no longer afraid" of their power seem in tension, if not at odds, with the silver cat brooch she wears so prominently throughout the scene, the presence of which may signal the very impossibility of Irena's transformation into well-ruled marital domesticity.

Indeed, the sense of Irena's pantherlike wildness returns forcefully in the striking image of her that closes this scene. Ordering Oliver out of their apartment, Irena turns her back on the camera and sinks onto the sofa. Her face hidden from view, she slowly strokes the sofa with her manicured hand, her painted fingernails rending the fabric, and leaving the trace of a dangerous cat claw. Irena can no longer harbor even the pretense of containing the drives and desires that position her outside of, and in resistance to, normative white American heterosexual culture. The visual effect is chilling, particularly in the shadowy flickers of candlelight on the panther-skin texture of Irena's black dress. The image of the dark woman-beast clearly engages with standard metaphors from the horror genre; yet the camera angles evoke sympathy for, or at least identification with—rather than condemnation of—Irena's position as the dark female unsuited to marital domesticity. The camera is positioned neither above her (an angle that might emphasize her vulnerability) nor below her (an angle that might emphasize her threat); instead the shot positions the viewer on the same level as Irena.

The film's movement toward Irena's death also feeds off the tensions between her position within patriarchal structures and her resistance to these same structures. Met in her apartment by Dr. Judd, Irena goes toward him with a look of blank acquiescence or seductive encouragement on her face—either of which would place her within appropriate feminine positions within the patriarchy. At Judd's touch, of course, Irena turns into a panther and kills him. Is Irena thinking of this while she walks across the room toward Judd? Is she enacting a masquerade of female sexual availability or vulnerability because she knows this is what Judd will respond to and that this response will trigger the panther in her? How conscious is she that this meeting will end in the death of the man she has transformed into King John in her nightmares? As with many things concerning Irena's desires and motives, the film remains vague about all this. But that may be the point. Women like Irena have profoundly anxious and complicated relationships with the patriarchy: whether to fit predetermined roles or stand outside of them in spaces marked as powerful yet "evil."

Within this complicated position—both inside and outside, individual and collective, evil and empowering—Irena meets her death. Whereas Judd has wounded her with the phallic sword cane he carries everywhere, he has not killed her. Deciding to end her anguish from being "torn between two worlds," Irena goes to the zoo. Using a key she has stolen from the (male) zookeeper (a key that has been prominently displayed in a close-up at the time she steals it and has appeared as a visual parallel to King John's sword in her nightmare), Irena unlocks the black panther's cage. Standing before the cage like a soldier or spy awaiting the firing squad, Irena allows the panther to jump on her and kill her by embedding Judd's sword cane further into her. By the logic of the narrative, in using the key to unlock the panther's cage, Irena has simultaneously taken up a (phallic) symbol of the patriarchy (the zookeeper's key that keeps animals caged) to free the queerly gendered animal. But she has freed it to drive Judd's phallic weapon into her, thus helping to rid the world of a queer Panther Woman. In this sense, Irena's death might be added to the long list of suicides and other deaths that have been the common fate of pathetic or dangerous homosexuals in literature, theatre, and films. However, there is something to be said for the fact that the narrative does not allow Judd (or some other representative of dominant culture) to end Irena's life or to lock her up. *Cat People* gives Irena a choice in the end. In this light, one might see her final moments as a return to the embrace of the Panther Women, granting that this is associated with death.

This quasi-suicidal ending, similar to those of Kate Chopin's novel *The Awakening* and the film *Thelma & Louise* (1991), shows women with outlaw desires backed up against a wall by "The Man," taking what would seem to be a brave and noble way out—brave and noble, that is, if they were men (see the finale of *Butch Cassidy and the Sundance Kid* [1969], for example). But what, then, are we to make of the shot of the panther that hit Irena itself being hit and killed by a police car? Is the film attempting to reclaim narrative and cultural normativity after Irena confuses things with her quasi-suicide, attempting to show that although Irena may have thought she was freeing the queer panther to roam around New York, the Law has quickly and efficiently put an end to that? But what about the Cat Woman in the Serbian restaurant? She's still roaming around New York, is she not?

Finally, then, and like Irena, the film itself remains caught between complicity with American patriarchal ideology and an ambiguously marked queer "medieval" resistance to this system. The film establishes the dramatic deaths of a couple of queer panthers in its finale, while it less prominently keeps alive the possibilities of a powerful resistance to dominant culture by suggesting "foreign" and ancient, if fraught, spaces are still open for expressing queer gender, sexuality, race, and ethnicity. It is no coincidence that the film's doubled interest in complicity and resistance is imagined as the result of a return to a set of collective desires linked with the medieval. As an imaginary space that is at once both the ancestor to contemporary regulatory systems and a time outside those very structures, the "medieval" evokes a collective scene of outlaw freedom that both resists the boring bright light of order and dominance and simultaneously seems to demand its own regulation and containment. Just as the forthright Oliver both desired and derided Irena's mysterious foreignness, so twentieth-century America is fascinated by a set of queer possibilities that are coded here in this troubling film both as "evil medieval" and as dangerously female.

WORKS CITED

Dinshaw, Carolyn. 1999. *Getting Medieval: Sexualities and Communities, Pre- and Postmodern*. Durham: Duke University Press.

Kaplan, E. Ann. 1997. *Looking for the Other: Feminism, Film, and the Imperial Gaze*. New York: Routledge.

Modleski, Tania. 1988. *The Women Who Knew Too Much: Hitchcock and Feminist Theory*. New York: Methuen.

Newman, Kim. 1999. *Cat People*. London: British Film Institute.

FIGURE 16. The fetishizing of the youthful body presents us with the evil specter of aging. Late in her career, as Tanya in Orson Welles's *Touch of Evil* (Universal, 1958), Marlene Dietrich still adored being the "adored object" of the male gaze and the camera. (Frame enlargement)

CHAPTER SIXTEEN

Wicked Old Ladies from Europe: Jeanne Moreau and Marlene Dietrich on the Screen and Live

E. ANN KAPLAN

As I have argued elsewhere, women's social position as objects "to be gazed at" makes aging especially traumatic in relation to the sheer changes in the human body (Kaplan 1997; 1999). In western culture, "menopause" retains some of its now-archaic biological implications, despite women's roles and positioning no longer being tied to such implications. Through misplaced association, menopause connotes the idea that after it is over women cease to be, or feel, sexual, as if in the patriarchal mindset reproduction and sexuality are inherently linked. Because of this ideology—more than because of the dramatic change in bodily schema—aging can be traumatic for women (Kaplan 2001). The ideology of the status "to be looked at," of being an object of the admiring male gaze, has been conditioned in women to the point that they bear the brunt of bodily changes as changes in identity.

Hollywood's aging women have been consistently portrayed in negative light, typically as socially maladapted in one way or another. They have been seen often as crotchety hags (Bette Davis in *What Ever Happened to Baby Jane?* [1962]), as tipsy and eccentric (Ruth Gordon in *Harold and Maude* [1971]), as gabby and doddering (Jessica Tandy in *Fried Green Tomatoes* [1991]) or possessive and controlling (Jessica Tandy in *The Birds* [1963]), as wicked but senile sprites (Judi Dench in *Chocolat* [2000]), as secretive and self-indulgent (Gloria Stuart in *Titanic* [1997]), as manipulative (Talia Shire in *The Godfather III* [1990]), or as smarmily desperate to hold onto lost youth (Eve Arden in *Grease* [1978]). They are not infrequently downright malevolent—Maggie Smith in *Gosford Park* (2001), for example, or Helen Mirren's aging sorceress in *Excalibur* (1981) or Patricia Neal in *Cookie's Fortune* (1999). Old women onscreen are shown as decrepit (Catherine Deneuve in *The Hunger* [1983]) or energetically mad (Katherine Hepburn in *The Madwoman of Chaillot* [1969]) or as cold as ice and as monstrous as vipers (Flora Robson as the Empress Tzu-Hsi in *55 Days at Peking* [1963]). But they are very rarely dramatized as people trying to live reasonable lives under trying circumstances, in short, as real.

In particular, Hollywood has long been fascinated with depicting the horrors that face aging stars, as if to cement this ideologically produced situation. As Jean Kozlowski notes, male stars' sex "can be stretched into a fantasy of ageless sexual potency," whereas women stars are summarily dismissed from sexy roles after menopause (1993, 8). The many well-known constructs of aging female film stars and performers include Gloria Swanson's powerful film star Norma Desmond in *Sunset Blvd.* (1950) and Shirley MacLaine's star-rapt mother competing with Meryl Streep in *Postcards from the Edge* (1990) (based loosely on the life of Debbie Reynolds and her daughter Carrie Fisher). *Postcards* shows the difficulty for the narcissistic—but, significantly, not evil—mother to recognize that she is aging, losing her beauty, and that it is time to cede center stage to her daughter. From the daughter's perspective, the film is about learning to empathize with her mother's aging difficulties and her narcissistic needs to be the center of attention. The scene in the hospital after MacLaine's drunk driving accident captures Streep's growing ability to help her mother through this stage of life: Streep finds her mother looking weary and plain without her wig and makeup; she pulls out her cosmetics and gradually constructs MacLaine's image for her so that she can go out and face the reporters. It is precisely such constructs of sad, aging stars, forced to take a back seat, that may have unconsciously revolted Marlene Dietrich—or at least may have led her to resist becoming the stereotype of a forlorn "aging star."

Aging women on the screen are not just old, they are usually bad. Indeed, in women age and badness appear equivalent, as if the very refusal to slip quietly into oblivion—as patriarchal ideology demands—is problematic. Western culture does not know what to do with old women and so in representing them it shows them either getting into mischief as they work at fending for themselves or else adamantly defending against the signs of age and trying to stay young. Even this is interpreted as being "bad."

Herein I discuss these issues with regard to two particular actresses, Marlene Dietrich and Jeanne Moreau.

DIETRICH: THE REFUSAL OF AGING AND AGING REVEALED

Images of Marlene Dietrich in Chris Hunt's docufilm, *Marlene Dietrich: Shadow and Light* (1996), along with information supplied by people interviewed in it, support the idea that Dietrich attempted to repress her aging, to simply refuse to "age" onscreen or in performances—this, regardless of how historically true or untrue are the events related in the film because it is the representation itself, the language used by the interviewees, that provides the ultimate telling. Perhaps most striking in *Shadow and Light* is the role played by Dietrich's only daughter, Maria. A main interlocutor, Maria has an investment in aging having been a trauma for her mother. Also important (although speculative) is the implied impact on Dietrich of Maria's scorn for her mother's difficulties in losing her beauty. According to Maria, Dietrich struggled to retain her image and to continue to perform, well into her seventies. In the documentary, viewers see Dietrich bravely trying to preserve the shimmering beauty for which she had been so renowned. However, the struggle shows on her face, which is so tight that expression is impossible. (Glynis Johns, her co-star in *Stage Fright* [1950], describes how Dietrich managed to pull her skin back taut to remove the wrinkles by plaiting her hair around her head—this in addition to many cosmetic surgeries Dietrich underwent.)

What impact is produced on viewers by the combination of image and testimony from Dietrich and people who knew her? What contradictions emerge between Dietrich's view of herself and her daughter's view of her? Perhaps offering my personal response to the narrative that the film creates will advance understanding of how images of aging can affect a viewer. Certain images in the film proved problematic for me. Two that made me gasp, showing my identification with Dietrich's trauma about aging (my empathy with her position), came at the end of the film. The first shows a surprised, aged Dietrich, sitting up in bed, dressed all in white, with her hair pinned behind a bandana, showing an ugly forehead. Clearly, Dietrich was not expecting to be photographed and is in the midst of protesting as the shot is taken. Too late! Posterity has the image she so feared, that of a wrinkled, gaunt, aged face trying to hide behind the windows of her Paris flat. Presumably, this was the act of Maria, taking revenge on her mother's narcissism that must have pained her while she was growing up (indeed, certain footage in Hunt's film supports this point).

The second image was perhaps even more terrifying in relation to the trauma of aging: it was another still photograph from inside the flat, this time of the empty wheelchair, positioned at the tall glass windows. Presumably Dietrich, who did not leave this flat for ten years or so out of fear of being seen aged, sat here in the afternoons and watched the life go by in the street below—a life from which she had excluded herself because she could not bear the public to see the changes in her body. Seeing this shot it is difficult not to believe that in her own eyes she had become, simply through the passage of time, a pariah.

These two shots from the end of the film speak volumes about Dietrich's investment in her external image—in being the adored object of the male gaze and of the camera—and about the ideology of aging for women identifying with the male gaze. It also tells volumes about her daughter, whose voice-over accompanies the images and whose investment in ruining Dietrich's image is also clear. Both Maria and Hunt's film, in its implied criticism of Dietrich's continuing to perform into her seventies, seem to subscribe to a dominant ideology about aging as something to be accepted passively, something people should shuffle quietly into, taking a marginal, observer position as one waits for death. Old age is also, then, an undesirable condition, a kind of pollution. Without realizing the difficulties for aging women of Western culture's addiction to youth, the film seems to berate Dietrich not only for having tried to forestall aging, but also for refusing to be seen after her beauty faded and wrinkles predominated. She is presumably vain, self-absorbed, obsessive, and hopeless. But in fact, dominant ideology ought to be highlighted as creating the dilemma for aging women by establishing a fetish for the youthful, fresh body. Such a fetish naturally leads to an idea of aging as something to be dreaded and of aging as disfigurement and loss of identity, a social problem, a negative state.

Faced with the contradictions of dominant ideology, Dietrich chooses to repress her aging body and to do whatever might be necessary to keep it appearing young. If she aims to create a glittering surface that no one is to see behind, in doing so she denies the body as such. One cannot but admire the courage this effort took—the pain silently endured to keep the surface shined and youthful through her seventies, and the energy deployed to flirt and play at being sexy long after these were real pleasures. However, here Dietrich reads less as courageous than as desperate, groping, pathological.

Equally as interesting and problematic as Hunt's film is Maximilian Schell's semidocumentary, *Marlene* (1984), made when Dietrich was in her early nineties. Fascinating is that while the film is about Marlene, we never see her as she is at the time of making the film: we only hear her voice. What can we learn about the aging body when that body is not visible? How does the viewer's response differ when the aging body is not seen? Theoretically, if it is true that the aged physical body is what turns viewers off, we should have more opportunity for positive response. Schell's experiment is interesting precisely because it raises these intriguing questions. A condition of Dietrich's agreeing to do the film, indeed, was Schell's promise that he would not film her in the present. This demand confirms that Dietrich refused to let go of her glamorous image, refused to be seen in her bodily form as a very elderly woman. A severe split had evidently taken place between the reality of her aging body and her image of herself as she had been—and as she had become known to the world on film.

The concept of Marlene's body, her look, is foregrounded at the start. Unable to make the documentary he had planned, which would have taken place in Marlene's Paris flat and shown her being interviewed, Schell is faced with a lack, an absence. He has the taped interviews, and the images from films they watched together in the flat (this joint viewing is clear from the tape we hear), but no visuals of Dietrich to go along with or to support the project. Thus, the crisis of making the documentary itself becomes a central topic in the film. The "present" of the film is Schell's German studio, where editing is going on. Opening shots show the tape recorder with the sound of Marlene's voice, while Schell's assistants reconstruct her Paris apartment, as if to remedy the lacks. This editing studio is revisited from time to time, and increasingly toward the end, when we see strips of film footage hanging or being cut and assembled on the editing machine. Sometimes, assistants correct information that Marlene pronounces on the tape. The material aspects of the film—time, place, and space—are thus strangely disturbed, rendering the film in some sense postmodern. In one shot, we see several Marlene "look-alikes" dressed in top hats and tails lolling about the studio. In light of all this, someone asks, "What's real here?" Schell answers, predictably: the tape recorder, the editing table, photos, and film clips—what he mainly has to work with. He omits that he himself is real, like his assistants and friends on the set (including Marlene's long-time companion and composer-accompanist, Burt Bacharach).

In relation to Dietrich's absence, one of the assistants asks (referring to Schell's visit to tape the interviews in Paris), "What does she look like now?" The question hangs in the air for viewers to think about during the entire film, while Schell zooms in on the famous image of Dietrich from *Just a Gigolo* (1978), as if to get as close as possible to what Dietrich looks like now. Toward the end of the film, Schell uses this image frequently for the same reason. In other words, because of its very absence, the aged body moves to the center of the film in the viewer's imagination, a thing that is haunting but also virtually unmentionable. The viewer stretches to make her own image of how Dietrich is now out of the shards of images from late Dietrich films and performances. When Schell asks Dietrich if she likes watching her films, she replies, "No. Why would I look at myself? They [the films] don't interest me. . . . I don't give a damn about myself." A bit later on Schell asks, "Why don't you want to be photographed?" She replies: "Too much photography; I've been photographed to death. . . . My private life is completely separate from my professional life." Schell pushes her, saying it would help his project, that a large public is interested in her as a person, but she retorts uncooperatively that she has turned many important people down and will not do it.

Perhaps to provoke her, he mentions Von Sternberg's criticism of Marlene in his book. She responds in a pained voice, "Why be critical? We're not doing the documentary to be critical, but to tell them my life."

Given the absence of her body now, Schell treats us to images of Marlene from a wealth of her films, going back to footage from largely unseen German silent films through which Dietrich launched her career but that she first denies having made and then regards with utter scorn. Between these clips, Schell inserts interviews Dietrich made during her last years doing stage performances, and newsreel shots from some of the performances, including her very last show in London. We thus have the contrast between our imagination of Marlene (how she looks now) and images of her youthful, glamorous, often very lively body (as in the unforgettable fight with James Stewart in *Destry Rides Again* [1939]). Schell plays this scene to evoke the still fiery Marlene he has to deal with—for the form of this film is a battle of sorts, as Schell and Marlene fence with each other verbally about the terms of their contract, and indeed, almost all his questions. If Schell is the hero of the endeavor, Dietrich is his dragon, the wizened, narrow-minded, self-protective, often softly belligerent Other who cannot share his goodness. Meanwhile, the materiality of Marlene is profoundly present in her remarkable voice—a voice that tells so much and that (without her possibly being able to realize it) reveals much about her aging and her identity at this point. The range of emotions Schell is able to elicit and that we hear clearly in the voice perhaps conveys more—and is more effective—through only being heard, not seen.

As Schell tries to probe Marlene about the past, and especially her childhood, she increasingly resists, claiming to be a literalist, relentlessly practical, logical, living only in the present. Feelings, she says—for cities or things like that—are *"kitschik"* emotions. When Schell asks why she keeps saying everything is *"kitschik"* and refers to the heavily pink allure of her stage performances, she is definite about her performances not being *kitschik*. Schell, she says, is the dreamer, and she has no time for daydreaming. She claims not to know where she was born, says she came of a good Berlin family, but she scorns any notion that her father's early death affected her. Yet we learn about her love for Burt Bacharach, who looked after her dotingly during her last years in the Paris flat. Dietrich lies about having a sister (she claims she had none). She all but denies any inner life: all she will say about her mother is that she raised her to be "proper." This is why her crying over a poem that her mother loved becomes so powerful at the end of the film.

Things come to a head towards the end of the film when Schell asks Marlene about her work with different directors. This seems to annoy her the most. She denies putting herself into her characters: "I detest this psychological stuff," she says. "Why do we have to get into the character? I put nothing of myself into the parts. . . ." Marlene's voice becomes increasingly loud and angry and sometimes her words are slurred, suggesting she's been drinking or is on medication. She is rude to Schell. She complains about having to see her films. Asked about *Touch of Evil* (1958), she says: "We're through. We've talked about him [Orson Welles]. He would hate it. What can I comment? . . . I'm not a prima donna like you. Why should I look at an old film? This is not my business. We're making a documentary. We have ninety minutes together. You don't have to show me anything. I've done it all."

This is followed by a frustrated outburst and more abusive language toward Schell: it feels like a lover's quarrel. "I don't know what you're after. I wish I knew." She then accuses Schell of being a film buff and going to Film Institutes. "You walked out on me. Terrible, terrible. I've sat at tables with the greatest artists. You're a real Swiss with some German thrown in; you want to be idolized."

As if to express his frustration and his sense that his whole project is collapsing, Schell inserts a surreal scene, in which the cameras move about on their own, coming in a threatening way toward the viewer as streams of film float around out of control. A rapid montage of shots from throughout the film appear. Meanwhile, Dietrich is heard saying that she never took her career seriously and accusing Schell of a masochistic complex. Not only is she pictured as antagonistic and daunting, then, but she is diminished in her age as incompetent to judge her own past and work properly.

At this point, Schell inserts that shot from *Gigolo* with Dietrich's sad face seen through a veil or all but covered by a large hat. She sings the song that seems to apply to her current situation: "Youth will pass away, then what will they say about me; life goes on without me." This picks up the theme of death that has run through the film like a black thread woven into a colored carpet (for more on which, see Lucy Fischer 2002, 194–211). If Dietrich earlier claimed she had been "photographed to death . . . ," those photographs will now outlive her death. When Schell asks her about fearing death and her beliefs about an afterlife, Marlene is scornful of any worries or fears. Just as Schell contrasted images of a feisty Dietrich on the screen when she argues with him, so now he inserts images of narratives in which Marlene's character is shot, as in *Dishonored* (1931), or when she plays a character foretelling death (as in *Touch of Evil*). Death haunts the film with regard to all the friends and family Marlene has lost by living so very long. Particularly moving is the image of Dietrich weeping at Gary Cooper's funeral, belying her previous tough line about not worrying about death and living only in the present.

The film returns at its end, as it had opened, to the reading of a poem Marlene's mother loved—another reminder of death. Finally, the blocked emotion breaks through. She does have feelings about her past, after all. She does have memories that pain her, and regrets. The line, "O God I meant no harm," seems to move her (perhaps she is thinking of her husband and her mother?), and she finds the most beautiful line to be, "The Other leaves and complains." The poem is too sentimental, she says, but (significantly) she adds, "maybe."

For the viewer this is a profoundly moving moment precisely because of the hard exterior that Marlene has presented throughout and her scorn of emotions as *"kitschik."* Hearing her voice without seeing her image now brings us very close to her. One can hardly bear to hear her soft cries, her attempt to block the sobs from being heard. We cannot know what the recalled pain is, but the sense of regret, of a past not confronted or allowed to come through, is clear. Her defenses may have served her well as an old and lonely woman, but they have a price.

Although the belligerence and contest in the tone of the Dietrich-Schell interaction cast her as something of a monster, it is useful to remember that Schell's are the terms of reference that dominate this film. But Dietrich's voice penetrates his dominating space. The voice is a remarkably revealing part of a person: while cosmetic surgeries can hide wrinkles and expression, it is very hard to conceal emotion in the voice. The voice is rarely able to lie. Hearing her voice allows us to attend to Dietrich's personality rather than to her body. Thus, paradoxically, in refusing to be seen, Marlene opens herself to the viewer: she arguably reveals more about being old—its defiance, its energy, but also its losses, pains, frustrations—than she would have if we had been distracted by the aged face and body to contrast with the glittering film persona we know so well.

Meanwhile, Marlene's sharp, logical mind emerges in the exchanges with Schell. She is a perfect match for him as they enter into a kind of combat about what she will or will not tell about her personal life. For someone so aged, this reveals laudable energy and challenges our misconceptions about aging. Instead of the frail, submissive old lady or the monster, what emerges is a forceful, smart, alert, determined, and complex personality—a force that age has not withered.

JEANNE MOREAU AND IMAGES OF AGED WOMEN

In a brilliant move, Josée Dayan cast Jeanne Moreau as Marguerite Duras in her 2001 film, *Cet amour-là*. As one reviewer (revealingly) put it, "un monstre sacré du cinéma incarne un monstre sacré de la littérature . . ." (Strauss and Loiseau n.d.). For the general public and this journalist, both Moreau and Duras were inserted into the discourse of strong older women being "monsters."

Unlike Dietrich, Marguerite Duras openly resisted or defied social codes and expectations regarding aging women. A rebel from a young age (as immortalized in her novel *L'Amant* and the film made from it, *The Lover* [1991]), Duras refused the codes of her situation, nation, and gender by living as a kind of loner, being true to her own values and goals as a dedicated and prolific writer. Apparently impervious to aging, Duras (unlike Dietrich) gave visibility to herself as an aging woman in a film, *Le Camion* (1977) (basically an extended monologue by Duras) in which she is "invisible" to the male protagonist—a truck driver (played by Gérard Depardieu) who picks her up—but very visible to us, the viewers.

In her own life, Duras achieved a similar visibility by continuing to have love affairs with younger men, defying cultural norms again, just as she had in loving an older man at fifteen. Most remarkable is her fifteen-year relationship with Yann Andréa Steiner, a young man and an ardent fan who had read all her works before seeking her out, and whom Duras took into her life until she died. Yann Andréa and Duras's very last book, *C'est Tout*—a text I discuss briefly in an essay on trauma and aging (Kaplan 1999)—relates particularly to this friendship. In *C'est Tout,* a series of dialogues between herself and her lover, Yann Andréa, Duras confronts the void that death has to be for the nonreligious and discusses the importance of love and of writing for her as she anticipates death.

Very like Duras, Jeanne Moreau has seemed impervious to aging, while at the same time giving visibility to older women in astonishing cinematic performances. Even before making *La Vieille qui marchait dans la mer* (1991) for Laurent Heynemann—a film that deals with an older woman's infatuation with a very young man (comparable to Duras's relationship to Yann Andréa), Moreau acted roles where, as an older woman, she was involved with, or attractive to, younger men.

Moreau and Duras were friends during parts of their lives, but perhaps it is the particular context of artistic, intelligent women in pre– and post–World War II France that connects the two. Living in Nazi-occupied Paris like Duras must have toughened Moreau and provided an important insight into human evil. Moreau has shown exemplary daring in undertaking a wide range of controversial film roles, while steadily working in French theatre (for a while at the prestigious Comédie Française), occasionally on television, and occasionally behind the camera. Like Dietrich, Moreau also made films with some of the greatest Hollywood and New Wave "auteurs." Like Dietrich, she was at home in several nations. In her case, she spent time in England (having had an English mother), but also frequently visited the United States (Jean-Claude Moreau 1988; Gray 1994). Unlike Dietrich, however, and as noted earlier, Moreau has been willing to allow her visibly aged body to be seen on the screen. Indeed, her career flowered as she played older women in the 1990s, as for example in *The Proprietor* (1996) and *Balzac* (1999). In the latter, indeed, as Balzac's mother, Moreau plays one of the great screen monsters—ceaselessly shaming and reducing her son. The willingness to be seen aging and desperate is part of Moreau's declared attitude to getting older. According to Jean-Claude Moreau, Jeanne Moreau is not indifferent to aging but would never cover up her feelings about it. In 1963, a picture of her on the cover of a women's magazine accompanied the text: "No, I am not afraid of aging!" Rarely questioned about aging, when she is she answers that aging does not terrify her and that knowledge of death increases appetite for life. Although she would hate an aging that involved physical or mental impotence, she says, the thing to do is to live and not worry about the years slipping by (Moreau, 209). In taking this point of view, Moreau is contesting patriarchal expectations, blatantly denying the investment in being a youthful object of men's vision that we see motivating Dietrich's old age.

Here, I focus on Moreau playing the role of Lady M in the film made from San-Antonio's (Frédéric Dard) remarkable 1988 novel, *La Vieille qui marchait dans la mer*. Author of more than 175 novels written since 1949 and famous for his neologisms, Dard is, along with Albert Camus and Marcel Pagnol, one of France's most-read novelists. When he died in 2000, he had sold more than 220 million copies of his books. Many were thrillers, featuring the detective San-Antonio, who also became Dard's pseudonym for other novels, such as the one being studied here. Lady M was a particularly daring role precisely because it challenges many deeply held attitudes about the aging body and about sexuality among aging men and women as well as between old and young people. How does this figuration impact the viewer schooled in the pleasurable voyeuristic/sadistic or masochistic cinematic pleasures—pleasures that Dietrich struggled so hard to maintain for herself and for her viewers, precisely to shield us and her from knowing what San-Antonio wants us to know about the aging body and lustful desire?

The opening shots of *La Vieille* establish the old lady of the title, Lady M, as an unabashedly sexy old woman, living for sex and adoring "young flesh." This she admits speaking directly to viewers as the film opens and she arranges her dress. Nearly crippled with arthritis, Lady M, dressed in wide-brimmed sun hat and flimsy chiffon dress, wades into the warm Caribbean at Guadeloupe, and drums her walking stick into the sand—a signal that she needs Lambert, her young stud, to take her walking in the sea. We cut to Lambert (Luc Thuillier) having sex in the hotel with a young waitress, who laughs at his being at the old lady's beck and call. But Lambert knows where his bread is buttered. Lady M immediately senses that he's been having sex, checking the status of his erection herself before they take off on their walk and demanding details of the intercourse. As viewers, what are we to think? How do we respond to this lustful old lady? How do we reconcile her crippled, wrinkled body with her dirty mind, her interest in sex, and her earthiness? Everything she is seems to contradict established notions of old age—notions that Dietrich was running away from and trying not to know. We would have to return to Chaucer, Boccaccio, or Shakespeare for such bawdy females, but the parallels would not work: many of those old women were marginal to the main story or represented Western traditions of the "hag" or "witch." If Lady M's figure plays with these traditions, it essentially contravenes them.

San-Antonio's novel, and the film script closely adapted from his text, is unusual in its graphic details regarding the aging male and female body. More: the dialogue San-Antonio gives his elderly couple—Lady M and her longtime companion, Pompilius (Michel Serrault)—is rife with lusty effusions and deadly diatribes detailing each other's ghastly bodies and dried-up sex organs. Although this is clearly a game between the two, the dialogue is remarkably corporeal, remarkably frank about the aging body, its sexual desires, its lusty yearnings, and its painful losses. In her vibrant dotage, then, Lady M is thus as wicked as it's possible to be in Western culture.

The focus on the aging body makes *La Vieille* unique as a film about old people. Calling Lady M a monster would be easy—perhaps too easy. The traditional hag stereotype is indeed monstrous, but Lady M has many more aspects to her. She is outrageous in her desires, her ambition, and her clothing (one inevitably thinks of Stella Dallas and her outrageous outfits). But she has her own morality, her own limits, and above all her own perspective on herself, conveyed, interestingly, through her frequent appeals to "God," whatever she may mean by that term. These appeals are a narrative strategy whereby viewers may glimpse Lady M's vulnerabilities—the uncertainty beneath her apparently secure persona—and have some access to her inner consciousness.

Whereas the dialogues with Pompilius consist of expletives about the old body, its pains, losses, and ugliness, those between Lambert and Lady M offer a glimpse into how an old person views a younger one and vice versa. With their growing closeness, they need to confront their physical differences. The yearning for sex in old women is rarely discussed in Western film: it is somehow assumed that sex is far behind them, that no sexual urges, lusty attractions, or stimulating infatuations remain. *La Vieille* belies this, as did Marguerite Duras in life with Yann Andréa. But the catch here is that the aging body is indeed "dried-up," its juices refusing to flow, the bones arthritic—"decalcified" as Lady M puts it—its energies waning. The contrast between young and old bodies is highlighted in several scenes, such as that where Lady M and Pompilius enviously watch young people playing tennis; or another where the camera catches the two limping painfully up some steps, while below Lambert flirts with one of his young women.

Cunningly, Lady M tries to lure Lambert into her bed. Anticipating Lambert's reluctance, she cagily offers a lure, which is to promise to make him, not Pompilius, her heir without telling the old man (who after all his work with Lady M could only expect an inheritance). After showing Lambert her secret hoard of jewels—given to her by 2,000-odd famous lovers (princes, ambassadors, film stars)—she offers a further lure, urging him to put on an old sentimental record and then open a packet of photos of herself when young. Here the film foregrounds the aging body and allows viewers to enter into its realities, especially vis-à-vis sexuality. At first astounded by the images he sees of her at 17, 28, and 42, Lambert looks at Lady M's old face and says it is as beautiful as all three photos. However, he still cannot bring himself to have sex with her. Like the viewers, perhaps, he finds the idea revolting. But as his conception changes with the unfolding of the plot, so perhaps does ours. Lady M seems to suffer temporary dementia, confuses Lambert with an old lover, and does not know where she is; he has to pull off a heist she has arranged on his own—a job where he appears to have killed the victim. Somehow, after this, she recovers, and the film leaves them where it found them, promenading together by the warm sea.

While Lady M's attraction to Lambert is understandable, even if presented in an unusually explicit and physical way, the reverse attraction of a young man to an elderly woman is more remarkable. How exactly are we to understand Lambert's attachment? At first it is not apparently sexual at all— and whether it ever becomes really sexual is not clear—but at the same time, the film does not tell us why Lambert wants to be with Lady M once the obvious mercenary interest has waned. Even San-Antonio in the novel leaves Lambert's psychology uncertain on this point. Perhaps Lady M's very complexity and difference keep him with her. But until nearly the end, Lambert seems to be vacillating. It is the fortuitousness of Lady M's being unwell when she is planning a crime that seems to be the turning point for Lambert. As noted, he decides to undertake the robbery alone, and after this, they share an investment in crime for crime's sake, the secret life of outlaws.

WICKED OLD WOMEN?

The ideology of *La Vieille* is complex and in some ways contradictory. In allowing the attraction between Lady M and Lambert to develop over the course of the narrative, the film encourages viewers to change their ideas of the aged female body as unattractive, undesirable, even sexually disgusting. The film breaks with norms about aging by being frank about elderly people's ongoing sexual desires and about the realities of the aging body and its losses. But at times a genuine tension develops—at least in this viewer. I found myself struggling against a certain wish for Lambert to end up with his young sexy girlfriend, without being able to understand why. Perhaps I did not like the tricks Lady M was playing to keep him. Was she humiliating herself, getting caught up in the larger conservative gender politics that insists on women being sexy and beautiful enough to capture a male such as he? After all, it is only through the inspiration of Lady M's earlier beautiful self, as we saw, that Lambert begins to feel desire.

But I do not think this contradictory ideology means that *La Vieille* is not a "progressive" film about aging. Rather, I would say that the film is interesting because of its contradictory ideology: the contradictions allow the film to lay bare our preconceptions about age. That is, it cuts across entrenched codes about aging. The film challenges the viewer to confront and recognize concepts about aging she brought into the cinema with her—namely, concepts saturated with Western culture's reification of youth and disgust about age. Introducing the young sexy woman as a rival to Lady M provokes the viewer's preconceptions in providing an opening for our normalized views that Lambert should end up with a young woman. In allowing the wicked old lady to win, the film is revolutionary. It frustrates our attraction to the young girl and in so doing forces us to rethink age stereotypes. Even if Lambert's sexual desire had to be provoked by images of Lady M as a young girl (narratively, these images make his desire plausible), he *does* desire her. She, for her part, has played nasty tricks to win him. We are forced to honor the urgency of *her* desire that leads her to such tricks. This is an urgency and a determination rarely associated with elderly women.

In the end Lady M and Lambert are planning a new caper, the future seems eternal for them, old age seems to have conquered death and Lady M to have won her "young flesh" for keeps. Implied here is that Lambert has discovered genuine attachment to Lady M: he is not only interested in her money or because he has discovered a "youthful self" beneath her wrinkled surface.

San-Antonio and Heynemann, then, work to overcome the idea of old women as the "abject" (in Julia Kristeva's sense). That is, underlying patriarchy's approach to aging women is the idea that old people are what we have to push away from the social body, and even the individual body, for that body to remain clean, whole, and pure. Because of such ideas, the sixteen-year relationship (from 1980 to 1996) between esteemed aging novelist Marguerite Duras and her young fan and lover Yann Andréa was deemed scandalous in Paris at the time. Josée Dayan's *Cet amour-là*, as mentioned earlier, allowed Moreau to be engaged in a similar exploding of preconceptions about age. In an interview about her role in the film (Clements 2003, 29), Moreau notes that she too has "always liked younger men." Perhaps, then, in both these roles she was able to identify especially well with her character. Moreau admits that she has "more fun with 20–25-year-old boys. We talk, we argue . . . Except for geniuses. Geniuses or young men . . ."

Like Moreau and Duras in their lives, *La Vieille* blurs the binary oppo-
sitions between youth and age in a far more productive way than that currently
at work in our culture—namely, increasing scientific advances which begin to
destabilize youth/age boundaries through reworking the surface of the body
by getting rid of wrinkles. The broad discussion of Botox and other injections
as I write is merely the latest example of a technique to decrease the "wrinkled" (an "ultimate badness") in a world where cosmetic surgery is as readily
undertaken by the young as by the aging.

For the purposes of this chapter, I have taken a deconstructive attitude
toward evil. That is, I am interested in the social norms, here those of aging
women, that prescribe what behavior is, and is not, appropriate for such
women. *Evil* is perhaps too strong a word for how culture defines elderly
women who do not fit social norms; that is, who do not stand aside from the
public sphere and action, do not become contemplative and ease slowly
toward death. I use the term *wicked* rather than *evil* to make my general points
(and this is especially true for the discussion of Marlene Dietrich), although
at times Lady M in *La Vieille qui marchait dans la mer* comes close to being
evil, for instance when she steals jewels from rich people and perhaps even
more when she manipulates Lambert and his young girlfriend. Because of her
lust and jealousy she more or less causes Pompilius's death. The point is that
such behavior makes great stuff for stories about men, but it is seen as dis-
tasteful when the protagonist is a woman. Heynemann is playfully decon-
structing social norms vis-à-vis aging women. Meanwhile, Dietrich's aging
persona in *Marlene* also belies social norms for elderly women in that she more
or less abuses the director of the film, Maximilian Schell, and behaves in an
impossibly difficult manner with regard to his effort to make a film about her
past. Women who defy social norms become by default "evil," falling into a
very old literary and cultural stereotype of the wicked witch or hag.

Cosmetic surgery is not the solution to our deeply ingrained attitudes to
aged women. It is the underlying, deeply held ideologies in Western nations
about the aged body and aging in general that require our attention (Kaplan
2001). Those ideologies underpin the "wickedness" of the "wicked old
women" we see onscreen, exemplified in many ways by Marlene Dietrich and
Jeanne Moreau. To understand such characters more fully is to more fully see,
and appreciate, aging women on the screen and in life.

WORKS CITED

Clement, Marcelle. 2003. "A Mai-Décembre Romance, Rekindled Onscreen," *New
    York Times* (March 30), Section 2, 15; 29.

Fischer, Lucy. 2000. "Marlene: Modernity, Mortality and the Biopic," *Biography* 23: 1
    (Winter), 193–211.

Gray, Marianne. 1994. *La Moreau.* New York: Donald I. Fine Books.

Gullette, Margaret Morganroth. 1987. *Declining to Decline: Cultural Politics and the Politics of the Midlife.* Charlottesville: University of Virginia Press.

Kaplan, E. Ann. 1997. "Resisting Pathologies of Age and Race: Menopause and Cosmetic Surgery in Films by Rainer and Tom." In Paul Komesaroff, Philipa Rothfield and Jeanne Daly, eds., *Reinterpretring the Menopause: Cultural and Philosophical Issues.* New York and London: Routledge, 100–26.

———. 1999. "Trauma and Aging: Marlene Dietrich, Melanie Klein and Marguerite Duras." In Kathleen Woodward, ed., *Figuring Age: Women, Bodies, Generations.* Bloomington: Indiana University Press, 171–94.

———. 2001. "Trauma, Aging and Melodrama (With Reference to Tracey Moffatt's *Night Cries*)." In Marianne DeKoven, ed., *Feminist Locations.* New Brunswick, N.J.: Rutgers University Press, 304–28.

Kozlowski, Jean. 1993. "Women, Film, and the Midlife Sophie's Choice. Sink or Souzatzka?" In Jean C. Callahan, ed., *Menopause: A Midlife Passage.* Bloomington: Indiana University Press, 3–22.

Moreau, Jean-Claude. 1988. *Jeanne Moreau.* Paris: Éditions Ramsay.

San-Antonio (Fréderic Dard). 1988. *La Vieille qui marchait dans la mer.* Paris: Fleuve Noir.

Strauss, Frédéric and Jean-Claude Loiseau. n.d. "Moreau, forcément Moreau," *Cinéma/Entretien.* Télérama no. 2714. www.telerama.fr.

Woodward, Kathleen. 1991. *Aging and Its Discontents: Freud and Other Fictions.* Bloomington: Indiana University Press.

FIGURE 17. The Fuehrer has been the butt of satire and humor in film. Adenoid Hynkel (Charles Chaplin) plans to take over the world in Chaplin's *The Great Dictator* (United Artists, 1940). This film "discusses anti-Semitic activities more openly than might have been possible in more realistic melodramas." (Collection Lester D. Friedman)

CHAPTER SEVENTEEN

Darkness Visible:
Images of Nazis in American Film

LESTER D. FRIEDMAN

I am the expression of your most secret desires.
—Adolf Hitler in *Hitler: a Film from Germany*

TRIUMPH OF THE SEEN/SCENE:
REFLECTIONS ON THE ATTRACTIONS OF NAZI IMAGERY

It seems as though they have always been here, the stuff of waking nightmares. But, unlike their fictional counterparts who took shape in the deep recesses of our collective unconscious, these monsters walked among us. Flesh and blood beings, they triumphantly marched to power amidst distinguished cultural achievements in medicine and law, architecture and the arts: the poison within the rose. They listened to music, had romances, read books, shopped for food, went to the movies, attended church, got married, and loved their children. Yet these good citizens murdered—or ignored the murders of—millions whose only crime was to be seen as somehow different. They forever altered our conception of what was imaginable, what was evil, and what was possible. As Von Berg, the gentile character suspected of being

The author wishes to thank Lisa Gschwind, Leslie Lewis, David Cook, and Rae-Ellen Kavey for their help with this piece.

a Jew in Arthur Miller's *Incident at Vichy* says, "Win or lose this war, they have pointed the way to the future. What one used to conceive a human being to be will have no room on this earth" (Langer 1995, 168).

The Third Reich, according to historian Saul Friedlander, "remains the key reference point of contemporary history" and an "obsession for the contemporary imagination" (1984, 11, 19). Yet why do figures and images from that time still possess the power to haunt and frighten us? If anything, the newspaper accounts, newsreels, feature films, documentaries, and magazine articles that appeared during World War II vilified the Japanese even more than their German counterparts; their sneak attack on Pearl Harbor, forever burned into U.S. history as a "day that will live in infamy," along with their status as nonwhites and non-Christians, made them natural targets for racist stereotypes: the Yellow Peril made flesh (Schatz 1997, 279). But few today worry about neo-Imperial Army hate groups. The North Koreans and North Vietnamese, like the Japanese before them, were also demonized during conflicts with those countries. Yet musical rebels do not wear black pajamas to emulate Vietcong fighters or fill their lyrics with thumping references to North Korean ideals. These adversaries from our past wars remain frozen in their particular historical eras and, as such, represent no psychic or tangible threat to contemporary citizens.

Alone among America's former enemies, the Nazis remain a palpable presence in our daily literal and imaginary life. Try this experiment during the next week: see how often the words *Hitler, Holocaust,* and *Nazi* enter your world. My guess is that you will not be able to go more than one or two days without hearing or seeing some reference to those words. Images taken from and inspired by the Third Reich saturate our culture functioning as concrete representations of that specific historical era, free-floating signifiers of universal evil and, for some, emblems of purity, power, and erotic fascination. For many of us, neo-Nazi Skinheads, the National Alliance, the Church of the Creator, the Posse Comitatus, the Aryan Nations, and a host of other Nazi progeny stand as a clear and present danger. Florentine Strzelczyk aptly describes this situation:

> Far from being relegated to the garbage heap of history . . . the spectacles, visual fantasies and paraphernalia of National Socialism have assumed a privileged place not only in entertainment films but in American mass culture in general. . . . The fantastic forms and visual arrangements of fascism incite a continuing, captivating enticement for North American filmmakers and audiences. (2000, 94–95)

The reasons for this cultural obsession with the images, figures, and narratives of the Third Reich mark the starting point for any serious discussion of films containing Nazis. One must explore their power to understand their appeal. I want to delineate, however briefly, five constituent components of that appeal before turning to actual movies with Nazi characters: Nazi image power; sympathy for the devil; the erotic dimension; the Holocaust culture; and the thought that we might be *them*.

Image Power

With the possible exception of the pre-Stalin era of communist Russia, no regime in history has ever been more conscious of, or more fully understood, the power of visual imagery than the Third Reich: "Nazism's attraction lay less in any explicit ideology than in the power of emotions, images and phantasms" (Friedlander, 4). Its leaders designed massive events with camera positioning firmly in mind (most spectacularly the 1934 Nuremberg rally that Leni Riefenstahl filmed in *Triumph of the Will* [1934]), staged events for their maximum visual impact, and transformed their prolific national cinema into a dynamic vehicle for broadcasting their ideology throughout the world (see Leiser 1974; Schulte-Sasse 1996; Kaes 1989; Hall 1969; Rentschler 1996). "Fascism," says Rey Chow, "cannot be understood without a certain understanding of the primacy of the image" (1995, 32). Speaking specifically of Hitler's regime, Thomas Elsaesser argues that the "pleasure . . . of being seen, of placing oneself in view of the all-seeing eye of the state" was central for the German middle and working classes; he goes on to discuss what he labels "the massive specularization of public and private life" during the Third Reich (1986, 545). Strzelczyk goes even further: "Nazi Fascism can be understood as an idealism-producing machinery whose success was closely linked with theatrical staging and aesthetic display using film as a medium. . . . It is a cultural phenomenon whose power and success can only unfold within technology, especially the film medium" (96). Nazism both designed and performed itself for optical pleasures, but its appeal went beyond the merely visual.

The Nazis tapped into an apparently primal set of beliefs and feelings and, what remains equally crucial, found ways to capture and communicate these values visually. Susan Sontag's 1975 essay on Leni Riefenstahl's book of African photographs, *The Last of the Nuba*, remains one of the best explorations of the Nazi ideals and aesthetics, and of the continuing question of whether form can be separated from content, beautiful art from the vile messages it enfolds. Fascist aesthetics, says Sontag, are preoccupied with "situations of control, submissive behavior, and extravagant effort: they exalt two seemingly opposite states, egomania and servitude" (1976, 40). As such, the artistic products of this ideology remain obsessed with "physical perfection" (40), which manifests itself in a series of overt contrasts: "between the pure and the impure, the incorruptible and the defiled, the physical and the mental, the joyful and the critical" (39). Combine these underlying values with the awe-inspiring pageantry of large groups of people massed around "an all-powerful, hypnotic leader figure or force," (40) continues Sontag, and the result is a set of "romantic ideals" (the cult of beauty, the fetishism of courage, the dissolution of alienation in ecstatic feelings of community, the repudiation of the intellect, the family of man under the parenthood of leaders) which are "vivid and moving to many people . . . [and] to which many continue to be attached" (43). Thus, far from being an aberrant disruption in the generally humanistic flow of European culture, the art of Nazi Germany amalgamated powerful strands of intellectual ideologies with deeply felt emotional longings to formulate an alluring ideal, express it through a consistent and pleasurable aesthetic, commodify it within powerful visual images, and distribute it throughout the world.

Sympathy for the Devil

Creative works that juxtapose a clear "good" against an unmistakable "bad" inevitably risk having audiences identify with the seductive power of evil rather than the moral force of virtue. Milton's grand epic *Paradise Lost* remains one of the best examples of this tendency. Although the blind poet's avowed purpose is to "justify the ways of God to men" (I, 125), generations of readers have responded more to Satan's rebellious defiance than to God's stern demands. Even as he remains "Chain'd on the burning lake" (I, 210), the devil's refusal to bend to God's will and his brazen declaration that it is "Better to reign in Hell, than serve in Heav'n" (I, 263) strike many as far more alluring than do any lines uttered by the forces of good. To achieve renown demands the destruction of a seemingly unconquerable antagonist: every David needs his Goliath, each Luke Skywalker and Rick Blaine his Darth Vader or Colonel Strasser. Artists often make such evocative personifications of evil as compelling as possible so that readers and viewers will viscerally experience the tempting allure of dark forces. As such, these characters appeal to our human desire to possess and wield enormous amounts of power and free ourselves from social constraints and conventional rules of behavior.

The Nazis embody all these attributes and have emerged as the preeminent incarnations of evil in our time. Yet one wonders how often, as with Milton's Satan, viewers identify with bold displays of enticing Nazi evil rather than admire long-suffering good. Even the most malignant portraits of celluloid Nazis can play into private fantasies of brutality, sexual license, and domination some members of the audience undoubtedly harbor. The question, therefore, is whether filmic representations of Nazis encourage those who possess these tendencies to imitate them outside movie theaters or allow them to find a safe outlet for their fantasies by indulging them, imaginatively, while watching the movie. If the former is true, then even those movies that forcefully condemn Nazism function, paradoxically, as an influential recruiting vehicle for modern neo-Nazis and their cohorts by replicating the alluring and arresting aesthetics that made fascism appealing in the first place.

The Erotic Dimension

Replicated Nazi uniforms appear regularly in the erotic paraphernalia that composes the contemporary sexual terrain. In "Fascinating Fascism," Sontag argues that originally, "the fascist ideal is to transform sexual energy into a 'spiritual' force, for the benefit of the community. The erotic is always present as a temptation, with the most admirable response being a heroic repression of the sexual impulses" (1976, 41). Yet in their present incarnation, most notably highly polished leather boots and caps, steel helmets and pseudomilitary outfits, these Nazi-inspired accoutrements convey precisely the opposite meaning: they identify the wearer as a sexual rebel, heighten the erotic stimulations of sight and touch, and establish the essential relationship between submissive and dominant partners. Movies ranging from the pornographic *Ilsa, She Wolf of the SS* (1974), in which a well-endowed Nazi death camp warden tortures male and female patients in a series of hideous medical experiments, to more serious explorations of sexuality such as *The Night Porter* (1974), where an ex-Nazi and his victim continue their sadomasochistic relationship in postwar Vienna, and *Seven Beauties* (1976), where a man must seduce his grotesque female camp commander to survive, all foreground this erotic component. While American mainstream films have shied far away from exploring this eroticism, films starring handsome leading men in Nazi uniforms (see Uklanski 1999) may well contribute to the appeal of this costuming.

"Power," Michel Foucault said in a 1974 interview with *Cahiers du cinéma*, "carries an erotic charge"; he then went on to explore why "Nazism . . . in all the pornographic literature of the whole world [is] the absolute reference of eroticism" (quoted in Friedlander, 74). Beyond whatever intrinsic appeal shiny black leather may have, the appropriation of Nazi outfits into sexual realms clearly springs from the intimate connections between being powerful and being powerless. "Nazism [is] a temptation into a new order of romance," writes Rosenfeld. "Follow the black boot and the whip into a new kind of bliss, one so intense . . . that it may kill you. The impulse is not primarily political but erotic" (1983, 56). Friedlander characterizes the psychological hold of Nazism as "a particular kind of bondage nourished by the simultaneous desires for absolute submission and total freedom" (19), echoing, in his use of "bondage," "submission," and "freedom" those who rhapsodize about s&m. But as historians acknowledge, Nazism strenuously opposed any liberation of sexual desire, at least on a conscious level. How

ironic, therefore, that those who adopt Nazi-inspired apparel ignore the ideology that spawned it and would, themselves, have been prime targets of the
Third Reich.

Holocaust Cultures

Even though scholars protest the "Americanization" of the Holocaust arguing
that fictional narratives are too often a "vulgarization and trivialization"
(Rosenfeld, 58); that they are squeezed into "narrowly circumscribed conventions of storytelling" (Kaes, 20); and that they are "moral oversimplifications"
(Langer, 166), the centrality of this event in American life has been firmly
established: in the words of historian Tim Cole, it is "the most oft represented
event of the Twentieth Century" (1999, 3). Certainly the establishment of the
United States Holocaust Memorial Museum in Washington, D.C., just walking distance from the Washington Monument and Lincoln Memorial, dramatically attests to this tragedy's significance in American life and culture. Yet
how did it come to be that atrocities that occurred in Europe and that, in actu-
ality, directly affected a fairly small portion of the American public loom so
large in the mosaic of American life?

It was not always so. Historians generally agree that the Holocaust
played little part in our communal consciousness until the early 1960s and
1970s. Its emergence, according to Cole and others, resulted from the coales-
cence of several historical events: the 1961 Eichmann trial in Jerusalem, the
1967 Israeli-Arab War, the rise of identity politics in the United States, the
social disorientation caused by the Vietnam War, the vast popularity of
NBC's 9 1/2-hour mini-series "Holocaust" (1978), and the rise of academic
Jewish Studies programs and Holocaust classes. Even when they maintain a
historical focus on Nazis and their Jewish victims, Holocaust narratives popular in the United States tend to be treated more as universal examples of
intolerance and hatred, the triumph of the human spirit, and personal dignity
amidst tragedy, than as nihilistic documents in which moral vindication is
neither possible nor accepted. So, for example, commentators fondly quote
the uplifting words of young Anne Frank in the film: "I still believe, in spite
of everything, that people are truly good at heart. . . . When I look up at the
sky, I somehow feel that everything will change for the better, that this cruelty too shall end, that peace and tranquility will return once more." Few
remark that she uttered these words before being taken off to Bergen-Belsen
or that, as Langer puts it, the "horrible happens after the curtain falls" (159).

Given all we know, it seems easy to accept Cole's polemical assertion
that the "Holocaust has emerged as nothing less than a ruling symbol in our
culture" (18). Yet victims inevitably force us to consider persecutors. The
increasing attention paid to casualties of the Holocaust clearly spurred a pre-

occupation with the Nazis. Some of this activity stems from a sincere desire to comprehend how seemingly rational men and women could have become mass murderers, some from an intense fascination with particular aspects of Nazi culture that ranges from collecting Nazi memorabilia to mouthing lyrics sung by white supremacist rock groups to joining neo-Nazi organizations. I am not arguing that fascist hate groups would not exist without the prominence of the Holocaust in American life, but such attention may have increased their numbers and fueled their philosophy of hate and fear. Friedlander poses the most trenchant question: "Is such attention [to things Nazi] . . . only a gratuitous reverie, the attraction of spectacle, exorcism, or the result of a need to understand; or is it, again, and still, an expression of profound fears and, on the part of some, mute yearnings as well?" (19).

They Are Us

Finally, the Nazis remain a subject of intense fascination because they emerged from one of the most civilized nations in Europe. Unlike the Japanese, the North Koreans, or the North Vietnamese, who could easily be dismissed as foreign, nonwhite, non-Christian fanatics, the Germans represented the heart of European society. Their long tradition of exceptional achievements in the sciences and the arts, in architecture and law, stood as an inspiring symbol of majestic cultural accomplishment and enlightened social refinement. How could it be that the Third Reich sprang to life in the land of Goethe and Mann, of Bach and Handel, of Nietzsche and Kant? Add to this that countless citizens of the United States directly traced their lineage, and felt strong emotional ties, to Germany, and that many of our country's laws and customs were derived from German models and ideals, and one can easily understand the puzzlement and concern of American scholars and citizens who contemplated the rise and fall of the Nazis. After all, if the unthinkable could happen there, then it might be possible for it to raise its head here, on our own shores, as well. In the famous words from the comic strip *Pogo,* "We have met the enemy . . . and they are us."

GOOSE-STEPPING IN THE DARK:
REFLECTIONS ON NAZISM IN AMERICAN CINEMA

In doing research for this chapter, I was staggered by the sheer number of Nazis that appear on the American screen, not to mention the vast roll call of performers who played them—Ronald Reagan, Errol Flynn, Clint Eastwood, Marlon Brando, Ralph Fiennes, Christopher Plummer, Robert Duvall, Gregory Peck, Carl Reiner, Michael Douglas, Dennis Hopper, Tom Selleck,

Richard Burton, Peter O'Toole, George C. Scott, and many more (see Uklanski's book of portraits of such actors in costume as Nazis). Do Nazis become less threatening and more appealing when performed by stars such as these? Even limiting my parameters to American films with characters from the Third Reich—thus eliminating a vast amount of European products, movies about neo-Nazis, and films that use generalized Nazi imagery (such as the *Star Wars* series [1977–99], for example)—a huge number of films still remained stretching from the late 1930s until the present time. These I consider in five categories: period pieces—those made immediately before or during World War II; retrospectives—films set in World War II but made afterward; humoresques and satires; fantasies; and victimization narratives—particularly Holocaust stories.

Period Pieces

Because much has already been written about World War II combat movies, I need not rehash the general contours and conventions of this genre (see Schatz, Manvell 1974; Birdwell 1999; Dick 1985; Beidler 1998; Basinger 1986). As one might expect, combat films, many featuring Nazi characters, increased markedly once the United States entered the war: from only 12 (out of 477) war films in 1940, the numbers spiraled upward quickly to 121 (out of 488) in 1942, staying roughly even in 1943, and then starting to drop until they reached 13 (out of 378) in 1946 and fell to 2 (out of 369) in 1947 (Shain 1976, 31). I want to focus on noncombat films rather than on those spotlighting actual warfare and fighting. At first, as Michael Birdwell clearly documents, Warner Bros. was virtually alone in promoting anti-Nazi activity prior to the War (12). But almost immediately after the attack on Pearl Harbor, the Office of War Information (OWI) played a crucial role in charting the content of Hollywood's wartime films. As Thomas Schatz and others have noted, the OWI encouraged filmmakers not to make simplistic "hate pictures." Instead, they asked the studios to focus "on the doctrine of fascism and its ruling cliques, not the German . . . people" (278). The result was that "Hollywood followed the OWI's lead and created individual German characters and distinguished between good Germans and evil Nazis" (279). A good example is *The Seventh Cross* (1944), the story of seven concentration camp escapees who, one by one, are caught, tortured, hung on crosses, and finally murdered. Only George Heisler (Spencer Tracy) manages to elude the Gestapo and escape, this with the aid of good German citizens who reject the Nazi tenets. As Jan-Christopher Horak explains: "the Nazis are a minority in Germany, a terroristic and totalitarian dictatorship of storm troops" (1986, 126); "Almost all of the ordinary people are upright anti-Nazis or sympathizers with the Resistance" (127) and the film "places blame on a Nazi elite . . . while simultaneously valorizing American democratic values" (128).

The most famous of the early Nazi films is *Confessions of a Nazi Spy* (1939). A heavy-handed attack on Nazi activities in the United States, the film relies on a pseudodocumentary approach that Harry Warner claimed "was carefully prepared on the basis of factual happenings" (Friedman 1982, 81–83). It ignited a controversy when originally distributed, but rereleased in 1940 after sensational government disclosures about Nazi activities in the United States, *Confessions of a Nazi Spy* was seen to present what *New York Times* critic Frank Nugent now called "common knowledge [whose] scope of treachery has been immeasurably widened" (Friedman, 82). In retrospect, the film represents the most determined anti-Nazi statement Hollywood produced prior to the United States' entry into World War II.

Near the beginning of the movie, Dr. Kassell (Paul Lukas), head of German-American activities, calls on all true German Americans to "save America from the chaos that breeds in democracy and racial equality. Germans in the United States," he continues, "must be brought back to racial unity." As one of his major undertakings, Kassell traces Americans back four generations and classifies them according to blood type and race. He feverishly warns Inspector Renard (Edward G. Robinson), head of the F.B.I. team set up to investigate his activities, that all Americans must become aware of the "insidious, international conspiracy of sub-human criminals greedy for world power." American audiences, no doubt, clearly presumed that the "sub-human criminals" were Jewish, although they are never mentioned by name and no Jewish characters appear in the film.

Other noncombat films made during the war focus on more domestic issues. The way Nazi doctrines and policies rupture meaningful relationships between family members and friends is treated in *The Hitler Gang* (1944), *Reunion in France* (1942), *Tomorrow the World!* (1944), *Hitler's Children* (1943), *Address Unknown* (1944), and *The Man I Married* (1940). We see the plight of Americans on foreign soil in *Casablanca* (1942) and *Background to Danger* (1943); and in Nazi Germany in *Escape* (1940) and *Berlin Correspondent* (1942). Espionage stories frame *Dangerously They Live* (1942), *Hotel Berlin* (1945), *The Fallen Sparrow* (1943), *Journey Into Fear* (1942), *Man Hunt* (1941), *Spy Train* (1943), *Nazi Agent* (1942), and *All Through the Night* (1942). And *Hitler's Madman* (1943), *Hangmen Also Die* (1943), *Enemy of Women* (1944), *Women in Bondage* (1943), *Edge of Darkness* (1943), and *Four Sons* (1940) show the Nazis as cruel, sadistic, and sexually depraved.

One of Hollywood's earliest attempts to depict Nazi Germany and to confront the regime's anti-Semitism directly was *The Mortal Storm* (1940). Although identified only as a non-Aryan, the persecuted Dr. Viktor Roth (Frank Morgan) is forced to wear an armband with a "J" on it. Set in January

1933, on the eve of Hitler's appointment as chancellor, the film begins with a prologue about "the evil elements within man" and "the mortal storm" in which mankind finds itself today. The film focuses on Roth, beloved patriarch of a devoted family and revered teacher of students for many generations. As Hitler's policies disrupt fundamental aspects of German life, the professor's once respectful students, inspired by doctrines of racial purity, metamorphose into vehement Nazis. Fritz Marberg (Robert Young), once one of Roth's favorites, leads a boycott of the professor's classes. Finally, the government bars Roth from teaching, takes him into custody, and deports him to a concentration camp where he dies. Trying to flee the country, his daughter Freya (Margaret Sullavan) is shot as she and Martin Breitner (James Stewart), one of the professor's still-loyal students, attempt to smuggle his manuscripts across the border.

Particularly interesting is director Frank Borzage's contrasting the attitudes of Breitner and Marberg toward Freya and shaping them into political statements that illustrate two divergent viewpoints. "I do the thinking for both of us," says Marberg, the budding Nazi, echoing Hitler's attitude toward the German people in his treatment of her as unintelligent. Unlike her father, who prizes "tolerance and a sense of humor," and Martin, who sees her as an equal, Fritz believes that service to the Third Reich means blind dedication without the emotional restraint of personal feelings or the intellectual strength of independent thought. *The Mortal Storm*'s strong anti-Nazi sentiment signals Hollywood's growing desire to alert the nation to the dangers abroad, despite protests from isolationists and the loss of foreign distribution markets under the sway of Germany. The interethnic love story between Martin and Freya represents, of course, a truly American approach to political differences, reducing large-scale issues to personal narratives.

Retrospectives

Social anthropologist Jonathan Webber remarks, "The past becomes the present only through representation; we cannot know the past in any other way" (quoted in Selizer 1998, 239). Films made about World War II after its conclusion serve multiple, often divergent, functions for audiences, obliging them to explore what happened during those times but also safely investigating controversial issues that could never have been discussed under wartime conditions. Free from the social and political constraints that held wartime filmmakers in check, a film such as *Hart's War* (2002) can openly explore racism in the armed forces. In addition, as Neal Gabler notes, "war movies serve as a metaphor for American attitudes toward authority, both personal and moral, that armed forces as institutions symbolize" (2002, 4). They instill a sense of national pride, particularly at a time (during the Vietnam and

Watergate eras, for example) when our heroes and villains seem far less clear than in earlier eras. Finally, these pictures demonstrate how "history and memory have finally intersected with commodity on a scale commensurate with the long national love affair with creative self-mythologizing" (Beidler, 6). As such, these retrospective films provide yardsticks by which we appraise who we were then and who we are now, as well as what we once believed and no longer accept.

The most lavish attempt to confront the question of German guilt during the wars years is *Judgment at Nuremberg* (1961), a fictional reenactment of the famous postwar trials. The defense attorney, Hans Rolfe (Maximilian Schell), sets his argument for limited blame carefully: "The brutality was brought about by a few extremists, the criminals, and a very few Germans knew about what was going on." In fact, he assures Judge Dan Haywood (Spencer Tracy) that men such as Judge Ernst Jannings (Burt Lancaster) "stayed in power to prevent worse things from happening." His defense, therefore, argues that a judge such as Jannings does not make laws but carries them out and that Jannings was unaware of the excesses of the German leaders. Conversely, U.S. Army prosecutor Colonel Edward Lawson (Richard Widmark) shows documentaries of the liberation of Buchenwald and calls witnesses who testify to the cruelties of the Nazis that were surely known by men in powerful positions, such as Jannings. Although the judges find all the defendants guilty of war crimes and sentence them to life imprisonment, demonstrating that, in Haywood's words, "under a natural crisis men can delude themselves into vast and heinous crimes" and provoking Jannings to admit his own culpability—"What was going to be a passing phase became a way of life"—the film nevertheless ends on a bitterly ironic note. The painstaking Nuremberg decisions are reversed by a higher court, all the defendants are pardoned, and then freed.

In many post–World War II films, soldiers refight important battles in traditional combat epics: *Battleground* (1949), which Basinger highlights because of its combat sequences and huge critical and commercial success (158), *Battle of the Bulge* (1965), *The Big Red One* (1980), *A Bridge Too Far* (1977), *The Bridge at Remagen* (1969), *The Guns of Navarone* (1961), *The Longest Day* (1962), *Saving Private Ryan* (1998), *Tobruk* (1967), *The Thin Red Line* (1998), and *U-571* (2000). Some films establish antihero units, ragtag groups of misfits who use unconventional methods to fight the Germans: *The Dirty Dozen* (1967) or *The Secret Invasion* (1964). A few films focus on the German point of view—*The Young Lions* (1958), *The Last Blitzkrieg* (1958), *The Misfit Brigade* (1987)—whereas others set the scene in prisoner-of-war camps: *The Great Escape* (1963), *Stalag 17* (1953), *Von Ryan's Express* (1965), *Victory* (1981). Many films deal with individual bravery in the face of Nazi oppression: *Julia* (1977), *The Passage* (1979), *Shining Through* (1992), *The*

Sound of Music (1965), *Swing Kids* (1993), *The Train* (1964). A few illustrate attempts to bring Nazi war criminals to justice (*Arch of Triumph* [1948]), and others begin to explore life after the war, both in the United States and Europe: *Little Boy Lost* (1953), *The Search* (1948).

Humoresques and Satires

Can one make fun of Hitler and not offend those who suffered in the Holocaust (see Gilman 2000)? Apparently generations of movie clowns think so because from the earliest days of World War II right up to the present time, the Fuehrer has been the butt of celluloid humor and satire. The earliest attempt to use comedy as a weapon was Charlie Chaplin's *The Great Dictator* (1940). Chaplin, who bore an uncanny resemblance to Hitler, played two roles in the film: a Jewish barber and the dictator Adenoid Hynkel. Throughout the comedy, Chaplin discusses anti-Semitic activities more openly than might have been possible in more realistic melodramas. He shows, for example, how Hynkel's men paint "Jew" on barbershop windows and how after the little barber wipes it off he is attacked by thugs. After Jewish bankers refuse Hynkel a loan, he vents his rage on the hapless Jewish community. Chaplin's film ends with a long and impassioned plea for tolerance that (with what we now know about Hitler's death camps) seems both naïve and sadly understated. Two other early films, *Once Upon a Honeymoon* (1942) and *To Be or Not to Be* (1942), also used wit and charm to satirize the Nazis before the world was aware of just how brutal they really were.

Probably the most famous example of making fun of Nazis is Mel Brooks's *The Producers* (1968), recently turned into a Broadway extravaganza. Here Nazi playwright Franz Liebkind (Kenneth Mars) receives the brunt of Brooks's satire as the creator of the worst play ever written, *Springtime for Hitler,* a vehicle through which producers Bialystock (Zero Mostel) and Bloom (Gene Wilder) seek to recognize their dream of opening and closing on the same night and ensuring themselves a financial windfall. Liebkind describes *Springtime* as a "gay romp with Adolf and Eva in Berchtesgaden." He frequently longs for Hitler's resurrection—forcing Bialystock and Bloom to wear Nazi arm bands and to sing German war songs with him—and agrees to sell them his play only because he thinks it will be a "way to clear the Fuehrer's name" and show once and for all that Hitler "was a nice guy who could dance the pants off Churchill."

Surely something is going on here beyond the surface content of this absurd situation. The very fact that Bialystock and Bloom sacrifice their principles to join forces with this Nazi indicates a great deal about the willingness of modern Jews to ignore the tragedies of the past as they do business in the present. Brooks, like Chaplin before him, shoots for some larger issues; most important, he wants to make people laugh at the obscene absurdity of a master race and its lethal anti-Semitism by using farce not force. Yet he goes even further than his predecessor. The sheer audacity of a musical called *Springtime for Hitler*, and of its becoming a hit, satirizes an American public willing to find humor, however grotesque, in the Third Reich. Bialystock and Bloom pick a subject that seems universally repulsive and assume that no feeling person could find it otherwise. Ironically, their awareness and compassion far outstrips that of their callous audience, which with deadened sensibility totally ignores the historical reality that lurks beneath the surface of the musical. Thus, in a world drifting into moral subjectivity, even Hitler can be reborn as a figure of fun. Brooks bites the hand that feeds him, satirizing the viewers of his film and expecting us to reward him for his honest cleverness. And we do (see Desser and Friedman 1993, 147–53).

Most of the famous comedy teams made wartime films: Laurel and Hardy (*Air Raid Wardens* [1943]), Abbott and Costello (*Buck Privates* [1941]), the Marx Brothers (*A Night in Casablanca* [1946]), and the Three Stooges (*No Dough Boys* [1944]). Comedians such as Bob Hope (*Caught in the Draft* [1941]), Milton Berle (*Margin for Error* [1943]), Danny Kaye (*Me and the Colonel* [1958]), Carl Reiner (*Dead Men Don't Wear Plaid* [1982]), and Jerry Lewis (*Which Way to the Front?* [1970]) all made movies with Nazis in them. Finally, several animated films were made with famous cartoon characters taking on the Nazis: Donald Duck (*Der Fuehrer's Face* [1943]), Bugs Bunny (*Russian Rhapsody* [1944]), and Daffy Duck (*Scrap Happy Daffy* [1943]). After the war came more satiric movies critical of the military system—*Catch-22* (1970) and *Kelly's Heroes* (1970)—or films that used German figures to make commentaries on contemporary politicians, for example *Son of Hitler* (1978). Nazis become cartoonlike villains in both the first and last Indiana Jones films, *Raiders of the Lost Ark* (1981) and *The Last Crusade* (1989). And several films that use Nazi figures are simply weird: *Hard Rock Zombies* (1984), in which Nazi sex perverts kill members of a band who then, recalled from the grave, wreak revenge on their persecutors; *Snide and Prejudice* (1998), where a psychiatrist encourages his patients' fantasies of themselves as historical Nazis; and *Rented Lips* (1988), featuring the making of a World War II porn musical in the midst of which a well-endowed actress exclaims, "We are being attacked by the dreaded Lufthansa!"

Fantasies

Nazis are often inserted into established science fiction and horror series with clearly recognizable heroes, such as the Tarzan features (*Tarzan Triumphs* and *Tarzan's Desert Mystery* [both 1943]), Jungle Jim (*Voodoo Tiger* [1952]), the Invisible Man (*Invisible Agent* [1942]), or Dr. Frankenstein (*Frankenstein— 1970* [1958]). Many films also depict the fiendish plots of Nazi scientists either to kill vast amounts of people (. . . *And Millions Die!* [1973]) or to conduct evil experiments (*Elves* [1990]; *The Keep* [1983]; *The Loch Ness Horror* [1981]; *Puppet Master III: Toulon's Revenge* [1991]; *Rendezvous 24* [1946]; *Revenge of the Zombies* [1943]; *They Saved Hitler's Brain* [1968]; *She Demons* [1958]; and *Zaat* [1972]). Modern-day Nazi plots hypothesize what might happen if Nazis survived in our contemporary world and we were, once again, forced to confront them. Clearly, equal amounts of wish fulfillment and fear exist in these speculative films. They allow characters to transcend the facts and tragedies of history. This time around, on at least a one-to-one basis, Jews and other victims can defeat the Nazis, showing themselves to be both physically and mentally superior to their tormentors. On deeper levels, the films represent a persistent fear not only that the Nazis have survived but that, under the right circumstances, it could all happen again. Representing more than merely elderly figures who escaped the destruction of the Third Reich, characters in these films personify the endurance of the Nazi philosophy in our own time. The responses of modern Americans who face these villains range from awe (*Apt Pupil* [1998]) to horror (*Anima* [1998]) to fear (*The House on Carroll Street* [1988]) to confusion (*The Man in the Glass Booth* [1975] and *River of Death* [1989]).

Two of the most representative films of this subcategory are *Marathon Man* (1976) and *The Boys from Brazil* (1978). *Marathon Man* features a sadistic ex-Nazi dentist (Laurence Olivier) who tortures a Jewish graduate student (Dustin Hoffman) to obtain secret information. Eventually, the Jew forces him to feel some of the pain he caused others and, finally, kills him. *Boys* advances the fiction that rich former Nazis living in South America have placed clones of Hitler among ninety-four families throughout the world in hopes of duplicating his childhood and thus bringing another German dictator into the world. A Holocaust survivor, Ezra Lieberman (Olivier), based on the famous Nazi-hunter Simon Wiesenthal, confronts the Nazi leader Dr. Josef Mengele (Gregory Peck) at the home of one of the clones and eventually causes him to be ripped apart by a pack of killer Dobermans. What is most interesting about *The Boys from Brazil* is its conclusion: Lieberman burns the list showing where the clones have been placed, rather than allow a militant anti-Nazi to kill all the children on it. "We are not in the business of killing children," he tells the Jew who demands the list, "Any children." His instinctive morality is far more important than any lesson in genetics vs. environment. Not blinded by hatred or revenge, Lieberman understands that killing innocent children would put him in the same class as the Nazis: murderers who excuse their atrocities by claiming a higher purpose. Of course, breaking the chain of violence he shows the Jews and their fellow victims as morally superior to their fanatical oppressors.

Victimization Narratives

The enormous number of films made about the Holocaust has been talked about in several other books and numerous articles (see Avisar 1988). Here I wish to make passing mention of only the two main types one may find: those which detail life inside the death camps—*The Day the Clown Cried* (1972), *Jakob the Liar* (1999), *Schindler's List* (1993)—and those in which survivors of the Third Reich remain traumatized in the modern world—*Enemies: A Love Story* (1989), *I Love You, I Love You Not* (1996), *Sophie's Choice* (1982).

Of these, *The Pawnbroker* (1964) remains one of the American cinema's most powerful depictions of the pain and trauma felt by death camp survivors. The twenty-fifth anniversary of his wife's death causes Sol Nazerman (Rod Steiger) to confront the painful feelings he has long suppressed beneath his world-weary cynicism and pursuit of financial stability. To indicate Nazerman's state of mind, director Sidney Lumet employs "shock" cuts that feed us tiny, highly disjointed bits of information piled on each other, forcing the viewer to share Nazerman's confused mingling of past and present experiences. It is a vicious cycle the pawnbroker is powerless to escape: the present sparks memories of the past, these memories force him to act in the present, which propels him to think more deeply about the past. There is no solace for Sol Nazerman, no spiritual victory to compensate for his loss and guilt. Nothing can bring back his beloved family. He is condemned to life, obliged to remember the suffering of his wife and their friends in the camp, and sentenced to absorb the death of those around him whom he loves. For Nazerman, life is a fate worse than death. Lumet sees no triumph in simple survival; how one lives is what remains important, not simply that one continues to exist.

In both our movie theaters and our towns, the Nazis have survived. Given this reality, it seems appropriate to ask how incorporating Nazi images into popular entertainments affects our culture. Does it rob them of their power, or does examining them in any context whatsoever (including this chapter), even as objects of humor, reinforce their hold on our imaginations and keep the sentiments that inspired them alive in a world far too ready to support them? I have come to believe that the obsession with the Third Reich is part of what Alvin Rosenfeld labels our contemporary "hunger for the horrible" (53). Appropriating the style, or even just the dress, of the Nazis, and ignoring the policies and practices of those who created it, legitimizes an ahistorical worldview that transmutes monstrous acts into titillating fantasies. For me, the use of Nazi images in any context contributes to our flirtation with fascism. Incorporating them into our popular culture, no matter what the artistic intent, helps sustain the cult of fascism. Instead, I choose to cede Nazi imagery to those who venerate the swastika and all it represents. I am not advocating censorship; such restrictions would only increase the taboo value of the censored images, adding the fascination of the forbidden to their other attractions. But I truly doubt that any use of Nazi imagery—no matter how creative—will force viewers "to confront the very process of moral and ethical decision making [and] then leave them to ponder the inexorable complexity of ethics" (Kleeblatt 2001, 13). Such hopes seem both naïve and downright foolish because critical works about Nazism inevitably preach to the converted. The alternatives are neither easy nor clear. But, we must continue to search for ways to remember the victims of the night while not perpetuating the philosophies of those who brought the darkness upon them.

WORKS CITED

Andrew, H. 2000. "The Power of Surrender," *NewsLink* (Fall). http://www.gmsma. org/newslink/surrender.html

Avisar, Ilan. 1988. *Screening the Holocaust: Cinema's Images of the Unimaginable.* Bloomington: Indiana University Press.

Basinger, Jeanine. 1986. *The World War II Combat Film: Anatomy of a Genre.* New York: Columbia University Press.

Beidler, Philip D. 1998. *The Good War's Greatest Hits: World War II and American Remembering.* Athens: University of Georgia Press.

Birdwell, Michael E. 1999. *Celluloid Soldiers: The Warner Brothers Campaign against Nazism.* New York: New York University Press.

Chow, Rey. 1995. "The Fascist Longing in Our Midst," *Ariel* 26:1, 23–50.

Cole, Tim. 1999. *Selling the Holocaust: From Auschwitz to Schindler, How History Is Bought, Packaged, and Sold.* New York: Routledge.

Desser, David and Lester Friedman. 1993. *American-Jewish Filmmakers: Traditions and Trends.* Urbana: University of Illinois Press.

Dick, Bernard F. 1985. *The Star-Spangled Screen: The American World War II Film.* Lexington: University Press of Kentucky.

Elsaesser, Thomas. 1986. "Primary Identification and the Historical Subject: Fassbinder and Germany." In Phil Rosen, ed., *Narrative, Apparatus, Ideology: A Film Theory Reader.* New York: Columbia University Press, 535–49.

Friedlander, Saul. 1984. *Reflections on Nazism: An Essay on Kitsch and Death.* New York: Harper and Row.

Friedman, Lester. 1982. *Hollywood's Image of the Jew.* New York: Crossroads.

Gabler, Neal. 2002. "Seeking Perspective on the Movie Front Lines," *New York Times* (January 27), 4.

Gilman, Sander. 2000. "Is Life Beautiful: Can the Shoah Be Funny? Some Thoughts on Recent and Older Films," *Critical Inquiry* 26, 279–308.

Hall, David Stuart. 1969. *Film in the Third Reich*. Berkeley: University of California Press.

Horak, Jan-Christopher. 1986. "The Other Germany in Zinnemann's *The Seventh Cross* (1944)." In Eric Rentschler, ed., *German Film and Literature*. New York: Methuen, 117–31.

Kaes, Anton. 1989. *From Hitler to* Heimat: *The Return of History as Film*. Cambridge, MA: Harvard University Press.

Kleeblatt, Norman L., ed. 2001. *Mirroring Evil: Nazi Imagery/Recent Art*. New Brunswick, NJ: Rutgers University Press.

Langer, Lawrence L. 1995. "The Americanization of the Holocaust on Stage and Screen." In *Admitting the Holocaust: Collected Essays*. New York: Oxford University Press, 157–77.

Leiser, Erwin. 1974. *Nazi Cinema*. New York: Collier Books.

Lipman, Steve. 1991. *Laughter in Hell: The Use of Humor during the Holocaust*. Northvale, NJ: Jason Aronson, 189–212.

Lipsitz, George. 1990. *Time Passages: Collective Memory and American Popular Culture*. Minneapolis: University of Minnesota Press.

Manvell, Roger. 1974. *Films and the Second World War*. London: J. M. Dent and Sons.

Rentschler, Eric. 1996. *The Ministry of Illusion: Nazi Cinema and Its Afterlife*. Cambridge, MA: Harvard University Press.

Rosenfeld, Alvin H. 1983. "The Holocaust in American Popular Culture," *Midstream* 29/30 (June), 53–59.

Schatz, Thomas. 1997. *Boom and Bust: American Cinema in the 1940s*. Berkeley: University of California Press.

Schulte-Sasse, Linda. 1996. *Entertaining the Third Reich: Illusions of Wholeness in Nazi Cinema*. Durham, NC: Duke University Press.

Selizer, Barbie. 1998. *Remembering to Forget: Holocaust Memory through the Camera's Eye*. Chicago: University of Chicago Press.

Shain, Russell Earl. 1976. *An Analysis of Motion Pictures about War Released by the American Film Industry, 1939–1970*. New York: Arno Press.

Sontag. Susan. 1976. "Fascinating Fascism." In Bill Nichols, ed., *Movies and Methods*. Berkeley: University of California Press, 31–43. Originally published in *The New York Review of Books* (February 6, 1975).

Strzelczyk, Florentine. 2000. "Fascism-Fantasy-Fascination-Film," *Aranchne: An Interdisciplinary Journal of the Humanities* 7:1/2, 94–111.

Uklanski, Piotr. 1999. *The Nazis*. Germany: Patrick Frey Editions.

FIGURE 18. "Please, whatever I did, I'm sorry!" whines Bobby Kent (Nick Stahl) but in a murder scene that is "alarmingly, and appropriately, graceless and stupid" Marty (Brad Renfro) slits his throat. *Bully* (Larry Clark, Lions Gate, 2001). (Frame enlargement)

CHAPTER EIGHTEEN

"The Whole Fucking World Warped around Me": Bad Kids and Worse Contexts

CYNTHIA FUCHS

> They used their inherent gift of free will to choose to do and to be evil. Because they could.
> —Jim Schutze, author of *Bully: A True Story of High School Revenge,* in *Dallas Observer* (21 June 2001)

"I want you to suck my big dick." During the first few seconds of Larry Clark's *Bully* (2001), young Marty Puccio (Brad Renfro) appears in close-up, speaking into a cordless phone. He's seated on his bed, shirtless; his eyes are dull, his diamond stud earring catches the light. He's focused on what appears to be a phone sex call, but just as he speaks his line, he's distracted by his mother's voice coming from downstairs, calling him for dinner. The boy looks briefly annoyed, covering the receiver with his hand, then continues: "I want you to lick my balls."

Marty stares vacantly into the camera as the soundtrack music begins, JT Money's "Who Dat," a hiphop song about posing, trying too hard to fit in. "Who dat off-brand nigga trying to hang wit the clique?" he raps, "Sucker boys run they mouth, real niggaz run the yard." The camera cuts to a series of shots of Marty's neighborhood. As if you're riding in a car, you pass lawns, palm trees, and sidewalks. The panning speed increases as you pass an abandoned roller coaster track, a strip mall, a Seven–11 and a small church with steeple off in the distance, pausing briefly on a sign that reads, "Welcome to Hollywood."

At once disturbing and mundane, *Bully*'s first two scenes (the 20 seconds in Marty's bedroom and the slightly longer introduction to his Florida suburbs) establish a world defined by its contradictions: speed and immobility, boredom and overstimulation, expectation and hopelessness, affluence and pretense. At the center of this world is Marty's relationship with his "best friend" since childhood, Bobby Kent (Nick Stahl), the bully whom he and six friends will murder by the end of the film.

Based on Jim Schutze's 1997 true crime book, *Bully: A True Story of High School Revenge,* Clark's film was released by Lions Gate in late July 2001, unrated and bypassing the usual festival circuit. At the time, Clark was best known as the erstwhile notorious photographer of underclass youths and drug users (see for instance, his books *Tulsa* [1971] and *Teenage Lust* [1983]), as well as the director of 1995's *Kids.* Criticized for its frank, lascivious, and occasionally crude treatment of its subjects (Henry Giroux cites the film's refusal to "probe where identity resides for the urban youth he represents" [1997, 51]), *Kids* was also praised for that same subject matter and for Clark's startling vérité technique, including raucous handheld camerawork, lingering shots of young naked bodies, raggedy editing, and an aggressive soundtrack by Lou Barlow's yowling Folk Implosion.

Bully met with similarly divergent responses, although on a much smaller scale. The relative lack of outrage had to do with the film's limited release, its real life source, and a significant shift in political and social contexts. While its focus on middle-class kids who brutally stabbed and beat to death one of their peers is no doubt disconcerting, the truth is that by 2001, too many kids-killing-kids scenarios had played out on television to make the concept especially shocking. Indeed, *Bully*'s protagonists are more "typical" than not. They listen to hiphop, speak in rude slang, fall prey to peer pressure, and avoid contact with adults. Looking closely at the murderers' relationships, the film explores youth violence, media consumption, drug use, and sexual activity. Whereas it lays blame on the kids, it also, more subtly, interrogates and indicts the cultural contexts that produce them.

This chapter looks at such interrogations in *Bully* and in David Gordon Green's *George Washington,* another U.S. independent film released around the same time, platforming from late 2000 through 2001. On their surfaces, these films are quite different: *Bully* concerns white 18- and 20-year-olds, whereas *George Washington* focuses on an interracial group of 12- to 15-year-olds living in rural, underclass North Carolina; *Bully* is the work of an accomplished, roughhewn 57-year-old artist, *George Washington* is the first feature film by 25-year-old Green, a graduate of North Carolina School of the Arts' film school in Winston-Salem; and *Bully* considers kids who commit murder, whereas *George Washington* reflects on the effects an accidental, if violent, death, has on a group of kids. Yet, for all their differences, the films are alike in significant ways. For one thing, they treat seriously the kids' conceptions of morality and responsibility in contexts where tenets and consequences are distressingly unclear. And both resist formal conventions and cultural assumptions concerning youth.

If kids are functions of their contexts, so too are broader conceptions of youth. Charles Acland has observed that youth is a changeable category, not a fixed experience, notion, or set of expectations. "Generations," he writes, "are discursive constructs, marshalling certain meanings into a single imagined location, rather than statistical truths pure and simple" (1995, 25). Youth, in this sense, is not rebellious, but reconfirms social conventions by marking their limits and emphasizing their ostensible value. In *Bully*, Marty's startling first words not only suggest he is "deviant" but also establish his difference from (most) viewers, who can assume, in relation, a moral high ground. At the same time, however, the film is setting up "bad" Marty's relationship with "worse" Bobby. Marty's recollection of his first experience with pot establishes his vexed relationship with Bobby: upon smoking a joint that Bobby has apparently dusted with a hallucinogen, Marty remembers, he ran to his bedroom and pulled the covers over his head: "The whole fucking world warped around me, man. I had no idea how to handle it."

Bully is about various inabilities to "handle it." Its title obviously alludes to ongoing problems in contemporary youth cultures, although Clark reports that securing funding for the project following the Columbine shootings was difficult for him (it was delayed for 10 months). As he puts it, "It's funny that when you are making work that is issue oriented, people want to go the other way, when I think it would be interesting to explore these subjects that are impacting the way we're seeing kids in society today" (Crawford 2001). "The way we're seeing kids in society today" cuts multiple ways, of course, from the ways "we" see them in movies, to the ways they see and represent themselves for "us," to the ways "we" see them in other, ostensibly real life contexts. *Bully* shows kids "in society," and at the same time implicates "us" for seeing them there. Clark's vérité style suggests this is how kids "really" interact, at the mall, at the video game arcade, at the beach, and having sex and smoking marijuana in their bedrooms with their parents just down the hall watching tv.

Acland argues that in visual media "certain meanings" typically attach to bodies of "youth in crisis." Media depict particular youth whose overt anomaly or trouble makes their service as social and political "limits" explicit. This increased visibility of youth bodies is a function of adult fear and surveillance (an effort to control and/or "protect" youth), as well as adult desire (an effort to possess and/or become youth). "The visibility of youth," Acland continues, "under the eye of social investigation, exists in a threefold formation: as an object of the critical gaze, as a cultural concern, and as a social category with particular members, relations, and experiences" (25).

In *Bully*, surveillance becomes a complex process, in part because the kids are relentlessly in motion, even if they are not going anywhere. Consider, for example, the first driving scene, the speeding camera. The film's action begins as that vehicle takes a diegetic form, that is, a new silver Mustang belonging to Ali Willis (Bijou Phillips). As she pulls into a mall parking lot, she and her best friend Lisa Connelly (Rachel Miner) emerge, wearing shorts and smoking cigarettes. "His cock was beautiful," says Ali, caught in mid-conversation. "And he ate me out for like, an hour. Goddamn it, Lisa," she continues, draping her arm over her friend's shoulder as they walk as one, "It's all about attitude. If you want it, you can get it."

Right away, it is clear that the girls speak the same language as our boy Marty, whom they happen to be on their way to meet for the first time. The camera follows them inside a food court, where Marty and Bobby make sandwiches. Ali swings her narrow hips as she walks, well aware that her body draws attention; she wears a barely-there tube top, while Lisa slouches in a baggy t-shirt, her dark hair hanging down over her face. The girls flirt with sandwich-boys Marty and Bobby, then agree to go with them to the beach, to watch the guys surf. Although they spend some time watching the boys cavort in the golden light ("Nice butt," observes Ali of Marty), it's not long before the group is on the move again, heading off to drink tequila and have sex in Bobby's Camaro.

Here the film establishes the mutual rage and sense of competition that fuel Bobby and Lisa's relationship in two distinct but linked instances. First, she observes a second abuse of Marty (after slamming his head into a counter at the sandwich shop, here Bobby grabs Marty's ear and calls him a "bitch," as Lisa appears in close-up, looking on from the backseat); and secondly, Lisa and Bobby exchange looks while she and Marty have intercourse. Here the camera cuts between Bobby and Lisa, while she moans with pleasure for Marty; the shot of Bobby's face looking down and over at her is repeated later in the film, when she decides that his maltreatment of Marty brings on, in turn, Marty's abuse of her. If Bobby looks at her in a way that is unnerving, proprietary, and supercilious, Lisa sees him as a rival and threat.

The camera's emphasis on Lisa's scrutiny establishes her as a central subject of looking, even as her naked body is repeatedly put on display; she learns to use her body, much as she sees Ali use hers, as a means to get what she "wants," to perform an "attitude." Lisa's look at Marty is immediately possessive—she sees him as her ticket out of her endless boredom. Following the sex scene in the car, she wakes in her bedroom, the camera tracing her nude form then panning up to her walls, showing off her Dr. Dre poster, an array of muscle-boy pin-ups and underwear models, and a newspaper headline taped up: "What Women Want" (this set design, aside from the Dre reference—Clark's updating of 1993 'burban kids' tastes—is taken directly from Schutze's book; he calls the wall "a shrine to yearning" [Schutze, 1]). Lisa thinks she's found exactly what she wants, a boy of her own. Wandering into the kitchen, she announces to her mother (Elizabeth Dimon), "I got a new boyfriend, Ma." During their exchange, they never appear in the same frame, and are further separated by a large plant on the table, situated so that they look like they're talking to the plant instead of each other. Mom gathers her cigarettes, distracted, on her way to work. "What kind?" she asks. "A hunk. You're gonna meet him."

On this line, the scene cuts to a gay club—the spot for hunks, no doubt—where a group of too-young boys dance on a stage for older men with money. The disco drumbeat thunders, the camera focuses on hairless torsos, some adorned with studded leather straps or tattoos, all naked save for their cotton briefs (some of these packed). Marty and Bobby watch from the audience until one man offers Bobby "a hundred bucks" to see Marty perform ("I hear your cute friend gives good phone," he smirks, underlining that it is Bobby who pimps Marty for phone sex). Marty resists, Bobby cajoles, Marty downs his beer and gets up to dance. Awkward at first, tripping as he removes his shoes and jeans, Marty soon gets into it, his hips popping as patrons slip bills into his waistband. Cut to Bobby counting the cash in the car as Marty drives. "You enjoyed that back there, didn't you?" sneers Bobby, again (as he did when calling him a "bitch") impugning his masculinity and sexuality. "Hell no," protests Marty, camera now on him from Bobby's shoulder. "I ain't queer like those guys." Distracted, Marty does not see a car that cuts in front of him and, aided by Bobby grabbing the wheel, drives up on the curb. Enraged—"You fuck, you fucked up my fuckin' car!"—Bobby punches Marty, who proceeds to stop the car and jump out. Bobby panics. Marty runs at him, punching him in the stomach. Bobby's apology, as he puts his hand warmly on Marty's neck, indicates their typical abusive relationship: the abuser insists he "won't do it again" and the victim hopes he's telling the truth.

Significantly, the filmic Bobby differs from the historical Bobby and from the Bobby of Schutze's book. That is, the real-life Bobby Kent was Iranian, first generation born in the United States. Casting the white (and, contrary to life and conventions for "bullies," small and wiry) Nick Stahl changes Bobby's contexts, certainly in his friends' inclination to kill him, and also in his relationship with his own father. In the film, Mr. Kent (Ed Amatrudo) encourages Bobby to work with him in a car stereo/window tinting shop: "It's the best future you can have in this country, to be your own master." Without the background of Mr. Kent's immigration, the line hangs in the air, broadly ironic, in the context of Bobby's compulsion to be the master of all his friends.

As Clark and cinematographer Steve Gainer shoot the scene, Bobby looks trapped in his bathroom when his father enters; the boy is naked, having just washed himself after raping Ali (he forced her to watch his "queer shit," a gay porn tape he made, then beat her until she proclaimed him "the best I ever had"), and Mr. Kent takes him by his neck and pulls him close (the same gesture Bobby uses when wheedling Marty). Father and son are too "intimate," but also at odds. Dad begs him to stop seeing Marty ("Can't you see he's dragging you down?"), and finally Bobby agrees to go along with the stereo shop idea. But, he says, "If I do this for you, can we hire Marty?"

For all his aggression, Bobby is also somewhat sympathetic in this relationship with his overbearing father and even more so in his own self-hatred. In another bathroom scene, he observes himself in his bathroom mirror, again naked, then spits violently at the mirror just as he exits to his bedroom (where the sign just above his head on the door reads, "Beware of Dog"). There he finds Lisa astride Marty in mid-coitus. The camera, at a low angle, emulating Marty's point of view, cuts from Lisa to Bobby grabbing a heavy leather weightlifter's belt. Bobby lunges at Lisa, slaps her off Marty with the belt, then turns Marty over brusquely, declaring, "I'm next." Although what happens next is not entirely clear—does Bobby take his turn with Lisa or Marty or both?—the next scene shows Marty asleep on his own bed, his eye blacked. His mother (Irene B. Colletti) enters, checking in an offscreen voice if he's awake: "Lover bug?" The camera takes mom's view, looking down on her son from above; as she spots the contusion, she only mumbles, "Oh my god." The camera shows her face, indecisive and unsupportive. At breakfast with the entire family seated in white decor on the porch (looking out on a decent lawn, a lake, sunshine), the camera pauses on Marty's face, the black eye, as he pleads with his father, "Can we move?" Exasperated with his wussy son, dad (Alan Lilly) dismisses his request: "Marty, we can't just quit our jobs and leave just because our son's having problems."

Throughout the film, the kids' problems do not concern the adults, who only seem to show up to evade liability. Following the murder, Ali asks her mother (Judy Clayton) whether it would be "enough" if she called a hot line to report it—"This guy," she whines, "kind of got killed"—but didn't leave her name. Although Ali's question suggests a dire lack of understanding—of what it means to have killed someone, of how legal and penal structures work—her mother's response reveals a comparable ignorance: "What are you kids into now? Are you talking about a 'murder' murder?" Ali is driving and her mother sits in the passenger seat, both with their treated blond coiffures blowing in the wind, and the camera pans back and forth between the two as they speak, not cutting as in a typical movie conversation but swinging from side to side to emphasize the distance between them, their faces turned for the most part away from one another, gazing at the road ahead or glancing off to the side, avoiding eye contact. They're mirror images of one another, but again, not at all connected.

The kids' isolation is represented dramatically when Lisa and Marty first raise the possibility of killing their tormentor. They sit together on a beach, the camera watching from a distance at first, then moving in for alternating close-ups, always mobile and shooting from behind out-of-focus beach grass. Tellingly then, while they are on flat ground and alone in the scene, the two are separated by visual obstructions. Marty sobs, drool hanging from his mouth, his punched eye still green. "We could kill him," Marty offers, and Lisa jumps at the suggestion, her smile weak and strange, unable actually to look at Marty, just as he can only glance at her, while still facing away. When they finally do look at one another, the agreement is made based on their resentment of Bobby's continuing class privilege: "He's the source of everybody's troubles," asserts Lisa. "And even so, he's gonna finish high school and go to college and probably get rich." Marty winces, "And I'm gonna be delivering pizzas to him in Weston." Lisa leans in to Marty and the camera. "Let's kill him."

As they embrace, the camera focuses on her own bruised wrists—the result of an assault by Marty when she informed him she was pregnant, no small detail in this advancing calamity. From here, the two convince several friends to go along with the murder because it's "some cool shit," even though two of them have never even met Bobby and have only vaguely heard about his viciousness. Though all the kids agree to the plan, the film suggests that Lisa is the apparent "mastermind" (much as she was determined to be in court and in Schutze's estimation; after her conviction in 1993, her sentence was reduced in 1997 from life to 26 years). Having already established her fraught relationship with Bobby, the film hammers home—with repeated close-ups of Lisa looking wild-eyed—that she drives everyone else to do the deed.

Still, no one does much to stop events once they are in motion. It's worth mentioning in this context that Clark casts himself, uncredited, as the father of the twenty-year-old neighborhood "Hitman" (Derek Kaufman, played by *Kids'* Leo Fitzpatrick) to whom Lisa and Marty turn for advice and support: during their first consultation, the camera pans the group, as if standing inside the loose circle they form—Marty, Lisa, Ali and her boyfriend Donny (Michael Pitt), Lisa's cousin Derek Dzvirko (Daniel Franzese), and Ali's friend Heather (Kelli Garner)—as they twitch and smoke, act tough and wonder out loud how to kill Bobby. Derek the Hitman looks skeptical, but is performing his own tough-guy image (he hangs out with 12-year-old boys, drinking 40s and playing pool, leading some kind of small-time thieving cabal). "You need to chill out and plan this out a little better," offers the Hitman. "No," snaps Lisa, the camera picking up speed in its circling, signifying their imbalance, delirium, and sense of urgency. "I wanna do it now. Goddamn it. I want that son of a bitch dead. I want his sorry ass dead tonight." When, at film's end, Lisa is about to be busted by the cops and calls for Derek, Clark sits behind their family room bar, drinking, advising his younger son, the Hitman's brother, what to say: "Tell her you'll write her."

Just before the murder (actually the second attempt: in both instances, the kids lure Bobby out to an abandoned area ostensibly so he can have sex with Ali), the kids gather at Lisa's house, where her mother doesn't stop them from going out but kicks them all out, complaining, "When we lived in the Bronx, at least we had a family. Family kept things tight and safe. Down here in Florida, nobody's tight. Everybody's just . . . whatever." As inarticulate as her child, she abandons Lisa yet again, departing for her sister's house to play cards. While the parents retreat into their own worlds, the kids continue to sink into theirs. At the same time, Heather tells Ali a horrific story about her grandmother's murder by her grandfather, a "bad drunk" who took a claw hammer to her face. He kept her body in the house for days, she recalls, having repeated sex with it as her mother, still a child, sat in her room down the hall. Her mother, as an adult, involved herself with abusive men and kept newspaper clippings about the murder, and read them habitually to Heather as a child: "I think that's how I learned to read," the girl smiles, her makeup smeared, her eyes blurry.

Grim, and instructive. Heather's lack of perspective (enhanced by the fact that she is perpetually high) is only a more extreme version of her friends'. The other kids, meanwhile, gather outside Marty's garage, showing off their weapons—a baseball bat, a metal pipe, a hunting knife. High on a variety of drugs, as well as wired from a day playing video games, they excite themselves into such a frenzy that they begin dancing and chanting: "Let's kill the motherfucker! Dead! Dead! Dead!" The murder scene itself is alarmingly, and appropriately, graceless and stupid. As Thurston Moore grinds away on his guitar (a track written for the film, called "Bully Murder Scene"), Ali leads Bobby to a canal, and on a hastily arranged and badly delivered "signal" the boys begin to attack him. Donny comes at him from behind and Marty from the front, slashing wildly as Bobby screams: "Please, whatever I did, I'm sorry!" The scene takes on a frenzy of its own, cutting jarringly and repeatedly from the assault near the water to Heather screaming in the car in fetal position, to Lisa's face—pale and luminous, thrilled and shocked in the glare of the headlights. The brutality of the event is translated into dreadful, hysterical effect.

This scene, so appalling (and draining—it goes on and on), brings to a head *Bully*'s probing of kids who are overwhelmed by their contexts. By contrast, *George Washington* turns an equally abrupt tragedy into a kind of offbeat transcendence that has as much to do with the film's "vision"—its look and ethos—as with its respect for kids' terrible longings and numerous limits. This difference is perhaps most visible in the films' death scenes. Where *Bully*'s is climactic, rife with bloodlust and chaos, *George Washington*'s (which takes place just 35 minutes into the film) is startling but also provocative, an ethical and ideological starting point for the survivors.

The scene begins as young Buddy (Curtis Cotton III) and his friends George (Donald Holden), Sonya (Rachel Handy), and Vernon (Damian Jewan Lee)—all age 12 to 14 or so—are hanging out, tired from running around in an abandoned miniature golf range and now bored as they rest up in a public bathroom. They begin horsing around, pushing one another and giggling. One might anticipate here that something is about to "happen" because George has been established as vulnerable to roughhousing. Afflicted with a surreal ailment—his skull is soft so he must wear a helmet and avoid getting his head wet—he will purportedly die following even slight injury to his head. And for an instant the plot looks like it will go where one expects: George is bumped up against the wall and sways briefly. But then, he pushes back, maintaining the game. Buddy, however, slips in a puddle of water and falls out of frame, the camera frozen in shock on the faces of the kids who remain visible. They are out of focus, as they were when Buddy was in the foreground, softly blurred. Cut to Buddy's head hitting the floor, in slow motion. Fade to black.

The violence here is abrupt and affecting, and to a point chaotic, but also heightens awareness rather than thwarting it. Green and cinematographer Tim Orr, with whom he shares screen credit for the film, fashion this scene to underline the kids' sudden, profound sense of loss, acute self-awareness, and efforts to ascertain how something so "bad" has happened and who is at fault. In the next frame, Vernon is helping Buddy to his feet. George and Sonya watch as Buddy staggers to a bathroom stall. The three others pause, unsure what to do. Like the kids in *Bully*, they are dealing with a recent, fairly scary shift in romantic connections: Buddy and George are "rivals" in love, or more precisely, the object of Buddy's affection, Vernon's 12-year-old sister Nasia (Candace Evanofski), has dropped him and declared her preference for George, who seems to her more "mature." As George, Sonya, and Vernon look at the floor and wonder what to do, they hear a banging from offscreen: Buddy is in a bathroom stall, a slight blotch of blood becoming visible on his white wife-beater, as he slams a metal pole against the wall. The camera takes you inside the stall as Buddy slows and then falls against the wall, then cuts to outside the stall, the narrow, repetitive frames of stalls filling the composition, light filtering gently through a single window above them all. Buddy drops to the ground.

This stunning event hardly elicits a visible reaction. They don't speak or move at first. Vernon starts pacing, the other two seated on the shiny, cool floor. They ponder their options: "If we leave him here, man," Vernon worries, "Somebody gonna find out." They have no sense that they might go to "authorities," that an adult might help them through this disaster. "I killed him," George frets. "I grabbed his head. I pushed him. It's my fault he's dead. I killed him." Cut to a series of shots showing a bulldozer pushing trash at the brown, expansive town dump just before the kids move their friend's body, by taxi, his face covered in a dinosaur mask. They leave him behind an abandoned building with Vernon's last words: "Ain't nobody gonna find you here, Buddy."

The child's death and his friends' responses are put in some perspective when the film makes its only clear, if abstract, temporal claim in an intertitle: "The 1st of July." Where these kids live, the cars are heaps (12-year-old Sonya steals them with her boyfriend); trains and trucks, however, create constant background noise: crossing bells ringing, wheels grating and squealing, truck beds heaving. In other words, life goes on. George feeds his skinny dog gummy bears, Nasia comes calling, posters go up to announce that Buddy is "Missing." Nasia and George talk around the subject, as she worries that Buddy has run away because he "still has a crush on me." They sit on a rooftop, backs to the camera, gazing out on smokestacks in the distance. "You have nice hands," Nasia tells George, who can't begin to answer.

George's guilt persists, mostly unspoken, and he becomes increasingly isolated. At the same time, Vernon and Sonya grow closer as they make a point of discussing their feelings with one another. "People have been talking," Vernon tells Sonya when they meet in the bathroom where Buddy died. He continues:

> I can't do this. It's like I can't trust nobody man. All my life people have let me down. I just want to be by myself and just think about what I'm gonna do. Cause I know I ain't stayin' around here. I just wish I had my own tropical island. I wish I was . . . I wish I could go to China. I wish I could go to outer space, man. I wish I had my own planet. I wish I was born again. I wish I could get saved and give my life to Christ. Then maybe he'll forgive me for what I did.

Vernon's anxious inability to parse his options—to differentiate between going to China or having his own planet and being "born again"—lays out the extent to which the kids' immediate experiences, their assumption of moral and social order, are disrupted by the death, and also, more critically, the extent to which their adult-ordained contexts will never again feel stable. He accuses Sonya of callousness, of not showing any "emotion." He sighs, "I just wish there was one belief, my belief." Sonya, in turn, worries that her lack of emotion is a sign that she's born "bad," like her brothers who go around "tearing up stuff." "Vernon," she confesses, "I don't have much to look forward to. I ain't smart. I ain't no good. My whole family ain't no good. And for the first time in my life, I don't got no excuses for my future."

Dark, exposed, and incisive, young Sonya's self-evaluation sounds like she's living in *The Bad Seed* (1956). Green encourages his young performers to articulate their feelings in addition to acting them. He tells interviewer Jon Matsumoto:

> When we did improv during rehearsals, there was a natural tendency to cuss all the time. But when I gave them boundaries where that wasn't permitted, they had these bizarre, very rich things to say. They started speaking these very lyrical sentences. . . . I guess swearing has a more realistic element to it, but since I was playing God, I wanted them to say something cooler. (2000, F2)

Indeed. Nasia's voice-over structures the film delicately, in part because she is not privy to her friends' awful experience ("I would have never even thought of the truth that George knew," she says, as you watch him through a chain link fence), and in part because she speaks in such confident, evocative poetry: "When I look at my friends, I know there's goodness. I can look at their feet, or when I hold their hands, I pretend I can see the bones inside." Body parts, in this context, reveal truth, strength, and purity, not objects for lascivious looking.

As Sonya imagines the worst of herself and of her fate, Nasia sees beyond. Again, as George wanders the streets, pondering what he must do, Nasia narrates, "I seen through your skin and seen the words, the things you done, the chances you missed, the loss of all things." Cut to an empty public pool, the scene of George's first act of "greatness" (as Nasia has stated at film's opening, "He just wanted greatness"). This is the site where George saves a scrawny white boy from drowning one afternoon, happening by while the boy is floating in the pool, alone. George strips to his underwear (and how different the lithe, thin naked male body looks in this film, compared to Clark's), dives in, and hauls the boy to safety, just before he passes out himself, undone by the stress and soon hospitalized for the threat to his soft head. Within days he's recovered, and his Aunt Ruth (Janet Taylor) practically sings to him the newspaper headline that marks his new role: "Duh da nuh na: a new kind of hero."

George welcomes his role, donning Buddy's abandoned wrestling singlet and cape to go with his new, softer helmet—fashioned by his Uncle Damascus (Eddie Rouse) out of the skin of his skinny dog that Damascus killed out of irrational and sadly confessed fear. George visits his father in prison to tell him he loves him; he gathers Buddy's body, baptizes it in the local river, and leaves it for the authorities to find; and finally, he begins directing traffic, the most immediate and consistent way he can find to "help people." Rico (Paul Schneider), a local who spends time with the kids when he's not working on the railroad, asks if he can join in, helping George with his newfound responsibility. "You know, I respect you," says Rico. "People might laugh, but you push on. . . . The truth is, we're all fightin' for salvation. But at the finish line, you're probably a better man than me." The two are pictured on the street, waving their arms at passing traffic, their gestures at once comic and lyrical, energetic and earnest; no matter that they may be ineffective or inexpert.

Bully examines the complex contexts of youthful killers, not to label them as "bad," but to raise broader questions about social responsibility and ethical definitions. In this way, the film challenges the presumption of "bad kids," even in extreme circumstances: it closes on brief, roughly edited handheld images of the killers, seated in the courtroom, wearing their prison uniforms and arguing with one another about who is to blame. As their voices rise, the camera cuts to show the startled statement of those family and community members in attendance, as if they are hearing their kids for the first time. *George Washington,* by contrast, intimates that moral comprehension is less a function of social structures or systemic failure than a spiritual, psychic, and emotional—a very personal—experience, one that can be affected by contexts but is not determined by them. "We all want families who love us," says Nasia at the end of the film, "because friends go separate ways. Some of us know our place, our home, our comfort. But for some, it's not that simple." George, Sonya, and Vernon discover that they live beyond socially assigned labels, and with one another, even if that means parting ways: Sonya eventually tells the authorities what happened, her story recorded on tape, a new history: "Buddy was crazy. He was playing in the bathroom one time. He slipped" (a quick insert shot recalls the accident that turned into history—the sink, the dripping pipes). Vernon leaves town by train, the sound of his departure echoing as the camera tilts up to show a huge, blood-red sky. And George remains.

The film closes, as it opens, with Nasia's voice-over: "My friend George, he told me that he could read God's mind. He told me he knew what God was gonna create, who he was gonna let die, and stuff like that. He also knew the future. He said he was gonna fight great wars, lead nations, and build back up from a broken land." A brief montage of historical portraits leads a fireworks display, and then George becoming memorialized, turned into history, in a black-and-white photograph session, wearing a suit, the U.S. flag behind him: he is reborn, as the fireworks indicate. He looks into the future. The photographer pauses, instructs him to smile, shoots. The film cuts to George, just as his smile, so lovely, so fleeting, fades. Far from Hollywood—California or Florida—this image becomes history, but is not only and necessarily transparent. It doesn't tell who George is or who he will be. And yet, George's comfort will come, you see, in a continual process of self-making, a process that is pictured, in part, as he poses, performing as a "hero." If it's not that simple, it's not so bad, either.

WORKS CITED

Acland, Charles. 1995. *Youth, Murder, Spectacle: The Cultural Politics of "Youth in Crisis."* Boulder, CO: Westview Press.

Crawford, Travis. 2001. "Larry Clark's Loss of Sexual Innocence," *Moviemaker Magazine* 43. www.moviemaker.com/issues/43/bully.html

Giroux, Henry A. 1997. *Channel Surfing: Racism, the Media, and the Destruction of Today's Youth.* New York: St. Martin's Griffin.

Malanowski, Jamie. 2000. "A Child's World in No Man's Land," *New York Times* (22 October), Section 2; Page 13; Column 1; Arts and Leisure.

———. 2001. "Larry Clark, Moralist, in the Florida Suburbs," *New York Times* (8 July), Section 2; Page 12; Column 1; Arts and Leisure.

Matsumoto, Jon. 2000. "He's Giving Children an Intelligent Voice," *Los Angeles Times* (24 November), Part F; Page 2; Entertainment Desk.

Schutze, Jim. 1997. *Bully: A True Story of High School Revenge.* New York: William Morrow.

———. 2001. "My Day of the Locust; How a book I wrote got turned into a movie, and why I ain't rich," *Dallas Observer* (21 June). Nexis-Lexis online.

Sewell, Dan. 1993. "Murder Bares Sordid Teen Culture," *Los Angeles Times* (15 August), Part A; Page 10; Column 1.

FIGURE 19. A paragon of the "bug-eyed monsters, hideous and generally not to be trusted" who have infiltrated the culture in Barry Sonnenfeld's *Men in Black* (Columbia/Amblin, 1997) is Mikey, who has just snuck across from Mexico and been recognized by the border patrol as a different kind of "alien," indeed. (Frame enlargement)

CHAPTER NINETEEN

Searching for Blobby Fissures: Slime, Sexuality, and the Grotesque

REBECCA BELL-METEREAU

In popular films of the last 40 years an explosion of grotesque and slimy figures has filled the screen. Critics have discussed how such monstrous images signal a fear of the feminine (see Creed 1993; Clover 1992), but discussion of this phenomenon seldom appears explicitly in critical reception of these box-office successes. In reviewing films from *The Blob* (1958) through *The Exorcist* (1973), *Alien* (1979), and *The Elephant Man* (1980) to more recent works such as *Men in Black* (1997) and *The Sixth Sense* (1999), critics seldom attempt to account for audience enthusiasm for blood, vomit, slime, and deformities. Films that feature disgusting fluids or revolting images capitalize on the appeal of exactly the kinds of sights people are generally acculturated to avoid. The power of such images to tantalize and satisfy audiences is apparent in the commercial success of films that score box-office winnings by grossing people out.

What accounts for the appeal of this forbidden viewing of supposedly disgusting sights? Imagery of the grotesque is often explicitly or implicitly sexual, and frequently it resembles male or female genitalia. Some theorists would explain the power of such sights as drawing from the Oedipal or primal scene scenario, whereas others explain this phenomenon as an example of what Julia Kristeva identifies as the "abject"—often associated with the feminine: "a heterogeneous, corporeal, and verbal ordeal of fundamental incompleteness" (1982, 27). Rosalind Krauss writes:

The abject, understood as this undifferentiated maternal lining—a kind of feminine sublime, albeit composed of the infinite unspeakableness of bodily disgust: of blood, of excreta, of mucous membranes—is ultimately cast, within the theorization of abject art, as multiple forms of the wound. Because whether or not the feminine subject is actually at stake in a given work, it is the character of being wounded, victimized, traumatized, marginalized, that is seen as what is in play within this domain. (1985, 92)

Hal Foster argues, "In horror movies and bedtime stories alike, horror means, first and foremost, horror of maternity, of the maternal body made strange, even repulsive in repression" (1996, 149).

More recently, the Web site "Bodies in Beige Boxes" discusses how

the body represents society's fantasies and obsessions. Its surfaces can represent sites of cultural marginality, confrontation and compromise, places of social exit and entry. . . . Body fluids incite disgust, according to Luce Irigaray, because of their association with femininity and the corporeal, subordinated to the privilege in patriarchy of the self-identical, the one, the unified, the solid. (Dwyer 2002)

A comic take on the subject of Irigaray's "two lips" would argue that once men come out of the womb, they spend the rest of their lives trying to get back in. A defiant celebration of the aggressively feminine appears in Francesca Da Rimini's description of the "sheroes as 'having hostile MUCUS coming out of the CUNTS. . . . May the power of slime be with you'" (Dwyer).

Although these varied views point to fundamental similarities among the symbolic uses of slime, blood, semen, vomit, and excreta, a look at actual films featuring slime reveals that all "abject" fluids are not created equal. The gender and genre of the actors, viewers, and films affect the uses of fantasy material with the source of the slime having a potent effect on its reception. Any monolithic reception theory ignores the enormous variety of viewers by assuming that male and female viewers will respond similarly and that gay and lesbian moviegoers will have the same responses to slime, suspicious looking cracks, fissures, bulges, and protrusions as heterosexual audiences do.

One of the first films to popularize cinematic slime was *The Blob,* which launched Steve McQueen's career, later took on minor cult status, and eventually morphed into a Criterion Collection DVD. So, how did the Blob inspire actual terror in some moviegoers of 1958 and a continued cult fascination with viewers of the new millennium? In its initial appearance, baby Blob looks a lot like a menstrual clot, a sight perhaps only imagined by men, all too familiar to most women. In both sets of viewers, it calls up a slight thrill of horror and repulsion if it creates any visceral response other than laughter and groans. Men may find the prospect of being consumed by this blob horrific, whereas women sit in silent shame or smugness as they watch the giant congealed blood clot absorb male victim after male victim. Reviewers and critics ignore the menstrual appearance of the blob, but they have managed to see the slimy red liver-like substance as a symbol for the Red Menace of communism. Taking nothing away from the political interpretation, I speculate that both the revulsion and laughter come from viewers' unconscious response to the obvious blood-clot appearance of the Blob, not from musings about the Cold War.

Filmmakers are often quite aware of how grotesque imagery can be used to manipulate viewers. For example, H. R. Giger toned down the vaginal appearance of the slimy egg cases in *Alien* not to be too blatantly sexual in his imagery. Later, the camera goes from an extremely low-angle shot of Ripley's (Sigourney Weaver) bikini underwear-clad body to an ambiguously coded shot of the alien, with its dripping toothy mouth and helmet-shaped phallic head. Ridley Scott has Weaver sweating, panting, heaving, and groaning like a porn star through multiple filmic climaxes, after which she expels the slippery, limp alien from her ship.

Scott was not the first filmmaker to manipulate audiences in this way. Alfred Hitchcock talked of how he directed viewers in *North by Northwest,* "playing them like an organ" (quoted in Spoto 1984, 440). With *Psycho* (1960), which climaxes with a shot of the horrific disintegrated face of "Mother," he seems to have done this again. Stanley Kubrick later echoes Hitchcock's use of the grotesque female crone image in *The Shining* (1980), in which anxiety about parent-child relationships surfaces in images of parental derangement, infantile monstrosity, and sexual perversity throughout. One of the film's most dramatic moments occurs in a bathroom, with the shocking body transformation from a seductive naked woman embracing Jack to the mirror image of a hideous old crone clinging to him. This scene is the horrific centerpiece of the film, embodying quite literally the fear of punishment, death, and decay nestled alongside the fantasy of unbridled sexual fulfillment. The father chasing the mother and son with a knife is the physical enactment of Freud's castration anxiety, and the boy's rescue of the mother completes the male fantasy cycle of eliminating the father and having exclusive possession of the mother.

In the 1960s, 1970s, and 1980s, several popular films featured female bodies inhabited by evil within the domestic sphere, as the spectacle of horror, science fiction, and mixed action genres supplanted popular westerns and musicals of earlier years. *Rosemary's Baby* (1968), for example, turned the body transformation of pregnancy into possession by demonic forces. The horrific appearance of babies and children signals a more general repulsion with the physical during an age obsessed with material consumption. *The Exorcist* had thirteen-year-old Linda Blair's head spinning (actually) and vivid images of her pea-soup-colored vomit had audiences lurching out of the theater in nauseated disgust. Her change into a lesion-covered representative of Satan reflects the larger suspicion of youth culture and its movement toward greater sexual and political freedom. She spews obscenities reminiscent of the taunts of Vietnam War protestors, and her skin sores resemble the wounds of child victims of the war that were captured in shocking and unprecedented documentary footage on nightly newscasts. A few years later, *Carrie* (1976) profiled a teenaged girl using her kinetic powers over the body to bring about the destruction of her classmates.

All of these films that place evil in the bodies and minds of women recall the hysteria of the Salem witch trials, which also involved women and children as the primary victims and supposed perpetrators. Religious movements have often featured women and children in key roles, along with scenes of body violation, from earliest creation myths to contemporary tales of stigmata or demonic possession. Ken Russell's *The Devils* (1971) combined close-ups of bleeding stigmata, scenes of flagellation, and shots of Oliver Reed as a grotesque hunchback with hallucinatory scenes of naked women, Satan, and his rituals. In *Agnes of God* (1985), repulsive images of the violated bodies of both sexes signal spirituality and holiness. Making filmic associations between body parts and religious concepts has always been a risky venture, though, in spite of the clear biblical precedent. Martin Scorsese's *The Last Temptation of Christ* (1988) created an enormous public outcry over the dream sequence in which Christ removes his beating heart from a slit in his chest. Churches may have paintings of the "sacred heart" as part of their iconography, but it is essential that these pictures remain formulaic, avoiding the look of realism that Scorsese managed in his film. These images shocked and outraged some audiences because they combine sexuality and the ritual roots of religion in a threatening and sinister way. Yet such images often influence popular belief as much as conventional religious institutions do. A Gallup poll indicated that after the first showing of *The Exorcist* more people believed in the existence of Satan than in the historical Jesus (Tithecott 1999).

Religious and gender issues surrounding sexuality and domesticity appear vividly in the horror genre. In *Carrie*, Brian De Palma highlights the sexual nature of religious ecstasy and the concomitant guilt held over from a puritanical heritage. *Carrie* features a rite of passage that begins as the ritualized crowning of a "prom queen" and ends with a bloody spectacle of teenage cruelty and revenge. *Carrie*'s climax is stimulated when the eponymous heroine (Sissy Spacek) is symbolically humiliated in an explicit reference to menarche with the prank of crowning her head with pig's blood. This triggers the expression of her wrath, a release of uncontrolled id, cementing the nature of Carrie's relation to her society.

Carrie returns to the domestic world for comfort, but in response to the girl's request to "hold me" her mother mutters about the devil returning and then stabs her in the back. Carrie retaliates with some telekinetic knife throwing, leaving her mother sprawled in a Christlike position. The mother moans in what sounds like sexual ecstasy each time another knife hits her, and her final groans become more clearly sexual until she finally dies. While Carrie is apparently burned to death in her own house, she has the ultimate posthumous revenge against her teenaged tormentors in the nightmares that remain to haunt the lone survivor, Sue (Amy Irving). In the closing dream sequence, as Sue bends down to place flowers on Carrie's grave, a bloody hand emerges from Mother Earth and grabs her wrist. These gripping scenes remind us—and the characters within the film—of the threatening female power and agency Carrie represents.

Barbara Creed argues that "part of the problem with *Carrie* is that it plays on the debased meaning of woman's/pig's blood in order to horrify modern audiences; in so doing it also perpetuates negative views about women and menstruation" (80). She does not discuss the other mythological connection between women and pigs, namely that of the sorceress Circe, who turned most of Odysseus's men into swine. I would argue that Carrie's extreme humiliation makes the audience's vicarious identification with her revenge both justifiable and excusable. For a revenge film to work effectively, the audience must see those who are killed as unworthy of living; the affront to the hero or heroine must be so despicable that violence is justified.

As Carol Clover suggests in *Men, Women, and Chain Saws,* Stephen King's explanation of *Carrie* as a feminist revenge tale, similar to the biblical account of Samson, indicates that men also identify with the opposite sex across gender lines, just as females do. I would not go as far as to say that horror presents "a universe in which the sex of a character is no object" (20), however. Creed argues in *The Monstrous Feminine* that the references to menstruation in *Carrie* and *The Exorcist* and the "horror film's obsession with blood, particularly the bleeding body of a woman, where the body is transformed into the 'gaping wound,' suggests that castration anxiety is a central concern of the horror film—particularly the slasher sub-genre" (52). According to Linda Williams, "horror shows that one of the most important pleasures of film viewing resides in the journey made by one gendered identity (the male viewer) into the position of another gendered identity (the female victim-hero)" (quoted in Clover, 52).

Creed also deals with images of menstruation, the *vagina dentata,* and castration, and she reinterprets Freud's analysis of the castrating woman, who desires to emasculate the man who deflowers her, arguing that "man's fear of sexual intercourse with woman is based on irrational fears about the deadly powers of the vagina, especially the bleeding vagina" (121). Despite the daring quality of this analysis, most of her attention is focused on the perceptions and views of patriarchal culture. Relatively little of her analysis explores how contemporary female viewers derive their own pleasure or work through their own anxieties by identifying with filmic characters or situations. For instance, scenes reminiscent of childbirth (*Poltergeist*'s mother-daughter rescue scene [1982]), spectacular bloodbaths with female survivors (*Halloween* [1978], *Friday the 13th* [1980]), and tales of cannibalistic aggression (*The Texas Chainsaw Massacre* [1974], *Silence of the Lambs* [1991]) all resonate with female viewers, who may align themselves simultaneously with both victims and perpetrators.

Isabel Pinedo focuses on what is appealing for female viewers in the horror genre, making the astute observation that a lone woman survives and defeats the monster in many recent slasher films. Despite this temporary empowerment, once the narrative ends the woman is again trapped in the frame with no agency or reason for existing. Pinedo observes that "the success of the horror genre lies in its capacity to transgress" (1997, 109). But she does not fully explore what is transgressive about the horror film and what is satisfying, particularly for women. One neglected element is the relationship of women to blood, which is essentially different from that of men. Most adult women have monthly encounters with blood and therefore probably do not have the same sense of fear or revulsion at the sight of blood that some male viewers may have. At the same time, this monthly ritual is one that must remain hidden. In contrast, castration anxiety has been so thoroughly analyzed and integrated into public discussion that it can hardly be viewed as hidden or subconscious any more. Menstruation, a very important point of natural initiation into womanhood, is a cyclical event that profoundly affects the lives of most women, and yet it scarcely appears as a psychological phenomenon in the literature of psychoanalysis or film theory.

C. D. Daly (quoted in Creed, 112) explores why menstruation is the ultimate taboo in its connection to castration anxiety. He also argues that the smell "here negative and repulsive" is associated with "putrefaction" and death in the unconscious mind. It is doubtful that this stimulation of scent or sight conjures the same negative emotions for women; to the contrary, menstrual blood may have a subconscious appeal for women. This response takes place at a subliminal level, beneath the veneer of societal taboos and disgust generated by women acculturated to a masculine view of the phenomenon. Film acts on viewers at a physiological level, often creating physical responses of excitement, adrenaline release, and arousal that are indistinguishable from sexual desire.

One of the subconscious motives operating in female viewers may be the pleasure of seeing the blood taboo violated. In contrast to the control and secrecy women in society must practice, the monster in film sheds and spreads blood everywhere, in a spectacular display. People react in horror to the sight of dismembered bodies and blood spattered on furniture, bodies, and clothing. Nevertheless, *Friday the 13th*, made for less than $1 million, was the twentieth highest grossing film of 1980, with female and male viewers reveling in the sight of slashed throats, an axe through the middle of a forehead, and a final battle between the two girls next door, the young Alice (Adrienne King) and the matronly Mrs. Voorhees (played by the ever-wholesome Betsy Palmer). *Poltergeist* features mother-daughter female survivors (Jobeth Williams and Heather O'Rourke) covered in goo that resembles afterbirth or amniotic fluids. The image of the cannibal, based on a real-life incident from the 1950s, appears in *The Texas Chainsaw Massacre,* in which the apparently dead grandfather (John Dugan) suddenly begins sucking on the finger of the young woman (Marilyn Burns). A similar closeness and identification between woman and cannibal/monster occurs in *The Silence of the Lambs,* particularly in the scene in which Hannibal Lecter (Anthony Hopkins) cuts off the face of a guard and, like a woman putting on makeup to go out, literally "puts on a new face" to escape from prison. This transgressive behavior embodies the female anger at having to suppress and control a periodic natural process, and in the overdetermined nature of this extravagant spectacle we can read both aggression and pleasure in breaking the taboo. The female viewer may then take vicarious pleasure in identifying with the monster or killer and in the shock and horror of the victim or viewer. All of these events and responses occur routinely and repeatedly on the site of her body and within the mixed emotions of her own consciousness. I do not argue that most women consciously connect screen blood with their menstrual periods, but the unconscious association raises a welter of emotions: anger, fear, pride, resignation, shame, and acceptance. It has been argued that women who like horror films simply participate in a masochistic way in their own victimhood. To the contrary, some women's pleasure may derive from vicarious release of aggression along with a transgressive enjoyment of the spectacle of blood spilling.

Several critics have pointed out that the inviolable monster is a relatively new phenomenon in film, but moviegoers have always perceived the monster as unkillable because it appears again and again in literature, film, television, and video games. The cyclical nature of the monster's appearance also aligns it with menstruation, that bloodletting violation of pristine social order that occurs again and again and again in its own right. The horror film makes a dazzling, exciting, and public spectacle of what women are socialized to view as shameful, tedious, and private. Any aggression or anger occasioned by the role of women in this personal ritual is displaced onto the monster. Feelings of victimization are displaced onto the females who are terrorized by the monster. And finally, it is the female survivor who is able to defeat the monster, symbolically clean up the mess, and emerge cleansed, renewed, and ready to gird herself for another round tomorrow.

If older horror films demanded restoration of order, the new horror beginning in the 1970s, in films such as *Carrie* or *A Nightmare On Elm Street*

(1984, and sequels 1985, 1987, 1988, 1989, 1991, 1994, 2003), created an open-ended narrative, in which the monster is never finally destroyed, normal boundaries never reestablished. William Paul claims that this lack of closure is not calculated simply to establish possibilities for a sequel: "Rather, as the body lost its sense of boundaries in this period, so did the bodies of narrative. . . . In its search for the final thrill, the horror film began to take on a kind of comic rhythm, moving toward a last scream that parallels the last laugh of comedy" (1994, 405; see also Sobchack 2003, 204).

This sort of genre slippage and mixed messages regarding boundaries and gender operate in David Cronenberg's *The Fly* (1986), one of the slimiest love stories ever hatched and deposited in the top twenty grossing films any year. The scientist, Seth Brundle (Jeff Goldblum), is a typical nerd, spectacularly lacking in the all-American masculine virtues. Instead of being comfortable with the American icon of phallic power, the automobile, he immediately tells Geena Davis's character, Veronica (called, significantly, Ronnie, a masculine version of the feminine name) that he always gets carsick. His transformation into a fly makes him even sicker. One of his first actions as Brundlefly is to vomit on his doughnut, a behavior he initially does not realize is repellent to Ronnie.

But this isn't just a film that offers disgusting sights for women. It also has its share of "guy things." Two of the masculine fantasies enacted are Brundlefly's limitless sexual potency and his superhuman strength. Body disintegration and transformation begin to occur at the same time with growth of coarse hairs on his back and the loss of his fingernails and eventually other body parts. When he arm wrestles with the burly character Marky (George Chuvalo), Brundle breaks Marky's wrist open and the bone and flesh protrude (something of an inside joke since Chuvalo is a former Canadian boxing champion). Later on, Ronnie comes to visit him, and by this point hideous sores cover his body. Alternating camp comedy with sentimental moments of emotion, the film goes from the grossly humorous scene of Brundle regurgitating on his doughnut before eating it to the shocking sight of his ear dropping off. Although Ronnie's initial response is disgust, this immediately changes to sympathy and affection when he says to her, like a child, "I'm scared," and she enfolds him in a motherly embrace.

Brundlefly retains the parts of his body as fetishized objects that take the place of human contact. He has his fingers, teeth, and ears in jars in his bathroom, and at one point he offers to show them to Ronnie, who recoils in horror and sadness. Although he warns her of the fact that when he completes his transformation he will "hurt" her, she nevertheless returns to tell him of her pregnancy. In the event, she does not tell him, but he overhears her conversation with her former boyfriend (John Getz), whom he attacks, vomiting on his hand and foot with the corrosive substance he uses to predigest his food. Carrying Ronnie away to the roof, like King Kong carrying Fay Wray, he asks her to combine genetically with him and attempt to rescue what is left of him that is human. She refuses, but Brundlefly manages to get her into his teleportation pod anyway. Ironically, it is the slimy ex-boyfriend who manages to fire a gun at the last minute and break the electrical connection that might have transformed her into a similarly grotesque creature. When Brundlefly emerges, looking even less human and more monstrous, Ronnie has the gun, which she points but cannot shoot. In a moment of disgusting pathos, the creature pulls the gun barrel back toward his head, and amidst tears and wailing she finally kills him.

In the end of *The Fly*, a woman destroys the male central character. Her killing of Brundlefly is depicted as a mercy killing, and the creature clearly wishes it. Cronenberg has been accused of victimizing his female characters, but as a director he tried in this film to be sensitive to women. He describes his decision to play the gynecologist in *The Fly* himself, as a way of making Geena Davis feel more comfortable because, of course she wouldn't "want a stranger down there between her legs." On a thematic level, Cronenberg also seems to sympathize with female anxieties. The nightmare sequence of *The Fly* is horrific and yet typical of the kind of dreams pregnant women sometimes have about their unborn children. The giant, wriggling maggot echoes David Lynch's creature in *Eraserhead* (1977), and it also has a suggestively phallic appearance.

This film is filled with images of revolting fluids, and gender signs are mixed throughout. Fascination with the grotesque and a tolerance for sticky liquids may be considered more the domain of female viewers than of male because women have to cope with messy fluids on a regular basis. When they have babies, they are more often the ones who must cope with the child's messy digestive processes. As odd as it may seem, *The Fly* may bring out precisely the mothering impulse in some female viewers. As a variation on the Beauty and the Beast motif, it privileges female power and stereotypically feminine sensibilities in its choice of the horrific. The image of liquids oozing from Brundle when he wrestles and his newly developed habit of vomiting on his food before ingesting it make him appear infantile, as do his embarrassment and awkwardness; Ronnie's willingness to nurture and to try to help him is typical of a mother's reaction to her baby's messes. An interesting by-product of the female's strength is the change in the former boyfriend character. Whereas he seems hopelessly crude and ruthless in the first part of the film, by the end he docilely accepts the role of rescuer, taking her to get an abortion for a pregnancy from another man, giving an arm and a leg—literally—to save her, and firing the shot that keeps her from being destroyed. Furthermore, he sacrifices himself in a way that softens and feminizes his character as it liquidates his body. At the ending his relationship with Ronnie is left undefined.

The mass popularity of gross-out in horror and comedy became a historical phenomenon, shrinking to its core audience in the late 1980s. The rawness of these films expresses the zeitgeist of a period of ambivalence and disturbance. Films such as *The Shining, Alien,* and *The Brood* (1979) exemplify what Paul calls "the most powerful expressions of a period that was itself defined by fissures and disruptions" (430). At the close of the twentieth century, movies witnessed significant changes in genre boundaries and gender roles, with noir, horror, slasher, science fiction, and comedy slipping seamlessly into each other's territory. Charles Derry (1987) divides recent horror films into three general categories: (1) the horror of personality, a trend begun by Hitchcock's *Psycho;* (2) the demonic, as typified by such films as *Rosemary's Baby* and *The Exorcist;* and (3) the horror of Armageddon, as exemplified in a variety of films, ranging from *Scanners* (1981) to *Mad Max 2: The Road Warrior* (1981). Christopher Sharrett notes the phenomenon of apocalyptic vision in films in his *Crisis Cinema.* He argues that in "the traditional pre-1960 horror film, the monster never really looks like a human being; there is always something that sets the monster apart: an odd manner of dress, facial disfigurement, or an animal appearance" (quoted in Derry, 163). In films after *Psycho,* Derry sees an emphasis on "the anxiety of living rather than the fear of death: violence is the norm, and fear of bodily mutilation is very strong" (164).

This fascination appears as well in David Lynch's *The Elephant Man,* which invokes the sex act as something awful and threatening with stampeding elephants and all their phallic sexual imagery bringing to mind the child's point of view in watching the forbidden sight of his parents having sexual intercourse. The film hints that young John Merrick's punishment for desiring his mother is his awful deformity, one in which his face seems almost a caricature of the sexual organs, with what look like scrotal folds of wrinkled skin surrounding the phallic nasal feature that gave Merrick his popular nickname. Dream scenes demonstrate the comingling of sexual imagery, voyeurism, and the mirror that reflects the individual's grotesque face. In one dream, scenes from the industrial world hint at a connection between the hideousness of the Elephant Man and the inhumanity of a system that turns people into something less than human. This is a graphic example of Marx's notion of commodity fetishism in which the true nature of the relationship between labor and production is replaced by the "fantastic form of a relation between things" (1986, 164). Images of parts of the male torso, back, and arms dissolve into shots of machines, hammers, pieces of metal. The close-up portrait of the mother's face is supplanted by images of elephants and trampling, all accompanied by a sound track that superimposes the elephant screams with factory sounds. Going from a close-up of the mask and eyehole of John Merrick to these scenes subtly hints at primal scene fantasies. The horrific consequence of this viewing of forbidden sights is a conflation of sexual regeneration with degeneration, rape, animality, and the seamy horrors of the machine sweatshop.

Se7en, the eleventh top-grossing film of 1995, portrays a variety of mutilations and grotesque imagery in a cautionary tale that makes the seven deadly sins as disgusting as possible. This late-twentieth-century film demonstrates the apocalyptic spirit of gloom. Rather than allow the audience to enjoy these guilty pleasures vicariously, *Se7en* reflects the millennial zeitgeist by encouraging its audience to consider its mortality and repent. Body distortion and violation appear in hideous and sickening images, first in a grossly obese man who represents gluttony and then in a model whose face is cut off as punishment for her vanity. The visual darkness of the film almost makes it seem as if it is in black and white, and in moral terms *Se7en* indeed offers no grays. The protagonist, a detective searching for the serial killer who is systematically producing these tableaux of gore, must come like a character in a medieval morality play to see the error of his own ways.

Black and white, in moral and racial terms, is also an issue in the number one box-office success of 1997, *Men in Black.* The characters who cause all the trouble and who create the need for the Men in Black to exist in the first place are, fittingly, aliens from outer space. In a number of films of recent years, the movie industry seems to be returning to the era of the 1950s in films that depict the good guys and villains in clear, forthright terms. Villains are bug-eyed monsters, hideous and generally not to be trusted. The explanations for this phenomenon are not obscure. In a culture bordering on the millennium, apocalyptic fears abound, and politicizing of the Other—scapegoating aliens, extraterrestrial and otherwise—is a natural tactic, what with the loss of our former enemy, the Soviet Union. Affirmative action and women's liberation are still causing a degree of anxiety, but the topics are too politically charged for a demographically sensitive filmmaker to attack directly. Instead, we see women and people of color in the background, in the role of supporters, occasionally sacrificial heroines, and sometimes as a deus ex machina, even a "ghost in the machine." *Men in Black* features a black-and-white buddy team, with the unlikely and effective pairing of Tommy Lee Jones, the archetypal cracker, and Will Smith—hip enough to stand out, clean-cut enough to fit in.

The film mixes genres, genders, and levels of discourse in a gooey postmodern pastiche that suits its cynical, mixed audience, providing something for everyone, from the sophisticated viewer who catches phallic references to the under-twelve set that takes childish pleasure in seeing goopy humans morphing into creepy monsters. Will Smith's character, as the feminized member of the buddy duo, handles issues typical to a woman's domain. He is the one left to birth a baby alien, coo over its cuteness, and be spewed on by the newborn. Later he advises the wife of a transformed farmer to "go to Bloomingdale's, get some new clothes, get a facial." Here, again, commercial solutions to emotional problems are slipped into the dialogue in one of the many witty lines given to Smith's character. In fact, several of the best jokes—palliatives to the goo—are based on commercial products. When the heroes get out their really big guns, in a display of phallic domination over bugs, they recite in unison the famous line about roach motels: "Bugs go in; they don't come out."

Slime and wetness saturate this film, an echo of the popular *Ghost Busters* (1984), in which characters are "slimed" with a whitish fluid that looks suspiciously like semen. In the finale of *Men in Black*, when Jones blows up the giant monster cockroach from within, the heroes are both covered in slime, in this case more reminiscent of female fluid than of male glory. When the bug, not quite dead, rises again, the female soon-to-be partner (Linda Fiorentino) blows it away once and for all, delivering the line, in a low-angle shot that features the triple-barrel gun foregrounded in front of her pelvis, "Interesting work you guys do."

The Sixth Sense (the second top-grossing film of 1999) offers one of the more interesting renditions of the panoply of the grotesque. A visual narrator (Haley Joel Osment) "sees dead people," who are presented onscreen in various states of bodily disintegration. The series of images reads almost like a catalogue of the ills of our society from domestic abuse to troubled teens: one woman has been beaten to death by her husband; a teenaged boy reveals the self-inflicted hole blown in his head; a young girl vomits because she has been poisoned by her psychotic mother. The film's climax makes the most cunning use of fluids to manipulate audience responses. Bruce Willis, shot early in the film and then recuperated to act as counselor for the troubled boy who is seeing the dead, suddenly feels moisture seeping from his back. He flashes back to the scene of his initial wounding. The camera, hovering above his prostrate body on the bed, shows his wife (Jennifer Connelly) kneeling over him as he clutches his side, rather close to his groin. She whispers, "Let me see it," and then a close-up shot reveals her peeling his hands away from the wound; blood leaks from behind him onto the bed in a dark stain. The shameful sights and fluids hidden from us, and from Willis, are revealed and finally accepted. With a slight squinting of the eyes, a viewer could easily imagine that a sexual scene is being played out, but we are distracted from noticing the suggestive poses of their bodies by our curiosity over the plot. The film accomplishes its magic by creating a subliminal pseudosexual release at the same time that it releases viewers from the intellectual tension created by a suspenseful narrative.

With *Sixth Sense*, the end of the millennium heralded the closing of a cycle, however. Audiences seemed to lose their fascination with gross and slimy fare. Apocalyptic fears and terrorist attacks dampened viewers' desires for images of the grotesque. Supplanted by a crop of war pictures, these slimy disgusting movies passed out of fashion for a time, but just like reruns, remakes, the Blob, Carrie, the Ghost Busters, Aliens, the Fly, the Men in Black, and the Terminator, they will be back.

WORKS CITED

Clover, Carol J. 1992. *Men, Women, and Chain Saws: Gender in the Modern Horror Film.* London: British Film Institute.

Creed, Barbara. 1986. "Horror and the Monstrous Feminine: An Imaginary Abjection," *Screen* 27, 44–70.

Derry, Charles. 1987. *American Horrors.* Urbana: University of Illinois Press.

Dwyer, Natasha. 2002. June 5. http://art-slab.scsd.edu/ARTSLAB/VA131ProjFall95/laura/mary.html

Foster, Hal. 1996. *Return of the Real: Art and Theory at the End of the Century.* Cambridge, MA: MIT Press.

Halberstam, Judith. 1995. *Skin Shows: Gothic Horror and the Technology of Monsters.* Chapel Hill, NC: Duke University Press.

Krauss, Rosalind. 1985. *Originality of the Avant-Garde and Other Modernist Myths.* Cambridge, MA: MIT Press.

Kristeva, Julia. 1982. *Powers of Horror.* Trans. Leon S. Roudiez. New York: Columbia University Press.

Marx, Karl. 1986. *Capital.* Vol. 1. London: Pelican.

Paul, William. 1994. *Laughing Screaming.* New York: Columbia University Press.

Pinedo, Isabel. 1997. *Recreational Terror: Women and the Pleasures of Horror Film Viewing.* Albany: State University of New York Press.

Sobchack, Vivian. 2003. "Thinking Through Jim Carrey." In Murray Pomerance and John Sakeris, eds., *Closely Watched Brains,* 2nd ed. Boston: Pearson Education, 199–213.

Spoto, Donald. 1984. *The Dark Side of Genius: The Life of Alfred Hitchcock.* New York: Ballantine.

Tithecott, Richard. 1999. *Of Men and Monsters.* Madison: University of Wisconsin Press.

Williams, Linda. 1989. *Hard Core: Power, Pleasure, and the "Frenzy of the Visible."* Berkeley: University of California Press.

FIGURE 20. Despite his knowledge that the Krell must have called up something monstrous, Morbius (Walter Pidgeon) blindly believes that he is immune to whatever evil haunts the *Forbidden Planet* (Fred M. Wilcox, MGM, 1956). (Frame enlargement)

CHAPTER TWENTY

Crazy Like a Prof:
Mad Science and the
Transgressions of the Rational

INA RAE HARK

That's the excuse they usually give for evil. Hitler was mad, so
they say. So he may have been. But not necessarily. Evil does
exist. Evil *is*.
—Mass murderer George Brougham (Kirk Douglas)
in *The List of Adrian Messenger*

The "mad scientist" has become an enduring fictional type, like the gunfighter
or the boastful soldier. Psychologist Stuart Asch believes that a feeling of being
rendered passive to be manipulated by a mad scientist and his infernal machine
qualifies as a "universal delusion" (1991, 187). My Google search for the phrase
"mad scientist" in March 2002 generated 209,000 hits. A cursory survey of the
sites shows that they range from instructional materials to teach children science
to the International Society of Mad Scientists, described by Web master Igor as
"dedicated to disseminating information about unusual projects in any field,"
and whose "membership is open to anyone that in practice or spirit considers
themselves [*sic*] to be a Mad Scientist" (http://www.Mad-Scientists.org). Yet
many of the articles accessed reveal nonfictional contemporary scientists
bemoaning the distorted picture of their profession provided by fiction, film,
and television (see Heron 2001; Brockway 1998; Alcorn 2001). Indeed, when

we think of science as a destructive force, some archetypal "mad scientist" in the movies, be he Dr. Frankenstein or Dr. Strangelove, is likely to spring to mind. He is aptly categorized by Lady Caroline Lamb's appraisal of Lord Byron: "Mad, Bad, and Dangerous to Know," which serves as the title of the chapter devoted to fictional twentieth-century villainous scientists in Roslynn Haynes's *From Faust to Strangelove* (1994). Although her survey uncovers innumerable examples of evil, greedy, arrogant, and power-hungry geniuses who deserve the second and third terms, the evidence for their actual madness, in a clinical sense, is far less convincing. Indeed, the fictional scientist archetypes she enumerates are none of them mad, despite her chapter's title. Evil scientists may resemble the medieval alchemist or sinister contemporary biologist "driven to pursue an arcane intellectual goal that carries suggestions of ideological evil"; the absent-minded professor so "preoccupied with the trivialities of his private world of science [that] he ignores his social responsibilities"; the unfeeling empiricist "who has reneged on human relationships and suppressed all human affections in the cause of science"; or the well-intentioned scientist who fails to calculate the potential harm that can be caused by his discoveries that have "monster-like . . . grown beyond his expectations" (3–4). Why then, one wonders, do we always speak of mad scientists rather than simply of bad ones?

There are, to be sure, historical precedents for the connection, ancient and medieval beliefs that madness was merely a manifestation of demonic possession. Moreover, the scientist's quest for knowledge, inherent in the very derivation of his calling, the Latin *scientia* (see Haynes, 7), suggests the forbidden fruit of the tree of knowledge and the first cause of the entry of evil into the world. Michel Foucault suggests that this evil was at a certain point in history part and parcel of the discourse on what constituted madness:

> In the Middle Ages and until the Renaissance, man's dispute with madness was a dramatic debate in which he confronted the secret powers of the world; the experience of madness was clouded by images of the Fall and the Will of God, of the Beast and the Metamorphosis, and of all the marvelous secrets of Knowledge. (1988, xii)

Yet the mad scientist figure is generally conceded to spring fully to life only in the person of Dr. Frankenstein and his many nineteenth- and twentieth-century successors, products of an age when insanity was being recast as disease rather than moral defect. Nevertheless, if the madman was not automatically considered bad, the bad man was often (and more frequently) considered mad.

In general terms this asymmetry may spring from a refusal to accept evil as an existential category, a denial that "evil is" in favor of a claim that "evil is because." I would posit that the displacement of the bad by the mad in the case of the scientist has a more specific cause. Let me first articulate a paradigm for the mad scientist as I use the concept in this chapter. This is an individual who, in a quest to unlock the secrets of nature and harness them to his will, transgresses limits self-imposed by other men and in doing so creates, unleashes, or authorizes the monstrous. While this narrative trajectory plays itself out endlessly in horror and science fiction films, political thrillers, and muckraking documentaries of technology run amok, the intentionality and causality that propel it have endless permutations. We have empirical proof that something went wrong with the scientist's research, but we aren't always certain what happened to make it go wrong: working on applications for nuclear power, for example, the scientist never imagines that the radiation will produce giant ants or cause humans to shrink.

There are of course those power-mad individuals who knowingly use science and technology in a quest to rule the world. They are often characterized by a campy excess of villainy, in figures such as Dr. Mabuse, Ming the Merciless, Dr. No, *The Adventures of Buckaroo Banzai Across the 8th Dimension*'s (1984) Dr. Emilio Lizardo, or *The Fifth Element*'s (1997) Zorg. The motivations of the majority of mad scientist figures are, however, not nearly so unequivocally malevolent. During their experiments some sort of line was crossed, but is that because man was not meant to know some things or because men are incapable of taking into account all possible unintended consequences? Since we are loathe to relinquish the positive results that much untrammeled scientific research has brought us, and since we know that many of the evils it has also produced come from the same well-intentioned seekers after knowledge who brought us its benefits, we balk at totally condemning the creator of the monster and give him the benefit of the doubt: he would not have crossed the line if he had not lost his reason.

In fact, whether they create the monstrous through evil intention or mere lack of foresight, when mad scientists go astray, it is less because they have become irrational than because they have followed rationality too rigorously. Signs of impending disaster that might have been heeded through recourse to ethical principles, consultation with colleagues, or going on instinct are ignored because the scientist exercises a form of hyperrationality, leaping from syllogism to syllogism without noticing that his conclusions are valid but his premises fatally flawed. Such transgressive and excessive rationality may thus devolve into its contrary, become a form of the insanity that seems its negative pole. As Robert Wexelblatt muses, "Is it that what looks historically like a fear of reason, arising around two centuries ago, is actually a fear of reason leading to its opposite, as though irrationality, madness, were exactly where reason would take us all by itself?" (1981, 277). So, too, may initially benevolent purposes circle back to degenerate into amoral self-aggrandizement and megalomania. Like Schrödinger's cat, the scientist who is dangerous to know because he knows that which it is dangerous to know inhabits a realm of uncertainty wherein he either is or is not mad and bad, until an act of observation determines the matter.

For my act of observation in this chapter, I focus on the 1956 outer space adventure *Forbidden Planet*, which manages to place most of the characteristics of the mad scientist on view, as well as to foreground the inherent contradictions the character embodies. It is supremely fitting that the specific mad scientist in the film is Professor Edward Morbius (Walter Pidgeon). Although the name suggests a morbid, diseased imagination that links to mental disturbance, it is also an alternate spelling of Möbius, the name of the nineteenth-century German scientist who was one of the founders of the field of topology. "During the early 1800s, the works of German mathematician August Ferdinand Möbius helped develop a study in geometry that became known as topology. Topology explores the properties of a geometrical figure that do not change when the figure is bent or stretched," says the appropriately named (for my purposes) children's Web site Reeko's Mad Scientist Lab (*http://www.spartechsoftware.com/reeko/*Experiments/ExpMobiusStrip.htm). Möbius is best known to nonspecialists as the inventor of the Möbius strip. By twisting a piece of paper 180 degrees and fastening the two ends together, one creates a continuous surface by which both sides become one single side. Mo(r)bius is thus an apt appellation for a man both mad and sane, selfish and selfless. As J. P. Telotte notes, such a name "suggests a self-enclosed representational world, wherein the thing becomes its own double as it forms a spiral—a spiral that, like the doubling in this film, leads nowhere, only back to itself" (1995, 129).

Morbius is also a mad scientist once removed. Not physicist or biologist but philologist, he translates his science from the records and still functioning machinery of a long-dead race, the Krell of Altair IV. Just as they had increased their mental powers to the extent of making an evolutionary leap, they were all wiped out, in one single night. The party of scientists with whom Morbius traveled to Altair suffered a similar fate as they were trying to leave the planet, against Morbius's wishes. Spared by whatever has killed his colleagues, Morbius is stranded with his wife, who dies soon after, apparently in giving birth to their daughter, Altaira (Anne Francis). In a situation that borrows from Shakespeare's *The Tempest*, Morbius is a Prospero who perfects his "magic" arts by studying the Krell records and using their machinery to enhance his intellectual capabilities. He designs an Ariel, Robby the Robot, to carry out all his wishes. Despite his knowledge that the Krell must have called up something monstrous that led to their destruction and the subsequent murders of the rest of his party, Morbius blindly believes that he is immune to whatever evil haunts the "forbidden" planet. Unlike Prospero, he neither acknowledges nor fears the mysterious Caliban with whom he shares a home. Morbius also insists that his own science is completely benign. In one sense he is right. Robby is programmed with a version of Isaac Asimov's three laws of robotics and is incapable of doing harm to any "rational" being. Thus Morbius can assure the nervous United Planets Cruiser officers (Leslie

Nielsen, Warren Stevens, Jack Kelly, Richard Anderson, Earl Holliman, and company) that he could not turn the robot into a deadly weapon, "Not even were I the mad scientist of the taped thrillers." Likewise, nothing in the Krell technology created monsters external to themselves.

However, the monsters were not external to themselves, but within—"monsters from the id." Although the Krell had "conquered their base selves" and eliminated most social ills (including insanity), the powerful technology that allowed them creation by mere thought gave their subconscious desires physical form, quite independent of the conscious superego that previously reined them in. Despite their "million years of shining sanity," their vast ethical and technological progress, the Krell are obliterated by the return of the repressed, "the mindless primitive," which the film insists can never be eliminated from the most rational of beings. In its evocation of a Freudianism believed to be long outmoded by Morbius but at the heart of *Forbidden Planet*'s ideology, the film gives us insight into a crucial distinction that representations of the mad scientist can often obscure.

The chain of causality in many books and films suggests that the scientist is mad because he goes ahead with questionable experiments that would give any sane man pause, thus producing a deadly monster. *Forbidden Planet* implies that madness does not produce monsters as much as monsters manifest madness. Michel Foucault in *Madness and Civilization* points out that this was a fundamental tenet in theories of madness that appeared during the Renaissance:

> In a general way, then, madness is not linked to the world and its subterranean forms, but rather to man, to his weaknesses, dreams and illusions . . . madness no longer lies in wait for mankind at the four corners of the earth; it insinuates itself within man, or rather it is a subtle rapport that man maintains within himself. (1988, 26)

"We're all part monsters in our subconscious," Adams (Nielsen) sternly lectures Morbius, who belatedly realizes what the dark force on the planet really is: "Guilty, guilty, my evil self is at that door, and I have no power to stop it."

If mad monstrosity dwells universally in the subconscious, a problem arises. Can we comfortably draw any distinctions between the mad man and the sane one? The answer that *Forbidden Planet* appears to give, one echoed in many treatments of mad scientists, is that one is only a carrier of madness until that moment when the monstrous breaks away from the subconscious and takes a physical form in the world. This incarnation can literally transform the body of the mad scientist, as in *Dr. Jekyll and Mr. Hyde* (1931) and its descendants, or can occur at the moment when the scientist's researches bring the "secret devil" to independent sentient existence. (Dr. Hannibal Lecter [Anthony Hopkins] of *The Silence of the Lambs* [1991] marks an interesting variant in that he does not so much disgorge monstrosity as engorge it, through dining on some of his patients.) At the same moment when Dr. Moreau (Charles Laughton) breeds his first beast man in *The Island of Dr. Moreau* (1933) or Rotwang activates the robotic Maria in *Metropolis* (1927) the scientist leaves sanity behind. Dr. Frankenstein's cry of "It's alive!!!" in the James Whale film (1931) is in this formulation also a code for "I am mad." "The purity of the mad scientist's obsession is both his science and his madness," says Wexelblatt. "He can even be said to become mad at the moment when his professional obsession becomes pure possession: not when he has it, but when it has him" (271).

The monstrous mad is, however, a primal madness. It is beyond—or, perhaps better, *before*—good and evil. Yet the operations that loose it can be seen to result from a kind of secondary madness. When Peter Goodrich speaks of the mad scientist's identification with his monstrous creation as "narcissistic and atavistic," arising from "the uncontrolled and jealous nature of his own ego turned inward upon itself" (1994, 83), he is describing the two forms of madness. The atavistic is the "mindless primitive" dwelling in the id, while the narcissistic is the overweening arrogance Morbius acquires after 20 years of living in his "egomaniac empire." The chief symptom of this narcissistic egomania appears when the scientist develops a distorted view of his own powers and a concomitant belief that he has the right and the ability to control the destinies of lesser mortals. Morbius is easily goaded into admitting to this delusion. When Ostrow (Stevens), the ship's medical officer, sarcastically inquires, "Whereas Morbius with his artificially expanded intellect is now ideally suited to administer this power for the whole human race?" he replies, "Precisely doctor. Such portions then of the Krell science as I may from time to time deem suitable and safe I shall dispense to earth. Other portions I shall withhold. And in this I shall be answerable exclusively to my own conscience and judgment."

Mad scientist texts generally attribute these mental disorders to the fact that the transgressive researcher allows himself to be isolated and therefore grows out of touch with the needs of other human beings and forgetful of the moral precepts that govern them. Morbius is an extreme case because he has an entire planet to himself, except for his daughter, who has never known any other human beings with whom to compare him. Even before his monster emerges, he has been pathologically inclined to solitude. He and his wife were the lone dissenters in the plan to leave Altair IV because they had a "boundless love" for a place "away from the scurry and strife of humankind." Morbius is disingenuous when he assures Adams that he is only a "simple scholar with no ambition beyond a modest measure of seclusion," but clearly both the desire for isolation from other living humans, in favor of the extinct, and nonhuman, Krell, and the fulfillment of that desire contribute to the mad manifestation of the monster from his id.

In the Renaissance world from which his precursor Prospero springs, Morbius would be diagnosed as suffering from melancholia, one of whose salient characteristics is the love of solitude and the shunning of companion-ship (Foucault, 118). To seventeenth-century British physician Thomas Sydenham melancholics were "people who, apart from their complaint, are prudent and sensible, and who have an extraordinary penetration and sagac-ity. Thus Aristotle rightly observed that melancholics have more intelligence than other men" (quoted in Foucault, 118). Clinching the diagnosis of Mor-bius as melancholic is the fact that he always dresses completely in black, the same "inky cloak" worn by Shakespeare's "melancholy Dane," Hamlet.

Despite the intersections of some of his behaviors with discourses that have been applied to madness over the centuries, Morbius, and most of his "mad scientist" kin, are not clinically insane. (Worth noting, however, is that the 2001 Academy Award for Best Picture, the biopic of a nonfictional, literally mad sci-entist, the schizophrenic mathematician John Nash, paints him as anything but wicked. Although the film links his madness to his genius, and does admit that he could be dangerous to know, it is not a horror film but a sentimental tale of triumph over adversity and redemption through love from someone who sees him not as an evil genius but as the possessor of *A Beautiful Mind*.) "A scientist who has gone mad, so the implication runs, would no longer be doing science or much of anything else; he would be doing lunacy," Wexelblatt says. "But the mad scientist, that dark yet white-clad figure out of the underside of modern theology, that creature running out of dreams and onto our screens, would not only still be functioning as a scientist just fine, thank you, but would be doing so to all sorts of amazing effects . . ." (269). Their secondary madness, that which leads them to actions that loose the primal madness residing within, is finally of the metaphorical kind invoked when we say "Are you crazy?" to some-one who seems bent on a reckless or transgressive course. In the 2001 film ver-sion of J. R. R. Tolkien's *The Fellowship of the Ring*, the treacherous wizard Saruman (Christopher Lee) is given all the characteristics of one of those sor-cerer precursors of the mad scientist, particularly his Promethean creation of the monstrous Uruk-Hai out of the mud. Fellow wizard Gandalf (Ian McKellen), aghast that Saruman would league himself with the source of ultimate evil, Sauron (Sala Baker), exclaims, "Has Saruman the White abandoned wisdom for madness?" Because Gandalf will soon wager all hope of defeating the enemy on sending a Hobbit on an apparent suicide mission into the heart of the Dark Lord's territory, one might well ask who is the madman here. Although Saru-man imagines that he can make himself an exception to Sauron's tendency to tolerate no allies but only subjects, and may perhaps be slightly mad in this regard, he has quite reasonably, if immorally, decided to seize the main chance to manipulate events to his best advantage.

From such an example it appears that the case for mad scientists being literally mad is a tenuous one; the case that they are bad appears to be much stronger. Yet a character such as Morbius calls the unequivocal badness of the type into question almost as much as he does its madness. Robert Plank analyzes the Prospero and Morbius figures as "outcast through their volatile interaction of hubris and blasphemy (the Promethean and the Faustian) with society's psychological defenses against them" (Goodrich, 76). Goodrich observes that the "madness" of such figures "is socially determined because all extraordinary genius provokes doubt in ordinary mortals" (82–83). *Forbidden Planet* takes the position that high intelligence is just as much a guarantor of evil as malicious intention. If Krell genius had not fashioned the power to turn thought to matter without the use of instrumentality, then the monsters from the id would never have gotten loose. If Morbius had not augmented his intellectual capabilities with the brain-boosting "plastic educator," his subconscious could never have tapped into that power to destroy the comrades who wanted to remove him from his private Eden and to attack the crew of the ship sent to rescue him. When Morbius, Commander Adams, and Doc Ostrow measure their intelligence with the educator, a rising arrow marks the amount of brainpower detected, rather like one of those devices seen at carnivals that measures the force with which someone strikes a hammer blow. Although they would all register as "low-grade morons" by Krell standards, Morbius outscores Ostrow two-to-one, despite their being only 20 points apart in IQ score. Adams, on the other hand, barely registers at all, prompting Morbius's scornful remark: "It's all right, sir. A commanding officer doesn't need brains, eh—just a good loud voice." Because both the captain of the Bellerophon and Ostrow were killed when they used the educator to enhance their intelligence, while Morbius survived the experience, Morbius's 183 IQ would seem to be a bare minimum for interfacing with Krell technology and enabling its attendant disasters. The film thus implies that Adams is the better, saner man for being the stupider. This is a persistent theme in mad scientist texts. Wexelblatt observes, "Now it is rather odd that, in our imaginings about scientists, we should associate incompetence with safety, not to mention benevolence (are they just too dumb to transgress?), and genius with catastrophe (is this merely the revenge of the poor math students on the precociously brilliant ones?)" (269).

I would contend that there is indeed a good deal of anti-intellectualism and defensive envy behind the creation and long persistence of the figure of the mad scientist. Such people *are* smarter and more knowledgeable than the average. So if the case were only against their hubris in thinking themselves superior to their less gifted fellows, condemning them would be harder. Mad scientist narratives therefore usually imagine that it is impossible for the superior intellect to draw the line at deciding what is best for others and at using its greater expertise and reasoning power for the common good. Inevitably, these narratives tell us, the superior intellect will conclude that its own desires and goals are so far above those of the common herd that there is nothing wrong with sacrificing others in the pursuit of these goals.

In the 1957 Hammer Film version of Mary Shelley's tale, *The Curse of Frankenstein,* Victor Frankenstein (Melvyn Hayes), an arrogant prodigy who has contempt for his teachers, grows into an obsessive, egotistical scientist (Peter Cushing) who wants to create life all on his own. His transgressions advance through increasingly ghastly collections of various body parts from the recently deceased until he gets impatient and harvests the brain of the brilliant and kindly Professor Bernstein only after pushing him down a flight of stairs. Behind his self-justifying palaver about breaking boundaries in the name of science lurks a not-so-superior and not-so-uncommon grubbing after fame and personal advancement, which many fictional mad scientists share. The equation of mad science with arrogant and cutthroat competitiveness may explain this rather odd passage in a *Washington Times* article about St. Louis Rams football coach Mike Martz entitled "Martz is 'mad scientist'":

> Opponents labeled Martz an egotist for the high scoring. The criticism stings, but Martz won't back off.
> "I do worry about insulting people," he said. "I don't like that, and it's certainly not our intent, but we take an aggressive approach to things, and I guess that's interpreted as being somewhat arrogant."
> However, his players are ardent Martz supporters. His temper can sometimes erupt, but they know Martz is simply challenging them to produce.
> "Mike loves the label of 'mad scientist.' He loves living up to that," Warner said. "He loves designing things. I think he got away from that last year, but he delegated responsibility this season and got back in the laboratory." (Snider 2002, www.washtimes.com/sports/20020201-79302.htm)

Or consider the epigraph of a personal Web site whose content is dubbed "a mad scientist's views on other mad scientists. And mad doctors, monsters, murderers, psychopaths." It is the following portion of dialogue from another 1950s science fiction film, *I Was a Teenage Werewolf* (1957):

DR. HUGO WAGNER (Joseph Mell): But you're sacrificing a human life!

DR. ALFRED BRANDON (Whit Bissell): Do you cry over a guinea pig? This boy is a free police case. We're probably saving him from the gas chamber.

DR. HUGO WAGNER: But the boy is so young, the transformation horrible—

DR. ALFRED BRANDON: And you call yourself a scientist! That's why you've never been more than an assistant! (Anonymous 2002)

It's really all about getting that next promotion.

But what about the scientific genius who really does not intend evil or turn his less gifted fellows into guinea pigs or organ donors? Does he not have the right to follow his superior intellect wherever it leads? The final trump that mad scientist texts play on the Promethean overreacher who claims superiority to most of his fellow humans is a reminder that there is someone he is not smarter or more powerful than: God, the omniscient and omnipotent. Christopher Toumey notes that the "antirationalism" that animates these stories casts the mad scientists as "depraved people" who "use science for amoral purposes. . . . They caution us to contain secular science within the ethical guidelines of traditional Judeo-Christian values" (1992, 411). *Forbidden Planet* resorts to this ultimate in superior beings to frame its containment of the monstrousness that the Krell and then Morbius enable on Altair IV. When the planet first appears on the viewscreen, Ostrow comments, "The Lord sure does make some beautiful worlds." After the last glimpse of its destruction—the only way to keep the Krell technology from allowing some other brainy researcher to loose his primitive, "secret devil" on any who oppose him—Adams comforts Altaira that her father's name will "shine again like a beacon in the galaxy. It will remind us that we are after all not God." When Morbius describes the Krell as an "all but godlike race of beings," the audience is being cued to conclude that their technology is somehow related to the dark force on the planet.

A mad scientist in a purely secular milieu cannot have a horrific resonance any different from that of the serial killer, the greedy plutocrat, the totalitarian oppressor. In a secular narrative, science is simply the weapon this villain employs, rather than a gun, an army of thugs, or death camps. For this reason, mad scientists who use technology to create death rays or cause earthquakes or alter climate to achieve world domination often find themselves consigned to pulp serials or campy spy thrillers, interchangeable with criminal masterminds who use nonscientific means to gain power and wealth. The distinctive fascination the mad scientist inspires derives from his long descent from those who strove with the gods. This context renders his transgressions all the more terrifying, and removes such texts from the science fiction or the thriller genres. The *locus classicus, Frankenstein,* in its most famous screen incarnations, the James Whale films, employed the same German expressionist style that Universal used for its horror classics about supernatural and demonic monsters, its Draculas and Wolfmen, the same style that characterized both Rotwang's creation of the Maria robot in *Metropolis* and the resurrection of Rabbi Loew's Golem in Paul Wegener's *Der Golem* (1915). Despite the technological marvels Robby the Robot can perform, and the spaceships and blinking gauges in *Forbidden Planet,* the film's deadly threat still takes the form of the hideous monster at the door, more folkloric demon than unintended consequence of science.

The specific prerogative of the Divine upon which the mad scientist inevitably infringes is the power to create life. Either he bypasses the God-given means of normal reproduction or he makes modifications or enhancements that produce "offspring" contrary to nature. As Telotte observes in *Replications,* the Frankensteins and Moreaus sculpt and stitch and vivisect human and animal flesh to produce sui generis creatures both human and inhuman. An amusing twist on this paradigm is featured in the "DNA Mad Scientist" episode of the television series "Farscape." Here the lab specimen whom reckless experimenters have been "improving" gains power over them and compels them to extract genetic qualities it desires from unsuspecting beings, rendering the DNA donors monstrous while it achieves a superior form of existence. Although not intentionally created by Morbius, the monster from the id is a similarly chimerical composite that "just doesn't fit into normal nature." In each of these instances, the scientists' blasphemies are punished not by the offended gods, as were those of the *ur*-mad scientist Prometheus, but by their own unholy creations, who inevitably turn against them.

Ironically, of course, this is precisely what happened to God when he made man in his own image. It is not as if the scientist who dares to mimic his creator empowers a monstrousness that is in stark contrast to the end result of the Creator's little experiment. Life created the "natural" way is already a result of man's fall, which perhaps explains why the development of alternative forms of procreation is so roundly condemned in the mythic imagination. It is a replication of original sin. Whatever the means employed, the result is some variation of "man," who is quite potentially monstrous even without scientific interventions. Interestingly, in *Forbidden Planet* the two forms of (pro)creation are specifically linked. As John Jolly notes:

> Demonstrating the machine's primary function for Ostrow and the commander, Morbius projects a three dimensional image of Altaira which is "alive," and it is significant that he chooses this familiar subject out of myriad possibilities. Having previously endowed his daughter with life via the conventional method of sexual reproduction, he creates her once more, albeit fleetingly, through volition. (1986, 89)

Although this chapter is not long enough to address the relationship of mad science to gender, I would point out with Haynes (100) that Frankenstein and his descendants spend a lot of time trying to devise a means of procreation that does not require the participation of women. Current cloning science has however accomplished the opposite—to make procreation possible without the participation of men.

Because the "forbidden" knowledge in the Eden story is carnal knowledge, it is no accident that the monster from the id manifests to the sounds of heavy breathing or that several commentators see the Morbius-Altaira-Adams relationship to take on the contours of a sexual triangle. Margaret Tarratt writes of Morbius and Altaira, "The word *incest* is never mentioned, but his suppressed incestuous desires are clearly implied to be at the root of all the trouble" (1986, 262). Joseph Milicia claims that "Dr. Morbius' attachment to Altaira [is] a major factor in the resurrection of his id monster," who appears following significant mileposts in the Adams-Altaira romance (1978, xii). These analyses are too much influenced, I contend, by the Freudian terminology of the id that the script bandies about. Rather than a participant in some Oedipal struggle, Adams, despite his name, actually plays serpent in the Garden to shatter the asexual union of Morbius and Altaira, just as his attentions cause her trusting pet tiger to turn on her. Although putatively a product of Morbius's primal self, the monster from the id conveniently kills off every male who is in competition with Adams for Altaira's affections. We might wonder whether the Krell machinery is sensitive enough to pick up the stronger libidinal impulses of the less intellectually endowed hero of the piece, as well as the rage of the brilliant mad scientist disturbed in his solitary laboratory.

In the final analysis Dr. Morbius is not mad; he's just slightly neurotic. Nor is he really bad; he's just blindly arrogant and self-absorbed. Evil does exist in the world of the film, springing from the irrational impulses that all sentient beings possess and that their reason, their morality, and their religion normally hold in check. Science and technology unintentionally give this evil extraordinary strength and a way to circumvent the forces that constrain it. Jolly remarks, "Dr. Morbius, the paradigm of the creative genius, learns (as Bellerophon learned) that he cannot escape his nature, that there is no mechanical shortcut to godhead" (89). Yet this supposedly reassuring moral, this minatory example that should teach man not to play God, isn't really much help at all. The Krell's "shining sanity" and utopian society, founded on their extraordinary technology, lasted a million years. How were they to know that this one additional scientific advance, out of so many, was to be the one to loose their secret devils? Nor does Adams destroy every last trace of the elusive, alluring Krell science. He brings Robby with him, even lets him pilot the ship. Telotte notes that if films of this era might caution against unbridled technology, at the same time "American audiences of the 1950s, with their global power and technological leadership, could hardly have disavowed so much of what had come to signal their status in the world" (125). If it is neither inherently insane nor inherently wicked for the human mind to exercise mastery over the physical and natural worlds to whatever extent reason makes possible, it is very hard to determine just what sorts of transgressive rationality these texts are targeting.

Mad scientist films purport to comfort us with the assurance that we can anticipate when such mastery will boomerang with deadly consequences, either because the scientist loses his mind or knowingly strikes a bargain with evil. The truth, and the fear the "mad scientist" figure contains, is that following knowledge like a sinking star can lead to miracles and monsters indiscriminately, and there are few signposts along the way to map the fatal wrong turns.

WORKS CITED

Anonymous. 2002. "And You Call Yourself a Scientist!" http://twtd.bluemountains. net.au/Rick/liz.htm

Alcorn, Gay. 2001. "Pity the Poor Mad Scientists." SMH.com.au. July 4. http://www. smh.com.au/news/0107/04/features/features1.html

Asch, Stuart. 1991. "The Influencing Machine and the Mad Scientist: The Influence of Contemporary Culture on the Evolution of a Basic Delusion," *International Review of Psycho-Analysis* 18: 2, 185–93.

Brockway, Kim. 1998. "Dialogue Aimed at Getting beyond 'Mad Scientist' Stereo-types in Film," *Columbia University Record* 23: 21 (April 17), 25.

Foucault, Michel. 1988. *Madness and Civilization: A History of Insanity in the Age of Reason.* Trans. by Richard Howard. New York: Vintage.

Goodrich, Peter H. 1994. "The Lineage of Mad Scientists: Anti-types of Merlin." In Branmir M. Reiger, ed., *Dionysus in Literature.* Bowling Green OH: Bowling Green State University Popular Press, 71–88.

Haynes, Roslynn. 1994. *From Faust to Strangelove.* Baltimore: The Johns Hopkins University Press.

Heron, Nicola. 2001. "Erasing the 'Mad Scientist' Stereotype," *Chemical Engineering News* 79: 13, 144.

The International Society of Mad Scientists Home Page. http://www.mad-scientists.org/ madsci

Jolly, John. 1986. "The Bellerophon Myth and *Forbidden Planet*," *Extrapolation* 27: 1, 84–90.

Milicia, Joseph. 1978. "Introduction" to W. J. Stuart, *Forbidden Planet* 1956; rpt., v–xvii. Boston: Gregg Press, 1978.

Reeko's Mad Scientist Lab. 2002. "Where Inside and Outside Are the Same," *Reeko's Mad Scientist Lab.* http://www.spartechsoftware.com/ reeko/Experiments/Exp-MobiusStrip.htm

Snider, Rick. 2002. "Martz is 'mad scientist,'" *Washington Times* (1 February), www. washtimes.com/sports/20020201-79302.htm

Tarratt, Margaret. 1986. "Monsters from the Id." In Barry Keith Grant, ed., *Film Genre Reader.* Austin: University of Texas Press, 258–77.

Telotte, J. P. 1995. *Replications: A Robotic History of the Science Fiction Film.* Urbana: University of Illinois Press.

Toumey, Christopher. 1992. "The Moral Character of Mad Scientists: A Cultural Critique of Science," *Science, Technology, & Human Values* 17: 4 (Autumn), 411–37.

Wexelblatt, Robert. 1981. "The Mad Scientist," *Midwest Quarterly* 22:3, 269–78.

FIGURE 21. Tom Ripley (Matt Damon) suffers an "explosion of shame and humiliation as he is rejected by the object of his amorous suit," Dickie Greenleaf, in Anthony
Minghella's *The Talented Mr. Ripley* (Paramount, 1999). In a social climate where
homosexuality is openly shunned, there is also intense fear. (Frame enlargement)

CHAPTER TWENTY-ONE

Tom Ripley's Talent

MURRAY POMERANCE

How can you expect a man who's warm to understand one who's cold?

—Alexander Solzhenitsyn,
One Day in the Life of Ivan Denisovich

COLD

The Talented Mr. Ripley is a house of fabrications. No turn of the plot of Anthony Minghella's "nightmarish and highly apt" (Rich, 30) 1999 film, or of Patricia Highsmith's 1955 novel on which (along with René Clément's 1960 *Plein soleil,* a film it frequently adores) it is based, is made without reference to Tom Ripley's (Matt Damon) talent for spontaneous invention—*authorship*—and to his desperate conviction for maintaining the fantasy architecture he builds. The story (of the film) is simple enough: penniless Ripley is cajoled by Herbert Greenleaf (James Rebhorn) to take his money and voyage to Italy, where the man's rambunctious heir Dickie (Jude Law) has set himself up in the company of some flip American young people, refusing to come home. Tom's mission is to influence Dickie to change his mind. Instead, however, he falls in rapture with both Dickie's fabulous life and the seductive Dickie, a viper who, capturing Tom's loyalty and love, finally rebuffs him. Infuriated and impassioned, Tom is responsible for Dickie's death and now, to hide the deed, he takes over Dickie's identity. The body of the film is devoted to Tom's—"Dickie"'s—body in nonstop flight: from agents of the law, eager to speak with the dead Dickie's closest friend; from Dickie's girl, Marge (Gwyneth Paltrow), who has been told Dickie is hiding out in Rome and must not be allowed to catch Tom in his impersonation; and from others. In the end, Tom has committed two more murders of necessity, has come close to committing a fourth, and gets away free. In all of this we see more than a character study of a "monster," as critical comment has decided (Rich), but an incisive allusion to the slippery post-Reaganist world of pose, mannerism, class inequality, self-interest, and merchandising, contexted in a fascinating exploration of the limits of sincerity and truth. Most interesting in some ways is the containment within this film—itself a pure construction—of a chain of social constructions: Tom's fibs, Marge's postures, Dickie's pretenses, and so on. The film is thus a construction about construction, thematically related to Fellini's *81/2* (1963) which it frequently admires in spirit.

Class experience—not mere personal malevolence—is at the heart of the Ripley story. Herbert Greenleaf, though he once had no money, is now a consummately rich man inhabiting a penthouse overlooking Central Park. He is funding his son Dickie in Italy with the great liberality of the newly wealthy. Dickie is an irrepressibly impulsive snob, willing to be entertained by other people's lives and possessing a lavish—almost automatic, and thus feelingless—generosity, which does not spring from the heart. His puissant future he can afford to delay with momentary pleasures strung together in what promises to be an unending chain. In this he is a child of his class, where "sons were brought into their fathers' economic world" (Stearns 1990, 109). Tom Ripley, on the other hand, has nothing but his talent—for sensitive pianism and for singing, the latter in its broadest sense since he uses his voice to impersonate and also to chant a merry tale. A scene created for the film shows Tom and Dickie jamming with a jazz band in a nightspot; Tom bashfully goes onstage to perform a haunting rendition of "My Funny Valentine" (Damon here artfully replicating the look and recorded performance of Chet Baker doing this song). It is in singing out tales of his friendships and associations in the golden days at Princeton, and back home in New York, for Dickie's regalement that Tom's voice approaches its greatest strengths. Paid by Dickie's father to meet Dickie and persuade him to go home, Tom—a charming enough boy not loathe to form romantic relationships with other charming boys—lapses into captivation for Dickie and the world Dickie inhabits—for the world Dickie inhabits, indeed, precisely *because* Dickie is inhabiting it.

What is played out onscreen for us, then, is a double desire and a double infraction: Tom wants Dickie (the film is set in 1955 in Italy and homosexuality is vigorously denied by the state); and Tom wants Dickie's class. The lies he spins for Dickie to approximate himself to this luxurious world are tools for penetrating the boundaries of masculinity and privilege at once. In a telling scene in Dickie's bathroom, where Dickie is lolling in a tub filled with luscious emerald green water, Tom's request to share the pleasure—

> TOM *(Dipping his finger into the water):* Can I get in? I'm so cold.
>
> DICKIE *(Looking at Tom, while a smile grows on his face):* No!
>
> TOM: Not with you in it!

—while appearing on the surface to signal a homoerotic feeling he can no longer stifle is in fact displaying the depth of Tom's penetration already into Dickie's private space. Although Tom's self-issued invitation to sex is rebuffed, no challenge is made to his presence in this secret, naked, completely erogenous zone.

A TALENT FOR UGLINESS

It is possible to read this film as the story of a "monster," as I have suggested critics have done (in *Plein soleil,* ironically and revealingly, it is Greenleaf who acts like, and is openly labeled, with this epithet): one may think, Tom Ripley has produced no achievements that stand on property, has sponged off a decent family (taking advantage of a man whose wife lives in a wheelchair!), has misled an innocent boy who is merely spending the last days of his youth in a blithe dream state in Italy, has connived to place himself in the position of a penniless friend for every one of whose hungry pleasures the affable Dickie must feel obliged to pay. Furthermore, when, off the coast of San Remo, Dickie tells Tom he plans to marry the not-quite-sophisticated Marge (a young woman who makes little effort to hide her understandable disdain for Tom Ripley), Tom is quite monstrous in his outrage, his accusation that Dickie "follows [his] penis around" a badge of his petulance. Dickie's bald statement to Tom, out on the blue, blue waters under the blue, blue sky, that he doesn't love Tom at all and that Tom is nothing but a bore and a mooch, are only so many categorical truths after all, and Tom's feverish shock at hearing this is nothing but a self-indulgence. Tom is therefore nothing but sociopathic when he responds to Dickie's comments as though they constitute an insult that has wounded him to the core, picks up one of the oars, and smacks Dickie in the head. And when Dickie protests, Tom is only a fiend from hell when he uses that oar again to bash Dickie's brains out, then removes Dickie's ring, and slides Dickie's body into the sea. Afterward, it is with not only caution but also snideness that Tom parades around as Dickie Greenleaf, swift to switch back to Tom Ripley if Marge or Dickie's clubbish old friend Freddie Miles (Philip Seymour Hoffman) or Marge's tweedy British buddy Peter

Smith-Kingsley (Jack Davenport) show up. Leading a double life in this way, continuing to use Dickie's money, killing Freddie because Freddie has become too suspicious, frightening Marge to the point of being terrified for her own life in his presence, evading the police, and finally dispatching the peaceable Peter, Tom is nothing but the very essence of evil personified. In all of this, too, it is the lie that is Tom Ripley's signal utility, his mendaciousness that is his saving talent. So, at any rate, the film can be seen.

But what is missing from this rather conventional approach to the story?

First, it takes no account whatever of the narrative structure, that artful placement of the viewer in proximity to Tom. Because we see the world through Tom we are within his bubble and identify with his perspective; and no person is a monster unto himself. We do not discover objectively that Tom is a liar and find ourselves in a position for evaluating him; we see, as he does, a social world that is beautiful but unobtainable, and watch him tell lies from a proximate vantage that allows us to understand the lying as the only action open to him that merits any hope of success. Using the most meager supplies of straw he makes bricks with the devotion of a slave, indeed. Tom is without capital resources in a world built upon capital. Why, we may ask sententiously, could he not get a job? To answer twice: because he already has one—working for Herbert Greenleaf as a spy checking on Dickie and trying to lure him home—and because menial labor is not very beautiful, and Tom Ripley admires beauty. So do we all, indeed, gazing from our theater seats, and that is why we can understand his desire to climb into Dickie's bed and Dickie's exotic universe. Dickie's universe has luxury, excitement, the promise of satisfying in every way, and freedom from taxation. Who would not desire to inhabit such a world, and on what grounds can we fault Tom for displaying that desire, other than by saying he lacks demeanor? In the sense that the film makes possible a reading that Tom is a bad boy precisely because of this, it can be seen as a trap for our *ressentiment*.

But the reading of Tom as a nefarious liar and murderer omits much of the action, too, and much of the depicted social structure that supports that action. Truth isn't a natural substrate, but a set of circumstances—by which I mean no one is taken as telling the truth but by grace of the resources he can muster to substantiate his tale. Authors seem truthful when they have vocabularies adequate to the demands of their fictional situations (don't write about what you don't know) and so fictions seem true when they are eloquent. But knowledge, language, style of expression, the clothing that supports that style, the gestures with which one makes decoration, the familiarity with cultural situations that makes possible cagey timing—all these are culturally apprehended and mastered. Tom lacks, Dickie has. There's no particular reason for suspecting Dickie of being truthful himself except that his performance is so well established upon resource. We are shown that he has impregnated a local girl who ultimately drowns herself because of his false promises: Dickie, then, is no paragon of honesty. Nor is Marge, who bad-mouths Tom to Dickie but smiles ingenuously into his face soon afterward. What makes Tom's lies so problematic for the ressentient viewer is precisely that although he lies from strength (he is an accomplished charlatan, and therefore a pleasure to watch) he doesn't lie from wealth. Through lying, then, he manages the success that evades his critics in the audience, relatively poor like him and equally admirers of Dickie Greenleaf's world. Our conviction that Tom is a fiend rests on another conviction, that nobody who doesn't already have it should ever have what we want but cannot have. Who is this bumpkin Ripley who dares to sit at breakfast with Dickie and Marge—at breakfast with them naked all three, eating toast and marmalade, according to a play script based on Highsmith's novel by Phyllis Nagy (1999, 99)?

Without lies, Tom has no hope at all of getting close to a fellow like Dickie Greenleaf. And a failure to achieve closeness would be a betrayal of his promise to Dickie's father, but also problematic for the viewer, who would have no other access to the pleasurable world Dickie possesses. If in *Plein soleil*, shot by Henri Decae, this was a world of starkly contrasting color, in which to music by Nino Rota Alain Delon's Ripley was present as ruddy flesh and black hair, as lithe animal line, in the Minghella film, shot by John Seale and scored by Gabriel Yared, the world is a dazzling, confusing feast of coloration without contrast and Damon's Ripley is a paragon of withheld desire. For us to bask in the sunlight of Mongibello, bounce to the clubby jazz, jaunt to Rome to go shopping for linen suits, watch the devouring of good food, and in other ways admire the good life, Tom's chain of deceits is absolutely necessary. He represents, in fact, a type of perfect pupil, a watcher who becomes and ingests, a stand-in for the middle-class film audience. His ultimate status as stand-in for Dickie Greenleaf is a reflection of his more general condition as a character, his being a marker for Highsmith's sensitivity to her reader's class aspiration and Minghella's respectful treatment of that sensitivity.

A more serious objection to the simplistic reading of Tom as a "leech" (Clark 2000) and premeditative murderer—the prevailing critical reception of him—is that Tom does not, strictly speaking, premeditatively murder Dickie Greenleaf in the film. Minghella is most precise in his mise-en-scène of the boat scene, filming it first from just outside the craft as the boys begin their spat, and bringing us aboard as the emotions climb. Tom's swipe at Dickie is pure reflex, the explosion of shame and humiliation as he is rejected by the object of his amorous suit. Fear would accompany these emotions in a social climate where homosexuality was openly shunned. Dickie now pounces upon Tom in a mad rage, screaming into his face while grasping his neck, "I'm going to kill you!" Because Dickie has already produced an emotional assault by admitting his loathing for Tom and has also just drawn Tom out of the closet in a manner sufficiently brutal to signal Tom that his social future may be in question, Tom has every reason to believe, thrown onto the bottom of the boat under Dickie's weight, that Dickie means precisely what he says. When he struggles free and takes up the oar again, may he not be trying to save himself?

Why, viewers protest, does Tom not at this point go to the police? Because, as Minghella meticulously shows, the police serve primarily the vested interests of the monied class. Tom is not in the right class to benefit from equable treatment under arrest. He does not go to the police for the same reason that in *Thelma & Louise* (1991), Louise does not call the police after she has murdered Harlan. Tom's only option now is to hide the death of Dickie for as long as possible—a project that requires his skills in performance and construction, to be sure, but more: the capital upon which to found Dickie's persistence, which means in effect, rent for the hotel rooms in which "Dickie" is staying and for "Dickie"'s apartment in Rome, access to the clothing in which "Dickie" can manifest himself, say, at the opera, a supply of lira for eating the way Dickie would eat at the restaurants Dickie would frequent. Without mobilizing Dickie's resources under his own control, Tom will be incapacitated in keeping "Dickie" alive no matter how good he is at spontaneous invention, verbal dexterity, physical agility, and imitation. If Herbert Greenleaf was producing his performance during the period when Tom was "befriending Dickie," he cannot be counted on indefinitely to continue as producer once Dickie has gone "missing." Dickie must simply be cast as being "incognito." But even in hiding, "Dickie" would spend money, and so Tom must engineer even that aspect of the performance. He is not, therefore, so much a thief as a systematic and devoted actor deeply engaged in a role—not unlike Matt Damon, or any of the rest of us.

Some will argue, "Yes, but a performance to save his own life." Well, for what other reason do actors give performances? Performance is the only way out of the trap of circumstance, condition, and history.

CONTINGENCIES

In Philip Seymour Hoffman's masterful rendition we see all of the facets of Freddie Miles that Highsmith describes: ". . . the belligerence growing . . . as surely as if his huge body were generating a heat that he could feel across the room. . . . Tom was afraid of his eyes. . . . Freddie wouldn't stop now until he had found Dickie." He circles around Dickie's apartment like a contemptuous satrap, taking no pains to conceal his distrust of Tom who is "staying for a few days." His eyes glare with the supercilious squint of "the kind of ox who might beat up somebody he thought was a pansy, especially if the conditions were as propitious as these." Because Dickie is out "having dinner," Freddie takes himself off, but on the staircase he encounters the padrona Signora Buffi, who says, quite loudly, she is sure Dickie is upstairs in his apartment. "Then Tom heard Freddie's footsteps running up the stairs."

For Tom to allow Freddie back into the apartment at this point is more than problematic. "Tom stepped back into the apartment and closed the door. He could go on insisting that he didn't live here, that Dickie was at Otello's, or that he didn't know where Dickie was, but Freddie wouldn't stop now until he had found Dickie. Or Freddie would drag him downstairs and ask Signora Buffi who he was."

There are no other possibilities discernable at this moment, to Tom or to us. His social standing a pretext for only denial and diminution, no avowal he makes will have weight against Freddie's mandarin voice. "Wasn't there another way out?" he asks himself quite reasonably, but "He couldn't think. This was the only way out." Or should he confess to Freddie instead, and terminate our story, since our story is Tom's life, and our pleasure in its continuance is his self-preservation? Could Freddie, the ox who might kill a pansy, tolerate the explanation of Dickie Greenleaf's death that Tom would provide if he told the entire truth? (In Nagy, he bizarrely *does*, just before stabbing Freddie with a letter opener: "You'll be pleased to know that his brilliant efforts at the wing position made it very difficult for me to actually, finally *kill* him. His lung capacity was truly amazing." [82])

It is worth mentioning at this point that the killing of Dickie has been transposed altogether in the Minghella film. In the novel, Tom and Dickie are on the beach at Cannes and Tom sees some acrobats wearing yellow G-strings. Dickie mocks him for his homophilic gaze, mobilizing Tom's shame and hatred ("Tom's fists were clenched tight in his trouser pockets"), largely, as Chris Straayer has it, because of:

> a homosexuality that [Tom] resolutely resists and denies. He wants Greenleaf to leave Marge behind in Mongibello during their travels. He fantasizes a committed, idyllic bond between Greenleaf and himself that transcends sexuality. In other words, Tom adamantly seeks an exclusively male homosociality with Greenleaf. (2001, 117)

When subsequently they rent a boat and go out to sea, Tom wants to kill Dickie and thinks of how to do it, where, when. The moment presenting itself, as Dickie is dropping his trousers in preparation for a swim, Tom swats him with an oar, over and over and over until Dickie lies dead at the bottom of the boat.

The film version has Dickie and Tom discussing love, Tom prodding Dickie with the insinuation that he loves him and wondering if Dickie reciprocates. The "resolute denial" of homoeroticism is hardly present. Dickie sneers—humiliatingly, brazenly—that he finds Tom utterly beneath consideration of any kind. Inflamed, impassioned, Tom goes at Dickie's head with the oar, drawing blood. Immediately frozen with guilt and remorse, he moves forward to embrace Dickie's head. At the proximity Dickie comes unleashed and attacks Tom, strangling him. Tom's struggle and eventual lethal assault is self-defense, against both Dickie's physical threat and Dickie's mortifying accusations. Although we are in a position to witness this optically because of Minghella's camera, the sensibility substantiating our reading depends even more on a readiness to accept the homophilic choreography that has been played out so far—Tom's desire for, and fear of, Dickie, a complex of feeling and motive that has mobilized our earnest attention and seduced our affiliation. We, too, find Dickie appealing and a little awesome—"Dickie" is a "role very likely to confer stardom" (Rich, 82). And in approximating himself to Dickie, Tom is earnestness, even innocence, personified.

What sympathy, then, either for Tom's story or for Tom's person, can be expected of Freddie Miles, a young man of consummate scornfulness and supreme self-importance, whose view of Tom from the beginning of their connection is that he is a lowly hanger-on with pretensions to a social world in which he has no rightful place but that is Freddie's birthright. Tom the usurper can hold no appeal for the scathing Freddie. Our feeling in the scenes between them, indeed, is that Freddie would cheerfully squash Tom like an irritating fly on any pretext whatever. In fact, he is instrumental in producing the social death that alienates Tom from Dickie's lighthearted affection.

No, Freddie is a problem. He has been lied to, and he has seen through the lies. He is at the door. He is entering. Nothing will suffice but to end him, because this is Tom's story, not Dickie's, not Freddie's, and Tom has a need to continue. Intriguing (and somewhat Hitchcockian) about the treatment onscreen is the conjunction between our shock at the brutality with which Tom smashes Freddie's head in with a statue (it is the statue, indeed, and not Freddie's skull we see covered with blood [I am indebted to Michael Bickerton for this observation]) and our relief that having killed Freddie he can escape undetected from the uncomfortable situation. As he walks the dead Freddie out of the building as a "drunk," sits him in his red Fiat under the eyes of a man strolling with his girl, and drives into the suburbs of the city to slough off the body, we urgently hope no other cars, no other persons, will intrude to watch him even as, equivocally, we take note of the awkwardly self-conscious construction of the scenes as empty boxes for containing Tom's action. Although we surely enough want Freddie to disappear, we are unprepared for the messiness involved in eradicating him ("It takes a very long time to kill a man," said Hitchcock [Truffaut 1985, 311]), yet the loneliness of the night scene is unbearable in its way, and since it's imaginable he really *is* drunk we hate to see him go.

There is a most charming moment in which Tom's game is almost up, not to be confused with a number of moments quite without charm in which the same is true. At a bar he has met and picked up Marge to drive her back to meet "Dickie" at his apartment. ("Dickie" will surely not happen to be there when she arrives.) Mopedding past the doorway he sees the police. He drives on and lets her off, saying they do not know yet that Tom Ripley is in Rome and he does not wish to meet them. She should go to Dickie's on foot. Swiftly he rides away and, as "Dickie," arrives at the apartment before her. The police are there. He lets them in to question "Dickie," affirming that he does not want to see anybody, not even his fiancée Marge Sherwood. During the interrogation, however—a deliciously awkward scene—there comes a rap at the door and the carabiniere comes in from the atrium to say that Marge is in the corridor. If she enters the gig is up. And for a moment, a blissful moment, it is clear the idea has crossed Tom Ripley's mind to just retire from the stage. Have her come in, let the terrifying identification be made, have the barrage of questions begin: "But Signor Ripley, why would you pretend to be Signor Greenleaf?" He has been moving far too fast, eluding too many pursuers with too many leaden weights upon his soul. Stop, sighs the fox; they can have me. It will finally be over. So, "Let her in," he says in a breath, with a beatific smile the police inspector doesn't quite know how to read. And then, just as the carabiniere disappears from view, he has had a resurgence of command. "Wait—"

Tom is not, then, merely a slave to his own desire; the performance is extended now, and has been extended until now, not merely on his whim or because it pleasures him, but because it can be. The performance has its own logic and life, its own will to life, and continues to the degree that conditions and circumstances make continuance possible. It does not curtail itself, even when curtailment is both logical and easy and likely to produce the reward of profound rest. Committed to acting, Tom must engage himself in whatever actions—murder included—seem most coherent with the extension of his role, which is his being, through time.

THE FIRST LAUGH

Bergson writes:

> There are innumerable comedies in which one of the characters thinks he is speaking and acting freely, and consequently, retains all the essentials of life, whereas, viewed from a certain standpoint, he appears as a mere toy in the hands of another, who is playing with him. (1956, 111)

That such comedies are innumerable does not lessen the shock—comic to the observer—of learning one is playing in them. For Dickie's dressing-down of Ripley on the boat at San Remo—

> Who are you? *He slaps Tom in the face.* Who are you to say anything to me? Who are you to tell me anything? That's why I really really do not want to be on this boat with you. I can't move without you moving. It gives me the creeps. You give me the creeps. Can't move without "Dickie, Dickie, Dickie!" like a little girl all the time!

—is surely nothing less than a confession that Tom has been misemployed, used for purposes beyond his ken and out of alignment with his own intentions. Tom, then, apparently is now and has been for Dickie a mere thing, precisely in the (Bergsonian) sense as lacking "a vitality which we regard as derived from the very principle of intellectual and moral life" (92). Tom has been precisely what Bergson suggests a body becomes for us at a comedic moment, "no more in our eyes than a heavy and cumbersome vesture, a kind of irksome ballast" (92). Thus it is that in becoming aware of his state, Tom can offer a perfect gesture of reciprocation, turning Dickie into an irksome ballast, then dropping him overboard.

But social form is in general for Bergson a rigid and material weight that burdens the spirit, and so propriety is most properly seen as yet another exemplification of the comic. Here for the first time the film offers Tom as a naked butt of laughter, and we see in all its hideous irony the thick mantle of shame that Dickie has laid upon Tom's soul in order to reduce him. The capacity to lay burdens upon other peoples' shoulders in a systematic way is class advantage, after all, the hallmark of those whose expression of superiority is always that they can enjoy the laugh. For all his manipulativeness, Tom's desire is to penetrate the brittle sociability of Dickie Greenleaf and elicit feeling from him. All of Dickie's effete class-conscious style—"I could *fuck* this icebox, I love it so much!"—is baggage, made explicit as such, indeed, when in Rome Tom packs "Dickie" up hyperbolically through his jewelry and clothing, to store him in the basement of the apartment building when he has decided that "Dickie" must "commit suicide." Freddie is utterly preposterous, an affront to genuine feeling because a monument to honor (like the sculpture that is his undoing), because for him the world is a place that "ought" to conform to certain regulations or assume a proper perspective or be measured in certain proportions. "This place come furnished? It doesn't look like Dickie. It's horrible, isn't it? So . . . uh . . . bourgeois." What is characteristic of Tom's murder of Freddie is the spirited way in which it is carried off, as contrasted with Freddie's stolid and judgmental officiousness—"You're a quick study, aren't you. Last time you didn't know your ass from your elbow and now you're giving me directions. That's not fair—you probably do know your ass from your elbow." What should it be to Freddie, after all, if Tom and Dickie have had a fight, and if the fight has led to Dickie's death or disappearance? But Freddie's world is properly what he configures it to be, and has no room for the feelingful zephyr. In the sense of its being a rejection of the classism of Freddie and Dickie, then, *The Talented Mr. Ripley* is an homage to Forster's *A Room with a View*.

THE LAST LAUGH

Ripley's comedic structure has eluded analysis in the critical audience: Kenneth Turan of the *Los Angeles Times* called the Tom of the novel "a shark among guppies," for example, and Janet Maslin describes the film as "the story of a homoerotic Faustian bargain played for keeps." This is perhaps because the exegesis has seemed to attach itself to Tom's miscreancy, rather than to his character, this notwithstanding the continual references to character made by Dickie, Freddie, Mr. Greenleaf, and Tom himself. His unerring violation of social form, coupled as it is with a profundity of pleasure signaled with great delicateness and sureness by Damon, suggest precisely the Bergsonian spirit, an effervescent substrate associated with freedom, feeling, sensibility, and sublimity, and antithetical to formality, expectation, requirement, stipulation, category, judgmentalism, and economy. Dickie and Freddie are notably economical and rational in a systematic way, while Tom is rapaciously expressive, even explosive; giddily impulsive; a reveler in the delights of the senses. The cinematography, notable for its use of diffuse lighting and a film stock and treatment that make possible extremely saturated color (a vision, as Frank Rich put it, of the "Technicolor 1950s")—especially in the Greenleaf killing sequence—shows the world as Tom sees it vibrantly, not as Dickie does in fear.

Only one other character has Tom's vision, Marge's friend and a middle-class refugee from England, Peter Smith-Kingsley. Taking up with him in Venice, Tom settles into a comfortable homosexual ménage: Peter, too, has musical training, and they can share sensibilities, their memories of friendship with Dickie and Marge, and the illicit nature of their genuine unaffected love. Tom confesses to Peter, indeed, that he wishes deeply that he could share all of his past, but he has stowed it in a room in the basement where he never goes and will never let anyone penetrate (a macabre reference to *Ripley Under Ground,* in which a grotesque murder is committed by Tom in just such a place). In the novel Peter is merely an acquaintance of Tom's, whom he visits in Venice briefly after evading the police in Rome. Peter invites Tom to come stay with him at his place in Ireland:

> "It's deadly quiet there, I can assure you."
> Tom glanced at him. Peter had told him about his old Irish castle and had shown him pictures of it. Some quality of his relationship with Dickie

flashed across his mind like the memory of a nightmare, like a pale and evil ghost. It was because the same thing could happen with Peter, he thought, Peter the upright, unsuspecting, naïve, generous good fellow—except that he didn't look enough like Peter. But one evening, for Peter's amusement, he had put on an English accent and had imitated Peter's mannerisms and his way of jerking his head to one side as he talked, and Peter had thought it hilariously funny. He shouldn't have done that, Tom thought now. It made Tom bitterly ashamed, that evening and the fact that he had thought even for an instant that the same thing that had happened with Dickie could happen with Peter.

In the film, Peter does not escape so easily, but becomes Tom's final victim in a moment of tragic irony. At the beginning of the film, sailing from America to find Dickie Greenleaf, and acting out his fantasy life by pretending to be the Dickie he is on his way to find and retrieve, Tom has a shipboard friendship with an American girl, Meredith Logue (Cate Blanchett). Now at film's end, it turns out she is aboard the same ship as Peter and Tom sailing away from Venice. She runs into "Dickie" again, and Peter is so placed as to hear enough of their conversation to realize that she is calling Tom "Dickie." Tom sees this. Meredith is sailing with her family, and is thus protected. Peter has only Tom. Peter is both loyal and loving, and though he is wondering about Tom, he is wondering entirely in devotion, yet Tom has no choice. The film ends with him strangling Peter and hunching in remorse in the silent shadows of the cabin as the ship sails on to an indeterminate future.

While the novel ends with Tom heading off happily to find the best hotel in Athens, the film leaves him in darker and colder circumstances. It forces him to sacrifice the love of his life for the coherence of his performance. Indeed, it is a performance he initiated out of curiosity and frivolity, then continued with excitement as he felt his strengths as a performer growing, and finally discovers he is locked into. Tom is the butt of our last laugh, then, for the mechanical skin of an alien identity has suffocated his affection and responsiveness; the need for persistent wariness has replaced his taste; efficiency and self-protectiveness, once aids to his expression of dignity and affection in the face of humiliating mockery, now mock him utterly.

Interestingly enough, in the four novels that follow *Ripley*, Patricia Highsmith has her protagonist living in France. (One of these, *Ripley's Game*, Wim Wenders filmed as *The American Friend* [1977] with Dennis Hopper as Ripley, and a second version of the same, with John Malkovich in the title role, appeared in 2002 from Liliana Cavani; Roger Spottiswoode's *White on White*, from *Ripley Under Ground*, is listed on the Internet Movie Database as "in production" with Barry Pepper as Ripley.) Dickie Greenleaf is accepted everywhere as the killer of Freddie Miles turned to suicide, and his old friend Tom marries and takes up residence in a charming house not far from Chantilly. More murders are required of him, each in the name of an honorable cause, but his talents for dissembling, masquerade, staging, and evasion never fail. If the "Dickie" he was attempting to be in the first Ripley novel is a figure of sunny if irresponsible playfulness—the real Dickie without the warts of arrogance—his "character" for the duration is something far less spontaneous, if wealthy and puissant in his own right. The "Tom Ripley" that Tom Ripley must be is still a character, but now a bourgeois one, the dutiful husband, the lover (and accumulator) of paintings, the citizen whose opinion should be listened to, the appropriate model for teenage boys. Under all of it, the "Tom" to come or the "Tom" we first met in the bar in New York in the first Ripley novel or playing the piano sweetly in the Greenleaf penthouse in the film, is who? Capability, attentiveness, memory, inspiration, daring, admiration, hunger are all there, yet no discernable personality. Who, then, is the actor beneath the characters Tom Ripley plays, even when they bear his name? He is the embodiment of the present, reaching out fully to experience in every dimension every conceivable taste, anticipating always what will come tomorrow, yet to save his life he must never look back.

OUTSIDE

"Every looking oozes with mendacity," Cortázar wrote, "because it's that which expels us furthest outside ourselves, without the least guarantee" (1967, 119). Or, it is not possible to regard the world without being unfaithful to ourselves in regarding it, without betraying where we have come from and everything we are; since all we can see is what we desire to see, though we call it the world. Having asked who he really is, we must wonder, finally, why it should be that Tom Ripley mobilizes our loathing as intensely as he apparently does: why his acquaintances are "guppies" and why he is a "shark." That he is a killer is morally problematic, of course, but hardly a cause for detesting him. Perhaps Tom Ripley's talent is not as rare as the glorification of the novel or film suggest by their isolation and framing. Perhaps in locking away his past in a room in the basement to which he has thrown away the key, he resembles any of us. Surely in the vapid and commercialized world that was America of the 1950s, and that was also America at the end of the twentieth century, the desire to escape from the confines of propriety and actually feel can hardly be seen as characteristic of only the deviant soul. Who has not wished for a life in which sensibility could be paramount, could triumph over economy?

Nor is Tom our only killer here. Dickie and Dickie's father have committed many crimes against the spirit. Herbert Greenleaf purchases Tom Ripley's existence; that is what the production of drama is all about, the agency through which persons are converted to actors and through which scripted roles are brought to "life." Because Tom is in many ways at the end of his rope when Herbert meets him, the arrangement they share is one Tom is in no position to escape, and so it resembles white slavery. For his part, Dickie experiences no moment in Tom's presence where he does not proceed toward the systematic assassination of Tom's spirit. Through superiority, through ridicule, through patronization, through the condescensions of education, and through the fear of touching he persists in positioning Tom beneath him, fueling Tom's (inutile) desire to climb. Marge Sherwood offers Tom what he thinks is her friendship but it is only an attachment sufficient to keep him near enough to entertain her with his clumsiness; in truth she is irritated by him, but will never admit it even when he has terrified her for her life. Is our outrage at the killing of Dickie not only a response to the physicality of the act but also a shriek of despair at the loss of an idol we have been worshipping? He represents, after all, the zenith of material desire, a gaudy enough package of all the amenities middle-class viewers desire now (and desired, too, in 1955): the ability to loll in Europe, the gay sailboat, access to exotic food and experience, lush garments, easy familiarity with both the pleasure dome of high culture and the hot secret den of jazz. Is there no self-hatred, then, in our distance from Tom? Is there no self-denigration in our bitter assessment of "Tom Ripley's talent"?

The sociopathy with which Tom is typically charged, a relentless subsistence on ever-shifting performance, is perfectly characteristic, if you will, of the capitalist age, in which personality is indexed as the capacity to labor and is marketed in an urban ecos of strangeness. Tom is a high priest of Baudrillard's "cult of the ephemeral" (1981, 52). But before we castigate him, we must see Ripley as a reflection of contemporary man. If we are all liars, and I suppose we can hardly be otherwise given the perilous difficulty of getting away from ourselves, we must seek to know why some lies seem more appealing than others to tell and to hear, the ones we call verities; why some, indeed, are so repugnant as to be the objects of our sneers. Dickie's lies, and Freddie's, Marge's, Herbert's—we have collaborated to accept and organize as truths: Dickie, we naturally believe, should properly return to his heritage and adopt the life his father has designed for him; he and Marge should live happily ever after, the ideal married prince and princess; Freddie's exclusivity should substantiate the creation of several blessed colonies of blissful isolates, who never catch a whiff of poverty or hunger or ignorance, who never meet a person they can't call by the first name. Privilege, in short, should continue indefinitely because it is not only beautiful—and therefore desirable to those who lack it—but also natural, the birthright of those who claim it. It is not that Tom has acquired a taste for the good life that niggles Freddie, after all, but that Tom has begun to make a claim upon that taste.

But Tom's lies—the true content of *The Talented Mr. Ripley*—seen from Tom's point of view, which is to say, from the outside, confront us with our own predisposition to adore the very process that excludes us. In that confrontation is our displeasure, our pain, and the gateway to understanding.

WORKS CITED

Baudrillard, Jean. 1981. *For a Critique of the Political Economy of the Sign.* St. Louis, MO: Telos Press.

Bergson, Henri. 1956. "Laughter." In Wylie Sypher, ed., *Comedy.* Garden City, NY: Doubleday Anchor, 59–190.

Clark, Mike. 2000. "A pretty young picture," *USA Today* (January 27). Available at http://www.usatoday.com/life/enter/movies/movie170.htm.

Cortázar, Julio. 1967. *End of the Game and Other Stories.* New York: Pantheon.

Highsmith, Patricia. 1992, © 1955. *The Talented Mr. Ripley.* New York: Vintage.

———. 1993, © 1974. *Ripley's Game.* New York: Vintage.

———. 1992, © 1970. *Ripley Under Ground.* New York: Vintage.

———. 1993, © 1980. *The Boy Who Followed Ripley.* New York: Vintage.

———. 1993, © 1991. *Ripley Under Water.* New York: Vintage.

Nagy, Phyllis. 1999. *The Talented Mr. Ripley.* London: Methuen.

Rich, Frank. 1999. "American Pseudo," *New York Times* (December 12), 80–87+.

Stearns, Peter N. 1990. *Be a Man! Males in Modern Society,* 2d. New York: Holmes and Meier.

Straayer, Chris. 2001. "The Talented Poststructuralist: Heteromasculinity, Gay Artifice, and Class Passing." In Peter Lehman, ed. *Masculinity: Bodies, Movies, Culture.* New York: Routledge, 115–32.

Truffaut, François. 1985. *Hitchcock.* Rev. ed. Trans. by Helen Scott. New York: Simon & Schuster.

CONTRIBUTORS

Aaron Baker teaches at Arizona State University. He has published essays about Italian American cinema and about the representation of social identity in sports, and is the author of *Contesting Identities: Sports in American Film* (Illinois).

Rebecca Bell-Metereau teaches film at Southwest Texas State University and directs the interdisciplinary Media Studies Program. She had a Fulbright to study media in Senegal (1999–2000), and she has published *Hollywood Androgyny* (Columbia); *Simone Weil: On Politics, Religion and Society* (Sage); and chapters and articles in *Ladies and Gentlemen, Boys and Girls: Gender in Film at the End of the Twentieth Century; Writing With; Cultural Conflicts in Twentieth Century Literature; Deciding Our Future: Technological Imperatives; Women Worldwalkers: New Dimensions of Science Fiction and Fantasy; College English; Journal of Popular Film and Television;* and *Cinema Journal.* She has also served as Special Assistant to the President at Southwest Texas State University and campus director for -ISM, a nationwide Ford Foundation grant to incorporate diversity and media literacy in the curriculum.

Wheeler Winston Dixon is the James Ryan Endowed Professor of Film Studies and Professor of English at the University of Nebraska, Lincoln, Series Editor for the State University of New York Press Cultural Studies in Cinema/Video, and the Editor-in-Chief of the *Quarterly Review of Film and Video.* His newest books are *Straight: Constructions of Heterosexuality in the Cinema* (SUNY), *Visions of the Apocalypse: Spectacles of Destruction in American Cinema* (Wallflower), *The Second Century of Cinema: The Past and Future of the Moving Image* (SUNY), *Film Genre 2000: New Critical Essays* (SUNY), and *Collected Interviews: Voices from 20th Century Cinema* (Southern Illinois). *Film and Television After 9/11* is forthcoming from Southern Illinois.

Alexander Doty is a Professor in the English Department at Lehigh University, Bethlehem, Pennsylvania. He has written *Making Things Perfectly Queer:*

Interpreting Mass Culture and *Flaming Classics: Queering the Film Canon* (both from Routledge), as well as co-edited *Out in Culture: Gay, Lesbian and Queer Essays on Popular Culture* (Duke). More recently, he has presented a clip-and-lecture show based on *Flaming Classics* at lesbian and gay film festivals across the country.

Kirby Farrell's latest book is *Post-Traumatic Culture: Injury and Interpretation in the 90s* (Johns Hopkins), which examines the idea of trauma and reads a variety of texts from late-Victorian fiction to contemporary black women writers, political memoirs, and recent films. His other work includes several books on Shakespeare and several novels. He is an editor of *English Literary Renaissance,* the European journal *Kritikon,* and several collections of Renaissance studies. He is currently working on *The Beserk Style in American Culture.*

Gwendolyn Audrey Foster is an Associate Professor in the Department of English, University of Nebraska, Lincoln, specializing in Film Studies, Cultural Studies, and Postfeminist Critical Theory. Her recent books include *Performing Whiteness: Postmodern Re/constructions in the Cinema* (SUNY), *Captive Bodies: Postcolonial Subjectivity in Cinema* (SUNY), *The Films of Chantal Akerman* (Flicks), and *Troping the Body: Etiquette, Conduct and Dialogic Performance* (Southern Illinois). Dr. Foster is also an editor-in-chief of *Quarterly Review of Film and Video.*

Lester D. Friedman has a joint senior appointment in the Program in Medical Humanities and Bioethics (Medical School) and the Department of Radio/TV/Film (School of Communication) at Northwestern University. He is the author/editor of many books and articles, including: *Hollywood's Image of the Jew* (Ungar), *Unspeakable Images: Ethnicity and the American Cinema* (Illinois), *American Jewish Filmmakers* (co-author; Illinois), *Fires Were Started: British Film and Thatcherism* (Minnesota), and *Arthur Penn*'s Bonnie and Clyde (Cambridge). His latest book, *Cultural Sutures: Medicine, Morals and Media,* forthcoming from Duke, examines the intimate connections between healthcare and mass communication systems. Currently, Dr. Friedman is finishing a book on the films of director Steven Spielberg. With Murray Pomerance he is co-editor of the Screen Decades Series from Rutgers University Press.

Cynthia Fuchs is Associate Professor of English, Film and Media Studies, and African American Studies at George Mason University. She is film, video, and TV editor for *PopMatters* (at popmatters.com), and weekly film reviewer for the *Philadelphia Citypaper* (citypaper.net), *Nitrate* (nitrateonline.com), *Reel Images Magazine* (reelimagesmagazine.com), and *Pop Politics* (poppolitics.com). She is co-editor of *Between the Sheets, in the Streets: Queer,*

Lesbian, Gay Documentary (Minnesota) has recently published *Interviews: Spike Lee* (Mississippi) as well as numerous articles on popular culture, and is at work on a book about Eminem.

Henry A. Giroux holds the Waterbury Chair Professorship in Secondary Education and is also the Director of the Waterbury Forum in Education and Cultural Studies at Penn State University. His most recent books include: *The Mouse that Roared: Disney and the End of Innocence* (Rowman & Littlefield); *Stealing Innocence: Corporate Culture's War on Children* (St. Martin's); *Impure Acts: The Practical Politics of Cultural Studies* (Routledge); *Beyond the Corporate University* (edited with Kostas Myrsiades; Rowman & Littlefield); *Public Spaces/Private Lives: Democracy Beyond 9/11* (Rowman & Littlefield); and *Breaking in to the Movies: Film and the Politics of Culture* (Blackwell).

Tom Gunning is a Professor in the Art Department and the Cinema and Media Committee at the University of Chicago. Author of *D. W. Griffith and the Origins of American Narrative Film* (Illinois) and the recently published *The Films of Fritz Lang: Allegories of Modernity and Vision* (British Film Institute), he has written numerous essays on early and international silent cinema and on the development of later American cinema in terms of Hollywood genres and directors as well as the avant-garde film. He has lectured around the world and his works have been published in a dozen languages.

Ina Rae Hark is Professor of English and Director of the Film Studies program at the University of South Carolina. She is co-editor of *Screening the Male* (Routledge) and *The Road Movie Book* (Routledge), editor of *Exhibition, the Film Reader* (Routledge), and the author of many articles and book chapters on gender, politics, and genre in Hollywood film.

Kristen Hatch is a Ph.D. candidate in the Department of Film, Television, and Digital Media at the University of California at Los Angeles. Her dissertation, "Playing Innocent: Shirley Temple and the Performance of Girlhood," traces Temple's performances to their roots on the nineteenth-century stage and considers how her career was shaped by emerging concerns about adult consumption of images of children. She has written on the two *Lolita*s in *Sugar, Spice, and Everything Nice: Cinemas of Girlhood.*

Patricia Clare Ingham is Associate Professor of English at Indiana University. She teaches courses on Medieval Literature, Popular Medievalism, and Gender Studies and is author of *Sovereign Fantasies: Arthurian Romance and the Making of Britain* (Pennsylvania) as well as of numerous articles on romance, and medieval colonial and gender relations. Her co-edited volume *Postcolonial Moves: Medieval through Modern* (Palgrave Macmillan) is forthcoming.

E. Ann Kaplan is Professor of English and Comparative Studies at SUNY Stony Brook, where she also founded and directs the Humanities Institute. She has written many books and articles on topics in women's studies, literary and media studies, and cultural studies, including *Women in Film: Both Sides of the Camera* (Methuen), *Women in Film Noir* (British Film Institute), *Rocking around the Clock* (Methuen), *Motherhood and Representation* (Routledge), and most recently *Looking for the Other: Feminism, Film and the Imperial Gaze* (Routledge). Recent co-edited books include: *Generations: Academic Feminists in Dialogue* (Minnesota) and *Playing Dolly: Technocultural Fantasies and Fictions of Assisted Reproduction* (Rutgers). An edited anthology, *Feminism and Film* (Oxford), appeared in 2000, and she is working on a new book, *Performing Trauma: Memory, Cinema and Witnessing*.

Peter Lehman is the Interim Director of the Interdiscplinary Humanities Program at Arizona State University. He is author of *Running Scared: Masculinity and the Representation of the Male Body* and *Roy Orbison: The Invention of an Alternative Rock Masculinity* (both Temple) and editor of *Masculinity: Bodies, Movies, Culture* (Routledge).

Gina Marchetti is an Associate Professor in the Department of Cinema and Photography at Ithaca College. In 1995, her book, *Romance and the "Yellow Peril": Race, Sex and Discursive Strategies in Hollywood Fiction* (California) won the award for best book in the area of cultural studies from the Association of Asian American Studies. She has essays in several anthologies and has published articles in *Journal of Film and Video; Genders; positions: east asia cultures critique; Postmodern Culture; Post Script,* and others, as well as *Jump Cut* (where she serves on the editorial board). Her current book, *From Tian'anmen to Times Square: China on Global Screens,* is forthcoming.

Dana Polan is Professor of Critical Studies in the School of Cinema-TV at University of Southern California. He is the author of five film books including *Power and Paranoia: History, Narrative, and the American Cinema, 1940–1950* (Columbia), *Pulp Fiction* (British Film Institute), and most recently *Jane Campion* (British Film Institute). He has a Doctorat d'État in film from the Sorbonne Nouvelle, and the French Ministry of Culture knighted him for his contributions to cross-cultural exchange between France and the United States.

Murray Pomerance is Professor and Chair in the Department of Sociology at Ryerson University. With Lester D. Friedman he is co-editor of the Screen Decades Series from Rutgers University Press and he is author, editor, or co-editor of numerous volumes including *Magia d'Amore* (Sun & Moon); *Bang*

Bang, Shoot Shoot!: Essays on Guns and Popular Culture (Pearson); *Closely Watched Brains* (Pearson); *Ladies and Gentlemen, Boys and Girls: Gender in Film at the End of the Twentieth Century* (SUNY); *Sugar, Spice, and Everything Nice: Cinemas of Girlhood* (Wayne State); and *Enfant Terrible! Jerry Lewis in American Film* (New York University). His *An Eye for Hitchcock* is forthcoming from Rutgers University Press, and he is working on a book about Johnny Depp's screen performance.

William Rothman is the author of *Hitchcock—The Murderous Gaze* (Harvard), *The "I" of the Camera* (Cambridge), *Documentary Film Classics* (Cambridge), and (with Marian Keane) *Reading Cavell's* The World Viewed: *A Philosophical Perspective on Film* (Wayne State). He is series editor of Cambridge University Press's Studies in Film series. He received his Ph.D. in philosophy from Harvard University, where he taught for many years, and is currently Professor of Motion Pictures and Director of the Graduate Program in Film Study at the University of Miami.

Christopher Sharrett is Professor of Communication at Seton Hall University. He is editor of *Mythologies of Violence in Postmodern Media* (Wayne State) and *Crisis Cinema: The Apocalyptic Idea in Postmodern Narrative Film* (Maisonneuve). His work has appeared in *Cineaste, Cineaction, Film Quarterly, Persistence of Vision, Millennium Film Journal, Journal of Popular Film and Television,* and numerous anthologies. He is on the editorial board of *Cinema Journal*.

Tony Williams is Professor and Area Head of Film Studies in the Department of English at Southern Illinois University at Carbondale. His books include *Structures of Desire* (SUNY); *Jack London: The Movies* (Drejl); *Hearths of Darkness: The Family in the American Horror Film* (Fairleigh Dickinson); and *Larry Cohen: Radical Allegories of An American Filmmaker* (McFarland). He has co-edited *Vietnam War Films* (McFarland) and *Jack London's The Sea Wolf: A Screenplay by Robert Rossen* (Southern Illinois).

Steven Woodward is Assistant Professor of Film and Literature at Clemson University. He has published essays on the films of Krzysztof Kieslowski and Roman Polanski, genre confusion in *Grosse Pointe Blank,* and the filmic depiction of girls who kill. He has had a libidinous fascination with the James Bond films since his childhood in England, a fascination that has been balanced by intellectual interest since he watched *The Spy Who Loved Me* with 100 inhabitants of Fanning Island, a remote atoll in the South Pacific.

INDEX

italic numeral indicates photograph

A.I. (Steven Spielberg, 2001), 68, 69
Abdul the Damned (Karl Grune, 1935), 162
Accused, The (Jonathan Kaplan, 1988), 3
Ackland, Rodney, 163, 164
Adam, Ken, 182
Address Unknown (William Cameron Menzies, 1944), 263
Adventures of Buckaroo Banzai Across the 8ᵗʰ Dimension, The (W. D. Richter, 1984), 303
Agnes of God (Norman Jewison, 1985), 290
Aigle à deux têtes, L' (Jean Cocteau, 1947), 130, 133
Air Raid Wardens [Laurel and Hardy] (Edward Sedgwick, 1943), 267
Airazian, Arshalouis, 146
Al Qaeda, 94
Alamo, The (John Wayne, 1960), 69, 70
Albigensians, 34
"Alcoa Hour, The" (1957), 158
Aldrich, Robert, 206, 207, 209
"Alfred Hitchcock Presents" (1960), 158
Alien (Ridley Scott, 1979), 2, 287, 289, 296
"All Girl Action: A History of Lesbian Erotica" (Susie Bright, 1990), 144

All Through the Night (Vincent Sherman, 1942), 263
Amadeus (Milos Forman, 1984), 90
Amatrudo, Ed, 277
Amazing Colossal Man, The (Bert I. Gordon, 1957), 12, 39, 40, 41
American Beauty (Sam Mendes, 1999), 118
American Friend, The. See *Der Amerikanische Freund*
American Pie (Paul Weitz and Chris Weitz, 1999), 118
"America's Most Wanted" (1988), 67–68
. . . And Millions Die! (Leslie H. Martinson, 1973), 268
Anderson, Paul Thomas, 12, 81, 88, 89
Anderson, Richard, 305
André, Marcel, 135
Andress, Ursula, 181
Anima (Craig Richardson, 1998), 268
Apollinaire, Guillaume, 130
Apt Pupil (Bryan Singer, 1998), 16, 268
Arch of Triumph (Lewis Milestone, 1948), 266
Arden, Eve, 240
"Are You Hot?" (2003), 67
Armageddon (Michael Bay, 1998), 69
Arnheim, Rudolf, 30
Arnold, Jack, 211
Ashton, Linda, 145

Asimov, Isaac, 304
Assayas, Olivier, 190, 195, 197
Astaire, Fred, 35
Astronaut's Wife, The (Rand Ravich, 1999), 3
Atomic Cafe, The (Jayne Loader, Kevin Rafferty, and Pierce Rafferty, 1982), 13, 96
Attack (Robert Aldrich, 1956), 68
Attack of the 50 Foot Woman (Nathan Juran, 1958), 11, 39, 40, 42, 43, 44, 45
Attenborough, Richard, 167
Auric, Georges, 130
Austin Powers: International Man of Mystery (Jay Roach, 1997), 180
Awakening, The (Kate Chopin), 236
Aznavour, Charles, 139

Bach, Barbara, 181
Bacharach, Burt, 243, 244
Background to Danger (Raoul Walsh, 1943), 263
Bad Seed, The (Mervyn LeRoy, 1956), 283
Badel, Alan, 157
Bailey, Robin, 178
Baker, Chet, 316
Baker, Sala, 307
Balaban, Bob, 115
"Ballad of Bonnie and Clyde" (Mitch Murray), 195
Balzac (Josée Dayan, 1999), 248
Bankhead, Tallulah, 163, 166
Bardot, Brigitte, 139
Barnes, Pamela, 175
Baron fantôme, Le (Serge de Poligny, 1942), 129
Barricade (Gregory Ratoff, 1939), 189
Basic Instinct (Paul Verhoeven, 1992), 9
Basler, Antoine, 194
Bataille, Georges, 21, 36
Batman & Robin (Joel Schumacher, 1997), 81
Batman Forever (Joel Schumacher, 1995), 81

Battle of the Bulge (Ken Annakin, 1965), 265
Battleground (William A. Wellman, 1949), 265
Battleship Potemkin, The (Sergei Eisenstein, 1925), 71
Baudrillard, Jean, 25, 33
Baudry, Jean-Louis, 26, 28, 30
Bauer, Christopher, *78*, 84
Bazin, André, 30
Bean, Sean, 183
Beast Within, The (Philippe Mora, 1982), 45
Beatty, Warren, 73
Beaumont, Étienne de, 133
Beaumont, Hugh "Binkie," 161–162
Beautiful Mind, A (Ron Howard, 2000), 307
Becker, Arno, 131, 140
Bedford Incident, The (James B. Harris, 1965), 163
Beecher, Rev. Henry Ward, 28
Behind the Green Door (Artie and Jim Mitchell, 1972), 80
Bel Geddes, Barbara, 216
Belasco, David, 191
"Belle et la Bête, La" (Madame Leprince de Beaumont), 134
Belle et la bête, La (Jean Cocteau, 1946), 13, 130, 132, 133, 134
Bellour, Raymond, 35
Beneath the Valley of the Ultravixens (Russ Meyer, 1979), 144
Bennett, Bruce, 51
Bennett, William, 113
Bequest to the Nation, A (James Cellan Jones, 1973), 158
Bérand, Christian, 130
Bergman, Ingrid, 128, 214, 216
Berle, Milton, 267
Berlin Correspondent (Eugene Forde, 1942), 263
Bernard, Jacques, 137
Bernard, Paul, 128
Bernard, Sue, 147
Bernays, Edward, 65

Berry, Halle, 183
Beyond the Valley of the Dolls (Russ Meyer, 1970), *142*, 144, 148, 152
Big Red One, The (Samuel Fuller, 1980), 3, 265
Big Trouble in Little China (John Carpenter, 1986), 189
Bin Laden, Osama, 103, 104
Binder, Maurice, 181
Birch, Thora, *108*, 115
Birds, The (Alfred Hitchcock, 1963), *212*, 217, 239
Birth of a Nation, The (D. W. Griffith, 1915), 12, 46, 65
Bitter Tea of General Yen, The (Frank Capra, 1933), 189
Bitter Victory (Nicholas Ray, 1957), 209
Black Hawk Down (Ridley Scott, 2001), 2, 12, 67
Blackmail (Alfred Hitchcock, 1929), 217
Blackman, Honor, 182
Blackton, John Stuart, 32
Blade Runner (Ridley Scott, 1982), 103
Blair, Linda, 289
Blair Witch Project, The (Daniel Myrick and Eduardo Sánchez, 1999), 8
Blanche Fury (Marc Allégret, 1947), 165
Blanchett, Cate, 326
Blin, Roger, 138
Blind Goddess, The (Harold French, 1948), 162
Blob, The (Irvin S. Yeaworth Jr., 1958), 16, 287, 288
Blood Alley (William A. Wellman and John Wayne, 1955), 189
Blood of a Poet, The. See *Sang d'un poète, le*
Blown Away (Stephen Hopkins, 1994), 2
Boatman, Michael, 60
Boccaccio, Giovanni, 249
Bodeen, DeWitt, 229
Bogarde, Dirk, 167
Böhm, Karlheinz, 164
Bolger, Frank, 147
Bonnie and Clyde (Arthur Penn, 1967), *64*, 73, 202

Boogie Nights (Paul Thomas Anderson, 1997), 12, 79, 81, 85, 86, 88–90
Boop, Betty, 35
Born to Be Bad (Nicholas Ray, 1950), 15, *200*, 201–211
Boudu Saved from Drowning [Boudu sauvé des eaux] (Jean Renoir, 1932), 49
Bowser, Eileen, 35
Box, Betty, 163
Boxer Rebellion, The (1900), 187
Boys from Brazil, The (Franklin J. Schaffner, 1978), 2, 268
Boyz N the Hood (John Singleton, 1991), 59, 60, 61–62
Brain That Wouldn't Die, The (Joseph Green, 1962), *38*, 39, 48
Brando, Marlon, 146, 261
Brandon, Henry, 189
Braque, Georges, 131
Braveheart (Mel Gibson, 1995), 70
Bray, Yvonne de, 135
Bread and Roses (Ken Loach, 2001), 98
Bride Wore Black, The [La Mariée était en noir] (François Truffaut, 1967), 3
Bridge at Remagen, The (John Guillermin, 1969), 265
Bridge Too Far, A (Richard Attenborough, 1977), 265
Broccoli, Albert R. "Cubby," 177
Brood, The (David Cronenberg, 1979), 296
Brosnan, Pierce, 173, 183, 184
Brown, Robert, 184
Browning Version, The (Terence Rattigan), 161
Bryce, Ivar, 177
Brynner, Yul, 139
Buck Privates [Abbott and Costello] (Arthur Lubin, 1941), 267
Buckaroo Banzai. See *The Adventures of Buckaroo Banzai Across the 8ᵗʰ Dimension*
Bully (Larry Clark, 2001), 2, 16, *272*, 273–280, 281, 284
Bully: A True Story of High School Revenge (Jim Schutze), 274

"Bully Murder Scene" (Thurston Moore), 280
Burgess, Guy, 162
Burns, Marilyn, 293
Burr, Raymond, 216
Burton, Richard, 262
Buscemi, Steve, 116
Busch, Dennis, 147
Bush, George H. W., 69, 103
Bush, George W., 66, 96, 112, 217
Butch Cassidy and the Sundance Kid (George Roy Hill, 1969), 236
Byron, Lord George Gordon, 302

Cage, Nicolas, 81
Cahiers du cinéma, 195
Caine, Michael, 49, 168
Calder, David, 184
Camion, Le (Marguerite Duras, 1977), 247
Camus, Albert, 248
Cannes Film Festival (1953), 133–134
Canterbury Tale, A (Michael Powell, 1944), 14, 159, 162, 164, 165, 167
Cape Fear (Martin Scorsese, 1991), 4
Capri, Alaina, 151
Cardinal, The (Sinclair Hill, 1936), 162
Carey, Harry Jr., 3
Carradine, John, 50
Carrey, Jim, 106
Carrie (Brian De Palma, 1976), 16, 290, 291, 293
Carroll, Leo G. , 214
Carter, Helena Bonham, 75
Carter, Myra, 81
Casablanca (Michael Curtiz, 1942), 2, 263
Casares, Maria, 128, 137, 139
Casey, Bernie, 62
Casey, William, 103
Castel, Lou, 191
Castle, William, 35
Castro, Fidel, 177
Cat People (Jacques Tourneur, 1942), 15, *224*, 225–236
Catch-22 (Mike Nichols, 1970), 267

Catcher in the Rye, The (J. D. Salinger), 118
Caught in the Draft (David Butler, 1941), 267
Cavani, Liliana, 326
C'est Tout (Marguerite Duras and Yann Andréa Steiner), 247
Cet amour-là (Josée Dayan, 2001), 246, 251
Chan, Jackie, 195
Chanel, Coco, 130
Chaplin, Charles, *254*, 266
Chaucer, Geoffrey, 249
Cherry, Harry, and Raquel! (Russ Meyer, 1969), 144, 145, 148
Cheung, Maggie, 14, 191, 192, 193, 194, 195, 197
China Syndrome, The (James Bridges, 1979), 102
Chinatown (Roman Polanski, 1974), 59, 60
Chinese Exclusion Act, The (1882), 187
Chocolat (Lasse Hallström, 2000), 240
Christie, John Reginald, 166
Christopher, Warren (U.S. Secretary of State), 56
Chuvalo, George, 294
Cinderella (Clyde Geronimi, Wilfred Jackson, and Hamilton Luske, 1950), 9
Civil Action, A (Steve Zaillian, 1998), 102
Clark, Ernest, 157
Clark, Larry, 273
Clayton, Judy, 278
Clear and Present Danger (Phillip Noyce, 1994), 68
Clemens, Paul, 45
Clifford, Clark, 103
Clowes, Daniel, 115
Cocteau, Jean, 13, *126*, 127–140
Colbert, Claudette, 39
Colditz Story, The (Guy Hamilton, 1955), 14, 159
Cole, George, 163
Cole, Nat King, 207
Colette [Sidonie Gabrielle Claudine Colette], 130

Collateral Damage (Andrew Davis, 2002), 66–67
Colletti, Irene B., 278
Colors (Dennis Hopper, 1988), 12, 56, 57, 58, 60, 62
Comédie Française, La, 247
Commando (Mark L. Lester, 1985), 2
Committee on Public Information (Creel Committee), 65
Common Law Cabin (Russ Meyer, 1967), 145, 147, 151
Confessions of a Nazi Spy (Anatole Litvak, 1939), 16, 263
Connelly, Jennifer, 298
Connery, Sean, 173, 182
Contender, The (Rod Lurie, 2000), 4
Conway, Tom, 227
Cookie's Fortune (Robert Altman, 1999), 240
Cooper, Gary, 167, 245
Copley, Peter, 157
"Cops" (1989), 67
Coq et l'arlequin, Le (Jean Cocteau, 1918), 130
Coriolan (Jean Cocteau, 1950), 133
Corridor of Mirrors (Terence Young, 1948), 162, 164, 165
Cosima, Renée, 136
Cosmic Man, The (Herbert S. Greene, 1959), 50, 51
Costello, George, 146
Cotten, Joseph, 214
Cotton, Curtis III, 281
Craft, Robert, 131
Creel, George, 65
Crimes of Stephen Hawke, The (George King, 1936), 162
Cromwell, James, *54*
Cronenberg, David, 190–197, 295
Cruise, Tom, 4, 90
Crumb (Terry Zwigoff, 1995), 115
Crying Game, The (Neil Jordan, 1992), 196
Cuneo, Ernest, 177
Curry, Tim, 196
Curse of Frankenstein, The (Terence Fisher, 1957), 309

Cushing, Peter, 46, 157, 309
Custer, Gen. George Armstrong, 66

Dalai Lama, 190
Dall, John, 215
Dalton, Timothy, 173
Dames du Bois de Boulogne, Les (Robert Bresson, 1945), 128, 137
Damon, Matt, *314*, 315, 316ff
Dances With Wolves (Kevin Costner, 1990), 98
Dangerously They Live (Robert Florey, 1942), 263
Daniel (Sidney Lumet, 1983), 3
Daniels, Leslie, *38*
Dard, Frédéric. See *La Vieille qui marchait dans la mer*
Darkman (Sam Raimi, 1990), 2
Daudet, Lucien, 133
Davenport, Jack, 318
Davenport, William Henry and Ira Erastas (The Davenport Brothers), 29
David (Jean Cocteau), 130
Davidson, Jaye, 196
Davis, Bette, 239
Davis, Elmer (The Davis Committee), 65
Davis, Geena, 294, 295
Dawn of the Dead (George Romero, 1978), 72, 73
Dawson, Anthony, 178
Day, Doris, 39
Day, Josette, 134
Day of the Dead (George Romero, 1985), 72
Day the Clown Cried, The (Jerry Lewis, 1972), 269
Daybreak (Compton Bennett, 1947), 159, 162, 165
De Jesus, Wanda, 62
De Niro, Robert, 4
Déa, Marie, 137
Dead Man Walking (Tim Robbins, 1995), 3
Dead Men Don't Wear Plaid (Carl Reiner, 1982), 267

Dead Ringers (David Cronenberg, 1988), 195
Deadfall (Bryan Forbes, 1968), 160, 167–169
Deadly Deception (Deborah Chasnoff, 1991), 94
Dean, James, 210
Dean, Jimmy, 181
Dear Murderer (Arthur Crabtree, 1947), 159, 162, 165
Debord, Guy, 26
Decae, Henri, 319
Deep Blue Sea, The (Terence Rattigan), 166
Deep Blue Sea, The (Anatole Litvak, 1955), 166, 167, 168
Deep Impact (Mimi Leder, 1998), 4, 69
Deep Throat (Gerard Damiano, 1972), 80
Delon, Alain, 319
Dench, Judi, 184, 240
Deneuve, Catherine, 240
Depardieu, Gérard, 247
Der Amerikanische Freund [The American Friend] (Wim Wenders, 1977), 326
Der Fuehrer's Face [Donald Duck] (Jack Kinney, 1943), 267
Dermithe, Édouard, 136, 138, 139
Desbordes, Jean, 129
Descartes, René, 28, 32, 33
Destry Rides Again (George Marshall, 1939), 244
Deutsch, John, 103
"Devil Got My Woman" (Skip James), 117
Devil in Miss Jones, The (Gerard Damiano, 1972), 80
Devils, The (Ken Russell, 1971), 290
Dhiegh, Khigh, 189
Diaghilev, Serge de, 130
Diamonds Are Forever (Guy Hamilton, 1971), 176, 178, 181
Die Another Day (Lee Tamahori, 2002), 175, 180, 183
Dietrich, Marlene, 15, *238*, 239–246, 247, 248, 249, 252
Dimon, Elizabeth, 277

Dirty Dozen, The (Robert Aldrich, 1967), 265
Dirty Pictures (Frank Pierson, 2000), 79
Discoverie of Witchcraft, The (Reginald Scott), 31
Dishonored (Josef von Sternberg, 1931), 245
Doctor Zhivago (David Lean, 1965), 2
Dog Day Afternoon (Sidney Lumet, 1975), 2
Doherty, David, 103
Dole, Sen. Robert, 71
Donat, Robert, 213
Dors, Diana, 168
Dorziat, Gabrielle, 136
Douglas, Illeana, 115
Douglas, Kirk, 70, 71
Douglas, Michael, 58, 82, 101, 261
Downs, Cathy, 40
Dr. Jekyll and Mr. Hyde (Rouben Mamoulian, 1931), 305
Dr. No (Terence Young, 1962), 173, 175, 176, 178, 179, 182
Dr. Terror's House of Horrors (Freddie Francis, 1965), 46
Dracula (Francis Ford Coppola, 1992), 8
Dugan, John, 293
Dulles, Allen, 103
Dulles, John Foster, 103
Dunaway, Faye, *64*, 73
Duras, Marguerite, 246, 247, 249, 251, 252
Durey, Louis, 130
Duvall, Robert, 58, 261

Earthquake (Mark Robson, 1974), 69
Eastwood, Clint, 261
Eaton, Shirley, 182
Edge of Darkness (Lewis Milestone, 1943), 263
Edison, Thomas Alva, 34
8 1/2 (Federico Fellini, 1963), 316
8MM (Joel Schumacher, 1999), 12, *78*, 79, 81–90
Eisenhower, Dwight D., 70
Eisenstein, Sergei, 30

Ekland, Britt, 181
Elephant Man, The (David Lynch, 1980), 16, 287, 296
Elves (Jeffrey Mandel, 1990), 268
Ely, Larissa, 145
Eminem, 74
Enemies: A Love Story (Paul Mazursky, 1989), 269
Enemy of Women (Alfred Zeisler, 1944), 263
Enfants terribles, Les (Jean-Pierre Melville, 1950), 13, 128, 133, 136, 137, 139
Eraserhead (David Lynch, 1977), 295
Erin Brockovich (Steven Soderbergh, 2000), 102
Escape (Mervyn LeRoy, 1940), 263
Éternel retour, Le (Jean Delannoy, 1943), 129, 133
Evanofski, Candace, 281
Evans, Edith, 168
Evans, John, 151
Eve and the Handyman (Russ Meyer, 1961), 144
Evers, Jason, *38*, 48
Excalibur (John Boorman, 1981), 240
Exorcist, The (William Friedkin, 1973), 6, 287, 289, 291, 296

Face/Off (John Woo, 1997), 8
Fallen Sparrow, The (Richard Wallace, 1943), 263
Falling Down (Joel Schumacher, 1993), 4, 58, 60, 81, 82
Fantasia (James Algar, Samuel Armstrong, Ford Beebe, Norman Ferguson, Jim Handley, T. Hee, Wilfred Jackson, Hamilton Luske, Bill Roberts, Paul Satterfield, and Ben Sharpsteen, 1940), 5
Farley, Carole, 128
"Farscape" (1999), 311
Faster, Pussycat! Kill! Kill! (Russ Meyer, 1965), 13, 144, 146, 147, 148, 150, 151
Fatal Attraction (Adrian Lyne, 1987), 6

Feminine Mystique, The (Betty Friedan), 205
Ferguson, Jessie Lawrence, 61
Ferrer, Mel, 46, *200, 204*
Fiennes, Ralph, 68, 261
Fifth Element, The (Luc Besson, 1997), 303
55 Days at Peking (Nicholas Ray, 1963), 189, 210, 240
Fight Club, The (David Fincher, 1999), 74, 75
Finch, Jon, 219
Finders Keepers, Lovers Weepers! (Russ Meyer, 1968), 144, 146, 148
Fiorentino, Linda, 298
First Blood [Rambo: First Blood] (Ted Kotcheff, 1982), 5, 103
Fishburne, Laurence, 61
Fisher, Carrie, 240
Fitzpatrick, Leo, 3, 279
Flare Path (Terence Rattigan), 161
Fleming, Ian, 173, 174
Flicker (Theodore Roszak), 11, 34, 35
Flock of Seagulls, A (Frank Maudsley, Paul Reynolds, Mike Score, Ali Score), 139
Flower Drum Song (Henry Koster, 1961), 193
Fly, The (David Cronenberg, 1986), 16, 294–295, 298
Flying Leathernecks, The (Nicholas Ray, 1951), 210
Flynn, Errol, 261
Folk Implosion (Lou Barlow, John Davis), 274
Fonda, Henry, 216
Fontaine, Joan, 204
For Your Eyes Only (John Glen, 1981), 175, 176, 179, 181
Forbes, Bryan, 168
Forbidden Planet (Fred McLeod Wilcox, 1956), 16–17, *300,* 301–312
Ford, Henry, 94, 97
Forman, Milos, 12, 81, 89
Forty-Ninth Parallel (Michael Powell, 1941), 14, *156,* 158, 162, 163, 164

Foster, Barry, 219
Foster, Jodie, 71
Foucault, Michel, 26
4 Non-Blondes (Christa Hillhouse, Linda Perry, Dawn Richardson, Roger Rocha), 144
Four Sons (Archie Mayo, 1940), 263
Francis, Anne, 304
Francis, Coleman, 146
Frank, Horst, 48
Frankenstein (James Whale, 1931), 306, 310
Frankenstein—1970 (Howard W. Koch, 1958), 267
Franzese, Daniel, 279
Fraser, Sally, 40
Frenzy (Alfred Hitchcock, 1972), 213, 214, 219
Freud (John Huston, 1962), 167
Friday the 13ᵗʰ (Sean S. Cunningham, 1980), 292
Fried Green Tomatoes (Jon Avnet, 1991), 239
Friedan, Betty, 205
Frobe, Gert, 179
From Beyond the Grave (Kevin Connor, 1973), 158
From Russia with Love (Terence Young, 1963), 175, 178, 184, 190
Fuller, Samuel, 206
Furman, Mark, 56

Gable, Clark, 39
Gainer, Steve, 278
Gaines, Kevin, 56
Gandolfini, James, 82
Garcia, Andy, 59
Garner, Kelli, 279
Garr, Teri, 115
Gates, Bill, 112, 175
Gates, Darryl, 56
Gavin, Erica, 149, 151, 152
General Died at Dawn, The (Lewis Milestone, 1936), 189
George Washington (David Gordon Green, 2000), 16, 274, 280–284

Gere, Richard, 59, 190
Germon, Nane, 135
Getz, John, 294
Ghost Busters (Ivan Reitman, 1984), 298
Ghost World (Terry Zwigoff, 2001), 13, *108*, 114–122
Gide, André, 130, 132
Gielgud, John, 158, 161, 167
Giger, H. R., 289
Glass Shield, The (Charles Burnett, 1994), 60, 61, 62, 63
Glover, Bruce, 181
Glover, Julian, 181
Go-Betweeen, The (Joseph Losey, 1970), 158
Godfather, The saga (Francis Ford Coppola, 1972, 1974, 1990), 81, 104, 240
Goldblum, Jeff, 294
GoldenEye (Martin Campbell, 1995), 176, 181, 183
Goldfinger (Guy Hamilton, 1964), 2, 4, 182
Golem, Der [The Golem] (Paul Wegener, 1915), 310
Gone With the Wind (Victor Fleming, 1939), 144
Good Companions, The (J. Lee Thompson, 1957), 168
Good Morning . . . and Goodbye! (Russ Meyer, 1967), 145, 147, 151
GoodFellas (Martin Scorsese, 1990), 2, 4
Gooding Jr., Cuba, 61
Gordon, Ruth, 239
Gorky, Maxim, 25
Gosford Park (Robert Altman, 2001), 3, 240
Gough, Michael, 46
Gould, Florence, 131, 132
Graham, Heather, 87
Grant, Cary, 39, 214, 216
Grant, James Edward, 70
Grant, Richard E., 157
Gray, Charles, 179, 181
Gray, Dulcie, 163
Gray, Sally, 165

Grease (Randal Kleiser, 1978), 240

Great Day (Lance Comfort, 1945), 162, 165

Great Dictator, The (Charles Chaplin, 1940), *254*, 266

Great Escape, The (John Sturges, 1963), 265

Greatest Generation, The (Tom Brokaw), 68

Greco, Juliet, 138

Green, Seth, 180

Green Mile, The (Frank Darabont, 1999), 3

Greene, Angela, 51

Greene, Graham, 167

Gremlins (Joe Dante, 1984), 8

Grier, Roosevelt, 51

Griffith, D. W. , 144, 217

Guffey, Burnett, 73

Guns of Navarone, The (J. Lee Thompson, 1961), 4, 265

Gynt, Greta, 165

Haigh, John George, 165

Haji, 146, 150

Halloween (John Carpenter, 1978), 292

Hand, The (Henry Cass, 1960) , 39, 47

Hand, The (Oliver Stone, 1981), 49

Hands of a Stranger (Newt Arnold, 1962), 47

Hands of Orlac, The (Edmond T. Gréville, 1960), 46, 48

Handy, Rachel, 281

Hangmen Also Die (Fritz Lang, 1943), 263

Hanna, Mark, 44

Hannibal (Ridley Scott, 2001), 8

Hard Rock Zombies (Krishna Shah, 1984), 267

Hardy, Robert, 157

Harold and Maude (Hal Ashby, 1971), 239

Harrelson, Woody, 86

Harris, Ed, *92*

Harris, Eric, 93, 99

Harris, Theresa, 232

Hart, Veronica, 88

Hartley, Nina, 88

Hart's War (Gregory Hoblit, 2002), 264

Harvey, Don, 61

Harvey, Laurence, 70

Hatchet Man, The (William A. Wellman, 1932), 189

"Hawaii Five-O" (1968) , 189

Hawke, Ethan, 57, 59

Hawkins, Jack, 157

Hawks, Howard, 202, 208

Haye, Helen, 214

Hayes, Allison, 42

Hayes, Melvyn, 309

Hays Office, 80, 206

Head, The [Die Nackte und der Satan] (Victor Trivas, 1959), 39, 48, 49

Heald, Anthony, 84

Hearts of Humanity (John Baxter, 1936), 162

Heath, Neville, 165

Heavenly Bodies! (Russ Meyer, 1963), 144

Heavenly Creatures (Peter Jackson, 1994), 9

Heaven's Gate (Michael Cimino, 1980), 71

Hedley, Jack, 175

Hedren, 'Tippi,' 217

Heidegger, Martin, 26

Hell Is for Heroes (Don Siegel, 1962), 68

Heller, Lt. Gerhard, 132

Helmore, Tom, 215

Hepburn, Katharine, 240

Heroic Trio, The (Johnny To, 1992), 194

Hertz, Nathan. See *Attack of the 50 Foot Woman*

Hickok, James Butler "Wild Bill," 66

High Noon (Fred Zinnemann, 1952), 98

Hinckley, John, 71

His Excellency (Robert Hamer, 1952), 168

Hitchcock, Alfred, 15, 34, 144, 161, 213–220, 289, 322

Hitler, Adolf, 266, 268

Hitler Gang, The (John Farrow, 1944), 263

Hitler's Children (Edward Dmytryk and Irving Reis, 1943), 263
Hitler's Madman (Douglas Sirk, 1943), 263
Hoffman, Dustin, 268
Hoffman, Philip Seymour, 317, 320
Holden, Donald, 281
Holder, Eric (Former Deputy Attorney General), 1
Holliman, Earl, 305
Hollis, John, 179
Home Alone (Chris Columbus, 1990), 4
Honegger, Arthur, 130
Hoover, J. Edgar, 162
Hope, Bob, 267
Hopkins, Anthony, 7, 157, 305
Hopper, Dennis, 261, 326
Hopper, Hedda, 70
Horton, Rena, 148
Hotel Berlin (Peter Godfrey, 1945), 263
House on Carroll Street, The (Peter Yates, 1988), 268
House Un-American Activities Committee, 70, 134
Howard, Leslie, 162
Hucksters, The (Frederick Wakeman, 1947), 205
Hudson, William, 42
Hugo, Jean, 130
Human Sexual Response, The (Virginia Masters and William Johnson), 149
Hunger, The (Tony Scott, 1983), 240
Hunt for Red October, The (John McTiernan, 1990), 68
Huston, John, 59
Huygens, Christian, 28
Hwang, David Henry, 190
Hyde Park Corner (Sinclair Hill, 1935), 161, 165

I Love You, I Love You Not (Billy Hopkins, 1996), 269
I Want To Live! (Robert Wise, 1958), 3
I Was a Teenage Werewolf (Gene Fowler Jr., 1957), 309
Ice Cube (O'Shea Jackson), 60, 61
Ice Storm, The (Ang Lee, 1997), 2

Ilsa, She Wolf of the SS (Don Edmonds, 1974), 259
Immoral Mr. Teas, The (Russ Meyer, 1959), 143, 144
In A Lonely Place (Nicholas Ray, 1950), 210
In Cold Blood (Richard Brooks, 1967), 3
Inauguration of the Pleasure Dome, The (Kenneth Anger, 1954), 138
Incident at Vichy (Arthur Miller), 256
Incredible Shrinking Man, The (Jack Arnold, 1957), 11, 39, 49, 50
Incredible 2-Headed Transplant, The (Anthony M. Lanza, 1971), 39
Independence Day (Roland Emmerich, 1996), 4, 69
Indiana Jones and the Last Crusade (Steven Spielberg, 1989), 267
Internal Affairs (Mike Figgis, 1990), 12, 56, 57, 59, 60, 62
International Society of Mad Scientists, 301
Intolerance (D. W. Griffith, 1916), 13, 65, 94
Invisible Agent (Edwin L. Marin, 1942), 267
Irma Vep (Olivier Assayas, 1996), 14, 190–197
Irons, Jeremy, 190, 196
Irving, Amy, 291
Island of Dr. Moreau, The [Island of Lost Souls] (Erle C. Kenton, 1933), 306

Jackson, Andrew, 66
Jacob, Max, 128, 130
Jagger, Mick, 137
Jakob the Liar (Peter Kassovitz, 1999), 269
Janssen, Famke, 184
Jarmusch, Jim, 83
Jaws (Steven Spielberg, 1975), 2
Jeannie (Aimée Stuart), 162
Jeremy, Ron, 80
Johansson, Scarlett, *108*, 115
Johnny Mnemonic (Robert Longo, 1995), 103
Johns, Glynis, 241

Johnson, John Eddie, 60
Jones, Grace, 184
Jones, Tommy Lee, 297
Journey Into Fear (Norman Foster and
     Orson Welles, 1942), 263
Judgment at Nuremberg (Stanley Kramer,
     1961), 265
Julia (Fred Zinnemann, 1977), 265
Jurassic Park (Steven Spielberg, 1993), 2
Jurgens, Curt, 181
*Just a Gigolo [Schöner Gigolo, armer
     Gigolo]* (David Hemmings, 1979),
     243, 245

Kael, Pauline, 35
Kalifornia (Dominic Sena, 1993), 13,
     100
Karloff, Boris, *186*, 188
Kaye, Danny, 267
Keener, Catherine, 82
Keep, The (Michael Mann, 1983), 268
Kelly, Claire, 168
Kelly, Jack, 305
Kelly's Heroes (Brian G. Hutton, 1970),
     267
Kennedy, John F., 70
Kernke, Karin, 49
Key Largo (John Huston, 1948), 4
Khanjian, Arsinée, 193
Kids (Larry Clark, 1995), 3, 118, 274
Kiel, Richard, 180
King, Adrienne, 293
King John of Serbia, 226ff
King Kong (Ernest Shoedsack and
     Merian C. Cooper, 1933), 13, 95
King, Rodney, 55, 56, 62, 63
Kinski, Klaus, 140
Kiss Me Deadly (Robert Aldrich, 1955),
     207
Klebold, Dylan, 93, 99
Knight, Esmond, 163
Knight, Marion (Suge), 56
Krongard, A. B. Buzzy, 103
Kubrick, Stanley, 68, 70, 289
Kundun (Martin Scorsese, 1997), 190
Kwan, Nancy, 193

L.A. Confidential (Curtis Hanson, 1997),
     12, *54*, 56, 57, 59, 60, 62
*La Vieille qui marchait dans la mer [The
     Old Lady Who Walked in the Sea]*
     (Laurent Heynemann, 1991), 15,
     247–252
La Vieille qui marchait dans la mer (San-
     Antonio [Frédéric Dard]), 248–252
Labourdette, Elina, 129
Lady Caroline Lamb (Robert Bolt, 1972),
     158
L'Amant [The Lover] (Marguerite
     Duras), 247. See also *The Lover*
Lamb, Lady Caroline, 302
Lancaster, Burt, 265
Lancaster, Stuart, 147
Landau, Martin, 214
Lang, Doreen, *212*, 217
Lang, Fritz, 134
Langan, Glen, 40
Lange, Hope, 209
Lansbury, Angela, 189
Larson, Lola, 181
Last Blitzkrieg, The (Arthur Dreifuss,
     1958), 265
Last Emperor, The (Bernardo Bertolucci,
     1987), 196
Last of the Nuba, The (Leni Riefenstahl),
     257
Last Temptation of Christ, The (Martin
     Scorsese, 1988), 2, 290
Laughton, Charles, 306
Law, Jude, 315
Lay, Kenneth, 102
Lazenby, George, 173
Léaud, Jean-Pierre, 191, 195
Leave Her to Heaven (John M. Stahl,
     1946), 4
Lee, Bernard, 184
Lee, Christopher, 46, 47, 181, 189, 307
Lee, Damian Jewan, 281
Lee, Will Yun, 184
Left Hand of God, The (Edward
     Dmytryk, 1955), 189
Leigh, Janet, 218
Leigh, Vivien, 158, 166

Leigh-Hunt, Barbara, 219
Leighton, Margaret, 158
Leith, Virginia, *38*
Lenya, Lotte, 184
Les Vampires (Louis Feuillade, 1915),
    191
Leslie, Joan, 204
Lewis, Jerry, 267
Lewis, Juliet, 4
Lewton, Val, 229
Licence to Kill (John Glen, 1989), 175
Lifar, Serge, 139
Life and Death of Colonel Blimp, The
    (Michael Powell, 1943), 164
Lifeboat (Alfred Hitchcock, 1944), 215,
    216
Lilly, Alan, 278
Linder, Cec (Cecil), 182
Little Boy Lost (George Seaton, 1953),
    266
Live and Let Die (Guy Hamilton, 1973),
    174
Livesey, Roger, 164
Livingston, Princess, 148
Loch Ness Horror, The (Larry Buchanan,
    1981), 268
Lodger, The (Alfred Hitchcock, 1926),
    15, 215, 219
Lone, John, 14, 190, 196
Long, John Luther, 191
Longest Day, The (Ken Annakin, Andrew
    Marton, and Bernhard Wicki, 1962),
    265
Lonsdale, Michel (Michael), 179
Look Back in Anger (John Osborne), 159
*Lord of the Rings: The Fellowship of the
    Ring, The* (Peter Jackson, 2001), 307
Lorna (Russ Meyer, 1964), 13, 143, 144,
    145, 147, 151
Los Angeles Police Department
    (L.A.P.D.), 55–63
Love, Courtney, 86
Lovell, Raymond, 163
Lover, The (Jean-Jacques Annaud, 1991),
    247. See also *L'amant*
Loy, Myrna, 188

Ludd, Ned, 97
Lukas, Paul, 263
Lumière, Auguste and Louis, 34
Lusty Men, The (Nicholas Ray, 1952),
    206
Lynch, Alfred, 168

M. Butterfly (David Henry Hwang), 190
M. Butterfly (David Cronenberg, 1993),
    14, 190–197
MacGinnis, Niall, 157
Mack, David, 56, 57
MacLaine, Shirley, 240
Maclean, Donald, 162
Mad Max 2: The Road Warrior (George
    Miller, 1981), 296
Madama Butterfly (Giaccomo Puccini),
    191, 194
Madame Chrysanthème (Pierre Loti), 191
Madwoman of Chaillot, The (Bryan
    Forbes, 1969), 240
Magnani, Anna, 128
Magnificent Ambersons, The (Orson
    Welles, 1942), 4
Magnolia (Paul Thomas Anderson,
    1999), 90
Maitland, Lorna, 147, 151
Malkovich, John, 326
Malraux, André, 132
Maltese Falcon, The (John Huston,
    1941), 35
Man Hunt (Fritz Lang, 1941), 263
Man I Married, The (Irving Pichel,
    1940), 263
Man in the Glass Booth, The (Arthur
    Hiller, 1975), 268
Man Who Fell to Earth, The (Nicholas
    Roeg, 1976), 2–3
*Man with a Movie Camera, The [Chelovek
    s kinoapparatom]* (Dziga Vertov,
    1929), 29
Man with the Golden Gun, The (Guy
    Hamilton, 1974), 176, 183
Man Without a Body, The (Charles
    Saunders and W. Lee Wilder, 1957),
    39

Manchurian Candidate, The (John Frankenheimer, 1962), 3, 189
Mann, Anthony, 206
Mannheim, Lucie, 215
Manson, Charles, "family," 59
Mapplethorpe, Robert, 79
Marais, Jean, 128, 129, 130, 131, 134, 137, 139
Marathon Man (John Schlesinger, 1976), 2, 268
Marceau, Sophie, 179
Marcovicci, Andrea, 49
Margin for Error (Otto Preminger, 1943), 267
Maria Marten, or The Murder in the Red Barn (Milton Rosmer, 1935), 162
Mark of Cain, The (Brian Desmond Hurst, 1947), 165
Marker, Chris, 194, 195
Marlene (Maximilian Schell, 1984), 15, 242
Marlene Dietrich: Shadow and Light (Chris Hunt, 1996), 15, 241
Mars, Kenneth, 266
Marshall, Herbert, 214
Martin, Melvyn, 137
Martz, Mike, 309
Mask of Fu Manchu, The (Charles Brabin and Charles Vidor, 1932), *186*, 188
Mask of Zorro, The (Martin Campbell, 1998), 4
Mason, James, 157, 214
Massey, Raymond, 162
Masters, Steve, 146
Matewan (John Sayles, 1987), 98
Matrix, The (Andy and Larry Wachowski, 1999), 2, 99, 105, 138
Mauriac, Claude, 127
Mauriac, François, 131, 140
Max, Édouard de, 133
McAnally, Ray, 157
McClory, Kevin, 177
McCowen, Alec, 213
McKellen, Ian, 157, 307
McKenna, Justice Joseph, 22, 23, 24, 25, 26, 27, 30, 33

McNamara, Robert, 97
McQueen, Steve, 288
Me and the Colonel (Peter Glenville, 1958), 267
Méliès, Georges, 32
Mellen, Albert, 43
Melville, Jean-Pierre, 136, 139
Men in Black (Barry Sonnenfeld, 1997), 16, *286*, 287, 297, 298
Men in Black II (Barry Sonnenfeld, 2002), 2
Men of Two Worlds (Thorold Dickinson, 1946), 162
Merrick, John, 296
Merry Christmas, Mr. Lawrence (Oshima Nagisa, 1983), 2
Metropolis (Fritz Lang, 1927), 13, 94, 183, 306, 310
Metzger, Radley (a.k.a. Henry Paris), 81
Meyer, Russ, 13, 143–154
Middleton, Charles, 189
Miles, Bernard, 157
Milhaud, Darius, 130
Milken, Michael, 102
Millions Like Us (Sidney Gilliat and Frank Launder, 1943), 162, 168
Milo, John, 145
Mineo, Sal, 210
Miner, Rachel, 276
Minority Report (Steven Spielberg, 2002), 8
Mirren, Helen, 240
Misfit Brigade, The (Gordon Hessler, 1987), 265
Missing Persons (Dale Bozzio, Terry Bozzio, Warren Cuccurullo), 139
Mission Impossible II (John Woo, 2000), 4
Mitchell, Artie and Jim, 79
Mitry, Jean, 30
Möbius, August Ferdinand, 304
Moderns, The (Alan Rudolph, 1988), 196
Montalban, Ricardo, 189
Moonlight Sonata (Lothar Mendes, 1937), 162
Moonraker (Lewis Gilbert, 1979), 179, 180, 182

Moore, Roger, 173, 183, 189
Moreau, Jeanne, 15, 240, 246–252
Morgan, Frank, 263
Morgan, J. P., 101
Morgan, Kenneth, 166
Mortal Storm, The (Frank Borzage, 1940), 263–264
Mostel, Zero, 266
Motion Picture Association of America (MPAA), 81
Motor Psycho (Russ Meyer, 1965), 13, 144, 146, 148
Mouse That Roared, The (Jack Arnold, 1959), 96
Mudhoney (Russ Meyer, 1965), 144, 147, 148
Mullen, Barbara, 165
Murder! (Alfred Hitchcock, 1930), 214
Murder by Numbers (Barbet Schroeder, 2002), 4
Murdoch, Rupert, 175
Mutual Film Corporation v. Ohio Industrial Commission (Supreme Court decision), 11, 21, 22, 23, 25, 35
"My Funny Valentine" (Richard Rodgers and Lorenz Hart), 316
Myers, Mike, 180
Mysterious Dr. Fu Manchu, The (Rowland V. Lee, 1929), 188

"Naked City, The" (1960), 158
Naked Edge, The (Michael Anderson, 1961), 167, 168
Napier, Charles, 145
Narcotic (Dwain Esper and Vival Sodar't, 1934), 189
Nash, John, 307
Natural Born Killers (Oliver Stone, 1993), 71
Nazi Agent (Jules Dassin, 1942), 263
Neal, Patricia, 240
Neeson, Liam, 68
Newton, Thandie, 4
Ney, Marie, 168
Nicholson, Jack, 59
Nielsen, Leslie, 304–305

Night in Casablanca, A (Archie Mayo, 1946), 267
Night of the Living Dead (George Romero, 1968), 72
Night Porter, The [Il Portiere di notte] (Liliana Cavani, 1974), 259
"Nightingale, The" (Igor Stravinsky, 1917), 130
Nightmare On Elm Street, A series (Wes Craven, 1984; Jack Sholder, 1985; Chuck Russell, 1987; Renny Harlin, 1988; Stephen Hopkins, 1989; Rachel Talalay, 1991; Wes Craven, 1994; and Ronny Yu, 2003), 293–294
Nijinsky, Waslaw, 130
Nineteen Eighty-Four (George Orwell), 94, 102
1900 (Bernardo Bertolucci, 1976), 71
Niven, David, 173
No Dough Boys [Three Stooges] (Jules White, 1944), 267
Noailles, Anna de, 133
Norma Rae (Martin Ritt, 1979), 98
Norman, Jessye, 128
North by Northwest (Alfred Hitchcock, 1959), 214, 216, 289
Norton, Edward, 86
Nosferatu, eine Symphonie des Grauens (F. W. Murnau, 1922), *268*
Notorious (Alfred Hitchcock, 1946), 214, 215, 216
Nouvelle Revue Française, La (NRF), 127
Novak, Kim, 215
Novello, Ivor, 219
Nyby, Christian, 211

"Oedipus Rex" (Igor Stravinsky, 1927), 131
Office of War Information (OWI), 262
Oland, Warner, 188
Old San Francisco (Alan Crosland, 1927), 189
Oldman, Gary, 157
Oliver, Stephen, 146
"Oliver Twist" (1959), 158
Olivier, Laurence, 71, 158, 162, 268

On Her Majesty's Secret Service (Peter R. Hunt, 1969), 178

Onassis, Jacqueline, 86

Once Upon a Honeymoon (Leo McCarey, 1942), 266

Once Upon a Time in the West [C'era una volta il West] (Sergio Leone, 1969), 71

Ondra, Anny, 217

One of Our Aircraft Is Missing (Michael Powell, 1942), 159, 162, 164, 168

Organizer, The (Mario Monicelli, 1963), 98

O'Rourke, Heather, 293

Orphée (Jean Cocteau, 1949), 13, 130, 133, 137, 138, 139

Orr, Tim, 281

Osment, Hayley Joel, 298

O'Toole, Peter, 262

Outland (Peter Hyams, 1981), 2

Outrage (Ida Lupino, 1950), 43, 45

Owen, Bill, 163

Pagnol, Marcel, 248

Palmer, Betsy, 293

Palmer, Geoffrey, 184

Paltrow, Gwyneth, 316

"Parade" (Erik Satie, 1917), 130

Paradise Lost (John Milton), 258

Parély, Mila, 135

Parents terribles, Les (Jean Cocteau, play), 131

Parents terribles, Les (Jean Cocteau, 1948), 128, 130, 133, 135, 136, 137

Paris, Henry. *See* Radley Metzger

Parker, William H., 56, 63

Parkin, Duncan "Dean," 40

Parks, Trina, 181

Passage, The (J. Lee Thompson, 1979), 265

Patriot Games (Phillip Noyce, 1992), 68

Pawnbroker, The (Sidney Lumet, 1964), 269

Peck, Gregory, 261, 268

Peeping Tom (Michael Powell, 1960), 164

Penn, Sean, 58

People v. Larry Flynt, The (Milos Forman, 1996), 12, 79, 81, 85, 88, 89, 90

Pepper, Barry, 326

Percy, Esme, 214

Perez, Rafael, 56, 57

Performance (Nicholas Roeg and Donald Cammell, 1970), 137

Périer, François, 138

Perkins, Anthony, 214, 218, 220

Perry, Linda, 144

Peter Pan (Clyde Geronimi, Wilfred Jackson, and Hamilton Luske, 1953), 4

Petty, Lori, 60

Phillips, Bijou, 276

Phoenix, Joaquin, 82

Picasso, Pablo, 130, 131, 139

Pidgeon, Walter, *300*, 304

Pillsbury, Garth, 149

Pitt, Michael, 279

Plato, 28

Playbill (Terence Rattigan), 158, 161

Pleasence, Donald, 157, 179

Plein Soleil [Purple Noon] (Réné Clément, 1960), 315, 317, 319

Plummer, Christopher, 189, 261

Poe, Edgar Allan, 132

Pohlmann, Eric, 178

Pollard, Michael J., 202

Poltergeist (Tobe Hooper, 1982), 292, 293

Poor of New York, The (Dion Boucicault), 27

Pope John Paul, 11

Pornstar: The Legend of Ron Jeremy (Scott J. Gill, 2001), 79, 80

Portman, Eric, 14, *156*, 157–170

Postcards from the Edge (Mike Nichols, 1990), 240

Poulenc, Françis, 128, 130

Powell, Jenny, *78*

Powers, Ed, 88

Powers, Mala, 43

Pressburger, Emeric, 164

Pretty Woman (Garry Marshall, 1990), 101

Price, Dennis, 165
Prince and the Pauper, The (William Keighley and William Dieterle, 1937), 158
Prince of the City (Sidney Lumet, 1981), 2
Producers, The (Mel Brooks, 1968), 266
Proprietor, The (Ismail Merchant, 1996), 248
Pryce, Jonathan, 175
Psycho (Alfred Hitchcock, 1960), 2, 214, 218, 289, 296
Pullman, Bill, 69
Puppet Master III: Toulon's Revenge (David DeCoteau, 1991), 268

Quesada, Veronica, 57
Quick and the Dead, The (Sam Raimi, 1995), 6
Quills (Philip Kaufman, 2000), 79

Radiguet, Raymond, 129
Raiders of the Lost Ark (Steven Spielberg, 1981), 267
Rains, Claude, 214, 216
Ralli, Giovanna, 168
Rambo: First Blood. See *First Blood*
Randolph, Jane, 229
Rated X (Emilio Estevez, 2000), 79
Rattigan, Terence, 160, 161, 162, 166, 168, 169
Ray, Man, 130
Ray, Nicholas, 14, 15, 201–211
Reagan, Ronald, 71, 261
Rear Window (Alfred Hitchcock, 1954), 216
Rebel Without a Cause (Nicholas Ray, 1955), 203, 204, 210
Rebhorn, James, 315
Red Corner (Jon Avnet, 1997), 190
Red Harvest (Dashiell Hammett), 103
Red Lantern, The (Albert Capellani, 1919), 189
Red Line 7000 (Howard Hawks, 1965), 202
Red Shoes, The (Michael Powell, 1948), 164

Reed, Oliver, 290
Reiner, Carl, 261, 267
Rendezvous 24 (James Tinling, 1946), 268
Renfro, Brad, 273
Renoir, Jean, 132
Rented Lips (Robert Downey Sr., 1988), 267
Reunion in France (Jules Dassin, 1942), 263
Revenge of the Zombies (Steve Sekely, 1943), 268
Reynolds, Burt, 86
Reynolds, Debbie, 240
Reynolds, Peter, 168
Rickman, Alan, 157
Ridgely, Robert, 86
Rimbaud, Artur, 27
Ripley Under Ground (Patricia Highsmith), 325, 326. See also *White on White*
Ripley's Game (Patricia Highsmith), 326
Ripley's Game (Liliana Cavani, 2002), 326
Ritchard, Cyril, 217
Riva, Maria, 241
River of Death (Steve Carver, 1989), 268
Robbins, Toby, 175
Roberts, Julia, 101
Robinson, Edward G., 133–134, 263
RoboCop (Paul Verhoeven, 1987), 103, 105
Robson, Flora, 240
Rockefeller, John D. Jr., 66
Rocky Horror Picture Show, The (Jim Sharman, 1975), 196
Roger and Me (Michael Moore, 1989), 94, 101, 102
Rohmer, Sax, 188
Rolfe, Guy, 165
Room with a View, A (E. M. Forster), 325
Rope (Alfred Hitchcock, 1948), 2, 215
Rosemary's Baby (Roman Polanski, 1968), 289, 296
Ross, Michael, 43
Rota, Nino, 319

Roth, Tim, 157
Rouse, Eddie, 283
Rove, Karl, 66
Russian Rhapsody (Robert Clampett, 1944), 267
Ruy Blas (Pierre Billon, 1947), 133
Ryan, Robert, 204

Sabotage (Alfred Hitchcock, 1936), 216, 209
Sade, Marquis de, 79
Saint, Eva Marie, 214, 216
Saint Augustine, 34
Saint-Blaise-des-Simples, chapel of, Milly-la-forêt, 139
Salaire de la peur, Le [The Wages of Fear] (Henri-George Clouzot, 1953), 133–134
Saltzman, Harry, 177
Sanders, George, 157
Sang d'un poète, Le [The Blood of a Poet] (Jean Cocteau, 1930), 13, 129, 130, 133
Sartre, Jean-Paul, 26, 132
Satan Never Sleeps (Leo McCarey, 1962), 189
Satana, Tura, 147
Satie, Erik, 130
Saturday Night Fever (John Badham, 1977), 2
Satyricon (Federico Fellini, 1969), 2
Savalas, Telly, 179
Saving Private Ryan (Steven Spielberg, 1998), 4, 68, 69, 70, 73, 90, 265
Scanners (David Cronenberg, 1981), 296
Schell, Maximilian, 242, 243, 244, 245, 246, 265
Schindler's List (Steven Spielberg, 1993), 8–9, 16, 68, 69, 101, 269
Schneider, Paul, 283
Schreck, Max, *220*
Schumacher, Joel, 12, 81, 88, 89
Schwarzenegger, Arnold, 66, 68
Scorpio Rising (Kenneth Anger, 1963), 138
Scott, George C., 262
Scott, Pippa, 3

Scott, Ridley, 192
Scott, Zachary, 204
Scrap Happy Daffy (Frank Tashlin, 1943), 267
Seale, John, 319
Search, The (Fred Zinnemann, 1948), 266
Searchers, The (John Ford, 1956), 3, 71
Secret Invasion, The (Roger Corman, 1964), 265
Selleck, Tom, 261
Sellers, Peter, 189
Selznick, Richard, 144
Separate Tables (Terence Rattigan), 158, 160, 161, 167
Serrault, Michel, 249
Sert, Misia, 130
Seurat, Georges, 27
Se7en (David Fincher, 1995), 2, 74, 297
Seven Beauties [Pasqualino Settebellezze] (Lina Wertmüller, 1976), 259
7 Women (John Ford, 1966), 158, 189
Seven Years in Tibet (Jean-Jacques Annaud, 1997), 190
Seventh Cross, The (Fred Zinnemann, 1944), 262
Sevigny, Chloë, 3
Sexual Behavior in the Human Female (Alfred Kinsey), 149–150
Shadow, The (Russell Mulcahy, 1994), 196
Shadow of a Doubt (Alfred Hitchcock, 1943), 214
Shakespeare, William, 249
Shanghai Express (Josef von Sternberg, 1932), 189
Shanghai Gesture, The (Josef von Sternberg, 1941), 189
Shanghai Story, The (Frank Lloyd, 1954), 189
She (Edwin S. Porter, 1908; Timothy Bond, 2001), 47
She Demons (Richard E. Cunha, 1958), 268
Shining, The (Stanley Kubrick, 1980), 289, 296

Shining Through (David Seltzer, 1992), 265

Shire, Talia, 240

Sidney, Sylvia, 216

Silence of the Lambs, The (Jonathan Demme, 1991), 4, 7, 292, 293, 305

Silkwood (Mike Nichols, 1983), 102

Simon, Michel, 48, 49

Simon, Simone, *224*, 226

Simpson, O.J., 56

"Simpsons, The" (1989), 102

Singing Marine, The (Ray Enright, 1937), 162

Sixth Sense, The (M. Night Shyamalan, 1999), 287, 298

Skull, The (Freddie Francis, 1965), 47, 48

Slezak, Walter, 215

SLON (Société de Lancement des Ouvres Nouvelles), 194

Smith, Dick, 5

Smith, Kent, 226

Smith, Maggie, 240

Smith, Putter, 181

Smith, Roger, 101, 102

Smith, Will, 297

Snide and Prejudice (Philippe Mora, 1998), 267

Some Like It Hot (Billy Wilder, 1959), 4

Son of Hitler (Rodney Amateau, 1978), 267

Sophie's Choice (Alan J. Pakula, 1982), 269

Sound of Music, The (Robert Wise, 1965), 265–266

Spacek, Sissy, 290

Spartacus (Stanley Kubrick, 1960), 69, 70, 71

Spider and the Fly, The (Robert Hamer, 1949), 159, 162, 165

Spielberg, Steven, 8, 68, 80

Spy Train (Harold Young, 1943), 263

Spy Who Loved Me, The (Lewis Gilbert, 1977), 176, 180, 182

Squadron Leader X (Lance Comfort, 1942), 164

Stage Fright (Alfred Hitchcock, 1950), 215, 241

Stagliano, John, 88

Stahl, Nick, *272*, 274

Stalag 17 (Billy Wilder, 1953), 265

Stallone, Sylvester, 68

Stapleton, James, 47

Star Trek films (Robert Wise, 1979; Nicholas Meyer, 1982; Leonard Nimoy, 1984; Leonard Nimoy, 1986; William Shatner, 1989; Nicholas Meyer, 1991; David Carson, 1994; Jonathan Frakes, 1996; Jonathan Frakes, 1998; Stuart Baird, 2002), 2, 189

Star Wars series (George Lucas, 1977; Irvin Kershner, 1980; Richard Marquand, 1983; George Lucas, 1999; George Lucas, 2002), 2, 4, 262

Stardust Memories (Woody Allen, 1980), 2

Starship Troopers (Paul Verhoeven, 1997), 4

Steiger, Rod, 269

Steiner, Yann Andréa, 247, 249, 251

Stepford Wives, The (Bryan Forbes, 1975), 9

Stéphane, Nicole, 136

Stephens, Toby, 184

Stevens, Warren, 305, 306

Stewart, James, 215, 216, 244, 264

Stone, Sharon, 9

Stormare, Peter, 82

Strange Days (Kathryn Bigelow, 1995), 79, 88, 89, 103

Strangers on a Train (Alfred Hitchcock, 1951), 214

Stravinsky, Igor, 130, 131

Streep, Meryl, 240

Strike (Sergei Eisenstein, 1925), 71

Stuart, Gloria, 240

Stuart, Randy, 49

Sullavan, Margaret, 264

Sum of All Fears, The (Phil Alden Robinson, 2002), 2

Sunset Blvd. (Billy Wilder, 1950), 240

Supervixens (Russ Meyer, 1975), 144

Swanson, Gloria, 240

Swing Kids (Thomas Carter, 1993), 266

Swordfish (Dominic Sena, 2001), 2

Tailleferre, Germaine, 130

Tale of Two Cities, A (Charles Dickens), 158

"Tale of Two Cities, A" (1958), 158

Talented Mr. Ripley, The (Patricia Highsmith), 315ff.

Talented Mr. Ripley, The (Anthony Minghella, 1999), 17, *314*, 315–329

Talented Mr. Ripley, The (Phyllis Nagy), 319, 321

Tandy, Jessica, 239

Tarzan the Ape Man (W. S. Van Dyke, 1932), 47

Tarzan Triumphs (Wilhelm Thiele, 1943), 267

Tarzan's Desert Mystery (Wilhelm Thiele, 1943), 267

Tate, Sharon, 59

Taxi Driver (Martin Scorsese, 1976), 71

Tearle, Godfrey, 213

Teenage Lust (Larry Clark), 274

Tempest, The (William Shakespeare), 304

Temple, Shirley, 39

10 Rillington Place (Richard Fleischer, 1971), 167

Terminator, The series (James Cameron, 1984, 1991; Jonathan Mostow, 2003), 99, 101, 103

Testament d'Orphée, Le (Jean Cocteau, 1960), 133, 138, 139

Texas Chainsaw Massacre, The (Tobe Hooper, 1974), 72, 75, 147, 292, 293

Thelma & Louise (Ridley Scott, 1991), 236, 320

They Saved Hitler's Brain (David Bradley, 1968), 268

Thin Red Line, The (Terrence Malick, 1998), 265

Thing with Two Heads, The (Lee Frost, 1972), 50, 51

Third Reich, the, 8, 256–270

39 Steps, The (Alfred Hitchcock, 1935), 15, 213, 214, 216, 218

Three Days of the Condor (Sydney Pollack, 1975), 2

Three Kings (David O. Russell, 1999), 103

Thuillier, Luc, 248

Thunderball (Terence Young, 1965), 176, 178, 182

Titanic (James Cameron, 1997), 3, 13, 100, 240

To Be or Not to Be (Ernst Lubitsch, 1942), 266

Tobruk (Arthur Hiller, 1967), 265

Todd, Richard, 215

Todorov, Tzvetan, 35

Tom Horn (William Wiard, 1980), 3

Tomorrow Never Dies (Roger Spottiswoode, 1997), 175, 184

Tomorrow the World! (Leslie Fenton, 1944), 263

Tong Man, The (William Worthington, 1919), 189

Topol, 181

Total Recall (Paul Verhoeven, 1990), 2

Touch of Evil (Orson Welles, 1958), 5, *238*, 245

Tourneur, Jacques, 229

Towering Inferno, The (Irwin Allen and John Guillermin, 1974), 69, 76, 93

Tracy, Spencer, 262, 265

Trader Horn (W. S. Van Dyke, 1931), 47

Traffic (Steven Soderbergh, 2000), 2

Train, The (John Frankenheimer, 1964), 266

Training Day (Antoine Fuqua, 2001), 12, 56, 57, 59, 60, 62

Traité de bave et d'éternité (Jean-Isidore Isou, 1950), 133

Trewey, Felicien, 32

Triesault, Ivan, 215

Trinka, Paul, 148

Triumph of the Will [Triumph des Willens] (Leni Riefenstahl, 1934), 257

True Romance (Tony Scott, 1993), 100

True Story of Jesse James, The (Nicholas Ray, 1957), 209–210
Truffaut, François, 139, 195
Truman Show, The (Peter Weir, 1998), *92*, 106
Trumbo, Dalton, 70
Tulsa (Larry Clark), 274
Tynan, Kenneth, 163

U-571 (Jonathan Mostow, 2000), 265
Ullman, Liv, 128
Ulmer, Edgar G., 35
United States Commission on Civil Rights, 56
United States Holocaust Memorial Museum, 260
Up! (Russ Meyer, 1976), 144

Vadim, Roger, 139
Valenti, Jack, 66, 81, 82
Valley of the Dolls (Jacqueline Susann), 149
Van Susteren, Greta, 11
Venice Film Festival (1950), 138
Vertigo (Alfred Hitchcock, 1958), 164, 215, 216
Vickers, Yvette, 43
Victim (Basil Dearden, 1961), 167
Victors, The (Carl Foreman, 1963), 68
Victory (John Huston, 1981), 265
View to a Kill, A (John Glen, 1985), *172*, 176, 179, 184
Villa Santo Sospir, 139
Villa Santo-Sospir, La (1952), 133
Vixen! (Russ Meyer, 1968), 13, 143, 144, 149, 151, 152, 153
"Voix humaine, La" (Jean Cocteau), 128
Voix humaine, La (Francis Poulenc, 1959), 128
Von Ryan's Express (Mark Robson, 1965), 265
Von Sternberg, Josef, 244
Voodoo Tiger (Spencer Gordon Bennet, 1952), 267

Wagner, Richard, 27
Wahlberg, Mark, 87

Walbrook, Anton, 162, 164
Walken, Christopher, *172*, 176
Walker, Robert, 214
Wall Street (Oliver Stone, 1987), 101
Walsh, Dermot, 165
Wanted for Murder (Lawrence Huntington, 1946), 14, 159, 162, 164, 165
War of the Colossal Beast (Bert I. Gordon, 1958), 12, 40, 41, 43
Warhol, Andy, 76, 83
Washington, Denzel, 57
Watergate (Hotel) scandal, 2
Waters, John, 144
Watling, Jack, 161
Wayne, John, 3, 69, 70
We Dive At Dawn (Anthony Asquith, 1943), 162, 168
Weaver, Sigourney, 289
Weisweiller, Francine, 139
Welles, Orson, 5, 35, 103, 245
West 11 (Michael Winner, 1963), 167, 168
What Ever Happened to Baby Jane? (Robert Aldrich, 1962), 239
Which Way to the Front? (Jerry Lewis, 1970), 267
Whisperers, The (Bryan Forbes, 1966), 167, 168
White on White (Roger Spottiswoode, 2004), 326
Whitehead, Robert, 160
"Who Dat" (JT Money), 273
Widmark, Richard, 163, 265
Wild Bunch, The (Sam Peckinpah, 1969), 73
Wild Gals of the Naked West! (Russ Meyer, 1962), 144
Wild One, The (Laszlo Benedek, 1954), 146
Wilder, Gene, 266
Williams, Edy, *142*
Williams, Grant, 49
Williams, Jobeth, 293
Williams, Kenneth, 163
Williams, Willie, 55

Willis, Bruce, 298
Wilson, Woodrow, 65
Wind Across the Everglades (Nicholas
   Ray, 1958), 209
Winfrey, Oprah, 11
Winters, Holle K., 146
Wise, Robert, 211
Wiseman, Joseph, 179, 181
Woman in White, The (Wilkie Collins), 27
Women in Bondage (Steve Sekely, 1943),
   263
Wong, B. D., 196
Woo, John, 195
Wood, Natalie, 210
World Is Not Enough, The (Michael
   Apted, 1999), 176, 179, 184
World Trade Center, 1, 93, 94, 95, 104
"World's Scariest Police Chases, The"
   (1997), 68
Wray, Fay, 95
Wrong Man, The (Alfred Hitchcock,
   1956), 216
Wymark, Patrick, 47

Yamasaki, Minoru, 104
*Yangtse Incident: The Story of H.M.S.
   Amethyst* (Michael Anderson, 1957),
   189
Yared, Gabriel, 319
Year of the Dragon (Michael Cimino,
   1985), 196
You Only Live Twice (Lewis Gilbert,
   1967), 2, 176, 178, 182
Young and Innocent (Alfred Hitchcock,
   1937), 214
Young Lions, The (Edward Dmytryk,
   1958), 68, 265
Young, Robert, 264
Yune, Rick, 180

Zaat (Don Barton and Arnold Stevens,
   1972), 268
Zabriskie Point (Michelangelo
   Antonioni, 1970), 4
Zee and Co. (Brian G. Hutton, 1972), 158
Zinnemann, Fred, 208
Zoroastrianism, 34

UNIVERSITY H.S. LIBRARY

UNIVERSITY H.S. LIBRARY 9/14/2011